THE

EVERYTHING

TRIVIA

BOOK

From the fascinating to the frivolous—everything you wanted to know about TV, music, movies, famous people, scandals, and more!

Nat Segaloff

Adams Media Corporation
Holbrook, Massachusetts

FOR

Ruth Baschkopf and Jesse Baschkopf
who made so much possible

Copyright ©1999, Adams Media Corporation.

An Everything Series Book. The Everything Series is a trademark of Adams Media Corporation.

Published by Adams Media Corporation
260 Center Street, Holbrook, MA 02343

ISBN: 1-58062-143-0

Printed in the United States of America.

J I H G F E D C B A

Library of Congress Cataloging-in-Publication Data
The everything trivia book / by Nat Segaloff.
    p.   cm. — (An everything series book)
ISBN 1-58062-143-0
Includes index.
1. Questions and answers. 2. Curiosities and wonders. I. Title. II. Series: Everything series.
     AG195.S39   1999
    031.02—dc21   98-47694
               CIP

This publication is designed to provide accurate and authoritative information with regard to the subject matter covered. It is sold with the understanding that the publisher is not engaged in rendering legal, accounting, or other professional advice. If legal advice or other expert assistance is required, the services of a competent professional person should be sought.
    — From a *Declaration of Principles* jointly adopted by a Committee
of the American Bar Association and a Committee of Publishers and Associations

Signed essays in *The Everything Trivia Book* were written specifically for it by the credited author. Entries appearing as Q&As were conducted by the author either for this book or in his capacity as a journalist. Some material by the author previously appeared in a different form in other periodicals which purchased first North American publishing right only, after which the copyrights reverted to, and remain the property of, the author.
    Many of the designations used by manufacturers and sellers to distinguish their products are claimed as trademarks. Where those designations appear in this book and Adams Media was aware of a trademark claim, the designations have been printed in initial capital letters. Any omission is purely accidental and unintentional. Every effort has been made to verify the accuracy of the information contained in this book as of the date of its writing. Nevertheless, the author and publisher are NOT responsible for lost bar bets.

Illustrations by Barry Littmann

This book is available at quantity discounts for bulk purchases.
For information, call 1-800-872-5627 (in Massachusetts, call 781-767-8100).

Visit our home page at http://www.adamsmedia.com

Contents

Chapter 1: TelEvisiOn 1

• Quiz: Service with a Smile • Quiz: Horses and Riders • Quiz: Heroes and Sidekicks • Quiz: Hosts • Top TV Shows • Jackie Gleason • Quiz: The Honeymooners • Quiz: Making a Living • Brilliant Endings • Andy Griffith • Quiz: Andy Griffith Show • The Brady Bunch • Quiz: The Brady Bunch • Quiz: Wacky Neighbors • Quiz: Harry Morton Lives • Quiz: Good Eeeeeevening • Rod Serling • Star Trek to the Prairies • PTM: Stirling Silliphant • PTM: Stan Levin on Red Skelton • TV Schedules • Quiz: TV-1 • Quiz: From Series to Stardom • Quiz: Catchphrases • PTM: Don Kopaloff • PTM: Jim Varney • PTM: Superman's Pal, Jack Larson

Chapter 2: MoviEs 35

• Quiz: Famous Last Words from Movies • Quiz: Less Famous Last Words from Movies • Quiz: Hype Me Hollywood • The Truth about Oscar® • Quiz: Un-reel Quotes • Quiz: Biopics • PTM: Gary Fleder • Quiz: No Credit, Please • Quiz: Read the Book, Miss the Movie • PTM: Christopher Darling • Go Figure • Quiz: Films á Clef • PTM: Tom Cruise • PTM: Stirling Silliphant on Winning an Oscar® • PTM: Abbott and Costello • The Marx Brothers • Quiz: Dying Words • Quiz: Disneyana • Strange but True • Contract Capers • Quiz: Before They Were Stars • The Write Actor • Acting Directors • Oscar's Oops • Billy Wilder • Wit and Wisdom of Hollywood • Black Cinema • Women in Film • PTM: Eleanor Perry • Quiz: Screen Lovers • Quiz: Casablanca • Small Fry • PTM: Liane Brandon • Brainstorm

Chapter 3: MusiC 69

• Woodstock • Quiz: Bop Till You Drop • Quiz: Paul Is Dead • Quiz: Commercial Music • Quiz: Sing Me a Story • Quiz: Odd Person Out • Quiz: Question and Answer Songs • Quiz: Pips, etc. • Disco • Quiz: Who's Who in Music • Quiz: Dances • Quiz: Musical Bios • The King and the President • Hit List • Fifth Beatles • Dick Clark • Alan Freed • Payola • "Top 40"

Acknowledgments

Thanks to Pamela A. Liflander who edited this book with her customary good humor and wisdom; to Agnes Birnbaum of Bleecker Street Associates, Inc. for her encouragement and counsel; and to Bob Adams for having so many varied interests and the gumption to publish books about them.

No contribution to any book—even one on trivia—is ever trivial. In addition to those who graciously consented to interviews, I would like to thank (alphabetically) Steve Allen, John de Lancie, Susan and Harlan Ellison, Mark Evanier, Peter and Joan Graves, Gary H. Grossman, Gloria Heiser, Stephen Israel, Robin Amann Levien and Ed Levien, Christine Lamonte, Jane Lanouette, Malcolm Leo, Susan Bay Nimoy and Leonard Nimoy, Barbara and Lan O'Kun, Penn & Teller, Pamela A. Perry, John Randolph, Jeremy Ritzlin, Guy Rodgers, Stephen F. Rohde, Danny Schechter, Steve Sherwin, Mike Sierra (*Flummery Digest*), Tiana (Thi Thanh Nga) Silliphant, Stirling Silliphant, Jr., Dave Smith, Jack Sparks (Sen. John Glenn's office) and Maggie Thompson (*Comic Buyer's Guide*), all of whom helped make the words appear, whether they know it or not.

Last, but really first, thanks to Ed Goodgold and Dan Carlinsky whose 1966 book got it all going.

Introduction

Some of us are cursed with memories like flypaper, and stuck there is a staggering amount of miscellaneous data, mostly useless.

— Billy Wilder and I. A. L. Diamond, screenplay, *The Private Life of Sherlock Holmes (1972)*

If the old saying is correct—that small matters amuse small minds—what does that say about people who are amused by Trivia? On one level, Trivia is a way of re-creating that delicious feeling you used to get in elementary school when the teacher asked the class a question and you knew the answer. That may not mean much in the cosmic scheme of things, but boy, when you had it and that brownnosing Jimmy Ledbetter in the first row didn't, was that sweet or what? (Jimmy Ledbetter isn't his real name. But he represents the dork who always sat in the front row and waved his hand shouting "Oooh, Me! Me!" at the teacher.)

To anyone interested in the bigger picture, of course, Trivia is but a way station on the road to higher knowledge, falling somewhere between nostalgia and the SATs. Yet the random factoids that go into Trivia also form a snapshot of popular culture, a common reference that serves to bind this sprawling culture together when so much else seems to tear us apart. For instance, ask a gathering of baby boomers for the four novels in Durrell's *Alexandria* quartet. Go ahead; I dare you. Even if anybody's ever read them, he or she will probably have to head for the library to get the answer. (Answer: *Justine, Balthazar, Mountolive,* and *Clea.*) Ask the same group to whistle the theme from *The Andy Griffith Show,* however, and you've started a songfest. (The actual theme was called "The Fishin' Hole," and it was com-

posed by Earle Hagen and Herbert Spencer.) Does this make Aunt Bee more important than Justine? Or is it just a case of popular priorities? Well, flibbertigibbet!

If the truth be told, people really ask Trivia questions for one basic reason: to prove that they know more than you do. If someone asks a Trivia question without already knowing the answer, it's not Trivia, it's research, and you can tell the difference by the lack of smugness in the asker's voice. It's like flexing at the beach: the joy of Trivia isn't the quest, it's the *con*quest. Perhaps this is why there are radio shows, books, syndicated columns, Web sites, and the entire database of *Jeopardy,* all of which celebrate the rote retention of factoids without the interest in applying them.

And this is the key to understanding the appeal of Trivia: *It doesn't involve thinking, just memorizing.* It's like cramming for an exam; no value judgment or historical context should complicate the accretion of Trivia. There is no guiding concept of truth, only its accumulation. Why, some people even memorize the answers on Trivial Pursuit™ game cards. Trivia *does* nothing; it just *is.* And it sure is a lot of fun!

But where did it start? There are several myths about how the word *Trivia* came to its current meaning. Clearly of first declension Latin origin (an observation that would please Lillian Goodwin, my beleaguered tenth-grade Latin teacher), *Trivia* is the place where three (*tri*) roads (*via*) meet. By this facile explanation, the tri-via served as the route by which news was conveyed from the farthest outposts of the Roman Empire to the Forum. More recently—if you consider the Middle Ages to be recent—*Trivia/Trivium* became the designation for the "lower" division of the seven liberal arts taught at University. These so-called "inferior" studies included grammar, rhetoric, and logic, while the "higher" studies, called *quadrivium*, consisted of music, arithmetic, geography, and astronomy. Perhaps it was this secondary regard for writing skills that has stigmatized Trivia, and its practitioners, ever since. Well, lah-de-dah.

Some insist that Trivia has been around longer. Although it's doubtful that Adam and Eve ever got drunk on applejack and sang the theme song from *The Brady Bunch,* Trivia didn't become a fad until around 1965. That's when two Columbia College students—Edwin Goodgold and Dan Carlinsky—turned a dormitory nostalgia game into a national phenomenon. Their first book on the subject, *Trivia*—now a collector's item—was published by Dell in 1966, and it became the first quiz book to break into the *New York Times* bestseller list. It was followed by *More Trivial Trivia* and additional sequels, both by Goodgold and Carlinsky, and by scores of other buffs.

Trivia changes with the times. In addition to the more ephemeral Web sites, radio call-in shows, and news-filler services devoted to it, there are reference books such as Charles Panati's titles, Tom Parker's *Rules of Thumb,* Tom Burnham's *Dictionary of Mis-information,* and, most notably, David Feldman's immensely popular *Imponderables*® series. And then there's *The Everything Trivia Book.*

This is not purely a reference book, nor is it nostalgia, although it is a bit of both. *The Everything Trivia Book* is designed to set Trivia into the context of the times that produced it.

Each chapter starts with an essay that provides a kind of orientation to the subject at hand as well as a point of view about the way Trivia has shaped the century, and vice versa.

Notably, there is no sports Trivia (except for a few inescapable examples). There are two reasons for this: First, sports statistics change more frequently than typeset can keep up with, and, second, there are already enough radio shows, Web sites, and brewery sweepstakes to cover the passionate subject.

What you *will* find in *The Everything Trivia Book* are tons of items about popular culture. Many of them appear as discrete mini-essays called *sidebars,* but interspersed among them are three challenging types of items:

Quizzes: Quizzes consist of lists of questions and answers. They can be Match-ups, True/False, Fill-in-the-Blank, or Multiple Choice.

Get a Life: These sections consist of really obscure questions that you either know or you don't.

Personal Trivia Memories (PTMs): PTMs are recollections from celebrities, scholars, and wags who bring their unique experience and authority to a subject.

A note for fussy linguists: The word *Trivia* is capitalized for purely stylistic reasons. Just like it isn't really dinner without a big spoon, who wants to read a book about something that isn't capitalized? (Three exceptions are k.d. lang, e e cummings, and archie and mehitabel.)

Emphasis is placed upon Trivia that has some connection with the experience of growing up in America in the second half of the twentieth century. But be warned: Just because a fact is obscure does not make it Trivia. It also has to be fun.

With that in mind, let's get trivial.

Nat Segaloff
Los Angeles, Spring 1999

PTM: Ed Goodgold and Dan Carlinsky

While they were Columbia College students in 1965, Edwin Goodgold and Dan Carlinsky wrote Trivia *and captured a verbal snapshot of an era. The era may have changed, but not the emotions of the pop culture that came out of it.*

Dan Carlinsky: The most powerful Trivia, with a capital *T*, which is to say the nostalgia-based Trivia, is based on experiences from childhood, or from adolescence. When you were a kid, you weren't so cluttered with other things. It had more importance. I think, for most people, a comic book read at the age of ten has more impact than any movie seen at the age of thirty.

Ed Goodgold: Here's an interesting thing to keep in mind: Simone Signoret's autobiography was called *Nostalgia Isn't What It Used to Be Any More.* So is Trivia. Take a look at the period of time from which we garnered this information (1950–1965): You had three networks, you had sixteen major league baseball teams, and a tighter knit media world. Now you have cable, you have the Internet, you have thirty baseball teams, a proliferation of sports— the amount of information that people can share is so much more than the communal aspect of trivia. Back then, you could run into somebody from a different part of the country with a different background, but you still shared the same cultural elements. The chances of that are diminished when you have more choices.

Carlinsky: One of the most fertile areas for Trivia is the early days of television. If you were a kid in the fifties or if you were an adult in the fifties, you still grew up, in a way, as television was growing up. Television was terribly important culturally because it was so new and pervasive. If you are, today, forty-something or sixty-something or eighty-something, you still remember the early days of television with almost the same kind of impact. You almost didn't watch a specific program, you watched television.

Goodgold: What you really want are questions that evoke a response—like the ingredient in chocolate that makes people feel good, it releases the endorphins. In the same way, a good Trivia question should release that kind of feeling. It's not just the fact, but it evokes a time, a period, a place. It's not just a yes, no, true, false; it's Proustian, if you will.

Carlinsky: We distinguished between the flower of *Trivia* and the weed of *Minutiae.* Trivia always had to evoke the "Aha!" response; even if you didn't know the answer, you knew the question. It would make you say, "Ah, I should know that! I should remember that because I lived that when I was eleven years old." And then when someone told you, you would say, "Aha!" Whereas, if you asked, "Which state is the largest consumer of Jell-O?" and you said, "It's Delaware, and the average per capita consumption is 4.7 gallons per year," you would never say "Aha!" You would say "Who gives a shit?" The difference in response from Trivia to minutiae is the difference between "Aha" and "Who gives a shit?"

Ed Goodgold works in the School of Education at New York University in the Office of Academic Affairs and is writing books of a spiritual nature. Dan Carlinsky also writes books, magazine articles, and is an agent. They have collaborated on The Beatles Trivia Book *and* Movie Monsters Trivia, *among other titles.*

Chapter 1

TelEVisiOn

The quizzes, lists, items, and memories that follow are about the good things that television does. They're about favorite characters, memorable scenes, historic shows, obscure sidekicks, noble steeds, and the myriad moments that an entire generation discussed at work or school or over the fence the day after they saw them on TV. Instead of gossiping about the neighbors, people talked about JR.

But there's a dark side to television, too. And since it is arguably the most powerful and pervasive communication device in the history of the human race, perhaps a little thought should be given to how it has changed the world, not to mention the people in it.

If music ever abdicates its position as the universal language, first place will inevitably fall to television. No human endeavor has done more to spread culture—or distort truth—than that ubiquitous electronic device that coldly trades sound and pictures for direct human experience.

Television doesn't convey facts as much as impart impressions; for some reason—maybe because viewers don't take notes—people don't retain specific information that they see on TV, but they do remember the gist of it. For example, ask someone who has just watched a weather forecast what the high temperature is going to be tomorrow. Then ask him/her simply if it's going to be "a good day" or "a bad day." His/her answer defines the difference between fact and impression.

Most of the time, when the TV is on, people don't watch shows as much as they just watch television. Like an offhand remark half heard in the elevator, people are seldom able to remember exactly where they picked up an idea, yet they will often feel comfortable repeating it. This is essential to making commercials effective, whether they are trying to convince people to switch beer brands or elect a public official. All people remember is that they saw something, or someone, on TV, and the experience becomes self-fulfilling.

Television legitimizes. It captivates. It secures, sedates, and sells. In the beginning, however, it only seduces.

It's hard to remember now, more than fifty years after it first went on sale, that television was originally praised as an invention that would bring families together. The reasoning was simple, if cynical: Since the first television sets were so expensive, the typical American family would only be able to afford one of them, so logic dictated that they would gather in one place (probably the living room) to watch it as a group.

That didn't last long, of course, as time and technology made TV sets cheaper and families more mobile. By the early 1960s, "the boob tube" was being blamed for fostering juvenile delinquency, raising the divorce rate, lowering IQ scores, and, oh yes, making kids go blind because they sat too close to the screen. Come to think of it, the same bad things were being said about comic books, rock 'n' roll, skateboards, and monster movies.

Quiz: Service with a Smile

In TV sitcoms the servant has the final word, and it's usually funny. From the list that follows, match the performers' names with their roles, and then identify the series. (Extra credit: Who played Beulah on radio, and why was the casting notable? Extra special credit: Name a second person who played a similar role in *McMillan and Wife*.)

Performer	Character	Series
1. Shirley Booth	Mildred	*Batman*
2. Esther Rolle	Beulah	*Rawhide*
3. Alan Napier	Alice Nelson	*The Brady Bunch*
4. Ethel Waters	Mrs. Livingston	*McMillan and Wife*
5. Paul Brinegar	Benson	*Bonanza*
6. Ann B. Davis	Florida Evans	*Courtship of Eddie's Father*
7. Victor Sen Yung	Hazel	*Maude*
8. Miyoshi Umeki	Hop Sing	*The Beulah Show*
9. Nancy Walker	Wishbone	*Hazel*
10. Robert Guillaume	Alfred Pennyworth	*Soap*

Quiz: Horses and Riders

Match the horse with the hero or heroine who rode in the saddle:

Rider	Steed
1. Johnny Mack Brown	a. Diablo
2. Roy Rogers	b. Tony
3. Hopalong Cassidy	c. Silver
4. Tom Mix	d. Buttermilk
5. The Lone Ranger	e. Scout
6. Tonto	f. Marshal
7. Gene Autry	g. Rebel
8. Zorro	h. Rex
9. Matt Dillon	i. Trigger
10. The Cisco Kid	j. Champion
11. Dale Evans	k. Tornado and Phantom
12. Sgt. Preston	l. Topper

Quiz: Heroes and Sidekicks

Match the heroes (mostly from TV, but also from other media) with their comical sidekicks. (Note: Some had serial sidekicks.)

Hero

1. Lash La Rue
2. Roy Rogers
3. Gene Autry
4. Wild Bill Hickok (Guy Madison)
5. Red Ryder
6. Super Chicken
7. Spider-Man
8. Hopalong Cassidy
9. Captain Midnight
10. Crusader Rabbit
11. Rocket J. Squirrel

Sidekick

a. Little Beaver
b. Ichabod Mudd
c. James Ellison
d. Al "Fuzzy" St. John
e. Rags the Tiger
f. Pat Brady
g. Andy Clyde
h. Andy "Jingles" Devine
i. Pat Buttram
j. Smiley Burnett
k. Fred
l. Edgar Buchanan
m. Bullwinkle J. Moose
n. George "Gabby" Hayes
o. Russell Hayden

Quiz: Hosts

Who hosted the original versions of the following TV shows? (Hint: Some shows had multiple hosts.)

1. NBC *Tonight* (before Johnny Carson)
2. NBC *Today* show
3. *The Breakfast Club*
4. *House Party*
5. *Video Village*
6. *Let's Make a Deal*
7. *Pantomime Quiz*
8. *You Asked For It*
9. *Beat the Clock*
10. *I've Got a Secret*
11. *People Are Funny*
12. *What's My Line?*

Choices:

Steve Allen, Art Baker, Al "Jazzbo" Collins, Bud Collyer, John Charles Daly, Dave Garroway, Monty Hall, Bob Hilton, Jack Lescoulie, Art Linkletter, Don MacNeill, Garry Moore, Jack Narz, Jack Paar, "Whisperin'" Jack Smith, Mike Stokey

Top TV Shows

People love happy endings, and when television promises one, viewers tune in. The last episode of *M*A*S*H*, the resolution of *The Fugitive*, the closing chapter of *Roots*, the climax of *Lonesome Dove* were just four of the most popular shows of all time (if you believe the ratings). Even though there are more people watching more TV nowadays, they are spread over so many additional networks that it is doubtful that any single program will ever again match the viewership of those from more than twenty years ago. The fragmentation of the audience by cable as well as other uses of the tube (Internet, VCR, satellite, etc.) have made it virtually impossible for the country to ever again be unified by a single broadcast on a single station on a single night. Only the Super Bowl remains a sure thing. For the record, these are the ten shows that set ratings records that may never be surpassed:

Program	Date	Viewers
1. *M*A*S*H* (final episode)	February 28, 1983	50,150,000
2. *Dallas* (Who shot JR?)	November 21, 1980	41,470,000
3. *The Day After* (ABC TVM)	November 20, 1983	38,550,000
4. *Roots* (final chapter)	January 30, 1977	36,380,000
5. *Gone with the Wind* (Part 2)	November 8, 1976	33,750,000
6. *Gone with the Wind* (Part 1)	November 7, 1976	33,390,000
7. *Roots* (Part 6)	January 28, 1977	32,680,000
8. *Roots* (Part 5)	January 27, 1977	32,540,000
9. *Bob Hope Christmas Show*	January 15, 1970	27,260,000
10. *The Fugitive* (last chapter)	August 29, 1967	25,700,000

Jackie Gleason

"I'm no alcoholic," Jackie Gleason once said. "I'm a drunkard. There's a difference: A drunkard doesn't like to go to meetings."

But that hardly mattered to Jackie Gleason's millions of fans, the ones who saw him sip something other than tea from his teacup every week on *The American Scene Magazine* (1962–1968). "I just had a little booze," Gleason later joked without embarrassment. "I'm on a strict diet: just booze."

Far from tarnishing his image, Gleason's celebrated bad habits—food, smoke, and liquor—actually defined it. He was the eternal *bon vivant* whose behavior could be equally maddening and endearing. People loved Gleason, respected his range, and laughed at his jokes—even though, at times, he seemed to be his own biggest fan. Somewhere along his five-decade show business odyssey he acquired the title "The Great One," and it fit.

Born in Brooklyn, New York, in 1916 into circumstances that could charitably be called abject poverty, Gleason ambled through vaudeville and supper clubs, never climbing higher than second banana and generally getting fired for his bad attitude. His break came in 1949 when he was hired to play the lead in television's The *Life of Riley*, after William Bendix, who had created the title role on radio, became tied up with movie commitments. Gleason's Riley was a revoltin' development and lasted one season; rather than play Chester A. Riley as a lovable lug, Gleason (who had listened to the suggestions of others), played him as a buffoon.

Thereafter, he vowed, he would never take advice from anyone else. (*The Life of Riley* returned, with Bendix, from 1953–1958.)

Next hired for the Dumont Network's *Cavalcade of Stars* in 1950, Gleason's ability to ad-lib made him a treasure. That, plus the gift of a photographic memory and an impatience with delay, added an edge to every performance. You either kept up with Gleason or got trampled; only Art Carney and Audrey Meadows consistently survived, and their ensemble work in *The Honeymooners*—a recurring skit that began in *The Jackie Gleason Show* in 1952 and that took on a life of its own—made them all into legends.

Ironically, to a generation too young to have seen most of his live TV work, the thirty-nine *Honeymooners* episodes filmed for the 1955–1956 season and endlessly rerun were what brought Gleason his greatest fame. The other *Honeymooners* skits, produced in varying lengths through 1971 on kinescope, had been thought lost. In 1985, however, they were found.

"They weren't lost," Gleason later admitted, "they were in my basement. It just took someone a long time to find the money." The "someone" was cable TV.

In his later years, Gleason, who once weighed in excess of 300 pounds, shed much of his bulk as his health, weakened by emphysema, declined. He died on June 24, 1987, at age seventy-one, not of emphysema but of cancer. His final feature film appearance was in Garry Marshall's sensitive comedy *Nothing in Common*, opposite Tom Hanks.

Quiz: The Honeymooners

The phenomenon of *The Honeymooners* is that the public never tired of watching its thirty-nine episodes, which were in near-constant rerun until the "lost" episodes were found in 1985. Those original thirty-nine half hours—shot in 1955–1956 on film as part of a complicated spin-off deal with Jackie Gleason Enterprises—contain the essential lore of this beloved series. (For definitive Honeymoonia consult *The Official Honeymooner's Treasury* by Peter Crescenti and Bob Columbe, cofounders of RALPH™: The Royal Association for the Longevity and Preservation of the Honeymooners.)

1. What was the name of the "Lodge" to which Ralph and Ed belonged? What was the name of their bowling team?
2. What romantic line did Ralph invariably say to Alice at fade-out?
3. Where—and how—did an irritated Ralph threaten to send a recalcitrant Alice?
4. What phrase did Ralph invariably utter when he was in trouble or confused?
5. What was Ralph's favorite meal?
6. What did Ralph say if he didn't think something was funny?
7. Which item was not among those in the Kramden's kitchen?
   a) Refrigerator b) Table and chairs c) Sink d) Cabinets e) Telephone
8. At what address did the Kramdens and Nortons live?
9. What musical talent did Ed Norton have, and what's the catch?
10. For whom did Ralph and Ed work?

Quiz: Making a Living

Nobody seriously believed that the television sitcoms of the '50s and '60s accurately reflected American life. Yet, while such social issues as unemployment were virtually unknown on network shows, some of them were a little vague about exactly what Dad did for a living. Match Pop to his profession:

TV Father	Profession
1. Ozzie Nelson (Ozzie Nelson)	a. Accountant
2. Mike Brady (Robert Reed)	b. Aviation engineer
3. Rob Petrie (Dick Van Dyke)	c. Magazine publisher
4. Steve Douglas (Fred MacMurray)	d. Who knows?
5. Dr. Alex Stone (Carl Betz)	e. Consulting engineer
6. Jim Anderson (Robert Young)	f. Architect
7. Tom Corbett (Bill Bixby)	g. TV head writer
8. Chester A. Riley (William Bendix)	h. Pediatrician
9. Bill Davis (Brian Keith)	i. Insurance agent
10. Ward Cleaver (Hugh Beaumont)	j. Aircraft hard hat

Brilliant Endings

When most TV series are canceled, they just shuffle off into the land of reruns. A few, however, end so brilliantly that the memory not only lingers but also it reminds us why they were successful in the first place. Here are some of the more satisfactory fade-outs. (Caution: contains spoilers.)

Mary Tyler Moore Show (September 3, 1977): New management takes over WJM-TV and fires everyone on the news staff—except Ted Baxter.

Newhart (September 8, 1990): After eight seasons of running a Vermont inn with his wife, Joanna (played by Mary Frann), Bob wakes up to find himself in bed next to Emily (Suzanne Pleshette), his wife from *The Bob Newhart Show*, having dreamed about running an inn in Vermont.

St. Elsewhere (August 10, 1988): Six seasons of inventive, taut, and frequently surrealistic dramas are revealed to have been the unexpressed daydreams of an autistic boy looking at a snow-globe of a hospital.

*M*A*S*H* (February 28, 1983): The adventures of America's combat surgeons in Korea (which lasted some eight years longer than the Korean conflict itself) concluded with the end of hostilities and the dramatic wrapping up of its numerous story lines.

Get a Life: Ponsonby Britt

Question: Who is Ponsonby Britt?

Answer: When Jay Ward and Bill Scott set up shop to create such memorable characters as Rocky and Bullwinkle, George of the Jungle, Super Chicken, Boris and Natasha, Mr. Peabody and Sherman, etc., they were more interested in producing TV shows than answering mail. So they invented an executive producer and named him Ponsonby Britt. That way, if anybody called or wrote looking for Mr. Britt, Ward and Scott knew it was no one they had to pay attention to.

Jay Ward was unquestionably one of the geniuses of TV. Not only did he possess the gift of devising a world in which every young fan thought that he or she was the only one who "got it," but Ward, himself, attained that level of wit in a medium not known for encouraging it.

He was also an eccentric who rarely allowed photographs, was famous for pulling bizarre publicity stunts, and even sent a life-sized cutout of himself to stand in the receiving line at the wedding of his daughter, Tiffany.

His legacy endures not only on home video, theatrical features, and in theme parks but also at the eclectic family-run gift shop-cum-shrine that sells merchandise and mementos:

Dudley Do-Right Emporium
8200 West Sunset Boulevard
West Hollywood, CA 90069
(323) 656-6550

The Fugitive (August 29, 1967): After nearly four years of running from Lt. Gerard (Barry Morse), Dr. Richard Kimble (David Janssen) is finally cleared when the one-armed man (Bill Raisch), who Kimble insisted murdered his wife, is uncovered but dies before he can be taken into custody. This resolution—watched by 72 percent of TV viewers—wasn't so much a clever surprise ending as much as it was simple approbation. Unfortunately, once Kimble was exonerated, the producers had a hard time selling the show in syndication.

Andy Griffith

The Andy Griffith Show was everything America wanted to be in the 1960s but wasn't. As a matter of fact, by the time the show hit its stride in its first season, the America that Mayberry, North Carolina, so warmly represented was preparing to fade into the mist of nostalgia.

Over eight seasons and 249 episodes, the show was always among the ten top-rated programs on television and remains a sturdy evergreen in syndication. Its April, 1986 reunion special, *Return to Mayberry*, was the highest rated movie of the season.

The series was also the inspiration for at least three subsequent bucolic shows: *The Beverly Hillbillies* (1962–1971), *Petticoat Junction* (1963–1970), and *Green Acres* (1965–1971), as well as its own sequel, *Mayberry R.F.D.* (1968–1971), which came after Griffith left his own series.

The Andy Griffith Show embodied the values of its star, who was born in Mt. Airy, North Carolina, in the Blue Ridge mountains. After college at the University of North Carolina—where he had considered the ministry—Griffith became a performer on the Rotary Club circuit. His first notice came with the monologue *What It Was, Was Football*, in which he played a naive backwoods boy confronted with the mysteries of organized sports. It was a small jump from playing that hayseed character to starring as Will Stockdale in the Broadway hit, *No Time for Sergeants*. Griffith entered movies in 1957 in Elia Kazan's *A Face in the Crowd*, in which he played a dynamic down-home TV talkmaster who, when the camera was off, was a power-mad bigot.

Griffith, a gifted actor, proved difficult to cast in films, so pronounced was his country persona. Fortunately, he fit right into the population of Mayberry and the character of Sheriff Andy Taylor, a widower with a young son, Opie (Ron—then called Ronny—Howard). Andy and Opie lived with Andy's Aunt Bee (Francis Bavier) in a community full of lovable zanies: Gomer Pyle (Jim Nabors), Floyd Lawson (Howard McNear), Otis Campbell (Hal Smith), Goober Pyle (George Kindsey), and the irredeemably inept but consistently lovable Barney Fife (Don Knotts). Andy's love interest at first was Ellie May Walker (Elinor Donahue), then Helen Crump (Aneta Corsaut), although he never remarried. Since there was no crime in Mayberry, Sheriff Taylor had little to do but serve as father figure to the village eccentrics, which pretty much covered everybody who lived there. Of course, that helps explain the show's broad appeal.

Quiz: Andy Griffith Show

There is such a wealth of Trivia to *The Andy Griffith Show* that the best way to handle it is with off-the-wall questions:

1. What does the name "Gomer" mean?
2. Which of the following persons did *not* appear as guest stars on *The Andy Griffith Show*:
    a) Bill Bixby
    b) Edgar Buchanan
    c) Doodles Weaver
    d) Raymond Burr
    e) Buddy Ebsen
3. Name the theme song and its composers.
4. Which of the following is Barney Fife's middle name:
    a) Milton
    b) Oliver
    c) P (initial)
5. Where does Barney Fife keep his bullet?
6. What was the name of Andy Taylor's wife (Opie's mother)?
7. Where do Andy, Opie, and "Aint" *(sic)* Bee live?
8. Name the town newspaper.
9. What is Gomer Pyle's job at the fillin' station?
10. Recite Gomer's signal phrases.

The Brady Bunch

Stand-up comedians long ago recognized it as the comedy club circuit's equivalent of the "Star-Spangled Banner": If you're dying on stage, there's no better way to get an audience's attention than to start them singing the theme song from *The Brady Bunch.*

The ABC-TV series is remarkable not only for what it is but also for what it isn't. Nominally, it's the story of a lovely lady (for God's sake, don't sing it!), a widow with three daughters, who marries a widower with three sons. The shows were produced between 1969 and 1974, during the years that were, outside the studio walls, the most tormented in recent American history. Nevertheless, the show offered pure escapism; relevance was limited to fashions not politics, and on those few occasions when the world at large dared enter the Clinton Avenue Brady home, it only raised issues such as sexism, women's liberation, or sex to set up a gentle joke.

And *gentle* is the word for *The Brady Bunch* (not to mention *gentile*). It is a show about a close family whose members support each other. There is no negativity. Even the put-downs are clearly rooted in affection. The series is "sweet" in the best sense of the word.

It is also grotesquely dated, more so than others of the era, probably because it starred so many young people who, in order to relate to their viewers, had to dress and act just like them (big mistake). Accordingly, the series' use of mores, slang, music, and attitudes have frozen its 116 episodes (plus pilot) in time. And that, of course, is why it is timeless.

Somehow *The Brady Bunch* became the darling of both the 1970s and the 1990s without ever having anything to do with the 1980s. Although there were furtive efforts to revive the series in 1977 and 1990 (with a few reunion movies thrown in along the way), it remained for *The Brady Bunch Movie* (1995) to make the connection between past and present. Coproduced and cowritten by Sherwood Schwartz, creator of the television series, *The Brady Bunch Movie* literally dragged the Bradys lock, stock, and bell-bottoms into modernity. The plot was so old that it had osteoporosis: The Bradys had to raise back taxes or lose their house. But the conflict between '70s optimism and '90s cynicism could not have been more profound, or funnier, and the film made the most of it.

Isolation in a fantasy culture may explain the Bradys' original appeal, but what has sustained it? In one sense, they are like the pictures you and your friends took of each other in college but no longer dare show anyone: long hair, tinted shades, epaulets, bell-bottoms, flowered shirts, miniskirts, sideburns, love beads, and using words like *groovy*, *hip*, *do your own thing*, *outasite*, *with it*, *far out*, and *funky*. *The Brady Bunch*—more than any other TV show of the era—tried so consciously to be contemporary that it's now a time capsule living in rerun purgatory.

Quiz: The Brady Bunch

True or False:

1. Carol Brady was the first divorced female character to star in a sitcom.
2. The Brady house had a double bed but no toilet.
3. Tiger, the Brady dog, was replaced mid-season.
4. *The Brady Bunch* is based on the feature film *Yours, Mine and Ours*.
5. Paul Lynde was the center square.
6. The show was a ratings success.
7. Horror meister Vincent Price found himself among the Bradys.
8. Dennis the Menace's dad and Richie Cunningham's mom once appeared on the show.
9. Desi may love Lucy, but Desi, Jr., loves Marcia.
10. Mike Lookinland, Susan Olsen, and Maureen McCormick all filmed scenes for *The Brady Bunch Movie* but they were removed prior to release.

Quiz: Wacky Neighbors

Who were the wacky neighbors—as opposed to the zany housekeepers, flaky bosses, precocious kids, or ditzy females—on the following TV shows, and who played them? (Hint: Some families had serial wacky neighbors.)

1. *Ozzie and Harriet*
2. *Dick Van Dyke*
3. *I Love Lucy*
4. *December Bride*
5. *Bewitched*
6. *Dennis the Menace*
7. *The Jeffersons*
8. *All in the Family*
9. *Three's Company*
10. *Mr. Ed*

Quiz: Harry Morton Lives

One role in television went through more actors than any other, except maybe Lassie. In its eight seasons on the air, *The George Burns and Gracie Allen Show* had no fewer than four actors playing Harry to Bea Benaderet's Blanche, the Burns's faithful (and obviously sturdy) next-door neighbor. Why so many Harrys in the night? Was the strain too great putting up with Gracie's ditziness? Or did Blanche get back at Harry for all those wisecracks about her cooking? Name the four Harrys:

Quiz: Good Eeeeeevening

If he wasn't Alfred Hitchcock, they never would have allowed him to appear on TV. Yet in his slow-talking, corpulent, mischievous and funereal way, he was more sincere than any dozen other stand-up hosts (except, perhaps, Rod Serling).

The great suspense director introduced ten years of the anthology *Alfred Hitchcock Presents* and then, through the miracle of colorization, returned from the grave to host a revival series—some new, some remakes—in 1987–1988. The studio simply took his original intros (written dryly and brilliantly by James Allardice) and spliced them onto new productions that vaguely fit the themes. Grotesque? Certainly. But Hitch would have approved. (Obviously his estate did.)

One of the few directors to be recognized by the general public, Hitchcock was a master of publicity as well as suspense. Audiences savored his weekly appearances and even stayed tuned while he announced commercials, waiting to see how he would insult the sponsor each week. And he got away with it.

Ever the cost-conscious filmmaker, Hitchcock embraced television, or at least its ability to use smaller union crews and a faster shooting schedule in order to save money. At least, that's how he made *Psycho* in 1960 (with his TV crew) for theatrical release. But Hitchcock also directed eighteen of the series episodes, including at least one that has become a classic of the genre. How many can you describe or name?

Rod Serling

There is a fifth dimension beyond that which is known to man. It is a dimension as vast as space and as timeless as infinity. It is the middle ground between light and shadow, between science and superstition, and it lies between the pit of man's fears and the summit of his knowledge. This is the dimension of imagination. It is an area which we call the Twilight Zone.

—Rod Serling © 1959, 1987
Cayuga Productions

Only a writer could truly appreciate what Rod Serling—one of the first and greatest television writers—did for writers everywhere. Serling not only got to host a TV series but, what's more, *he talked on the air about the writers!*

They included Charles Beaumont, Ray Bradbury, John Furia, Jr., Earl Hamner, Jr., George Clayton Johnson, Richard Matheson, Montgomery Pittman, Reginald Rose, and Jerry Sohl, but mostly Serling, who was contractually obligated to deliver 80 percent of the scripts himself—and, remarkably, did. An astonishing number became classics.

But that shouldn't surprise anyone who watched *The Twilight Zone* every week. The haunting anthology, which first ran from October of 1959 to June of 1964, stands practically alone as an example of creative, literate, and compelling short-form television drama. In spite of this—or perhaps because of it—the series always had to struggle for ratings and network renewal orders.

Serling was already the acclaimed author of *Requiem for a Heavyweight*, *Patterns*, *The Rack*, and several adaptations for CBS's *Playhouse 90* when he proposed a fantasy script called "The Time Element" in 1958. It was a time-travel story about a modern man who finds himself back in 1941 and tries unsuccessfully to warn the army about the impending attack on Pearl Harbor. Even though it was contorted by sponsor pressure (an important element in 1958), it drew attention when it aired and opened the doors a little so that *The Twilight Zone* could squeak through for five bumpy seasons.

Everybody has at least five favorite *Zone* episodes, each of which featured unusually strong characters in a life crisis that was not necessarily resolved neatly by the end credits; in fact, most were distinctively unsettling, such as:

- "Time Enough at Last," in which Burgess Meredith is an avid reader who survives a nuclear blast only to break his glasses
- "Eye of the Beholder," in which a hideously ugly woman is revealed to be gorgeous by earth standards but deformed according to the aesthetics of her own alien race
- "A Stop at Willoughby," in which harried businessman James Daly gets off his commuter train and steps into the bucolic small town of his dreams—and he doesn't know he's dead
- "Monsters Are Due on Maple Street," in which a suburban community goes crazy at the prospect of space aliens among them, when, in fact, the space aliens are watching from above as an experiment in earthly paranoia
- "To Serve Man," in which alien visitors arrive on earth bearing a plan for happiness, which, when decoded, turns out to be a cookbook
- "It's a Good Life," in which a boy with horrific telekenetic powers punishes people by putting them "out in the corn field"

- "The Dummy," in which a ventriloquist is possessed by his dummy (years before *Magic* was ever written or filmed)

The first three years of *The Twilight Zone* featured lean, well-focused, snazzy half-hour dramas. Season number four saw the time slot expanded to an hour, but in adding sub-plots and, at times, blatant padding, the shows lost their punch. The series ended its first incarnation in 1965, and, thereafter, Serling devoted his time to feature films (*Seven Days in May*, *Planet of the Apes*, and *The Man*, which had been made for TV but released to theatres instead). He also found a second career doing commercial voice-overs and documentary narration. In 1970 he was brought aboard to host (and sometimes write) *Night Gallery* on NBC, an anthology series that tried to be spooky but seemed to be more scared of itself. Serling died in 1975 at the age of fifty, during open-heart surgery.

Any hope of bringing back *The Twilight Zone* died with him, or so it was thought until 1983, when interest was revived, ironically, after the ill-fated *Twilight Zone: The Movie* reminded Hollywood's decision-making puppies that there was a wealth of script material in the Serling estate. By 1985 *The Twilight Zone* was back on TV—this time in color, with violence, and as a showcase for big-name directors, but, more importantly, fueled by remaking some of the original series' best scripts.

Disappointingly, the new *Twilight Zone* was less in awe of the writing than the *idea* of the writing. It turned out that Rod Serling was more than just the *Twilight Zone*'s spokesman; he was also its soul. Although the new *Zone*'s producers fought bravely to keep the old spirit alive, it proved impossible in an age of short attention spans, cable-level budgets, and frightened bean counters with a focus on group mentality. By 1988 Serling's "dimension of imagination" had become a desert.

Yet *The Twilight Zone* lingers in the mind, which, of course, is where is was so effective. As vivid as a nightmare, as hypnotic as *film noir*, and as evocative as one's most primal urges, *The Twilight Zone* is probably the most consistently memorable dramatic series that was ever "submitted for your approval . . ."

Get a Life: Who Shot JR?

Question: Who shot JR?

Answer: Kristin Shepard (played by Mary Crosby) shot J. R. Ewing (played by Larry Hagman) on *Dallas* at the end of the 1979–1980 season, but her identity was kept secret until the series resumed in the fall. In the convoluted story, Kristin was carrying JR's child, and she shot him rather than leave town after learning that he was about to frame her as a prostitute. But let's face it, she really shot him for ratings: Some 80 percent of American homes were watching CBS on November 21, 1980, the night her identity was revealed (q.v.).

Star Trek to the Prairies

For years Gene Roddenberry recalled how he sold *Star Trek* to the network by describing it as a *"Wagon Train* to the stars." The quote has been faithfully—and endlessly—repeated for thirty years (as has *Star Trek*). There's only one problem: How many people today have a clue about what *Wagon Train* was?

Well, *Wagon Train* was an hour-long western series that ran not only from Missouri to California, but also from 1957 to 1965. It starred Ward Bond—who had provided gruff character support in so many John Wayne/John Ford films—as Major Seth Adams. (Bond was also Bert the cop in *It's a Wonderful Life*.) When Bond died in November of 1960, he was replaced by the somewhat more avuncular John McIntyre, as Christopher Hale.

Since the whole idea of a wagon train is that it is a traveling city, each episode brought its population to a new location—although somehow they all seemed to look like the Universal Studios ranch. Sometimes the enemy was "hostile Indians," for which their scout, the younger and sexier Flint McCullough, played by Robert Horton, would ride ahead and try to make peace. When Horton, himself, turned hostile and quit the show, he was replaced by Michael Burns and Robert Fuller.

At other times the jeopardy came from within. The episodic nature of *Wagon Train* allowed an extraordinary number of guest appearances by well-known stars, whom the settlers either encountered on the way west or who had been quietly among the Conestoga population all along. At least one of the shows ("The Colter Craven Story," 1969) was directed by John Ford as a favor to Ward Bond, which was fitting, since the series was arguably based on Ford's own 1950 film, *Wagon Master*.

If it appears that *Wagon Train* had more in common with *Star Trek* than Gene Roddenberry's coy comment acknowledged, it's only that both shows share Homeric roots with *The Iliad* and *The Odyssey*. What Roddenberry really had in the back of his mind was the quality of the *Wagon Train* shows. After its first season, it vied with the equally lauded *Gunsmoke* for ratings success, finally beating venerable Marshall Dillon in 1962, which is about the same time that Gene Roddenberry was going around town pitching *Star Trek*.

Wagon Train was an anthology series that didn't look like an anthology series. Plus, Major Adams could start fresh in Missouri at the beginning of every new TV season (presumably he rode back east alone during the summer hiatus). Where is it today? Unfortunately, *Wagon Train* is a black-and-white western, with mostly sixty-minute episodes (one season ran ninety minutes), and is therefore not easy to sell for reruns. But as an adult western with consistently fine writing and acting, it can be proud of going where not only no man has gone before but also very few TV shows, either.

PTM: Stirling Silliphant

Screenwriter Stirling Silliphant wrote an astonishing 73 out of 114 episodes for the 1960–1964 series Route 66. Starring Martin Milner as Todd Stiles and George Maharis and Buzz Murdock (Glenn Corbett replaced Maharis in shows airing from March 1963), the concept was simple: Two guys vroom across America in their 'vette and meet people—but the execution transcended it. The format allowed for new locations and new guest stars every week and a great deal of freedom, as Silliphant recounted.

By Stirling Silliphant

I have always felt that the most original writing I have done in the filmed medium was done in the period 1960 to 1964 when I wrote the majority of the one-hour *Route 66* filmed-on-location shows for CBS. These shows caught the American psyche of that period about as accurately as it could be caught. I wrote all of them out of an intense personal motivation, each was a work of passion and conviction.

We could have done many of the stories without [the main characters], but the stories, somehow, worked *better* with Marty and George involved. In a sense, *they* were the viewer—bringing the viewer into a new town, meeting new people, becoming involved, having the involvement either affect or not affect their own search for identity. Rather than feel they were a drag on the stories, I can tell you clearly that I would have been lost without them and their reactions and interplay.

Of course the guest stars got the juicy parts—as witness Anne Francis in "A Month of Sundays" or Julie Newmar in "How Much a Pound Is Albatross" or Tuesday Weld in "Love Is a Skinny Kid" or Bob Duvall in "Bird Cage on My Foot."

The series did attract some of the best actors from both New York and Hollywood. I remember Joan Crawford called us personally and asked if she could appear in an episode. I wrote a show just for her—"Same Picture, Different Frame." We had one of the most brilliant casting talents in the business, working on the show, Marion Dougherty. And she was working out of New York, where her judgment was based on performance, not fan mail.

With the exception of the Joan Crawford episode, I never wrote for any particular actor or actress. The characters came out of the writing—the casting then came out of the character. For example, I wrote an episode called "Kiss the Maiden All Forlorn," which required a debonair actor of clearly established class—and Marion signed Douglas Fairbanks, Jr., for the part. [Producer] Bert Leonard flew him from London to the location in Texas.

Without going into too much personal detail, there were few of the stories I wrote for "Route 66" during those four years which did not spring out of my own life.

Silliphant died in April of 1996. This is an excerpt of his career interview with Nat Segaloff for Backstory 3, *Patrick McGilligan, ed. (CA: University of California Press, 1997).*

PTM: Stan Levin on Red Skelton

Red Skelton was, with Lucille Ball, one of a tiny number of true, classic clowns to work in television. Film critic and playwright Stan Levin recalls Skelton in a way that helps explain his immense appeal.

By Stan Levin

When Red Skelton died in September of 1997 at the age of eighty-four, he had been semiretired for a number of years, but when he had his weekly network television variety show for a remarkable twenty seasons from 1951 to 1971, he was incredibly active.

The son of circus performers, Skelton held fast to this tradition, favoring the visual over the verbal and the carefully built routine over one-line gags. Even more astonishing, in the television field of the '50s, '60s, and '70s, he was not alone in this respect for the circus tradition; no less than Lucille Ball, Carol Burnett, and Jackie Gleason also embraced the art of classic clowning.

Although Skelton starred in a string of successful comedies at MGM in the '40s (most notably *Merton of the Movies* but also others), he is best known for his television appearances.

In 1971 I was living in Canoga Park, California, and trekked over the mountains into Los Angeles to watch a taping of the Skelton show at CBS Television City. Skelton did his standard repertoire: Clem Kadiddlehopper, Gertrude and Heathcliff, San Fernando Red, et al. The material was new each week, but he played it with the same panache and polish as if he had honed it to perfection in vaudeville for twenty years.

During the commercial breaks, he did something I'd never experienced before or since: Instead of chatting with his producer and director about the next segment, he played the studio audience. He asked if we were enjoying the show. He did material for us to keep us focused and entertained. Consequently, after each commercial break, we were progressively more laudatory. He called it entertainment; I called it seduction, and I loved every minute of it. Skelton was a consummate entertainer.

TV Schedules

It can't happen now that there are 99-plus cable channels, but back in the '60s, when there were only three networks and maybe an independent station in the bigger cities, kids used to memorize the weekly TV schedules. Was it because TV was so good in the days of Perry Como that you didn't want to miss a minute of it? Or was it just that when there was only one TV set per household, a ten-year-old didn't want to risk his daily viewing allowance on a time slot he wasn't sure about?

The choices have blossomed exponentially since, say, 1946, when Dumont featured *Cash and Carry* at 9 PM on Wednesdays and NBC alternated *You Are an Artist* and *Let's Rhumba* on Fridays at 8:30. Ten years later Dumont was out of business and the surviving ABC, CBS, and NBC were going head-to-head with full rosters of westerns, sitcoms, variety shows, and dramas.

Here are some snapshots of the fall prime time (7 to 11 PM) network lineups for average years. Programs that made their debuts as midseason replacements won't show up unless they ran five years into the next sample. (For a truly helpful research work, consult the most recent edition of *The Complete Directory to Prime Time Network TV Shows* by Tim Brooks and Earle Marsh.) Depending on how old you are, try to recall how many of these shows made you race through your homework (or lie that you finished) to be able to watch or plead with your folks to stay up "just ten more minutes" to tune in. (Note: "/" means alternating or replacement shows.)

1956 Prime Time Lineup

Sunday:

ABC: *You Asked For It, Amateur Hour, Press Conference, Omnibus*

CBS: *Lassie, Jack Benny/Ann Sothern, Ed Sullivan, GE Theatre, Alfred Hitchcock Presents, $64,000 Challenger, What's My Line?*

NBC: *Bengal Lancers, Circus Boy, Steve Allen Show, Goodyear Playhouse/Alcoa Aluminum Hour, Loretta Young Show, Bowling*

Monday:

ABC: *Kukla, Fran and Ollie, News, Bold Journey, Danny Thomas, Voice of Firestone, Life Is Worth Living, Lawrence Welk Talent Scouts*

CBS: *News, Adventures of Robin Hood, Burns and Allen, Arthur Godfrey Talent Scouts, I Love Lucy, December Bride, Studio One*

NBC: *Nat "King" Cole, News, Adventures of Sir Lancelot, Stanley, Medic, Robert Montgomery Presents*

Tuesday:

ABC: *Kukla, Fran and Ollie, News, Conflict/Cheyenne, Adventures of Wyatt Earp, Broken Arrow, DuPont Theatre, It's Polka Time*

CBS: *News, Name That Tune, Phil Silvers Show, The Brothers, Herb Shriner, Red Skelton, $64,000 Question, Do You Trust Your Wife?*

NBC: *Jonathan Winters, News, Big Surprise, Noah's Ark, Jane Wyman, Armstrong Circle Theatre/ Kaiser Aluminum Hour, Break the $250,000 Bank*

Wednesday:

ABC: *Kukla, Fran and Ollie, News, Disneyland, Navy Log, Adventures of Ozzie and Harriet, Ford Theatre, Wednesday Night Fights*

CBS: *News, Giant Step, Arthur Godfrey Talent Scouts, The Millionaire, I've Got a Secret, U.S. Steel Hour/Twentieth Century-Fox Hour*

NBC: *Eddie Fisher, News, Hiram Holliday, Father Knows Best, Kraft Television Theatre, This Is Your Life, Twenty-One*

Thursday:

ABC: *Kukla, Fran and Ollie, News, Lone Ranger, Circus Time, Wire Service, Ozark Jubilee*

CBS: *News, Sgt. Preston of the Yukon, Bob Cummings, Climax, Playhouse 90*

NBC: *Dinah Shore, News, You Bet Your Life, Dragnet, People's Choice, The Ford Show with Tennessee Ernie Ford, Lux Video Theatre*

Friday:

ABC: *Kukla, Fran and Ollie, News, Rin-Tin-Tin, Crossroads, Treasure Hunt, The Vise, Ray Anthony Show*

CBS: *News, My Friend Flicka, West Point Story, Dick Powell's Zane Grey Theatre, The Crusader, Schlitz Playhouse, The Lineup, Person to Person*

NBC: *Eddie Fisher, News, Life of Riley, Walter Winchell, On Trial, The Big Story, Cavalcade of Sports, Red Barber's Corner*

Saturday:

ABC: *Famous Film Festival, Lawrence Welk, Masquerade Party*

CBS: *Beat the Clock, The Buccaneers, Jackie Gleason, The Gale Storm Show, Hey Jeannie, Gunsmoke, High Finance*

NBC: *People Are Funny, Perry Como Show, Caesar's Hour, George Gobel, Your Hit Parade*

1962 Prime Time Lineup

Sunday:

ABC: *Father Knows Best, The Jetsons, ABC Movie, Voice of Firestone, Howard K. Smith*

CBS: *Lassie, Dennis the Menace, Ed Sullivan, The Real McCoys, G.E. True Theatre, Candid Camera, What's My Line?*

NBC: *Ensign O'Toole, Walt Disney's Wonderful World of Color, Car 54: Where Are You?, Bonanza, DuPont Show of the Week*

Monday:

ABC: *Cheyenne, The Rifleman, Stoney Burke, Ben Casey*

CBS: *News, To Tell the Truth, I've Got a Secret, Lucy Show, Danny Thomas, Andy Griffith Show, The New Loretta Young Show, Stump the Stars*

NBC: *It's a Man's World, Saints and Sinners, The Price Is Right, David Brinkley's Journal*

Tuesday:

ABC: *Combat, Hawaiian Eye, The Untouchables, Close-Up*

CBS: *News, Marshall Dillon, Lloyd Bridges, Red Skelton, Jack Benny, Garry Moore Show*

NBC: *Laramie, Empire, Dick Powell Show, Chet Huntley Report*

Wednesday:

ABC: *Wagon Train, Going My Way, Our Man Higgins, Naked City*

CBS: *News, CBS Reports, The Many Loves of Dobie Gillis, Beverly Hillbillies, Dick Van Dyke, Armstrong Circle Theatre/U.S. Steel Hour*

NBC: *The Virginian, The Perry Como Show, The Eleventh Hour*

Thursday:

ABC: *The Adventures of Ozzie and Harriet, The Donna Reed Show, Leave It to Beaver, My Three Sons, McHale's Navy, Alcoa Premiere Theatre*

CBS: *News, Mr. Ed, Perry Mason, The Nurses, Alfred Hitchcock Hour*

NBC: *Wide Country, Dr. Kildare, Hazel, Andy Williams*

Friday:

ABC: *The Gallant Men, The Flintstones, I'm Dickens—He's Fenster, 77 Sunset Strip*

CBS: *News, Rawhide, Route 66, Fair Exchange, Eyewitness*

NBC: *International Showtime, Sing Along with Mitch, Don't Call Me Charlie, Jack Paar Show*

Saturday:

ABC: *Beany and Cecil, Roy Rogers and Dale Evans, Mr. Smith Goes to Washington, Lawrence Welk, Fight of the Week, Make That Spare*

CBS: *Jackie Gleason, The Defenders, Have Gun, Will Travel, Gunsmoke*

NBC: *Sam Benedict, The Joey Bishop Show, NBC Movie*

1967 Prime Time Lineup

Sunday:

ABC: *Voyage to the Bottom of the Sea, The FBI, ABC Movie*

CBS: *Lassie, Gentle Ben, Ed Sullivan, Smothers Brothers, Mission: Impossible*

NBC: *Disney, Mothers-in-Law, Bonanza, The High Chaparral*

Monday:

ABC: *Cowboy in Africa, The Rat Patrol, Felony Squad, Peyton Place, The Big Valley*

CBS: *Gunsmoke, The Lucy Show, Andy Griffith Show, Family Affair, Carol Burnett Show*

NBC: *The Monkees, Man from U.N.C.L.E., Danny Thomas Hour, I Spy*

Tuesday:

ABC: *Garrison's Gorillas, The Invaders, NYPD, The Hollywood Palace*

CBS: *Daktari, Red Skelton, Good Morning World, CBS News Hour*

NBC: *I Dream of Jeannie, Jerry Lewis, NBC Movie*

Wednesday:

ABC: *Legend of Custer, The Second Hundred Years, ABC Movie*

CBS: *Lost in Space, Beverly Hillbillies, Green Acres, He and She, Dundee and Culhane*

NBC: *The Virginian, Kraft Music Hall, Run for Your Life*

Thursday:

ABC: *Batman, The Flying Nun, Bewitched, That Girl, Peyton Place, Good Company*

CBS: *Cimarron Strip, CBS Movie*

NBC: *Daniel Boone, Ironside, Dragnet, Dean Martin*

Friday:

ABC: *Off to See the Wizard, Hondo, Guns of Will Sonnett, Judd for the Defense*

CBS: *Wild, Wild West, Gomer Pyle, USMC, CBS Movie*

NBC: *Tarzan, Star Trek, Accidental Family, Actuality Specials/ Bell Telephone Hour*

Saturday:

ABC: *The Dating Game, Newlywed Game, Lawrence Welk, Lawrence Welk, Iron Horse, ABC Scope*

CBS: *Jackie Gleason, My Three Sons, Hogan's Heroes, Petticoat Junction, Mannix*

NBC: *Maya, Get Smart, NBC Movie*

1972 Prime Time Lineup

Sunday:

ABC: *The FBI, ABC Movie*

CBS: *Anna and the King, M*A*S*H, Sandy Duncan, New Dick Van Dyke Show, Mannix*

NBC: *Disney, Mystery Movie (Columbo, McCloud, McMillan and Wife, Hec Ramsey), Night Gallery*

Monday:
ABC: *The Rookies, Monday Night Football*
CBS: *Gunsmoke, Here's Lucy, Doris Day Show, New Bill Cosby Show*
NBC: *Rowan and Martin's Laugh-In, NBC Movie*

Tuesday:
ABC: *Temperature's Rising, Movie of the Week, Marcus Welby, MD*
CBS: *Maude, Hawaii Five-O, New CBS Movie*
NBC: *Bonanza, The Bold Ones, NBC Reports*

Wednesday:
ABC: *Paul Lynde Show, Movie of the Week, Julie Andrews Hour*
CBS: *Carol Burnett Show, Medical Center, Cannon*
NBC: *Adam-12, Mystery Movie (Madigan, Banacek, Cool Million), Search*

Thursday:
ABC: *Mod Squad, The Men, Owen Marshall*
CBS: *The Waltons, CBS Movie*
NBC: *Flip Wilson, Ironside, Dean Martin*

Friday:
ABC: *Brady Bunch, Partridge Family, Room 222, The Odd Couple, Love, American Style*
CBS: *Sonny and Cher, CBS Movie*
NBC: *Sanford and Son, Little People, Ghost Story, Banyon*

Saturday:
ABC: *Alias Smith and Jones, Streets of San Francisco, Sixth Sense*

CBS: *All in the Family, Bridget Loves Bernie, Mary Tyler Moore Show, Bob Newhart, Mission: Impossible*
NBC: *Emergency, NBC Movie*

1977 Prime Time Lineup

Sunday:
ABC: *Hardy Boys Mystery/Nancy Drew Mystery, Six Million Dollar Man*
CBS: *60 Minutes, Rhoda, On Our Own, All in the Family, Alice, Kojak*
NBC: *Disney, NBC Big Event*

Monday:
ABC: *San Pedro Beach Bums, Monday Night Football*
CBS: *Young Dan'l Boone, Betty White, Maude, Rafferty*
NBC: *Little House on the Prairie, NBC Movie*

Tuesday:
ABC: *Happy Days, Laverne and Shirley, Three's Company, Soap, Family*
CBS: *Fitzpatricks, M*A*S*H, One Day at a Time, Lou Grant*
NBC: *Richard Pryor, Mulligan's Stew, Police Woman*

Wednesday:
ABC: *Eight Is Enough, Charlie's Angels, Baretta*
CBS: *Good Times, Busting Loose, CBS Movie*
NBC: *Life and Times of Grizzly Adams, Oregon Trail, Big Hawaii*

Thursday:
ABC: *Welcome Back, Kotter, What's Happening, Barney Miller, Carter Country, Redd Foxx*

CBS: *The Waltons, Hawaii Five-O, Barnaby Jones*
NBC: *CHiPS, Man from Atlantis, Rosetti and Ryan*

Friday:

ABC: *Donny and Marie, ABC Movie*
CBS: *New Adventures of Wonder Woman, Logan's Run, Switch*
NBC: *Sanford and Son, Chico and the Man, Rockford Files, Quincy M.E.*

Saturday:

ABC: *Fish, Operation Petticoat, Starsky and Hutch, Love Boat*
CBS: *Bob Newhart, We've Got Each Other, The Jeffersons, Tony Randall, Carol Burnett*
NBC: *Bionic Woman, NBC Movie*

1982 Prime Time Lineup

Sunday:

ABC: *Ripley's Believe It or Not, Matt Houston, ABC Movie*
CBS: *60 Minutes, Archie Bunker's Place, Gloria, The Jeffersons, One Day at a Time, Trapper John, M.D.*
NBC: *Voyagers, CHiPS, NBC Movie*

Monday:

ABC: *That's Incredible, Monday Night Football*
CBS: *Square Pegs, Private Benjamin, M*A*S*H, Newhart, Cagney and Lacey*
NBC: *Little House: A New Beginning, NBC Movie*

Tuesday:

ABC: *Happy Days, Laverne and Shirley, Three's Company, 9 to 5, Hart to Hart*
CBS: *Bring 'em Back Alive, CBS Movie*

NBC: *Father Murphy, Gavilan, St. Elsewhere*

Wednesday:

ABC: *Tales of the Gold Monkey, The Fall Guy, Dynasty*
CBS: *Seven Brides for Seven Brothers, Alice, Filthy Rich, Tucker's Witch*
NBC: *Real People, Facts of Life, Family Ties, Quincy M.E.*

Thursday:

ABC: *Joanie Loves Chachi, Star of the Family, Too Close for Comfort, It Takes Two, 20/20*
CBS: *Magnum P.I., Simon and Simon, Knots Landing*
NBC: *Fame, Cheers, Taxi, Hill Street Blues*

Friday:

ABC: *Benson, The New Odd Couple, Greatest American Hero, The Quest*
CBS: *Dukes of Hazzard, Dallas, Falcon Crest*
NBC: *The Powers of Matthew Starr, Knight Rider, Remington Steele*

Saturday:

ABC: *T. J. Hooker, Fantasy Island, Love Boat*
CBS: *Disney Movie, CBS Movie*
NBC: *Diff'rent Strokes, Silver Spoons, Gimme a Break, Love, Sidney, Devlin Connection*

1987 Prime Time Lineup

Sunday:

ABC: *Disney Movie, Spenser: For Hire, Dolly, Buck James*
CBS: *60 Minutes, Murder, She Wrote, CBS Movie*

NBC: *Our House, Family Ties, My Two Dads, NBC Sunday Movie*

Fox (weekends only): *21 Jump Street, Werewolf, Married with Children, Tracey Ullman, Duel*

Monday:

ABC: *MacGuyver, Monday Night Football*

CBS: *Frank's Place, Kate 'n' Allie, Newhart, Designing Women, Cagney and Lacey*

NBC: *Alf, Valerie's Family, NBC Monday Movie*

Tuesday:

ABC: *Who's the Boss?, Growing Pains, Moonlighting, Thirtysomething*

CBS: *Houston Nights, Jake and the Fat Man, The Law and Harry McGraw*

NBC: *Matlock, J. J. Starbuck, Crime Story*

Wednesday:

ABC: *Perfect Strangers, Head of the Class, Hooperman, Slap Maxwell Story, Dynasty*

CBS: *Oldest Rookie, Magnum PI, The Equalizer*

NBC: *Highway to Heaven, A Year in the Life, St. Elsewhere*

Thursday:

ABC: *Sledge Hammer, The Charmings, ABC Movie*

CBS: *Tour of Duty, Wiseguy, Knots Landing*

NBC: *The Cosby Show, A Different World, Cheers, Night Court, LA Law*

Friday:

ABC: *Full House, I Married Dora, Max Headroom, 20/20*

CBS: *Beauty and the Beast, Dallas, Falcon Crest*

NBC: *Rags to Riches, Miami Vice, Private Eye*

Saturday:

ABC: *Once a Hero, Ohara, Hotel*

CBS: *My Sister Sam, Everything's Relative, Leg Work, West 57th*

NBC: *Facts of Life, 227, Golden Girls, Amen, Hunter*

Fox (weekends only): *Mr. President, Women in Prison, New Adventures of Beans Baxter, Second Chance*

1991 Prime Time Lineup

Sunday:

ABC: *Life Goes On, America's Funniest Home Videos, America's Funniest People, ABC Movie*

CBS: *60 Minutes, Murder, She Wrote, CBS Movie*

NBC: *Adventures of Mark and Brian, Eerie, Indiana, Man of the People, Pacific Station, NBC Movie*

Fox: *True Colors, Parker Lewis Can't Lose, In Living Color, ROC, Married with Children, Herman's Head, Sunday Comics*

Monday:

ABC: *MacGuyver, Football*

CBS: *Evening Shade, Major Dad, Murphy Brown, Designing Women, Northern Exposure*

NBC: *Fresh Prince of Bel Air, Blossom, NBC Movie*

Fox: *Fox Night at the Movies*

Tuesday:

ABC: *Full House, Home Improvement, Roseanne, Coach, Homefront*

CBS: *Rescue 911, CBS Movie*

NBC: *I'll Fly Away, In the Heat of the Night, Law and Order*

(no Fox on Tuesday or Wednesday)

Wednesday:

ABC: *Dinosaurs, Wonder Years, Doogie Howser, M.D., Sibs, Anything but Love, Good and Evil*

CBS: *Royal Family, Teach, Jake and the Fat Man, 48 Hours*

NBC: *Unsolved Mysteries, Night Court, Seinfeld, Quantum Leap*

Thursday:

ABC: *Pros and Cons, FBI: The Untold Stories, American Detective, Primetime Live*

CBS: *Top Cops, Trials of Rosie O'Neill, Knots Landing*

NBC: *Cosby Show, A Different World, Cheers, Wings, LA Law*

Fox: *The Simpsons, Drexell's Class, Beverly Hills 90210*

Friday:

ABC: *Family Matters, Step by Step, Perfect Strangers, Baby Talk, 20/20*

CBS: *Princesses, Brooklyn Bridge, Carol Burnett Show, Palace Guard*

NBC: *Real Life with Jane Pauley, Exposé, Dear John, Flesh 'n' Blood, Reasonable Doubts*

Fox: *America's Most Wanted, Ultimate Challenge*

Saturday:

ABC: *Who's the Boss, Growing Pains, Young Riders, The Commish*

CBS: *CBS Movie, PS: I Luv U*

NBC: *Golden Girls, The Torkelsons, Empty Nest, Nurses, Sisters*

Fox: *Cops, Totally Hidden Video, Best of the Worst*

Things You May Have Noticed:

1. Early on, the networks ceded their 7–7:30 slot to local affiliates; by 1976, thanks to the "prime time access" rule, they had given back an additional half hour from 7:30–8 PM (Eastern and Pacific). The rule was supported by Donald McGannon of Group W, who used it to license *Evening* and *P.M. Magazine* when most other local stations were showing game shows and reruns.

2. Yesterday's adult/family shows (*My Friend Flicka, Green Acres,* etc.) seem to have become today's—or at least cable's—kiddie fare. As a perspective of how American society has changed, it should be noted that when *The Flintstones* premiered in 1960, it was advertised as the first cartoon series for adults.

3. Astonishingly, CBS ruled the sitcom and Sunday Night lineups almost from the start, and did so until ABC and NBC started eroding CBS's supremacy.

4. The emergence of the Fox Broadcasting Company in 1987 challenged the "Big Three" webs into making their shows more "edgy" and mature. By the mid-'90s the addition of the Warner Bros./WB and Paramount/UPN networks would divide programming into a racial schism: Fox, WB, and UPN appealed to black audiences, while white audiences watched ABC, CBS, and NBC.

5. The writers' strike of 1988 nudged the networks toward creating "reality-based" (Read: nonunion) shows such as *COPS, America's Most Wanted,* and a zillion talk shows.

Quiz: TV-1

On what TV shows did the following characters appear, and who played them?

1. Kookie, the parking lot attendant
2. Brothers Bret and Bart (and sometimes Pappy)
3. Disguise expert Artemis Gordon
4. Disguise expert Rollin Hand
5. Sidekick Andamo
6. Gunther Toody and Francis Muldoon
7. Cha Cha O'Brien
8. Sam, the first receptionist
9. Martin Lane
10. Uncle Martin

Quiz: From Series to Stardom

Not counting *Saturday Night Live* or *Second City*, what television stars became movie stars after playing these roles?

1. Tom Jordache
2. Vinnie Barbarino
3. Bret Maverick
4. Simon Templar
5. Allison Mackenzie
6. Rodney Harrington
7. Rowdy Yates
8. Josh Randall
9. Tom Hanson
10. Steve Keller

Quiz: Catchphrases

Name the shows—and the stars—that made these catchphrases a part of everyday conversation:

1. "Lucy, you got some 'splainin' to do."
2. "Sorry about that, Chief."
3. "What a revoltin' development *this* turned out to be."
4. "Hamina, hamina, hamina, hamina."
5. "Bless your little pea-pickin' heart."
6. "Good Eeeeeeeevening."
7. "Your mission, if you choose to accept it . . ."
8. (coffee spit)
9. "He's dead, Jim."
10. "Will the real—John Jones—please—stand up!"
11. "Say the secret woid."
12. "That's French! You're speaking French!"
13. (nose wiggle)
14. "Man, woman, birth, death, infinity."
15. "The eye of an eagle, the hand of a woman, the heart of a lion . . ."
16. "Open channel D, please."
17. "Does not compute" and "Danger, Will Robinson!"
18. "Look that up in your Funk & Wagnall's"; "The Flying Fickle Finger of Fate Award goes to . . ."; "Sock it to me"; "Verrrry interesting."
19. "Would you trade this for what's behind that door?"
20. "Reallllly!"

PTM: Don Kopaloff

Every show business agent worth his or her 10 percent started off in the mail room. Don Kopaloff is no exception. Beginning in the legendary William Morris Agency—when it was, indeed, legendary—Kopaloff over the years has represented variety acts, actors, writers, and directors. At one time he was in charge of production for Avco-Embassy Pictures, under the colorful Joseph E. Levine. Now a partner in SGK and Associates in Los Angeles, he remembers one of his first jobs: carrying a message to NBC in the early 1950s, when comedian Milton Berle was "Mr. Television."

By Don Kopaloff

The second week I went to work for the Morris office, the biggest TV show in the world—the only one in the world that had any meaning—was *Milton Berle*. I was called in by my superiors at the mail room and told to take an envelope over to the *Berle* show at 30 Rock, around the corner from our offices next to Radio City Music Hall. So I go over and walk around the corner at NBC and go up to the sixth floor, and it's a mess. People buzzing all around, running back and forth, I'm saying, "Excuse me, could you tell me where . . ." Nobody would pay attention. So I saw a red light flashing. I had no idea what it meant.

As soon as I walked in, I was hit with this light and the words, "Who the f— is that schmuck? Get him out of there!" at which point I started to cry. Arnold Stang, who was the actor in the sketch, started to console me. Here I am, six feet one, and Arnold Stang was maybe five feet two, and the agent in charge of the show comes running down to me, and, by that time, I was so scared I started to cry. Bawling, because Berle embarrassed me. So they took me up to a bleacher section in the back, and they're consoling me, and with that the executive in charge of the show got Milton and pulled him over like a little kid and said to him, "You know, this is the young man who just started working for us. You scared the hell out of him." So Milton, at this point, came down and put his arm around me—he used to have a police whistle—and he asked me, "You wanna blow the whistle?" He spent ten or fifteen minutes trying to get me to smile. Meanwhile, I couldn't wait to get out and go home so I could tell my family that I was with Milton Berle.

Fast forward to a few years ago when I'm at the Friar's Club. I've known Milton over the years. He's sitting holding court at the first table with Dick Shawn and Tom Bosley and a group of cronies. As I walk out, he said, "Don, come over here. Tell the guys the story of how we first met." So I did. Two booths down is Zsa Zsa Gabor, who is having lunch with her husband, Baron von something. I tell the story and go through the whole story, down to the punch line, "Who the f— is that schmuck? Get him out of there!" And, with that, Zsa Zsa gets up with her husband, and as she walks out she says, "Milton, dahling, I've always wanted to ask, What's a schmuck?" And, without batting an eyelash, Milton points to her husband and says, "Him."

PTM: Jim Varney

If there is a more obnoxious presence on TV than Ernest P. Worrell, Jim Varney would like to know about it—and one-up him. Varney, the dog-faced actor who, as commercial pitchman, talks to his friend "Vern" somewhere off-camera—is proud of his omnipresence. And so are the eighty-five-plus clients who have hired him (and director John Cherry) to sell their products over the years. In real life, Varney is, indeed, earnest (if not Ernest), and recalled how his famous character was born.

Ernest came along out of the actors' strike (in 1981). I was back in Kentucky and Tennessee driving a truck by the hour. I had done television in LA—*Fernwood 2Night, Operation Petticoat*—and played the Comedy Store the whole time I was there, but I've never played Ernest as a club act, although he would work as one. I was one of the first graduates of the Comedy Store of their 1970–1971 season.

His name is Ernest P. Worrell. The *P* stands for "power tool," 'cause Ernest breeds power tools with larger appliances in his spare time. And the last name is the same as the Tennessee state treasurer that you write all your checks for parking tickets to.

John Cherry and I had known each other since 1972. The first commercial we ever did was a car commercial, where I was a guy with a nickel cigar looking in the window. (Since then, Ernest has easily done hundreds of commercials, all of them featuring him talking to the camera, photographed with a lens that distorts Varney's not normally unattractive face). We can't do a national commercial, though, because we have so many local and regional contracts that a national spot would violate them.

I was the class clown. They always said, "You'll never amount to anything." Then they said, "Okay, you'll have television, but you'll never amount to anything." And then they said, "Um, okay, you'll have television and movies but you won't amount to anything." And they're right; I don't know how many times I've used geography since school.

PTM: Superman's Pal, Jack Larson

Before Bob Woodward and Carl Bernstein inspired a generation of hopeful young people to become journalists in the 1970s, Jack Larson did the same thing; in fact, he even inspired Woodward! Larson played cub reporter Jimmy Olsen on 104 episodes of The Adventures of Superman, *airing from 1952–1957. Since then (and following the controversial death of George "Superman" Reeves in 1959), Larson has continued to work in the arts. As a writer and producer, he has collaborated with Virgil Thomson, Jerome Robbins, Ned Rorem, and, most significantly, filmmaker James Bridges (Urban Cowboy, The Paper Chase, 9/30/55). But it's Jimmy Olsen who continues to fascinate millions of fans as much now as when he first came to work at* The Daily Planet.

Jack Larson: My part in the show *was* to be rescued. The only time I felt victimized was when somebody went for water. They liked to have Jimmy facing death by water: He is in an airtight closet and the sprinkler system goes off and the water slowly rises, or he's in a cave and the tide is rising and bars block his escape. Well, every time you shoot the show, you're wet. And then after you're rescued you spend the next scenes wet. Sound stages are never heated, and I would catch a cold. I got tired of being sick.

Nat Segaloff: Did they give you hazard pay for this?

Larson: I always did my own stunts. Like an idiot. After the first season, Jimmy became the most popular character on the show; he was the one the kids identified with. That first year, Jimmy is pretty much a straight juvenile in peril.

Segaloff: Was there any discussion of a Jimmy Olsen spin-off series?

Larson: When George [Reeves] died there was some discussion about a Jimmy Olsen spin-off series. By that time I was typed and couldn't get another job in the United States. The *Superman* people wanted me very much to come back to work. But they could only do thirteen episodes. A story editor named Mort Weisenger had gone through all the old shows and found enough footage to piece together thirteen episodes showing George in the same scenes with me. And because we were always in the same clothes, they could try thirteen without George by reusing the old footage. If they needed Superman in the scene, they would use a weight lifter in a Superman outfit to run through. I refused to do it. I said to them, "You don't know it, but the show's over. And even if I could do it, I wouldn't, because the first time you sent through that weightlifter I'd start crying."

Segaloff: What sense did you and the other cast members have about the popularity of your show?

Larson: The *Superman* show was filmed in '51 but didn't go on the air till '53. Between that time I was just an actor. But when the *Superman* show went on the air, my life changed. I couldn't eat where I'd eaten; I was mobbed. Jimmy became very popular. I actually had to be rescued. I had a little basement apartment at 28 East 82nd Street, around the corner from the Metropolitan Museum, between Madison and Fifth. I used to eat a very late breakfast at a place called the Yankee Doodle. I met a friend there one day after the show had gone on, not thinking, and realized that there was a terrible commotion out on Madison Avenue. I didn't think about it and went on talking. And then I saw that kids were standing on each other's shoulders against the window of the restaurant. Just at that point a policeman came in. "Jimmy," he said, "I have to tell you that you're a public nuisance!" It seems that there was a school nearby and word had spread that Jimmy Olsen was at the Yankee Doodle. They had to bring me to the Metropolitan Museum to get me away from all those kids.

Segaloff: Thank you very much.

Larson: "Jeepers, we're finished?"

For thirty years Jack Larson held onto Jimmy Olsen's emblematic bow tie and, in 1987, presented it to the Smithsonian Institution in Washington, D.C. It is now displayed beside Archie Bunker's easy chair, the Fonz's jacket, Irving Berlin's upright piano and, of course, the ruby slippers.

Service with a Smile (Answers)

1. Hazel (Shirley Booth), *Hazel*
2. Florida Evans (Esther Rolle), *Maude*
3. Alfred Pennyworth (Alan Napier), *Batman*
4. Beulah (Ethel Waters, Louise Beavers). The character began on radio's *Fibber McGee and Molly* program played by a white male, Marlin Hurt.
5. Wishbone (Paul Brinegar), *Rawhide*
6. Alice Nelson (Ann B. Davis), *The Brady Bunch*
7. Hop Sing (Victor Sen Yung), *Bonanza*
8. Mrs. Livingston (Miyoshi Umeki), *The Courtship of Eddie's Father*
9. Mildred (Nancy Walker) and Agatha (Martha Raye) both played maids to *McMillan and Wife*.
10. Benson (Robert Guillaume), *Soap*

Horses and Riders (Answers)

1. g
2. i
3. l
4. b
5. c
6. e
7. j
8. k
9. f
10. a
11. d
12. h

Heroes and Sidekicks (Answers)

1. d
2. f
3. i, j
4. h
5. a
6. k
7. This was a trick question. Spider-Man had no sidekick. According to Stan Lee, "What teenager wants a kid for a sidekick?"
8. p, g, c, l, n
9. b
10. e
11. m

Hosts (Answers)

1. NBC *Tonight* (before Johnny Carson): Steve Allen. Jack Paar, Jack Lescoulie, Al "Jazzbo" Collins
2. NBC *Today* show: Dave Garroway (with Jack Lescoulie)
3. *The Breakfast Club:* Don MacNeill
4. *House Party:* Art Linkletter
5. *Video Village:* Jack Narz, Monty Hall
6. *Let's Make a Deal:* Monty Hall, Bob Hilton
7. *Pantomime Quiz:* Mike Stokey
8. *You Asked for It:* Art Baker, "Whisperin'" Jack Smith
9. *Beat the Clock:* Bud Collyer
10. *I've Got a Secret:* Garry Moore
11. *People Are Funny:* Art Linkletter
12. *What's My Line?:* John Charles Daly

The Honeymooners (Answers)

1. The International Order of Friendly Raccoons (sometimes called "The International Order of Friendly Sons of the Raccoons" and "The International Order of Loyal Raccoons"); the Hurricanes
2. "Baby, you're the greatest"
3. Either "Bang-Zoom" or some assortment of "To the Moon," "Right to the moon," or "You're goin' to the moon, Alice." But never "Bang-Zoom" *plus* any of the moon missions. (And here's a PC moment: Why was spousal abuse funny?)
4. "Hamina, hamina, hamina . . ."
5. Pot roast, dumplings, and sauerkraut
6. "Hardy-har-har-har"
7. e) Telephone
8. 328 Chauncey Street, Brooklyn, New York
9. Ed (like Art Carney) played the piano but (unlike Carney) had to warm up by playing "Way Down Upon the Swanee River."
10. Ralph was a driver for the Gotham Bus Company, and Norton's "place of business" was the Department of Sewers.

Making a Living (Answers)

1. d
2. f
3. g
4. b
5. h
6. i
7. c
8. j
9. e
10. a

Andy Griffith Show (Answers)

1. It's an acronym used by pragmatic doctors who apply it to arriving hospital patients beyond help: Get Out of My Emergency Room. It is not known if this was intended to apply to Jim Nabors's character.
2. Raymond Burr, who was busy playing Perry Mason, never appeared on Andy's show. Note that Edgar Buchanan was later hired as Uncle Joe Carson in Petticoat Junction.
3. The theme song is "The Fishin' Hole," composed by Earle Hagen and Herbert Spencer, with lyrics (that's right, there were lyrics) by Everett Sloane. But everybody whistled it instead (go ahead; you know you want to).
4. All of them were used at various times.
5. In the shirt pocket of his uniform.
6. As far as can be determined, she was never named.
7. Their address is 322 Maple Road (the old Parmaley place).
8. The Mayberry Gazette, a weekly published by Farley Upchurch
9. Just gas and oil, water and air
10. "Lots of luck to you and yours" and, of course, "Shazam!" (pronounced "sha-ZYE-um!")

The Brady Bunch (Answers)

1. True, as far as can be determined. Mike's wife died, but Carol's husband's absence never was explained.
2. True. Even married couples had to have twin beds in those days, but somehow the Bradys were permitted to, er, bunch. Potties were still taboo on TV, though.
3. Grotesquely true. In The Brady Bunch Book by Andrew J. Edelstein and Frank Lovece, coproducer Lloyd Schwartz reveals that the original Tiger got killed one night, and the owner went to the pound and bought a look-alike, hoping no one would notice (shades of Dick York/Dick Sargent!). Tiger II went on to play "Blood" in the 1975 cult classic A Boy and His Dog.
4. False. Although there are amazing likenesses between Sherwood Schwartz's TV series and Melville Shavelson's delightful feature film, both projects were developed independently, and the similarities are purely coincidental. (To top it off, Shavelson and Schwartz are friends.)
5. False. He was, but not on The Brady Bunch. Try Ann B. Davis. The supercilious Lynde was the perpetual center of The Hollywood Squares game show.
6. False. It ambled along and was only renewed in thirteen-week spurts.

7. True. Strange as it seems, when the Bradys visited Hawaii in 1972, the venerable Price guest-starred as a professor of the occult.
8. True. Herbert Anderson and Marion Ross played doctors treating the kids' measles in a 1969 episode that actually dealt with gender roles.
9. True. Desi Arnaz loves Lucille Ball, but Desi Arnaz, Jr., loved Marcia Brady—at least for one episode.
10. True (according to The Internet Movie Data Base). Plus, the movie was rated PG-13 for "racy dialogue." Oh, pork chops and applesauce!

Wacky Neighbors (Answers)

Show	Neighbor	Actor
1. Ozzie and Harriet	Thorny Thornberry	Don DeFore
2. Dick Van Dyke	Jerry Helper	Jerry Paris
	Millie Helper	Ann Morgan Guilbert
3. I Love Lucy	Fred Mertz	William Frawley
	Ethel Mertz	Vivian Vance
4. December Bride	Pete Porter	Harry Morgan
	Gladys Porter	never seen[1]
5. Bewitched	Gladys Kravitz #1	Alice Pearce
	Gladys Kravitz #2	Sandra Gould
	Abner Kravitz	George Tobias
6. Dennis the Menace	George Wilson	Joseph Kearns
	Martha Wilson	Sylvia Field
	John Wilson	Gale Gordon
	Eloise Wilson	Sara Seegar
7. The Jeffersons	Harry Bentley	Paul Benedict
	Tom Willis	Franklin Cover
	Helen Willis	Roxie Roker
8. All in the Family	George Jefferson	Sherman Hemsley
	Louise Jefferson	Isabel Sanford
	Lionel Jefferson	Mike Evans
9. Three's Company	Stanley Roper	Norman Fell
	Helen Roper	Audra Lindley
	Ralph Furley	Don Knotts
10. Mr. Ed	Roger Addison	Larry Keating
	Kay Addison	Edna Skinner
	Gordon Kirkwood	Leon Ames
	Winnie Kirkwood	Florence MacMichael

[1] Gladys was later played by Cara Williams in the spin-off Pete and Gladys.

Harry Morton Lives (Answer)

1. October 1950–January 1951: Hal March
2. January 1951–June 1951: John Brown
3. June 1951–August 1953: Fred Clark
4. September 1953–September 1958: Larry Keating

Good Eeeeeevening (Answers)

Caution: These are all spoilers.

1. "Revenge": A woman identifies her attacker, and her husband kills him. Then she identifies another man as her attacker. Vera Miles and Ralph Meeker costarred.

2. "Breakdown": Callew, a stern businessman, is paralyzed in an accident and is about to be sent to the morgue. Finally achieving emotion, he summons a tear, which alerts others that he is still alive. Joseph Cotton starred. (Hitchcock shot this episode as the debut show but delayed airing it for a month.)

3. "The Case of Mr. Pelham": Someone impersonating Mr. Pelham is taking over his life, and soon everyone believes him, include Mr. Pelham. Tom Ewell starred.

4. "Back for Christmas": Herbert and Hermione Carpenter plan to visit California on holiday, but Hermione doesn't know that her husband intends to make the trip alone—as a widower. He kills her and buries her in the cellar, then lives merrily in California, until he learns that a construction crew is about to excavate: Hermione had planned on building him a wine cellar whilst they were gone. John Williams and Isobel Elsom costarred.

5. "Wet Saturday": Mr. Princey plots an elaborate cover-up to keep his daughter off the gallows after she shoots the schoolmaster in a fit of jealousy. Sir Cedric Hardwicke and John Williams appeared.

6. "Mr. Blanchard's Secret": Babs Fenton suspects her neighbors, the Blanchards, variously of murder and theft, in Hitchcock's parody of his own film *Rear Window*. Mary Scott, Robert Horton, and Meg Mundy appeared.

7. "One More Mile to Go": Sam Jacoby kills his wife and stuffs her in the trunk of his car. A cop pulls him over for having a broken tail light, and the rest of the playful story builds suspense over whether Jacoby will be forced to open the trunk. David Wayne and Steve Brodie are the mouse and cat.

8. "The Perfect Crime": Charles Courtney is a detective so arrogant that he will not admit he convicted the wrong man, even when a defense lawyer comes to him with absolute proof. So he kills him. Vincent Price and James Gregory costarred.

9. "Lamb to the Slaughter": Mary Maloney kills her husband with a frozen leg of lamb after he announces he is leaving her. When police arrive to investigate, she serves them a lamb dinner and all three devour the evidence. Barbara Bel Geddes, Allan Lane, and Harold J. Stone starred.

10. "A Dip in the Pool": Gambler William Botibol bets a fellow passenger that their cruise ship will slow down on the high seas, and to make sure of it, he throws himself overboard after arranging for a woman passenger to scream for help. Alas, she is not playing with a full deck and does nothing. Keenan Wynn starred.

11. "Poison": Fun and deadly games abound as three plantation residents try to anesthetize a poisonous snake. People: 0; snake: 1. James Donald, Wendell Corey, and Arnold Moss appeared.

12. "Banquo's Chair": A Scotland Yard detective tricks a murderer into confessing by faking the appearance of the victim's ghost during a prearranged dinner. He gets his confession, but it turns out that the fakery didn't work and that the ghost was real. John Williams, Kenneth Haigh, and Hilda Plowright starred.

13. "Arthur": A chicken farmer insulates himself against the gold-digging of an ex-girlfriend by doing away with her and feeding her to his chickens, confounding the police—and cooking them dinner. Laurence Harvey and Hazel Court starred.

14. "The Crystal Trench": A young woman loses her husband when he becomes frozen in a glacier. She waits her entire life to see his perfectly preserved body when the glacier presents it once again, only to discover that the locket he wears contains the picture of another woman. Patricia Owens starred.

15. "Mrs. Bixby and the Colonel's Coat": A married woman is given an expensive coat by her lover but realizes she can never bring it home for fear her husband will learn of her affair. She contrives to have him fetch it from a pawn shop, but he hoodwinks her because he's having an affair, too. Audrey Meadows, Stephen Chase, and Les Tremayne costarred.

16. "The Horseplayer": A priest and a gambler have separate crises of conscience in this O. Henry-style story of prayer, fate, and dumb luck at the race track. Claude Rains and Ed Gardner appeared.

17. "Bang! You're Dead": Jackie Chester thinks his uncle has brought him a toy gun from Africa, but he doesn't know it is real—and loaded. Billy Mumy, Steve Dunne, Bill Elliott, and Lucy Prentiss appeared.

18. "I Saw the Whole Thing": A mystery writer is found innocent of murder by getting witnesses to his traffic accident to contradict each other. It turns out that he really *is* innocent; he has taken the blame for his pregnant wife. John Forsyth appeared.

(A superb reference for this series is *Alfred Hitchcock Presents: An Illustrated Guide* by John McCarty and Brian Kelleher.)

Answers

TV-1 (Answers)

1. Edd "Kookie" Byrnes, *77 Sunset Strip*
2. James Garner (also Pappy) and Jack Kelly, *Maverick*
3. Ross Martin, *Wild, Wild West*
4. Martin Landau, *Mission: Impossible*
5. Ross Martin, *Mr. Lucky*
6. Joe E. Ross and Fred Gwynne, *Car 54: Where Are You?*
7. Margarita Sierra, *Surfside Six*
8. Mary Tyler Moore, *Richard Diamond, Private Detective*
9. William Schallert, *The Patty Duke Show*
10. Ray Walston, *My Favorite Martian*

From Series to Stardom (Answers)

1. Nick Nolte, *Rich Man, Poor Man*
2. John Travolta, *Welcome Back, Kotter*
3. James Garner, *Maverick*
4. Roger Moore, *The Saint*
5. Mia Farrow, *Peyton Place*
6. Ryan O'Neal, *Peyton Place*
7. Clint Eastwood, *Rawhide*
8. Steve McQueen, *Wanted: Dead or Alive*
9. Johnny Depp, *21 Jump Street*
10. Michael Douglas, *Streets of San Francisco*

Catch Phrases (Answers)

1. Desi Arnaz, *I Love Lucy*
2. Don Adams, *Get Smart*
3. William Bendix, *The Life of Riley*
4. Jackie Gleason, *The Honeymooners* ("to the moon" and "baby, you're the greatest" would have been insultingly easy)
5. Tennessee Ernie Ford, *The Tennessee Ernie Ford Show*
6. Alfred Hitchcock, *Alfred Hitchcock Presents*
7. Steven Hill, *Mission: Impossible*
8. Danny Thomas and Sid Melton, *Make Room for Daddy*
9. DeForest Kelley, *Star Trek*
10. Johnny Olsen, *To Tell the Truth*
11. Groucho Marx, *You Bet Your Life*
12. John Astin, *The Addams Family*
13. Elizabeth Montgomery, *Bewitched*
14. Sam Jaffe, *Ben Casey*
15. Richard Boone, *Medic*
16. Robert Vaughn and David McCallum, *The Man From UNCLE*
17. Dick Tufeld (as the robot), *Lost in Space*
18. Dick Martin, Dan Rowan, Judy Carne, and Artie Johnson, respectively, *Rowan and Martin's Laugh-in* (the first show that consciously tried to introduce catchphrases, and it showed)
19. Monty Hall, *Let's Make a Deal*
20. Frank Gallop, *The Perry Como Show*

Chapter 2

MoViEs

Television
Movies
Music
Twentieth Century History
Sayings & Common Sense
Religion
Science & Geography
Home Frontier
Celebrity
Minutiae

As the major art form to be created in the twentieth century, motion pictures have now outlived most of the people who invented them. Part of this is simple attrition. At their birth, movies were a young person's medium; older, established stage actors, writers, and directors didn't want to come near the upstart child for fear of ostracism. Only upstarts (usually desperate or unemployed) saw fit to try their hand at the novelty of lights. They would quickly become the thousands of people who were created by the movies—stars, directors, producers, and, occasionally, writers—whom the public grew to know and, more critically, paid money to see. Movies conferred a unique kind of fame. Unlike royalty, politicians, or despots—and even unlike celebrities in theatre, dance, opera, or music—movies made people famous *in absentia*.

Before movies, would someone in Japan know who Charlie Chaplin was? For that matter, would there even *be* a Charlie Chaplin?

Movies are a conundrum: They are big, they are intimate, they are watched in a dark room, and hundreds of strangers share the individual experience.

But most of all, movies are seductive.

They are also commerce. "Just remember," said director Bob Fosse, "they don't call it show *art*, they call it show *business*."

The "art" may have been the fantasy, but the "business" was the reality. It began in the East but quickly moved to California, for it was to the Sunshine State that early filmmakers fled in the 1910s to escape the all-powerful Motion Picture Patents Trust, led by Thomas Edison, who controlled the rights to early filmmaking equipment. Using contraband cameras, enterprising producers set up shop in a sleepy town called Hollywood. There they found sun, varied locations, and cheap labor. More importantly, it was also an hour away from the Mexican border, which is where they raced when Edison's summons servers came looking for them.

The influence of Hollywood soon pervaded America, and then the world. The examples are well known: how people started dancing the carioca when they saw Astaire and Rogers do it in *Flying Down to Rio* (1933); how undershirt sales dropped 50 percent when Clark Gable didn't wear one in *It Happened One Night* (1934); how women cut their hair when Veronica Lake shortened hers in the 1940s; how rock 'n' roll grabbed teenagers when it was used in *The Blackboard Jungle* (1955); how *Bonnie and Clyde* (1967) and *Annie Hall* (1977) shaped women's fashions; how *Saturday Night Fever* (1977) sent people into discos; and how *Scream* (1996) sent them to the video stores.

Interestingly, for all the criticism that has been leveled at movies over the decades—from sex in the '30s, violence in the '70s, and both in the '90s—not one legitimate study has directly linked movies with either. A sweeping statement, to be sure, but it should be noted that most studies include TV in their sample, and the pervasive nature of the television medium makes it a special case. People must deliberately leave the house to see a movie; television programs (including movies on home video) enter the home and are merged into the domestic experience. There is a difference. Whether the movies lead, follow, or ignore public opinion has often been debated; what cannot be, however, is that they leave a legacy that holds the world in thrall.

That's what's in this chapter: the love of movies, the love of movie lore, and little things about our favorites that will add to their enjoyment. As befits Trivia, it offers closer looks at interesting subjects that may have been brushed, as it were, behind the screen.

Movies have changed since ninety million people went to see them every week during the late 1940s, grossing $1.5 billion in 1948 (from Motion Picture Association of America), the year before TV became a competitive factor. It took twenty-four years (until 1972) for the receipts to reach that same level, but it was due to rising ticket prices, not more people in the seats. And yet movies are making more money now than ever before: $6 billion/year in the late '90s. Of course, the average ticket price is nearing $10. But let's face it: Movies are doing better than ever.

That doesn't mean that movies, *themselves*, are better than ever. Regardless of the Oscars®, Golden Globes, People's Choice, MTV, or Blockbuster awards, movies of the late 1990s seem like retreads of earlier hits, except with better special effects. The current generation of filmmakers was raised not on life or literature but on other movies and TV. There is, for example, respect for the master when Brian DePalma directs an *homage* to Alfred Hitchcock, but there is only plagiarism when a lesser filmmaker rips off DePalma without even knowing who Hitchcock was. In any other art—painting, music, dance—it is incumbent on newcomers to study those artists who preceded them. When it comes to movies, however, the past exists only to the extent that it can be mined.

To be sure, the old-line studios didn't make pictures so much as they re-made them. If one Joan Crawford melodrama worked, a second one with the same plot was put right into production. That's why Cagney made more than one gangster movie, Powell and Loy made six *Thin Man* pictures, and James Bond has been 007 eighteen times since 1962. Hits happen because the public surprises Hollywood at the box office; trends happen because Hollywood thinks they want more. There's nothing wrong with trends, but it's important to remember that every one of them started with an original idea.

Quiz: Famous Last Words from Movies

Name the movies that end with the following dialogue:

1. "Louis, I think this is the beginning of a beautiful friendship."
2. "Hello, Ladies and Gentlemen. This is Mrs. Norman Maine."
3. "'Twas beauty that killed the beast."
4. "I used to hate the water."/"I can't imagine why."
5. "There's no place like home."
6. "Tomorrow is another day."
7. "And her daughter, Gypsy."
8. "I am, George, I am."
9. "All right, Mr. DeMille, I'm ready for my close-up."
10. "I was cured, all right!"

Quiz: Less Famous Last Words from Movies

Try these:

1. "Well, nobody's perfect."
2. "Shut up and deal."
3. "Throw that junk in, too."
4. "Its origin and purpose still a total mystery."
5. "Mein Fuhrer, I can walk!"
6. "Why, Mr. Rusk, you're not wearing your necktie."
7. "Ah, then it's a gift."
8. "Now what's all this crud about no movie tonight?"
9. "Well, sir, goin' home. (Hmm?) Goin' home!"
10. "Sing out, men. We open at Levenworth on Saturday night."

Quiz: Hype Me Hollywood

Identify the films that were originally advertised with these slogans:

1. In space no one can hear you scream.
2. A long time ago in a galaxy far, far away . . .
3. They're young, they're in love, and they kill people.
4. They met at the funeral of a perfect stranger. After that, things got perfectly stranger.
5. Bernie wanted romance in the worst way, and that's how he got it.
6. Nothing says goodbye like a bullet.
7. Up Madison Avenue
8. Something almost beyond comprehension is happening to a girl on this street, in this house, and a man has been sent for as a last resort.
9. Laugh or get off the pot.
10. Be afraid. Be very afraid.
11. 65 Million Years in the Making
12. She was the first.
13. From the studio that brought you *The Jazz Singer*.
14. Before Christ. After Fellini.
15. Of all the bright young men to make it through the hang-ups, the mix-ups, the foul-ups, and the grown-ups . . .
16. This is the weekend they decided not to go fishing
17. Sometimes reality is the strangest fantasy of all
18. The Ultimate Trip
19. Gable's Back and Garson's Got Him
20. What the Dickens have they done to Scrooge?

The Truth about Oscar®

The Academy Awards are the highest honor that the Hollywood community can bestow, but most of the time the films that win Best Picture merely confirm the status quo; they dare not challenge it. Typically, the Oscar® goes to the kind of movie that Hollywood wants the world to think that Hollywood makes all the time but, in reality, seldom does. Otherwise, why would almost every producer, while accepting his statuette for having made the best picture, invariably announce, "Nobody in town wanted to make this film." Here are some examples of ground-breaking films that either *lost* or *were never nominated* for Best Picture:

2001: A Space Odyssey
After Hours
American Graffiti
Apocalypse Now
Beauty and the Beast (1946)
Blue Velvet
Brazil
Bride of Frankenstein
Bringing Up Baby
Chimes at Midnight
Citizen Kane
A Clockwork Orange
The Color Purple
Crimes and Misdemeanors
David Copperfield
Do the Right Thing
Dr. Strangelove
Duck Soup
E.T.
Europa, Europa
Frankenstein
Goodfellas
Grand Illusion
The Grapes of Wrath
Hail the Conquering Hero
Hannah and Her Sisters

A Hard Day's Night
His Girl Friday
Hoop Dreams
I Am a Fugitive from a Chain Gang
In Cold Blood
The Informer
Jaws
Jean de Florette
King Kong
The Last Picture Show
Local Hero
The Magnificent Ambersons
Manhattan
Manon of the Spring
The Miracle of Morgan's Creek
My Life as a Dog
A Night at the Opera
North by Northwest
The Palm Beach Story
Paths of Glory
Petulia
The Philadelphia Story
Raging Bull
Ran

Rear Window
Red River
Roger and Me
The Rules of the Game
Salvador
Scarface (1932)
The Scarlet Empress
The Searchers
Shadow of a Doubt
The Shop Around the Corner
Show Boat (1936)
Singin' in the Rain
Some Like It Hot
Star Wars
Sullivan's Travels
The Sweet Smell of Success
The Thin Blue Line (1988)
The Thin Man
The Thirty-Nine Steps (1935)
To Be or Not to Be (1942)
Two for the Road
Vertigo
What Price Hollywood?
The Wizard of Oz
Wuthering Heights (1939)

Quiz: Un-reel Quotes

Which of the following people actually said (or didn't say) these *exact* phrases, which are usually credited to them:

1. "Come up and see me some time."
2. "Judy, Judy, Judy."
3. "You dirty rat."
4. "I vant to be alone."
5. "Are you sure you *have* everything, Otis?"
   "I haven't had any complaints yet."
6. "Pe-tah!"
7. "Fill your hands, you sonofabitch!"
8. "I do not like the panties drying on the rod."
9. "A toast, Jedediah, to love on my terms. Those are the only terms anybody ever knows: his own."
10. "Play it, Sam."

Quiz: Biopics

Who was the actor or actress who played the real-life subject on screen? (For extra credit, name the film.)

1. Red Nichols
2. George M. Cohan
3. Ruth Etting
4. Fannie Brice
5. Barbara Graham
6. Eddie Foy
7. Edwin Booth
8. Thomas More
9. Florenz Ziegfeld
10. Alexander Graham Bell

PTM: Gary Fleder

Although director Gary Fleder won acclaim for his first two feature films, Things to Do in Denver When You're Dead *and* Kiss the Girls, *he has also contributed highly regarded work to television's* Tales from the Crypt, From the Earth to the Moon, *and* Homicide. *Fleder is a film school graduate who, even before he enrolled, had been making films on his own from a young age. That infatuation with not only the craft but also the history of motion pictures distinguishes his work, and in this remembrance he recalls the masters who influenced him.*

By Gary Fleder

During my four-year stay at the University of Southern California School of Cinema, I came to realize that many aspiring filmmakers of my generation discovered their love for film after seeing one of two movies: *Star Wars* or *Jaws.* Obviously, there were exceptions to this (although those who cited Volker Schlondorff's *Young Torliss* as an early influence were slightly suspect), but this observation proved pretty consistent.

For me, the film that started it all was *Jaws,* and Steven Spielberg was the first to not only make me love film but also offer me the seeds of obsession for the medium. I was twelve when I first saw *Jaws* at the Pembroke Theater in Norfolk, Virginia; I saw it three more times that month. I loved it then, and now—even while understanding the mechanics behind it—I love it still.

But the king, for me, was Martin Scorsese. Scorsese, as I now know, was driven by his own muses/demons, ranging from Ford, Hawks, and Kazan's elegance in staging and composition to the liberating editing styles of the French New Wave. But, to me, he was, and is, an original who loves film as much as anyone possibly can; he is a true cinephile. I first saw *Taxi Driver* in 1976, but it took me almost ten years to appreciate the genius of its filmmaking. When I saw *Raging Bull* in 1980, I knew then that it was one of our great movies. For those who want to learn the rules of cinema and then, confidently, break them to effectively tell a story, Scorsese is the place to start. Films like *King of Comedy, After Hours*, and *GoodFellas*, among his others, have reminded me—inspired me—to look beyond convention. Always, in the end, when I'm about to shoot something, I go back to the source. To *Jaws.*

As a footnote, David Brown, who produced *Jaws,* was also my producer on *Kiss the Girls.* When things got tough during shooting (weather, studio conflicts), I could always count on David to get me through the day. He'd recall one of their days on *Jaws*—months over schedule, the mechanical shark not working, actors growing weary, a twenty-six-year-old director at wit's end—and I'd realize that my problems on dry land weren't so bad, after all.

Quiz: No Credit, Please

Modesty is not something we usually associate with actors, but these actually made unbilled appearances. Some of these are tough. Name the films:

1. Robin Williams
2. Robin Williams
3. Marlene Dietrich
4. Richard Burton
5. Ava Gardner
6. Walter Huston
7. Helen Hayes
8. Bill Murray
9. Groucho Marx
10. Elizabeth Taylor

Quiz: Read the Book, Miss the Movie

Sometimes the movie is better than the book, but occasionally the book *about* the movie is better than the movie itself. Name the films whose behind-the-scenes goings-on were exposed by these books:

1. *The Devil's Candy* by Julie Salaman
2. *Picture* by Lillian Ross
3. *Final Cut* by Stephen Bach
4. *Final Cut* by Paul Sylbert
5. *On Making a Movie* by C. Kirk McClelland
6. *Fatal Subtraction* by Pierce O'Donnell and Dennis McDougall
7. *Outrageous Conduct* by Stephen Farber and Marc Green
8. *Special Effects* by Ron LaBrecque
9. *The Magic Factory* by Donald Knox
10. *Double De Palma* by Susan Dworkin

PTM: Christopher Darling

Action films are Hollywood's trademark, and screenwriter Christopher Darling is an expert in crafting them. His original script for Paramount's Flight Distance *pulled down six figures, and his military techno-thriller,* Catapult, *is set up at another major studio. Several more projects are on Darling's horizon, as he speaks, as an insider, about what it takes, literally, to light a movie's fuse.*

Nat Segaloff: What are the elements you must have in an action film to make it satisfying to the audience?

Christopher Darling: You have to have an instantly identifiable hero because the audience has to be pulled through the adventure, and therefore you need to have someone the audience can immediately recognize as the person that's going to figure his way around the explosions.

Segaloff: Are there pyrotechnic requirements?

Darling: Nowadays the more you blow up, the better. Within the next few months, we're going to have films where they blow up the entire earth. I don't know what's left. It's gotten bigger and bigger as the years have gone on, and now with computer technology it's possible to smash spacecraft into each other and destroy death stars.

Segaloff: Is there a list you go through? A car chase, fire, shootings, explosions, and so on?

Darling: The really successful action films are like a wonderful orchestra piece, a Beethoven concerto, where they build to mini-climaxes, then a major climax in the middle, where the whole story turns around, and to a massive climax at the end. Most films nowadays start with what they call "Hollywood 101." This is a giant action scene which usually has very little to do with the story, but everything that people say in this scene is a foreshadowing of something that's going to pay off later in the film. I tell people that you can figure out how the ending of a film is going to play out by listening to the first two or three minutes of the film. If the hero happens to collect stuffed bunnies, then at the end of the film the only thing they can use to save the world will be a stuffed bunny.

Segaloff: If these films are such a ritual for the audience, why does anybody bother to see them, since they're all the same?

Darling: Why do audiences go back again and again and again to see opera? Or Gilbert and Sullivan musicals? Or a live concert of a performer whose music they've bought on tape? It's because it's an experience, and they get to share it. They know in advance what they're going to get. The trailers are a contract with the audience: They say, "This is what I'm going to blow up." The movies really haven't changed that much in seventy years. Action films probably count for 75 percent of the movie-going audience.

Segaloff: How do serious actors do in action films?

Darling: Quite often, they fail. The people who succeed, by and large, are people who may be good actors, but that's not what they're called on to do. Meryl Streep made a pretty good film, *The River Wild,* where she showed a fully developed character, but none of it was necessary—all she really had to do was row a boat and hang off a cliff. An action film actor's job is to stand there like a slab of steel with the bullets bouncing off. When John Wayne entered a room, you *knew* he was going to be the one who walked out of it.

Go Figure

The 1989 Warner Bros. movie *Batman,* which cost $50 million to produce, has amassed a worldwide gross in excess of $1 billion from all media, yet, as of 1995, was reportedly still at least $16 million in debt. This probably explains why the studio has had to keep making ever-more-expensive sequels, in a desperate and honorable move to pay off the deficit.

Get a Life: SMERSH

Question: We all know that Ian Fleming, the author of the James Bond books, was a former British MI-5 employee who created not only 007 but also Bond's arch-rival agency, SMERSH. Or did he? Is SMERSH real?

Answer: SMERSH was the predecessor to the USSR's KGB, whose mandate was to destroy enemies of the Soviet Union who resided abroad. Its name comes from its motto: *SMERt SHpionen* ("death to spies"). SMERSH is said to have been responsible for the 1940 murder of Bolshevik leader Leon Trotsky in Mexico (and, of course, of Tracy (*nee* Draco) Bond in *On Her Majesty's Secret Service*).

Quiz: Films á Clef

Can there be such a thing as an anonymous biography? For legal reasons (usually invasion of privacy), Hollywood sometimes can't use the actual name of someone about whom they're making a film. Despite the chicanery, the truth usually surfaces anyway. Match the real figure with the movie character. (For extra credit, name the movie and the actor who played the role.)

Real	Movie
1. William Randolph Hearst	a. Howard Hughes
2. James Michael Curley	b. John C. Holmes
3. Willie Stark	c. John Barrymore
4. Dirk Diggler	d. Thomas Merton
5. Tony Cavendish	e. Walter Winchell
6. Aram Nicholas	f. Frank Skeffington
7. Rochelle Isaacson	g. Bogdanovich
8. Henry Brubaker	h. Ethel Rosenberg
9. J. J. Hunsecker	i. Charles Foster Kane
10. Jonas Cord	j. Huey Long

Get a Life: Black Sunday

Question: What event happened on September 25, 1966, to earn the name "black Sunday" from movie theatre owners all across America?

Answer: That was the date that *The Bridge on the River Kwai* aired on ABC-TV. The 1957 Oscar® winner achieved an unprecedented rating of 38.3 and literally sucked audiences out of the nation's movie houses. Until that time, the best received movie broadcast had been reruns of *The Wizard of Oz*, but that was seen as a fluke that didn't threaten theatre-going habits. *Kwai's* appeal, however, proved that audiences would, in the words of producer Sam Goldwyn, "stay away in droves" from movie theatres. Here are some subsequent killer ratings for Hollywood movies on network TV:

1.	*Gone with the Wind*	1976	47.6	7.	*The Birds* (A theatrical flop,	1968	38.9
2.	*Airport*	1973	42.3		this atypical Hitchcock thriller		
3.	*Love Story*	1972	42.3		became an unexpected hit on		
4.	*Jaws* (It included additional	1979	39.1		TV, further driving programmers		
	footage that had been cut from				nuts and upping the financial		
	the theatrical release. This				ante for network sales.)		
	expanded version has not been			8.	*Patton*	1972	38.5
	aired since the first network run.)			9.	*Kwai*	1966	38.3
5.	*The Poseidon Adventure*	1974	39.0	10.	*The Godfather*	1974	38.2
6.	*True Grit*	1972	38.9				

PTM: Tom Cruise

I remember a lot of rejection. Maybe not as much as some, but I remember when I came out to California and was reading for television situation comedies. I was in a meeting and did a reading for a guy, and I was terrible. The guy said, "So how long are you gonna be in town?"

I said, "I dunno, a couple of days."
He said, "Oh, a couple of days?"

I thought he was going to ask me to come for a callback and read again. Instead, he said, "A couple of days, huh? Well, get a tan while you're here." Brutal.

Excerpted from interview comments to the author in 1988 for the film Cocktail.

PTM: Stirling Silliphant on Winning an Oscar®

What's it like to win an Oscar®? For screenwriter Stirling Silliphant, who got one in 1968 for adapting In the Heat of the Night, *it was a mixed experience. Although the film itself won Best Picture, its director, Norman Jewison, was overlooked.*

I adore Norman Jewison, did from the beginning, always will. He was a magnificent sport when the Academy passed him over. I can only tell you that those of us who went up to get our Oscars felt little personal triumph, because Norman—who made it all possible—wasn't up there with us. For that matter, neither was Sidney [Poitier]. But then the Academy had to decide: Sidney or Rod [Steiger]. It couldn't be both.

And, yes, I CAN recall that night. Every second of it. Mostly my disbelief to hear Claire Bloom call my name. And then I was whizzing down the aisles past all those smiling faces—wondering why are *they* smiling?—and as though fast-forwarded, I was in front of the mike and mesmerized by the backdrop of faces and tuxedos and . . . all the dazzling ladies who'd spent all day getting their hair done—all looking up at *me* and awaiting something more than "I want to thank, etc." Not having expected to win (would you—competing against *Bonnie and Clyde* and *The Graduate?*), I had prepared absolutely nothing. I do remember mumbling something about "We members of the Writers Guild are not allowed to write on spec—and so I have nothing prepared." That seemed to do the trick—the audience gave me a warm sweeping feeling of love and support—and I may or may not have said thanks to Norman and Sidney and Walter [Mirisch, producer] and especially to [agent] Marty Baum, who got me the job. At least I *hope* I said that—then I was whisked off with my Oscar®, far heavier than I had imagined—but then when had I ever imagined I'd be holding one?

Stirling Silliphant also scripted "The Towering Inferno," "Charly," "The Grass Harp" and TV's "Route 66" (q.v.). This extract is from his Backstory 3 *interview with Nat Segaloff (op cit).*

PTM: Abbott and Costello

Bud Abbott (the thin one) and Lou Costello (the fat one) are arguably the finest comedy team in talkies—the loophole being that Stan Laurel (the other thin one) and Oliver Hardy (the other fat one) started in silent pictures. Critic, teacher, and film historian Daniel M. Kimmel fondly remembers Abbott and Costello and explains why in ways that every TV-watching kid of the '60s will acknowledge.

By Daniel M. Kimmel

If you're an Abbott and Costello fan, you're either someone who saw their movies first run in the 1940s or on television in the 1960s. In the '40s they were the kings of the box office several times, beating out such competitors as Spencer Tracy and Clark Gable. In the '60s they were considered kiddie fare, but television was young and needed their movies (and their TV series) to fill gaps in the schedule, usually when kids were most likely to be tuning in.

By the early '70s, when I was in high school, I had seen their movies over and over again. Many of their best films were little more than showcases for their comic routines, such as the dice game in *Buck Privates*, where sup-

posed novice Lou Costello keeps beating sharpie Bud Abbott, or the cockeyed math lesson in *In the Navy,* where they "prove" several times over that 7 times 13 is 28. They had come out of burlesque and polished their routines until they shone. Their films contain a virtual encyclopedia of classic comedy.

Their most famous routine, of course, is "Who's On First," which derives its comedy from Lou's inability to understand that what he's taking as questions are actually statements ("When the first baseman gets paid, who gets the money?" asks Costello. "Every penny of it," replies Abbott). As a kid, I loved Costello. As an adult, I appreciate the genius of Abbott's work as straight man. He was, as Groucho Marx observed, one of the best in the business.

It has always been an uphill battle to convince people that Bud and Lou should be taken seriously. Some, from Carol Burnett and Jerry Seinfeld to director John Landis, are proud fans. Others, especially my critical colleagues, dismiss them with a wave of the hand, which may suggest that they haven't seen their films in years—or at all—and are at a loss to back up their views.

Perhaps it was the fate of all comedians to be taken lightly. With the exceptions of Charlie Chaplin and Woody Allen, most of those who labored on screen in film comedy have yet to earn the respect of the academic film historians. It's comedy, we're told, not *Citizen Kane.*

The Marx Brothers

By Stan Levin

Although the Marx Brothers are now considered outlandish, even surreal, comic performers, it is important to remember that Leonard, Adolph, Julius, and, sometimes, Herbert Marx—better known as Chico, Harpo, Groucho, and Zeppo—were mainstream comedy stars of the 1930s.

Their origins were in vaudeville, but their apotheosis came from the movies, starting in 1929 with *The Coconuts* for Paramount Pictures. After four more middling successes, they switched studios to MGM and hit their peak in 1935 with *A Night at the Opera,* under the aegis of MGM production chief Irving Thalberg.

The Marx Bros., in their heyday, never achieved the upper echelon comic status of Charlie Chaplin, Fatty Arbuckle, or Buster Keaton. They were, however, highly successful performers, wealthy men, and well-known personalities of their era.

Why, then, did these manic brothers become superstar cultural icons in the 1960s, twenty-five years after they made their best films?

Because times change. By the advent of the so-called "film generation" in the mid-'60s, Arbuckle's and Keaton's auras had long disappeared. Chaplin—who withheld his classics from distribution until the '70s—was not much more than a footnote (although he was still a working director with his last comedy, *A Countess from Hong Kong,* released in 1967).

But the Marx Bros. were more popular than ever. Why?

The Marx Bros. movement, contrary to their centrism in the 1930s, was suddenly seen as counterculture. It had its footing on college campuses where the anarchic spirit was consistent with the times. The peace/love/now generation wanted a cultural revolution, and the Marx Bros. were its perfect leaders (their last name ironically notwithstanding): They were of another era; Groucho was a known commodity because of his '50s quiz show *You Bet Your Life;* and the Marx Bros. were at their best when they were taking on the establishment and extending the comic middle finger. Where Chaplin's Little Tramp was the small guy struggling to cope with the world, the Marx Bros. were trying to subvert it.

There are thirteen films in the Marx canon:

Coconuts (1929)
Animal Crackers (1930)
Monkey Business (1931)
Horse Feathers (1932)
Duck Soup (1933)
A Night at the Opera (1935)
A Day at the Races (1937)
Room Service (1938)
At the Circus (1939)
Go West (1940)
The Big Store (1941)
A Night in Casablanca (1946)
Love Happy (1950)

Of particular value in the Marx renaissance were *Horse Feathers, A Night at the Opera*, and *Duck Soup.*

In *Horse Feathers,* Groucho played the newly appointed president of Huxley College. It was a satire on old-style campus life and the pre-eminence of college football; it certainly found favor with a "hippie" generation that blackballed fraternity life. *A Night at the Opera* attacks the pomposity of the *nouveau riche* and arts patronage as the path to high society. The film openly and savagely mocked the wealthy in 1935 and found renewed relevance in the late 1960s. The film that probably filled more campus movie theaters than any of the others, however, was *Duck Soup*. In an era torn by Vietnam, the film was overtly antiwar. Groucho, as the leader of Freedonia, declared war on Ambassador Trentino of Sylvania (Louis Calhern) for calling him an upstart. The college kids applauded the message of the same film that made the 1930s audiences wince.

Also adding to the interest in the Marx Bros. revival was intrigue: the film rights for *Animal Crackers*—rumored to be the most consummate example of their art—had been restricted by the estate of screenwriter George S. Kaufman and could not be shown. Here was a cause ready-made for their antiauthoritarian fans: Bring back *Animal Crackers!* Accordingly, college students responded to the call to arms, and, finally, in 1973, Universal Pictures (which by then owned the Paramount titles) freed the legendary film from its vaults for the first time since its initial release. The fans flocked to see it (and this was years before home video made revivals *de rigueur*).

Alas, the cultural coup—like most revolutions—could not last. Every generation has its social, political, and cultural events to define it. It was inevitable that the generation of the 1970s would eschew the values of the 1960s. After all, by mid-decade, the war was over, eighteen-year-olds could vote, and there was a vague belief that the *status quo* was not that bad after all. The Marx Bros.' followers of the 1960s passed the cultural crown to the Three Stooges aficionados of the 1970s, and the revival of interest in the Marx Bros. was over.

Stan Levin, a writer, director and film historian with a special affinity for the Marx Bros., also works for the government, which probably explains why he likes the Marx Brothers.

Get a Life: Citizen Kane

Question: In the movie *Citizen Kane*, Charles Foster Kane had *two* sleds. What was the name of the *other* one?

Answer: When Kane is taken away from his mother, he leaves Rosebud to gather snow outside of Mary Kane's boarding house. His second sled is the Christmas present given him by Walter P. Thatcher. It was called "Crusader." *(Courtesy of David Kornfeld)*

Quiz: Dying Words

What actor or actress made his or her final exit, so to speak, with these words? And in what films?

1. "We—belong—dead."
2. "Coulda been whole world Willie Stark."
3. "Mother of Mercy, is this the end of Rico?"
4. "What the hell happened?"
5. "I tripped."
6. "That's mighty brave talk for a one-eyed fat man."
7. "Good. For a minute I thought we were in trouble."
8. "Yahoo—yee-ha! yaaaa-hooooooo!"
9. "—upon the seat of a bicycle—built—for—two."
10. "Tell Manny he's got to go on—got to see our grandson—for both of us."

Quiz: Disneyana

Even though the Walt Disney Company now owns TV networks, film companies, record labels, sports franchises, music publishing, theme parks, and two or three of the major planets, it's important to remember—as Walt himself always said—"It all started with a mouse." Following are ten points of Disneyana. True or false:

1. *Steamboat Willie* was the first Mickey Mouse Cartoon.
2. Mel Blanc—the vocal genius behind Warner Bros.' Bugs Bunny and Daffy Duck—has his voice in Disney's *Snow White and the Seven Dwarfs*.
3. The animated *Fantasia* ran into censorship problems over nudity.
4. Walt Disney could never draw Mickey Mouse.
5. *Snow White and the Seven Dwarfs* literally scared children incontinent when it was released in 1937.
6. During World War II, Mickey Mouse starred in an army training film about VD.
7. After Walt died in 1966, they discovered a film he had made in advance. It was designed to be shown to his chief executives in the company screening room after he was gone. The men entered and sat in their assigned seats. Walt then spoke to each of them individually from the screen, staring right at them, and told them how they were to run the company over the next five years.
8. Secret messages are hidden in Disney animated features.
9. Real-life people sometimes make guest appearances in animated features.
10. Walt Disney, who died in 1966, is frozen.

Strange but True

In a town that thrives on fantasy, when the real thing comes along it is sometimes hard to believe. Here are some Hollywood tales that insiders swear are absolutely true (and if they're not, let's just pretend they are):

1. In *The Wizard of Oz,* actor Frank Morgan (Professor Marvel/The Wizard) wears a ratty Prince Albert–style coat. The coat was not made for the film but was, instead, bought off the rack from a second-hand shop on Main Street in Los Angeles by the MGM costume department. One day Morgan happened to turn out the pocket and discovered the name tag sewn inside: L. Frank Baum, the original author of *The Wizard of Oz.* This was later confirmed by the coat's tailor in Chicago, but it is often cited as a publicity stunt. (Aljean Harmetz researched this strange but true occurrence for her book titled *The Making of The Wizard of Oz.*)

2. When producer David O. Selznick filmed *Gone with the Wind,* he first shot the burning of Atlanta so that he could clear sets on the back lot. Among the buildings that can be seen on fire are the great gates from *King Kong.* Because Selznick had not yet cast the role of Scarlett O'Hara, a stuntman dressed as Scarlett rode in the wagon beside the stuntman dressed as Rhett Butler. Selznick's brother, Myron, was an agent, and he brought a new client to watch the spectacular burning. Myron introduced her to his brother by saying, "David, I want you to meet your Scarlett O'Hara." The client was Vivien Leigh.

3. In the 1973 movie *Sleuth,* Laurence Olivier plays a mystery writer who coerces a rival, played by Michael Caine, to rob him and ransack his house. Olivier demonstrates the level of carnage by sweeping a collection of glass figurines off the mantlepiece. In reality, Olivier sliced open his hand doing the move. He then blotted the blood on the back of an upholstered chair, hid his bloody hand in his trouser pocket, and calmly waited until the director said "Cut!" before asking to be taken to the hospital. The shot remains in the finished film; Olivier can be seen grimacing at the wound.

4. While filming *A Clockwork Orange* (released in 1972), director Stanley Kubrick asked actor Malcolm McDowell to sing a song while committing "ultra-violence." The only song McDowell could think of at the time was "Singin' in the Rain." Kubrick took a break, called MGM for the rights, got them instantly, and told McDowell to resume. Ever since then, critics have marveled at the irony of the song choice when, in fact, it was coincidence.

5. While filming *The African Queen* in what was then the Belgian Congo, director John Huston noted that there was a meat dish being served to the film crew by the local caterer who referred to it as "long pig." A few days later, authorities arrested the caterer. It seems that men had been disappearing from local villages and cannibalism was suspected.

6. The dialogue in *The Jazz Singer*—the first talking feature film—consists of only 354 words, none of which was scripted. All of them are ad-libs, mostly by Al Jolson but also by Eugenie Besserer and Warner Oland, who play his parents. The catchphrase "You ain't heard nothin' yet" had been used by Jolson in his act for years and was not supposed to be part of the movie.

7. Edna Purviance, who costarred with Charles Chaplin in most of the short films he made between 1915 and 1923, remained on full salary from Chaplin until her death in 1958. She made a brief appearance in his 1952 film *Limelight*.

8. The gunshot heard at the end of the Oscar-winning *policier The French Connection* has confused audiences since its release in 1971. In the scene, Gene Hackman, as a crazed narcotics detective, fires his gun at an unseen target after the screen goes black. What does it mean? Absolutely nothing, according to director William Friedkin, who admitted that he playfully told the editor, "Let's just end the film with a bang" and get it into theatres.

9. Sometimes directors talk actors into a performance, and sometimes they scare them into it. In *The Towering Inferno,* producer Irwin Allen—who directed the fire sequences—signaled the cast's reaction to the climax of the film by counting down from ten to zero on a bullhorn and firing a gun at the moment he wanted them to look surprised. They did.

Contract Capers

In the heyday of the studio system, stars were routinely signed to seven-year contracts that could be extended indefinitely by putting a naughty performer on "suspension." At Warner Bros. the problem was exacerbated by the tension between combative production chief Jack Warner and such headstrong stars as Bette Davis, James Cagney, Humphrey Bogart, Errol Flynn, and Olivia de Havilland.

Cagney, for one, wanted out of his deal, even though he was being paid $4,500 a week. In 1935 he got his chance when a billboard for *Ceiling Zero* placed costar Pat O'Brien's name before his, when he was guaranteed top billing. Cagney sued Warners for breach of contract and won in court, sending shockwaves through studio legal departments all over town. Eventually Cagney returned to Warner Bros.—but on much better terms.

But the person who actually broke the studio contract system was demure Olivia de Havilland. In 1941 she likewise sued Warners, not on breach of contract but rather on the principle that a self-extending contract was tantamount to slavery, a clear violation of the Thirteenth Amendment to the U.S. Constitution (q.v.). She won her case in court, but the litigation reduced the number of films she could make and her star faded for a while—until 1946, that is, when she won a Best Actress Oscar® for *To Each His Own*—made at Paramount.

Quiz: Before They Were Stars

Some people are born stars, others achieve stardom, and others wait on tables until Hollywood calls. Match the star with their prestar job:

1.	Steve McQueen	a.	Rodent exterminator
2.	Luke Perry	b.	Supermarket cashier
3.	Oliver Reed	c.	Bellboy
4.	Julia Roberts	d.	Doorknob factory worker
5.	Brad Pitt	e.	Live window dress model
6.	Michelle Pfeiffer	f.	Dance hall gigolo
7.	Jerry Lewis	g.	Barroom piano player
8.	Lee Marvin	h.	Driver for strippers
9.	Jack Lemmon	i.	Bouncer
10.	Jeremy Irons	j.	Carpenter
11.	Warren Beatty	k.	Theatre usher
12.	Lauren Bacall	l.	Plumber's assistant
13.	Charles Bronson	m.	Rodeo rider
14.	James Caan	n.	Hotel clerk
15.	Geena Davis	o.	Social worker
16.	Harrison Ford	p.	Ice cream parlor attendant
17.	John Wayne	q.	File clerk
18.	George Raft	r.	Coal miner
19.	Charles Laughton	s.	Fairground pitch man
20.	Walter Matthau	t.	Prop man

The Write Actor

Considering that screenwriters are seldom found on the sets of movies they have written, it is even more unusual for a scribe to be handed an acting role. Nevertheless, the following writers have appeared, usually in the background, in movies whose scripts or novels they have authored but not directed:

1. Dalton Trumbo, *Papillon,* as commandant
2. Michael Schiffer, *Lean on Me,* as teacher
3. Robert Bolt, *Lawrence of Arabia,* as bystander
4. Peter Benchley, *Jaws,* as TV reporter
5. Barry Levinson, *High Anxiety,* as bellman
6. Harold Pinter, *The Servant,* as society man
7. Jacqueline Susann, *Valley of the Dolls,* as first reporter
8. Gore Vidal, *Gore Vidal's Billy the Kid,* as bystander
9. Carl Gottlieb, *Jaws,* as town newspaper editor

Acting Directors

Other than Alfred Hitchcock—whose cameo appearances in his own films are legendary—and accomplished actor-directors such as Woody Allen and Warren Beatty, directors are not known for their acting abilities. Here are some who have proved otherwise in films that they did not direct themselves:

1. Sidney Pollack (*Husbands and Wives,* dir. Woody Allen)
2. Martin Ritt (*The Slugger's Wife,* dir. Hal Ashby)
3. Mark Rydell (*The Long Goodbye,* dir. Robert Altman)
4. Steven Spielberg (*The Blues Brothers,* dir. John Landis)
5. Fritz Lang (*Contempt,* dir. Jean-Luc Godard)
6. Lindsay Anderson (*Chariots of Fire,* dir. Hugh Hudson)
7. Cecil B. DeMille (*Sunset Boulevard,* dir. Billy Wilder)
8. Federico Fellini (*Alex in Wonderland,* dir. Paul Mazursky)
9. Jean Renoir (*The Christian Licorice Store,* dir. James Frawley)
10. Raoul Walsh (*The Birth of a Nation,* dir. D. W. Griffith)
11. Samuel Fuller (*The American Friend,* dir. Wim Wenders)
12. Oliver Stone (*Dave,* dir. Ivan Reitman)

Oscar's Oops

The best known activity of the Academy of Motion Picture Arts and Sciences is giving out their annual awards. But a service they perform that is even more highly valued (by outsiders, anyway) is their establishment of the Margaret Herrick Library, a superb research facility. Nevertheless, Oscar® occasionally gets it wrong, as a few inadvertent "goofs" from their awards reveal:

1. Screenwriter Robert Towne was so upset with the way his script, *Greystoke: The Legend of Tarzan, Lord of the Apes,* was filmed, in 1984, that he took his name off the credits, using the pseudonym of P. H. Vazak. To Towne's amusement, Vazak was nominated for an Academy Award. What amused him most was that P. H. Vazak was the name of his pet sheepdog.

2. William Friedkin's 1972 Oscar® for *The French Connection* made him the youngest director—age thirty-two—to ever win the coveted award. Except he wasn't the youngest. Norman Taurog (who won in 1931 at age thirty-two) was. In reality, Friedkin was thirty-six at the time.

3. When sample footage is shown on the Oscar® telecast for Achievement in Cinematography, it's usually shots of gorgeous sunsets or other vistas. This always makes insiders chuckle because, generally, these "beauty shots" were filmed by the second unit crew, not the cinematographer who was nominated for the award. He was too busy shooting scenes with the actors.

4. During the 1976 award telecast, presenter Marty Feldman, the comedian, dropped and broke a prop Oscar® statuette, causing the audience to gasp at the sacrilege. When the joke flopped, the rattled Feldman then opened the envelope and presented the live-action short film award to *In the Region of Ice,* without announcing the other nominees. When *Ice's* coproducers, Andre Guttfreund and Peter Werner, got to the stage, they showed their class by making a point of reading the names that Feldman had forgotten.

5. For years the legend persisted that Greer Garson, accepting her 1942 Oscar® for *Mrs. Miniver,* rambled for over an hour. Her acceptance speech was, in fact, five-and-a-half minutes. Nowadays the recipients are given forty-five seconds, after which the orchestra plays them off (unless they're really *really* famous—or old).

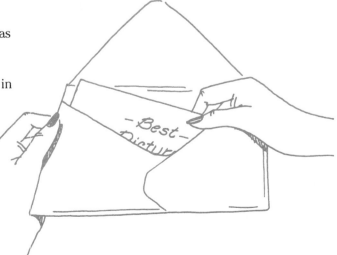

Billy Wilder

One of the most quotable—and certainly most brilliant—filmmakers is Billy Wilder. His screen credits include *Sunset Boulevard, Some Like It Hot, The Apartment, The Private Life of Sherlock Holmes, Ace in the Hole, The Fortune Cookie, One, Two, Three,* and *Double Indemnity.*

As if his films weren't brilliant enough, Wilder himself is a source of acerbic comments and witty insights. When an actor once dared to challenge a script by insisting, "Mr. Wilder, I don't think the character would say that line," Wilder shot back, "Oh yeah? Where was the character when the page was blank?"

Put in charge of a cadre of former SS officers in Germany after World War II, he responded to their request to perform an Easter passion play by saying, "Only if you use real nails."

And when his wife once asked him to bring a bidet home from a European junket, he wired back, "Unable obtain bidet. Suggest handstand in shower."

Born in Austria, Wilder first worked as a newspaperman and began writing scripts for the Berlin film industry. When Hitler came to power, Wilder fled to Hollywood where fellow *emigrés* helped him find work coscripting such films as *Midnight* and *Ninotchka* for MGM. In 1942 he moved to Paramount Pictures, where he began directing, although the studio insisted that he be paired with an American writing partner to help him learn English. A collaboration with the urbane Charles Brackett led to *The Lost Weekend, Sunset Boulevard,* and his first Oscars®. In the late '50s he began working with I. A. L. Diamond, with whom he created *The Apartment, Some Like It Hot,* and *Irma La Douce,* among other triumphs.

Wilder became an avid art collector and a connoisseur of conversation, an art form at which he excelled. Among his most famous (and legendary) quips are:

- "France is a country where the money falls apart in your hands and you can't tear the toilet paper."
- "What critics call dirty in our movies they call lusty in foreign films."
- To cameraman John Seitz (*Sunset Boulevard*): "Johnny, keep it out of focus. I want to win the Best Foreign Film award."
- Turning down a third film with Marilyn Monroe (after *The Seven Year Itch* and *Some Like It Hot*): "I have discussed this project with my doctor and my psychiatrist and they tell me I'm too old and too rich to go through this again."

An educated, progressive art collector, Wilder decided to thin his collection while he was alive, and in 1989 held an auction which brought in an astounding $32.6 million—more than he had ever made from filmmaking. At the traditional bidders' viewing that preceded the auction, Wilder was reportedly taken aside by his wife, Audrey, who asked him, "Billy, I wish you would stop referring to me as 'the future widow.'"

Finally, in accepting his Life Achievement Award from the American Film Institute in 1986, Wilder acknowledged the beating that creators routinely take at the hands of studio bosses but bolstered his fellow filmmakers' spirits by saying, "Remember: theirs may be the kingdom, but ours is the power and the glory."

Wit and Wisdom of Hollywood

Becoming impatient with a pretentious interviewer who was endlessly trying to define "a Clint Eastwood picture," Eastwood responded, simply, "To me, a Clint Eastwood picture is one that I'm in."

When Twentieth Century Fox debuted CinemaScope, studio chief Darryl F. Zanuck ordered his producers, "From now on we don't want stories with depth. We want stories with width."

Director Peter Bogdanovich tells of the time he was acting for Orson Welles in the legendary (but never-finished) *The Other Side of the Wind.* The camera was a good distance away when Welles, standing beside it, shouted to Bogdanovich to run toward him. "What's my motivation?" asked Bogdanovich. Responded Welles, "I'll tell you when you get here."

Alfred Hitchcock was once stopped by a customs inspector who asked him about his passport, which identified him as a producer. "What do you produce?" asked the customs inspector. "Gooseflesh," Hitchcock replied.

Actress Carroll Baker once asked director John Ford if she could wear her blond hair long, "like the women in Bergman's films."

"Ingrid Bergman?" the cantankerous Ford asked.

"No, *Ingmar* Bergman," Baker corrected. "The great Swedish director."

"Oh, *Ingmar* Bergman," Ford played along. "You mean, the fella that called me the greatest director in the world?"

"A film should have a beginning, a middle and an end," said Jean-Luc Godard, one of the founders of the French New Wave. "But not necessarily in that order."

"If a man enters a room through a door, you have a scene," said Billy Wilder. "But if he enters through a window, you have a *situation.*"

Producer David O. Selznick, concerned that *Gone With the Wind* was clocking in at over three and a half hours, asked fellow producer Sam Goldwyn, "How long should a picture be?" Goldwyn answered, "A picture should be as long as it is good."

Although Christopher Plummer has come around over the years, he originally had intense disdain for *The Sound of Music.* Supposedly he once said of his costar, Julie Andrews, that working with her was "like being hit over the head with a Valentine card."

Black Cinema

There are, to be broad with the brush strokes, three periods of African-American cinema: invisibility, exploitation, and arrival. At a time when black filmmakers are still struggling for recognition at Oscar® time, it may be helpful to look back toward the roots of the issue.

The invisibility existed almost from the start of movies and expressed itself through the "Negro Circuit" of racially segregated theatres that catered exclusively to black audiences, with films produced specifically for them. Pioneer filmmakers such as Oscar Micheaux (*Underworld, God's Step Children*) and Noble and George Johnson (*Trooper of Troop K*) made silent movies for these theatres in the 1920s. Given the alternative—the mainstream movies produced by whites and embodying the prevailing racial stereotypes (e.g., *The Dancing Nig* and *Wedding of a Coon*)—the Negro Circuit's programming was extraordinarily progressive. Even while *The Birth of a Nation* drew criticism in 1915 (and still does) for its racist portrayal of blacks, few white Americans were aware of the positive images of African-Americans that were presented in "race films," as they were then called in the press.

Talking pictures created a new generation of black stars, most of whom had to toe the stereotype in order to keep working in the 1930s. Stepin Fetchit, Clarence Muse, Bill "Bojangles" Robinson, Eddie "Rochester" Anderson, Hattie McDaniel, "Farina," Paul Robeson, Mantan Moreland, Louise Beavers, and Nina Mae McKinney were all subjected to pressures of conformity, despite that—partic-

ularly with Fetchit, Farina, McDaniel, and Robeson—many, if not all, of these artists were more cultured, and certainly better educated, than the white studio bosses who hired them.

While acknowledging the existence of what writers John McKee and Edward Mapp have called "a separate cinema," the Hollywood studios were hesitant to produce films specifically for it. *Hallelujah* (MGM, 1929), *Hearts in Dixie* (Fox, 1929), *The Green Pastures* (Warner Bros., 1936), and *Cabin in the Sky* (MGM, 1943) were four notable exceptions that had "crossover" potential—a studio code word for "the bookings we lose from Southern white theatres may be made up by the bookings we receive from Negro theatres."

It was, ironically, the civil rights struggle in the '50s and '60s that brought black cinema into the mainstream, and then nearly killed it. Although Hollywood had made furtive efforts to attract multiracial audiences with such films as *The World, the Flesh and the Devil* (1959), *One Potato, Two Potato* (1964), *A Raisin in the Sun* (1961), or *Lilies of the Field* (1963), it wasn't until the 1970s that the second era in black cinema began. And then it was *Shaft*.

Released in 1971 by MGM and directed by Gordon Parks—a black man and former *Life* magazine photographer whose previous film, *The Learning Tree,* was a bucolic paean to childhood—*Shaft* starred Richard Roundtree as a black detective who will use force where necessary—in other words, just like white movie detectives. The film was sold to black audiences with the line, "Rated R—if you wanna see *Shaft,* ask yo' mamma." If *Shaft* was a new look at an old genre, another 1971 production called *Sweet Sweetback's Baadassssss Song* broke all the rules. Made by Melvin van Peebles, it was at once revolutionary and revelatory, full of anger and wit, all of it directed against whites. Naturally it was rated X; naturally it had trouble getting bookings; naturally, when it did, it made a fortune.

The film that unified these two strains of black filmmaking in America—action and anger—was *Superfly*. *Superfly* (1972) starred Ron O'Neal as a drug dealer who outwits "the man," a.k.a, the white establishment. Its script by Philip Fenty, its light directorial touch by Gordon Parks, Jr., and O'Neal's playful presence came together with Curtis Mayfield's exciting music to create a sensation. It also created a schism within the black community: It was good for black artists to be working, but why did the message have to be so destructive? But the box office offered powerful approbation, and for the rest of the decade, Hollywood studios (and independents) would produce countless pictures with similar themes of disenfranchisement, empowerment, and revenge.

Notable titles at the time include *Cotton Comes to Harlem*, *Watermelon Man*, *Coffy*, *Across 110th Street*, *Blacula*, *Gordon's War*, *A Warm December*, *Uptown Saturday Night*, *Let's Do It Again*, *Buck and the Preacher*, *Book of Numbers*, *Hit Man*, and *The Mack*. No mater how skillful they were—and some were extremely so—the genre was quickly nicknamed *blaxploitation* by observers who pointed out that the only difference between some of these movies and *The Birth of a Nation* was that they were made by black people.

Black cinema in the '70s was doomed to fail by the sheer design of the film industry. The only theatres that would book them were those in major cities where, exhibitors felt, there lived sufficient black audiences to support the pictures. Since few suburban or rural theatres gave the films subsequent bookings, the movies had to recoup their entire budgets from the first-run theatres, and consequently the budgets were kept agonizingly low. Low budgets translated into poor quality, and the poor quality eventually drove audiences away, which curtailed the genre just when it was developing a generation of its own filmmakers (such as Gordon Parks, Jr., Lonne Elder III, Pam Grier, Michael Schultz, Stan Lathan, Ron O'Neal, and others).

The third phase of African-American cinema is the one currently represented by directors Spike Lee, Euzhan Palcy, John Singleton, Robert Townsend, Bill Duke, James Bond III, Mario Van Peebles (Melvin's son), Carl Franklin, Allen and Albert Hughes, Reginald and Warrington Hudlin, and many people named Wayans. What distinguishes their work—aside from the fact that most of it is financed by major studios and accorded wide theatrical and video release—is its breadth. Such widely differing films as *Malcolm X, One False Move, A Dry White Season, The Five Heartbeats, House Party,* and *Boyz in the 'Hood* testify to the willingness of the industry to include—although some would say *engulf*—the themes and spokespersons (mostly men) working in the genre. In order to get made, all commercial motion pictures must now address a wide, "crossover" audience and design themselves accordingly. After eighty years, "black cinema" has, indeed, found itself equal to "white cinema"—be that as it may.

Women in Film

When 1995 was declared "the year of the woman," in Hollywood, the leading joke around town was, "Really? Let's find that woman and congratulate her." Although women have been part of Hollywood since the very beginning—the first performer to be identified by name, for example, was Florence Lawrence in 1909—the business end of the industry has consistently excluded them from decision-making positions.

Women have always been accepted as actresses, writers, costume designers, casting directors, publicists, script supervisors, directors of development, film editors, and, occasionally, directors—positions arguably in service of male producers and company executives—but seldom are they accorded the ultimate Hollywood power: the ability to "green light" (authorize) a project.

Few women in film history received the recognition they were due, or, if they did, it was only by grace of the man to whom they were married.

The story of Daeida Beveridge Wilcox is a good example. According to the legend, Wilcox was taking a long train trip when she struck up a conversation with another lady, who spoke of her estate in the East called "Holly Wood." Smitten with the name, Daeida told her husband, Horace Henderson Wilcox, a real estate dealer who was selling off land parcels in Los Angeles. At his wife's urging, he named the development "Hollywood." Although Wilcox was accorded a street in the district he once owned, Daeida consistently has been refused credit—even a plaque—by the men whose addresses owe their very existence to her.

Other examples include Natalie Kalmus, wife of Herbert Kalmus, the inventor of Technicolor. She served as paid "technicolor color consultant" on dozens of feature productions. But it was not her taste that awarded her the job, rather it was a judge. The job was part of a divorce settlement, in lieu of alimony from Herbert.

Then there was the elegant Frances Goldwyn, who served as official story advisor to her producer-husband Samuel Goldwyn yet was never accorded a salary or title; Margaret Booth, MGM's ranking film editor, who, it was said, was the only person at the studio other than Louis B. Mayer who could demand retakes; Maya Deren, literally the "mother" of American avant-garde experimental cinema in the 1940s; and Elinor Glyn, whose "scenarios" in the 1920s defined the manners and morals of the Jazz Age.

And of course there was Mary Pickford, "America's Sweetheart," or, more accurately, the "Bank of America's Sweetheart"—thanks to all the revenue her pictures generated. She was so popular—and therefore so powerful—that, after cofounding United Artists in 1919, she won the unprecedented right to destroy any of her films, if she did not like them once they were finished.

It was not until Hollywood commerce became truly internationalized in the late 1980s and early 1990s that women were finally recognized as participants in the filmmaking process. Present-day Hollywood is inhabited by scores of women actively involved in the process of making commercial motion pictures. They include Kathryn Bigelow, director (*Blue Steel*), Bonnie Bruckheimer, producer (*Beaches*), Martha Coolidge, director (*Rambling Rose*), Amy Heckerling, director (*Clueless*), Marci Carsey, partner, Carsey-

Werner Productions (*Roseanne*), Debra Hill, producer (*The Fisher King*), Gale Anne Hurd, producer (*The Terminator*), Kallie Khoury, screenwriter, (*Thelma and Louise*), Barbara Kopple, director, (*Harlan County, USA*), and, the two highest ranking women, Sherry Lansing, president of Paramount Pictures, and Amy Pascal, president of Columbia Pictures.

Despite this presence at the executive level, actresses still have trouble finding good parts. Typically, movies are still aimed at the nineteen-year-old white male market, and female characters routinely exist solely to help the male characters work out their problems.

PTM: Eleanor Perry

Eleanor Perry was the acclaimed screenwriter of David and Lisa, Last Summer, The Swimmer, Truman Capote's Trilogy, *and* Diary of a Mad Housewife. *Although she was known chiefly for having written the scripts, which were directed by her then-husband, Frank Perry she also adapted and coproduced, for MGM,* The Man Who Loved Cat Dancing. *Her 1979 novel* Blue Pages *was about a woman writer who is exploited by her director-husband and is patterned closely after her relationship with Frank, whom she had divorced nine years earlier.*

I've thought about why women can't get power in Hollywood, believe me, many times. The money has the power. Creative people and business people make a very crazy mix. The business people put up the money; they deserve to have some power. But the trouble is, they don't really respect writers. They wish they could make up the whole script in computers because writers are just damn nuisances, as you can see from my book. They argue, they won't put in rewrites, they have all sorts of trouble with writers—meaning anybody creative who feels honor bound, who cares about something besides money.

When you write, you've got to at least delude yourself that you love it. And I'm not complaining, because, God knows, writers in Hollywood get paid very well so that, alright, it's a horrible pain sometimes, but at least we get paid for our agony.

Eleanor Perry died in 1981, but not before inspiring a generation of young writers—male as well as female—with her example, and often with her counsel.

Quiz: Screen Lovers

Actors and actresses sometimes costarred so often in movies that the public began to think that they were married in real life. Match the men with the women:

1. Spencer Tracy
2. Ronald Colman
3. William Powell
4. Percy Kilbride
5. Wallace Beery
6. Charles Chaplin
7. Dick Powell
8. Fred Astaire
9. Walter Pidgeon
10. Woody Allen

a. Ginger Rogers
b. Edna Purviance
c. Ruby Keeler
d. Marie Dressler
e. Marjorie Main
f. Mia Farrow
g. Vilma Banky
h. Katharine Hepburn
i. Myrna Loy
j. Greer Garson

Quiz: Casablanca

Everybody's favorite romantic movie is *Casablanca*. But how well do you really know it? Take this test:

1. What is Rick's last name?
2. What is Ilsa's maiden name?
3. Two TV series were later made of *Casablanca*. Who starred in the Bogart and Rains roles?
4. What were the names of waiters played by S. Z. Sakall and Leonid Kinskey?
5. What now-famous director created the montages?
6. What are the *other* songs Sam sings?
7. Ella Fitzgerald was considered for a role in the film. Which role?
8. What are "letters of transit" in real life?
9. What was the name of Rick's cafe in Paris?
10. "Colorization" be damned: What color are Rick's eyes?

Small Fry

Hollywood is usually concerned with bigness (*viz Titanic, Jurassic Park,* etc.), but there have been a few times when smaller was better—or at least more trivial. Put on your glasses.

1. Smallest fee paid for screenwriting: $10 was paid to Preston Sturges for writing *The Great McGinty* (1940)—if they would let him direct it, too.
2. Shortest color sequence: There was a two-frame red flash when a gun fires in Alfred Hitchcock's *Spellbound* (1945).
3. Shortest shooting schedule for an American theatrical film: It took two days and three nights for Roger Corman's original *Little Shop of Horrors* (1960).
4. Shortest run of any film: The film was *The Super Fight* (1970), a staged bout between Muhammad Ali and Rocky Marciano, who were both undefeated heavyweight champs. It was shown once on January 20, 1970. Thereafter, all prints were destroyed. (From: *The Guinness Book of Movie Facts and Feats, 5th. ed.*)
5. Smallest cast—not counting one-person performances (Note: contains a spoiler): *Sleuth* (1973) had two performers. Another kind of small cast was the all-little person western, *The Terror of Tiny Town* (1938).
6. Shortest leading man: It is probably Alan Ladd at five feet four inches.
7. Smallest big-screen effect: An exploding nebula during the stargate/trip sequence in *2001: A Space Odyssey* (1968) was a photographed chemical reaction in an area the size of a pack of cigarettes.
8. Shortest Oscar®-winning role: Beatrice Straight in *Network* (1976) whose single scene ran 10 minutes. In 1998, Judi Dench won with three scenes (total 10 minutes) in *Shakespeare in Love.*

PTM: Liane Brandon

Liane Brandon is a filmmaker whose 1972 short subject, Anything You Want to Be, *was one of the first films to address issues of gender stereotyping that were being raised by the Women's Movement, which was then in its formative period. The film concerned a teenage girl who wanted to believe society's assurances of equality, yet every time she aspired to a goal, she was offered a rung lower on the ladder. Facing similar resistance, Brandon and her fellow filmmakers began New Day Films, a distribution collective that today, twenty-five years later, has become the major source of social-issue films and videos.*

Nat Segaloff: What sort of reception were you accorded when you started making "feminist films"?

Liane Brandon: People didn't understand what feminist films were, or why a woman would want to make a film, or what kind of films would even appeal to women. The first distributor I went to told me he wanted a very short-term contract, which was unusual because most distributors want contracts "in perpetuity." This guy didn't want more than a two-year contract because he thought the women's movement would be dead in two years. That was 1972.

Here's another example of early attitudes, and I don't know how many of them have changed a whole lot. Another distributor—I won't mention their name—was interested in handling New Day Films, of which there were three at that point. They came to us after our work was shown at the First International Festival of Women's Film in New York, which, amazingly, drew an enormous crowd. It was a whole new genre of independent filmmaking—"girls with cameras," someone called it. This major distributor wanted to put together a package of women's films, and we thought it was wonderful that, at last, somebody wanted us. We were thrilled but not stupid, and one of the things that we asked for in the contract was approval of publicity. Thank goodness! They sent us a mock-up of the cover of the brochure, and it was a naked woman in an extraordinarily obscene and provocative pose. We were stunned and could not fathom why this major distributor would put that on the cover—after all, these were feminist films, the first films about the women's movement. I called the guy up and said that we were a little confused and did someone not understand what the films were about. He said, "Oh, yeah, honey, we got it, but we didn't think that anybody would even open the brochure if we didn't have a naked broad on the cover." We wound up not going with them, and, in fact, that is one of the reasons we started New Day Films.

Another time, one of my films was to be shown at a conference, and I was invited as a speaker, but they wanted to know whether I would be bringing "the opposition." I said, "What opposition? A guy?"

On still another occasion, I was driving to the University of New Hampshire with another woman filmmaker and Vito Russo (author of *The Celluloid Closet*, which is about homosexuality in films) to be on a panel, and we were intercepted by university police who detained us and wanted to now what we were going to say. I guess they thought we were going to corrupt the students—two feminists and a gay guy. They finally allowed us to speak. They didn't stop the program, but they were clearly uncomfortable with our being there.

Anything You Want to Be *won the Blue Ribbon at the American Film Festival in 1972. Among Brandon's other prize-winning films are* How to Prevent a Nuclear War, Betty Tells Her Story, *and* Once Upon a Choice. *She is a professor at the University of Massachusetts and a director of University of Massachusetts Educational Television.*

Brainstorm

When actress Natalie Wood drowned in 1981, toward the end of production of her MGM film *Brainstorm,* it placed completion of the movie in serious doubt. Although director Douglas Trumbull assured the studio that Wood had completed all her major scenes, the head of MGM, David Begelman (whose check forgery scandal had caused his ouster from Columbia Pictures), demanded that they cancel the picture and collect the insurance money. Adding to Begelman's zeal to suppress the picture was his resentment against Wood's costar, Cliff Robertson, whose name Begelman had forged, and whose honesty had led to his being caught.

Nevertheless, *Brainstorm* was finished and released, but with a secret that is even more haunting than its legacy as Natalie Wood's last film. Because it contained so many mechanical effects, actors Robertson, Christopher Walken, and Louise Fletcher were required to "loop" (rerecord) key dialogue. Since, obviously, Wood was unable to do so, sound technicians carefully filtered the background noises out of her scenes and used the sound that had actually been recorded on the set. Therefore *Brainstorm*—a dazzling film about scientists who access the human mind beyond the moment of death—contains the only "live" performance by a beloved actress who did not survive its completion.

Famous Last Words From Movies (Answers)

1. *Casablanca*
2. *A Star Is Born*
3. *King Kong*
4. *Jaws*
5. *The Wizard of Oz*
6. *Gone with the Wind*
7. *Gypsy*
8. *Who's Afraid of Virginia Woolf?*
9. *Sunset Boulevard*
10. *A Clockwork Orange*

Less Famous Last Words from Movies (Answers)

1. *Some Like It Hot*
2. *The Apartment*
3. *Citizen Kane*
4. *2001: A Space Odyssey*
5. *Dr. Strangelove*
6. Alfred Hitchcock's *Frenzy*
7. *Dr. Zhivago*
8. *Mister Roberts*
9. *Lawrence of Arabia*
10. *The Producers*

Hype Me Hollywood (Answers)

1. *Alien*
2. *Star Wars*
3. *Bonnie and Clyde*
4. *Harold and Maude*
5. *The Last of the Red Hot Lovers*
6. *The Long Goodbye*
7. *Putney Swope*
8. *The Exorcist*
9. *Tunnelvision*
10. *The Fly*
11. *Jurassic Park*
12. *Jaws*
13. *Blazing Saddles*
14. *Satyricon*
15. *The Graduate*
16. *Deliverance*
17. *Blow-Up*
18. *2001: A Space Odyssey*
19. *Adventure*
20. *Scrooge*

Un-reel Quotes (Answers)

1. Mae West said "Come up and see me some time" to W. C. Fields at the end of *My Little Chickadee* (not in *She Done Him Wrong*).

2. Cary Grant maintained that he never said "Judy, Judy, Judy."
3. James Cagney insisted he never said "You dirty rat."
4. Greta Garbo pined "I vant to be alone" in *Grand Hotel*.
5. Margaret Dumont and Groucho Marx said their lines in *A Night at the Opera*, but they were deleted by the censors before the picture was released on the grounds that they were too suggestive.
6. Bette Davis swore she never said "Pe-tah!"
7. John Wayne said this before shooting it out with Bruce Dern and his gang of baddies in *True Grit*.
8. Richard Dreyfuss de-pantied the bathroom of *The Goodbye Girl*.
9. Orson Welles toasted Joseph Cotton (but not with Gallo wine) in *Citizen Kane*.
10. A reel trick question: Humphrey Bogart never said "Play it, Sam" in *Casablanca* or any other picture. He said, "What's that you're playing?" and "Play it." It was Ingrid Bergman who said, "Play it, Sam. Play 'As Time Goes By.'"

Biopics (Answers)

Real Person	Played by	Film Title
1. Red Nichols	Danny Kaye	*The Five Pennies*
2. George M. Cohan	James Cagney	*Yankee Doodle Dandy*
3. Ruth Etting	Doris Day	*Love Me or Leave Me*
4. Fannie Brice	Barbra Streisand	*Funny Girl/Lady*
5. Barbara Graham	Susan Hayward	*I Want to Live*
6. Eddie Foy	Bob Hope	*Seven Little Foys*
7. Edwin Booth	Richard Burton	*Prince of Players*
8. Thomas More	Paul Scofield	*A Man for All Seasons*
9. Florenz Ziegfeld	William Powell	*The Great Zeigfeld*
10. Alexander Graham Bell	Don Ameche	*The Story of Alexander Graham Bell*

No Credit, Please (Answers)

Actor	Film
1. Robin Williams	*Baron Munchausen*
2. Robin Williams	*Shakes the Clown*
3. Marlene Dietrich	*Touch of Evil*
4. Richard Burton	*What's New, Pussycat?*
5. Ava Gardner	*The Bandwagon*
6. Walter Huston	*The Maltese Falcon*
7. Helen Hayes	*Third Man on the Mountain*
8. Bill Murray	*Tootsie*
9. Groucho Marx	*Will Success Spoil Rock Hunter?*
10. Elizabeth Taylor	*Elephant Walk*

Read the Book, Miss the Movie (Answers)

A special commendation for bravery should go to Brian De Palma for voluntarily letting journalists cover *two* of his movies from start to finish.

1. *Bonfire of the Vanities* (Brian De Palma, director)
2. *The Red Badge of Courage* (John Huston, director)
3. *Heaven's Gate* (Michael Cimino, director)
4. *The Steagle* (Paul Sylbert, director)
5. *Brewster McCloud* (Robert Altman, director)
6. *Coming to America* (John Landis, director)
7. *Twilight Zone: The Movie* (John Landis, segment director)
8. *Twilight Zone: The Movie* (John Landis, segment director)
9. *An American in Paris* (Vincente Minnelli, director)
10. *Body Double* (Brian De Palma, director)

Films á Clef (Answers)

1. i. (*Citizen Kane* starred Orson Welles as a newspaper magnate.)
2. f. (*The Last Hurrah* starred Spencer Tracy as a Boston mayor.)
3. j. (*All the King's Men* starred Broderick Crawford as a southern governor.)
4. b. (*Boogie Nights* starred Mark Wahlberg as a huge '70s porno star.)
5. c. (*The Royal Family of Broadway* starred Fredric March with actor-siblings Ina Claire as Julie Cavendish and Mary Brian as Gwen Cavendish.)
6. g. (*Death of a Centerfold* featured Roger Rees portraying a filmmaker who loved doomed model Dorothy Stratten, played by Jamie Lee Curtis.)
7. h. (*Daniel* starred Lindsay Crouse opposite Mandy Patinkin as Paul Isaacson, accused/convicted/executed atomic spies.)
8. d. (*Brubaker* starred Robert Redford as a reform-minded southern prison warden.)

9. e. (*The Sweet Smell of Success* starred Burt Lancaster as the newspaper columnist with a private agenda.)
10. a. (*Nevada Smith* featured Brian Keith as an industrialist-to-be.)

Dying Words (Answers)

1. Boris Karloff in *Bride of Frankenstein*
2. Broderick Crawford in *All the King's Men*
3. Edward G. Robinson in *Little Caesar*
4. Steve McQueen in *The Sand Pebbles*
5. Laurence Harvey in *The Outrage*
6. Bruce Dern in *True Grit*
7. Paul Newman in *Butch Cassidy and the Sundance Kid*
8. Slim Pickens in *Dr. Strangelove*
9. HAL 9000 (voice of Douglas Rain) in *2001: A Space Odyssey*
10. Shelley Winters in *The Poseidon Adventure*

Disneyana (Answers)

1. False. The first Mickey Mouse film to be produced was *Plane Crazy. Steamboat Willie,* produced third, was the first Mickey Mouse film to be *released* (1928) as the first sound cartoon. Later sound was added to *Plane Crazy,* and it, too, was released.
2. True. Although Mel Blanc was hired to play Dopey, Dopey's lines were all removed and the lovable character remained silent—except for a single hiccup. That's Mel Blanc.
3. True. Garlands of flowers were, indeed, added to *Fantasia* at the request of the Hays (censorship) Office early in the animation process to cover the breasts of the female centaurs.
4. False. Disney was an accomplished artist who could draw a passable Mickey, but he left it to his chief animator, Ub Iwerks, to engineer a Mickey that his artists could endlessly reproduce from Walt's concept. Walt also supplied Mickey's voice through 1946, when sound effects wizard Jimmy McDonald took over until his retirement in 1976.
5. Arguable. In *The Disney Version* (NY: Simon & Schuster, 1968) Richard Schickel writes that Dr. Benjamin Spock once reported that the Rockefeller family, which owned Radio City Music Hall, had to re-upholster the seats "because they were wet so often by frightened children" during the film's original 1938 run.
6. False. Although the Disney studios produced scores of extremely effective training films, none starred the "major" characters (who were too valuable doing theatrical shorts).

Answers

7. False. Despite a futile search by archivists to locate the film, the rumor persists.

8. True, but they are removed before the home video release. At least, they're supposed to be. Of those that are not (vulgarisms can be found in *Who Framed Roger Rabbit*), they can only be seen on DVD or the CAV laser disc editions. On original theatrical prints of *The Little Mermaid,* in the scene where Ariel signs Ursula's agreement, there are single-frame drawings on the contract scroll that show Mickey committing suicide.

9. True. For example, co-directors John Musker and Ron Clements "appear" as bystanders in an early scene in *Aladdin* (1992), and film historian John Culhane is Mr. Snoops in *The Rescuers.*

10. False. After Walt Disney died of cancer on December 15, 1966, his remains were cremated and quietly interred at Forest Lawn Cemetery in Glendale, California.

For Internet information on Disney (and other) urban legends, browse to: **http://www.snopes.com/disney**

Before They Were Stars (Answers)

1. s
2. d
3. i
4. p
5. h
6. b
7. c
8. l
9. g
10. o
11. a
12. k
13. r
14. m
15. e
16. j
17. t
18. f
19. n
20. q

Screen Lovers (Answers)

1. h
2. g
3. i
4. e
5. d
6. b
7. c
8. a
9. j
10. f

Casablanca (Answers)

1. Blaine
2. Lund
3. 1955: Charles MacGraw and Marcel Dalio; 1983: David Soul and Hector Elizondo
4. S. Z. Sakall (as S. K. Sakall) was Carl, the headwaiter; Leonid Kinskey was Sascha, the Russian waiter.
5. Donald Siegel (*Dirty Harry, The Killers*) was a Warner Bros. contract editor/second unit director who specialized in montage sequences.
6. "It Had to Be You," "Shine," and "Knock on Wood"
7. The great singer was tested for the role of Sam when producer Hal Wallis considered making Sam a woman.
8. There is no such thing, although a *reisepass* (travel permit) might come close.
9. La Belle Aurore
10. "Are my eyes really brown?"

Television

Movies

Music

Twentieth Century History

Sayings & Common Sense

Chapter 3

Music

Religion

Science & Geography

Home Frontier

Celebrity

Minutiae

As father time raises his baton for the downbeat on the twenty-first century, the music industry finds itself facing declining sales, frightening new technologies, conflicts over the definition of genres, and mounting public attack on content, or, in other words, business as usual. No single barometer of cultural taste is more accurate than pop music, or as guided by emotion. Of all the performing arts—film, theatre, dance—pop music is the most capricious. Anybody thinks he/she can be a star if only he/she just has a song, plays an instrument, and has a couple of friends, preferably one of whom owns a tape recorder. Oh, and the desire.

The reality is somewhat darker. But that hasn't stopped a steady stream of hopefuls (mostly male) who move from garages and gyms to Gotham and groupies looking to land a recording contract, a fancy car, and maybe a fashion model. Or they're urban kids who see music as a way out of the ghetto, raising hell and consciousness in equal parts, wielding nothing but a microphone and an attitude.

Although music has been around ever since Ugg the Caveman carried a tune on a hollow log ("It has a good beat, and I can dance to it"), it wasn't until the invention of the phonograph at the turn of the last century that it became entertainment for the masses. Before then, although every parlor had a piano and all children dutifully took lessons, popular songs existed silently on sheet music. Most of the money from sales was kept by the publishers, who paid the composer a penny a copy, which he had to split with the lyricist, if there was one. Selling ten thousand copies made a song a hit.

To be sure, not all sheet music was of the innocuous "Moon, June, Spoon" variety. The ragtime compositions of Scott Joplin were widely criticized for rousing the "baser" instincts among listeners, and in the '20s not a few torch singers (Helen Morgan and Ruth Etting, for example) found themselves vilified not so much for their music as the yearning with which they sang it.

The phonograph changed all that. Invented by Thomas Edison in 1877, it promised to permit the average person to hear, in his own home, music played by professionals, even stars, who had recorded it elsewhere. And the performance was the same every time—as long as the brittle wax cylinder didn't break. Ten years later the gramophone introduced the more stable flat discs, and by 1906 Eldridge Johnson, of the Victor Talking Machine Company, signed the great Enrico Caruso to record for him. What Milton Berle did for early television, Caruso did for the Victrola. Soon more people had heard Caruso sing on records than had witnessed him perform in Milan in twenty years.

Recorded music changed the public's recreational habits. People stayed home rather than venturing to concert halls. Small-town bands found themselves competing with record stores. Sheet music sales plummeted. Then came radio and talking pictures, and by the 1927 premiere of *The Jazz Singer,* pit orchestras all across the country began being laid off, as silent movie houses frantically converted to sound.

At almost every stage of its development, music has been a target, usually of the older generation against the younger, and always to no avail. The year doesn't even matter; in all likelihood, fans of Bach's baroque compositions fought a losing battle against Beethoven and his newfangled classical symphonies. Gershwin likewise shook up Friml, Dixieland drowned Lehar, and Kern & Hammerstein replaced Gilbert & Sullivan. Stravinsky scandalized Paris, the Charleston and jitterbug trounced the waltz and fox trot, and people are still trying to understand Philip Glass.

But that was then, and rock 'n' roll is now. Ever since Bill Haley and the Comets rocked around the clock in 1955, young people have found their voice in the strains of rock, R&B, soul, acid, rap, ska, punk, new wave, grunge, and all the fringes and shadings in between. Just as surely as parents shout "You kids turn down that damn music!" there will always be music, kids, and parents, and they will always be at odds.

What changed music was when kids became a commercial force in the '50s. That's when Little Richard was singing "tuti-fruiti," Elvis was swinging his hips, and Jerry Lee Lewis was marrying his cousin. And mainstream America didn't like it one bit.

Not much has changed since the mid-'50s except lapels. Sinatra yielded to Elvis, Elvis to the Beatles, the Beatles to each other, Rod Stewart to Springsteen to Madonna to Van Halen to Madonna again to Michael Jackson to Nirvana to Pearl Jam to Tupac to Babyface and to whomever is next (probably Sinatra reissues).

What has, indeed, changed is the music industry itself. In the last half century, it has consolidated its power, streamlined its operations, and diversified its holdings. Insiders call it *synergy*—the ability to integrate all aspects of the product, from movies to soundtracks to tours to records/CDs/tapes/DATs to merchandising to licensing to TV specials to video games to mail orders to screen savers. Rather than empower some other company to market an artist, record companies have acquired subsidiaries to do it.

But vertical integration hasn't made them invincible. With so much at stake, these publicly held companies still tremble at the first hint of government intervention. Whether it was Tipper Gore's support of the Fundamentalist-controlled PMRC (Parents Music Resource Center) in the mid-'80s, the pro-censorship alliance of C. Delores Tucker and William Bennett against gangsta rap and heavy metal in 1995, or congressional hearings into music and violence in general (and Marilyn Manson in particular) in 1997, the sides are pretty well drawn. Whatever music William Congreve heard in 1697 that had "charms to soothe a savage breast," it had become noticeably silent three hundred years later.

No question about it, music arouses emotions. It communicates nonverbally, and powerfully. It also seems to produce, for want of a better word, a kind of cultural aphasia that makes grownups deaf to the musical tastes of their children, and unable to remember that they went through the same thing when they were young. At the same time, music is a business. A huge business. Generally speaking, businesses do not have time for nostalgia—although, in the case of music trivia, everybody makes exceptions.

Woodstock

There were at least two births and one death at Woodstock, and a lot of people took trips there, most of them after arriving. Was the brown acid really "not specifically too good"? Did Alan Fay ever make it to the information booth? Did that nun get in trouble for flashing the peace sign? We may never know.

On the other hand, was Woodstock a commercial washout? Was it the confluence of everything good that the hippie era stood for? Or was it just one big mud-bath?

1. According to Roberts and Pilpel's *Young Men with Unlimited Capital,* young heirs John (Jock) Roberts and Joel Rosenman took an ad in the *New York Times* on March 22, 1967, looking for "interesting, legitimate investment opportunities and business propositions." They were all set to build a Manhattan studio to be called Media Sound when lawyer Miles Lourie introduced them to rock managers/producers Mike Land and Artie Kornfeld.
2. The Woodstock Music & Art Fair in 1969 grew out of a simultaneous desire to build a recording studio in Upstate New York so that such "local" residents as Bob Dylan, Tim Hardin, and the Band wouldn't have to schlep all the way into Manhattan to cut their albums. It was proposed that holding a rock concert might finance the studio through ticket sales.
3. John Roberts put up $1,300,000, which he obtained not from his trust fund but from his New York bank, as a lien *against* his trust fund. The deal was closed based upon his personal word, not his family's signature; nothing was signed until the day after the concert. By then Woodstock owed approximately $1,600,000.
4. The original plan was to hold the concert on the Wallkill, New York, farm of Howard Mills. When the townspeople passed laws that effectively barred the concert from taking place, a nearby Sullivan County farmer named Max Yasgur stepped forward. He was dismayed that his Wallkill neighbors had treated the hippies so badly and offered his own six-hundred-acre dairy pasture. He was also nobody's fool: his price was $50,000 plus $75,000 in escrow to cover damage. Since his offer came through less than a month before the August 15–17 concert, he got a fast yes. Deals for compensation and cleanup were made with adjoining landowners (who weren't too pleased with Yasgur's decision in the first place) to cover the anticipated spill-overs, sleep-overs, and trudge-overs by patrons.
5. Nobody knows how many people actually showed up. There were between fifty thousand and sixty thousand tickets sold. Crowd estimators figured five hundred thousand (which mysteriously went up to ten million once the movie came out in 1970).
6. Bottom line: By the end of 1973 there were $3,300,000 in receipts from tickets, records, licensing, and the movie. There were also $3,400,000 in debts, including $250,000 in talent fees. In other words, a $100,000 loss.

7. In 1994, Woodstock Ventures, the company run by Mike Lang, John Roberts, and Joel Rosenman, presented a Twenty-fifth Anniversary Woodstock Concert in partnership with Polygram Diversified Entertainment. Scheduled for August 12–14 in Saugerties, New York, the promoters went to court to prevent Sid Bernstein and Harry Rhulen of Shea Entertainment, Inc., from using the name *Woodstock* on their competing concert, for which they had managed to obtain Max Yasgur's farm (contrary to some reports, they did not try to enjoin the concert itself). The Shea event, however, was eventually scrapped due to low ticket sales.[1]

8. Tickets in 1969 were $18 *for all three days*. The average price of a ticket for Woodstock 25 in 1994 was $135.

---

[1] Source: *Daily Variety,* August 2, 1994.

Acts at Woodstock

The following acts appeared at Woodstock. Please note that Dylan, Bob was not among them (alphabetically):

Baez, Joan	Hardin, Tim	Santana
Band, The	Havens, Richie	Sebastian, John
Blood, Sweat and Tears	Incredible String Band, The	Sha Na Na
Canned Heat	Jefferson Airplane, The	Shankar, Ravi
Cocker, Joe	Joplin, Janis	Sly and the Family Stone
Country Joe and the Fish	Keef Hartley Band	Sommer, Bert
Credence Clearwater Revival	Menalie	Sweetwater
Crosby, Stills, Nash and Young	Mountain	Ten Years After
Grateful Dead, The	Paul Butterfield Blues Band, The	Who, The
Guthrie, Arlo	Quill	Winter, Johnny

Quiz: Bop Till You Drop

How did the following musical artists die?

1. Janis Joplin
2. Jimi Hendrix
3. Jim Croce
4. Phil Ochs
5. Keith Moon
6. Elvis Presley
7. Richie Valens
8. Buddy Holly
9. J. P. "Big Bopper" Richardson
10. Otis Redding
11. Spinal Tap drummers
12. Sid Vicious
13. Brian Jones
14. Dennis Wilson
15. Jim Morrison
16. Bob Marley
17. "Mama" Cass Elliott
18. Sam Cooke
19. Kurt Cobain
20. John Lennon

Quiz: Paul Is Dead

They're called "urban myths" because everybody has heard them and knows somebody who knows somebody who knows somebody who says they're true. This one has been traced back as far as a prank at a college radio station in northern Illinois, but it's only a fuzzy search.

Nevertheless, in 1969 everybody was saying that Paul McCartney had died in 1965 and had been replaced by an impostor—a fantasy that was supposedly supported by evidence, both visual and sonic, that was contained on Beatles albums. At best, the rumor was proof of the affection by an entire generation for the "Fab Four." At worst, it was probably a record company ploy to get kids to buy more albums (you had to, after you scraped the vinyl off the old ones playing them backward looking for clues).

Speaking of clues, which of these were NOT cited as "proof"?

1. On the cover of "Sgt. Pepper," a hand—symbol of death—is held over Paul's head, while on the back cover he faces away from the camera.
2. On the white album, during the cut "Revolution 9," there is a voice that mumbles "number nine, number nine." If you play it backward, it sounds like "turn me on, dead man."
3. On the Lennon song "Glass Onion," the now-dead-for-real Beatle sang, "And here's another clue for you all/the Walrus was Paul."
4. In *Magical Mystery Tour* (the movie), Paul wears a black carnation in the "Your Mother Should Know" sequence, instead of a white one.
5. If you hold "Yesterday . . . and Today" sideways, Paul looks as though he's laying in a coffin.
6. On "Revolver," if you play the inside groove on Side Two, you can hear Paul saying, "I was here, now I'm gone."
7. Paul is walking barefoot across Abbey Road on the cover of that album (corpses are buried without shoes), his eyes are closed, and he's out of step. The car license plate reads "28 IF," meaning IF Paul lived he'd be twenty-eight.
8. When he composed the music for the James Bond film, *Live and Let Die,* the fake Paul purposely included the redundancy lyric, "In this ever-changing world in which we live in," to confess that he is an impostor.
9. The line "He blew his mind out in a car" from "A Day in the Life" refers to Paul's suicide.
10. He was replaced by Pete Best.

Quiz: Commercial Music

People seeing the 1960 western *The Magnificent Seven* for the first time are usually struck by Elmer Bernstein's title music, which they hitherto knew only as the theme for Marlboro cigarette TV commercials. And Richard Strauss is probably not too happy in de-composer's heaven that his tone poem *Also Sprach Zarathustra* is referred to as "the theme from 2001." Rock musicians likewise face such dilemmas, and while some of them (notably the Beatles) refuse to sell out, those below did. Name the products that were advertised by these songs:

1. "Good Vibrations" (Beach Boys)
2. "Up, Up and Away" (The Fifth Dimension)
3. "Just One Look" (Doris Troy)
4. "Anticipation" (Carly Simon)
5. "My Sharona" (The Knack)

Quiz: Sing Me a Story

Identify the songs from the stories they tell, and give the artist:

1. A minister rebukes a soldier for playing cards in church until the boy explains that they are his bible.
2. A girl is killed by a train when she attempts to retrieve her boyfriend's high school ring from a stalled car.
3. An XKE and a Stingray drag race on Sunset Boulevard with predictably inescapable intersecting results.
4. A boy leaves his girl when her parents forbid her to see him anymore, but he is killed, as she watches, when he departs too quickly on his motorcycle.
5. A boy meets a girl on a mountain and they fall in love, but he accidentally stabs her.
6. A boy and girl have a secret affair in the South until she learns that he has inexplicably committed suicide by jumping off a bridge.
7. What's the use of singing rock 'n' roll now that Buddy Holly is gone?
8. A student uses a blunt instrument to kill his girlfriend, his science teacher, and his sentencing judge.
9. A devoted church-going woman dies a nonentity.
10. Be careful eating rotten legumes.

Quiz: Odd Person Out

All of these people had the misfortune to quit a rock group before the group hit it big. Some later made it on their own, but many remain footnotes in rock 'n' roll history. Identify the group that these people dis-membered:

1. Stuart Sutcliffe
2. Al Kooper
3. Al Jardine
4. Pete Best
5. Eric Clapton
6. Signe Anderson
7. Tory Crimes
8. Jeremy Spencer
9. Doug Sanden
10. Vinne Lopez

Quiz: Question and Answer Songs

In the days when singles could be cut and released in a matter of days, it was not unusual for singers to produce "answer" songs in response to a current hit. Some were parodies (ala Weird Al Yankovic), while some were merely an attempt to latch onto another's coattails. From the following answer songs, name the original question song and its artist:

1. "Ballad of the Yellow Berets" (Bob Seger)
2. "Come Back, Maybellene" (Big John Greer)
3. "Got a Job" (The Miracles)
4. "Single" (Bette Davis)
5. "My Girl" (The Temptations)
6. "Woman, Oh Woman" (Jose Ferrer)
7. "Your Generation" (Generation X)
8. "Battle of Camp Cucamonga" (Homer and Jethro)
9. "Day-O" (Stan Freberg)
10. "Ballad of Duvid Krocket" (Mickey Katz)

Quiz: Pips, etc.

Let's get the old joke out of the way: No, the Beatles were not Paul McCartney's first backup group. On the other hand, music isn't always made alone. Just ask the Pips. Name the featured artists who were ably supported by these performers:

1. Jerry Allison, Sonny Curtis, Niki Sullivan
2. Levon and the Hawks
3. Crazy Horse
4. The Famous Flames
5. Guam
6. The Silver Bullet Band
7. Mad Dogs and Englishmen
8. The Attractions
9. Big Brother and the Holding Company
10. Wonderlove

Get a Life: John Cameron Cameron

Question: Who was John Cameron Cameron and where was he?

Answer: The fictitious broadcaster always identified himself by saying, "This is John Cameron Cameron—downtown" while issuing updates on the adventures of "The Flying Saucer."

"Flying Saucer" records, produced by the team of Buchanan and Goodman for the independent "Luniverse" label, told frantic stories of alien invasions in the guise of news reports. The gimmick was that the records asked fake interview questions that were "answered" by out-of-context lines from popular songs. Such hits as "The Flying Saucer" and "The Flying Saucer Goes West" (in which General Elvis Presley [!] leads the U.S. Army against the spacemen) provided effective—and usually well-deserved—satire on the nonsense words (Nee-nee-na-na-na-na-nu-nu; day-o; oo-ee-oo-ahh-ahh/ting-tang-walla-walla-bing-bang, etc.) that passed for pop lyrics in the 1950s.

Disco

Disco. The word itself is enough to melt poly-ester; the memory is even more annoying. If you read any Jay McInerny books or lived through the disco era (roughly 1976–1983) you can remember the ritual. You found yourself at 2 AM entering a smoke-filled dance club, your eyes assaulted by laser shows and pin-point reflections of light from a spinning mirror ball hanging from the ceiling. The throb of woofers thumps up from the floor, through your legs and into your stomach, and your ears are assaulted by the caterwauling sound of genuine 100 percent real synthesized music. The disc jockey is locked inside a glass booth talking to his/her girlfriend/boyfriend, probably about you, while segueing from one record to another and smiling at the wit of juxtaposition as though it was possible to tell the tunes apart. Nevertheless, to impress the person you're with, you bite your lower lip as though turned on, start to move to the beat, and say "good song" even though you've never heard it before.

Maybe somebody on the floor passes you a popper, or you wonder if there's any Bolivian Marching Powder for sale in the bath-room. Otherwise you head for the bar, tug at the double-knit clothing that's giving you a bad case of Virginia Heartburn, and try to pick up somebody other than the person you came with. Gender becomes less important as the hour gets later. If all else fails, you head to the strobing dance floor and writhe to the rhythm, sublimely self-absorbed, yet trying not to lose your partner in the hazy crowd. You know how many drinks you had by counting the cocktail straws you saved. And you pray

you haven't lost the match book with the phone number.

That was disco.

Disco was more than music, it was a way of life, but a way of life that was not exactly what it appeared to be. With hindsight, it can be seen as providing five things:

1. **Ritual**. Following the free-form '60s and the "me decade" of the '70s, disco set down codes of dress and behavior that made high school cliques look positively Montessori. To a generation of young people con-fused by feminism, disco offered a somewhat more level (though still not easily navigable) playing field.

2. **Technology**. Sound got better in the late '70s; clarity became more impor-tant than decibels. Vinyl discs were yielding to tapes (cassettes as well as dreaded 8-tracks), with CDs just around the corner. While Hollywood was maturing into digital Dolby and THX through *Star Wars* and *Close Encounters,* home audio was blos-soming into a form so powerful it could make your eyes bleed.

3. **Commerce**. In the wake of techno-logical changes, the recording industry noticed its sales figures lev-eling off, even dropping, for the first time in decades. It was the age of all-star super-groups and a dearth of new talent. Popularity was becoming an all-or-nothing thing: Either everyone bought Bee Gees and Peter Frampton albums, or they bought nothing. The clothing industry, too, benefited from an increasing fashion awareness among young people. Admittedly, it

was threads they would be ashamed of in five years, but they were still buying white suits, black shirts, twirling dresses, and snazzy shoes, all of which separated the crass from the cognoscenti.

4. **Movement**. No more boys on one side of the room and girls on the other. Disco allowed anybody to ask anybody. Movement—provocative movement, especially—became part of the tradition. Disco was solo dancing in pairs; it's all in the show. And that leads to the most important single aspect of disco, and the most controversial:

5. **Disco was gay**. The glitz, the cruising, the poppers, the theatricality, the physicality, the style, and the chemistry was indisputably defined by the gay community. Gays had been well aware of "dance music" before it hit the ethnic urban areas, where *Saturday Night Fever* (1978) was set. Black couples, who for years had gone to gay clubs for the music, were soon joined by white couples who came for the same thing. Just as rock 'n' roll allowed white kids to share something of the black experience in the '50s, so did disco open the closet door a little to straight kids in the '70s.

It could be argued that disco died because it became its own parody: the rigid styles, the inflexibly same-sounding music, and the pressure to party take a toll if you have classes or work to go to the next day. It might also be posited that racism and homophobia eventually branded disco and limited its appeal. But more likely it dissipated simply because something newer and better came along: punk, new wave, grunge, and other movements of the late '80s. Soon "disco sucks" became a verdict as well as a battle cry.

You grow up, your tastes change, and you wish Mom and Dad would throw away those old pictures they took of you in that leisure suit. Or in those pink bell-bottoms. Or in the white bucks. Or in the sailor suit. Or on the bearskin rug.

Get a Life: Oversights

Question: Which of the following have won Grammy awards:

1. The Who
2. The Beach Boys
3. Jimi Hendrix
4. Chuck Berry
5. Smokey Robinson

Answer: As of this writing, none of them.

Quiz: Who's Who in Music

Match the professional names on the left with the recording artists' actual names on the right:

On the Record

1. Big Bopper
2. David Bowie
3. Chubby Checker
4. Jimmy Cliff
5. Alice Cooper
6. Elvis Costello
7. Bobby Darin
8. Connie Francis
9. Southside Johnny
10. Chaka Khan
11. Ben E. King
12. Lulu
13. Taj Mahal
14. Manfred Mann
15. Freddie Mercury
16. Van Morrison
17. ? (and the Mysterians)
18. Les Paul
19. Iggy Pop
20. Conway Twitty
21. Steve Tyler
22. Muddy Waters
23. Howlin' Wolf
24. Gene Simmons

Off the Record

a. Gene Klein
b. Mike Liebowitz
c. Henry Saint-Claire Williams
d. George Ivan
e. Marie McDonald Laurie
f. Steven Tallarico
g. Frederick Bulsara
h. Yvette Marie Holland
i. Lester Polfus II
j. Constance Franconero
k. Rudy Martinez
l. Declan Patrick MacManus
m. James Chambers
n. Ernest Evans
o. James Jewell Osterburg
p. Jiles Perry Richardson
q. David Robert Hayward-Jones
r. Vincent Furnier
s. Chester Burnett
t. McKinley Morganfield
u. Robert Warden Cassotto
v. Harold Lloyd Jenkins
w. John Lyon
x. Benjamin Nelson

Quiz: Dances

Which of the following were *not* dances in the '60s?

The Frug
The Twist
The Swim
The Monkey
The Skate

The Watusi
The Mashed Potato
The Shaggy Dog
The Jerk

Quiz: Musical Bios

Match the movie with the musician it was (supposed to be) about:

1. *Night and Day*
2. *Bound for Glory*
3. *Song of Norway*
4. *Amadeus*
5. *Rhapsody in Blue*
6. *Three Little Words*
7. *Song Without End*
8. *Impromptu*
9. *Yankee Doodle Dandy*
10. *The Five Pennies*
11. *Song to Remember*
12. *Words and Music*

a. Franz Liszt
b. "Red" Nichols
c. Woody Guthrie
d. Frederick Chopin
e. George M. Cohan
f. George Gershwin
g. Frederick Chopin
h. Rodgers and Hart
i. Cole Porter
j. Wolfgang Mozart
k. Edvard Grieg
l. Kalmar and Ruby

The King and the President

The most frequently requested photograph from the National Archives is that of Elvis Presley shaking hands with President Richard M. Nixon in the Oval Office of the White House. The picture was taken on December 20, 1970, under legendary circumstances.

Although his sensuous voice and swiveling hips made parents uneasy (we're talking about Elvis now), Presley was a deeply religious and unusually conservative American. He was also given to highly impetuous acts. One day in 1970 he decided that he wanted to become a drug enforcement agent and proceeded to Washington, D.C., to ask President Nixon to sign him up.

Well, why shouldn't the King want to meet directly with the president?

Never one to let an opportunity slip through his fingers, the chief executive consented to the impromptu summit. Elvis—higher than a B-52, by some reports—stated his case to Nixon, and Nixon gave him a handshake, a badge, and his thanks. Then Elvis gave Nixon something he'd brought with him: a silver-plated revolver. There is no record of what Nixon (or, more importantly, the Secret Service) said at the moment of presentation.

For years thereafter, Nixon would feel that he had made an important spiritual connection with the youth community and actually took an interest in Elvis's career. It is not known whether Agent Presley ever took part in any undercover drug sting operations; in most cases, the term *Elvis impersonator* refers to fans who want to look like Elvis, not Elvis wanting to look like one of the fans.

Elvis died in 1977. His stamp was released in 1997.

Nixon died in 1994. His stamp came out the next year.

Get a Life: Altamont

Question: What was the name of the man who was killed by the Hell's Angels at Altamont?

Answer: He was Meredith Hunter, and he was killed by a member of the Hell's Angels Motorcycle Club during the Rolling Stones' free concert on December 6, 1969. The fact that Hunter was black and the Angels were white didn't help matters. Of the three hundred thousand fans who attended the freebie at the Altamont Speedway in San Francisco, three other people also died: One drowned and two were run over in their sleeping bags. Afterward, Mick Jagger refused to perform "Sympathy for the Devil" for six years. The concert, the incident, and its aftermath were chronicled in the 1970 documentary *Gimme Shelter* by David Maysles, Albert Maysles, and Charlotte Zwerin.

Hit List

Nothing better demonstrates the transition from popular music to rock 'n' roll than lists of the "Top 10" hits and their artists during signal years of the '50s. (Note: Elvis was in the army from 1958–60, accounting for his absence from the charts.)

1950:
1. "Goodnight Irene" (The Weavers and Gordon Jenkins)
2. "It Isn't Fair" (Sammy Kaye)
3. "The Third Man" theme (Anton Karas)
4. "Mule Train" (Frankie Laine)
5. "Mona Lisa" (Nat "King" Cole)
6. "Music! Music! Music!" (Teresa Brewer)
7. "I Wanna Be Loved" (Andrews Sisters)
8. "If I Knew You Were Comin' I'd've Baked a Cake" (Eileen Barton)
9. "I Can Dream, Can't I" (Andrews Sisters)
10. "That Lucky Old Sun" (Frankie Laine)

1954:
1. "Little Things Mean a Lot" (Kitty Kallen)
2. "Hey There" (Rosemary Clooney)
3. "Wanted" (Perry Como)
4. "Young at Heart" (Frank Sinatra)
5. "Sh-Boom" (The Crew Cuts)
6. "Three Coins in the Fountain" (Frank Sinatra)
7. "Little Shoemaker" (The Gaylords)
8. "Oh, My Papa" (Eddie Fisher)
9. "Secret Love" (Doris Day)
10. "Happy Wanderer" (Frank Weir)

1955:
1. "Rock Around the Clock" (Bill Haley and the Comets)
2. "Ballad of Davy Crockett" (Bill Hayes)
3. "Cherry Pink and Apple Blossom White" (Perez Prado)
4. "Melody of Love" (Billy Vaughn)
5. "Yellow Rose of Texas" (Mitch Miller and the Sing-Along Gang)
6. "Ain't That a Shame" (Pat Boone)
7. "Sincerely" (The McGuire Sisters)
8. "Unchained Melody" (Les Baxter)
9. "Crazy Otto Rag" (Crazy Otto)
10. "Mister Sandman" (The Chordettes)

1956:
1. "Don't Be Cruel" (Elvis Presley)
2. "Great Pretender" (The Platters)
3. "My Prayer" (The Platters)
4. "Wayward Wind" (Gogi Grant)
5. "Whatever Will Be, Will Be" (Doris Day)
6. "Heartbreak Hotel" (Elvis Presley)
7. "Lisbon Antigua" (Nelson Riddle)
8. "Canadian Sunset" (Hugo Winterhalter)
9. "Moonglow" and "Theme from *Picnic*" (Morris Stoloff)
10. "Honky Tonk" (Bill Doggett)

1959:
1. "Mack the Knife" (Bobby Darin)
2. "Battle of New Orleans" (Johnny Horton)
3. "Venus" (Frankie Avalon)
4. "Lonely Boy" (Paul Anka)
5. "There Goes My Baby" (The Drifters)
6. "Personality" (Lloyd Price)
7. "Three Bells" (The Browns)
8. "Put Your Head on My Shoulder" (Paul Anka)
9. "Sleep Walk" (Santo and Johnny)
10. "Come Softly to Me" (The Fleetwoods)

Fifth Beatles

There were at least four "Fifth Beatles." Numbers one through four are, of course, undisputed: Paul McCartney, John Lennon, George Harrison, and Ringo Starr. The first number fives are alternately guitarist Stuart Sutcliffe and drummer Pete Best. Both men performed with Lennon, McCartney, and Harrison in Liverpool beginning in the late '50s. At that time, the five musicians called themselves the Quarrymen, although within the next year they would be known variously as the Moondogs, Moonshiners, and Silver Beatles.

By the end of the group's 1960 sojourn in Hamburg, Germany, Sutcliffe was out and Best had been replaced by Ringo Starr. (Sutcliffe died in Hamburg in 1962 of a brain hemorrhage.)

When the Beatles returned to England in 1961, their increased profile and popularity with young British music fans brought them to the attention of manager Brian Epstein. Epstein, who had gumption as well as music connections (his father owned an appliance store), quickly signed them as clients and aggressively secured them a record deal. Epstein literally created the image of the group, which anointed him the "the fifth Beatle." And therein begins the controversy.

When the Beatles first visited America in 1964, they were practically adopted by New York radio station WINS-AM, which was riding the crest of—as well as being responsible for generating the majority of—Beatlemania in the U.S. WINS's leading disc jockey, Murray "the K" Kaufman, became so closely identified with the quartet that he began calling himself "the fifth Beatle." Brian Epstein's reaction to this is not recorded, although there exists a faction that insists Epstein led Kaufman to think of himself in that capacity as a means of gaining increased airplay. Epstein died in 1967 at age thirty-two; Kaufman died in 1982 at age sixty.

Pete Best is alive as of this writing. He penned his own reminiscence, *Beatle!*, in 1994.

Dick Clark

"The World's Oldest Teenager" was born in 1929 and decided he wanted to be a disc jockey in 1942. Since rock 'n' roll wasn't even a gleam in the eye of Alan Freed (who introduced the term in the early '50s), the upstate New York Clark worked his way through several local radio stations until he landed a summer replacement gig at WFIL in Philadelphia in 1952.

Dick Clark didn't invent *American Bandstand,* but he certainly popularized it after taking over the show from its troubled host, Bob Horn, in 1956. With Clark's clean-cut image, gift of gab, and genius for picking and promoting musical groups, he convinced the ABC network to carry the show to an ever-growing number of its affiliates by 1958. The formula was basic: Attractive teenagers danced while up-and-coming performers moved their lips to prerecorded songs.

Because Philadelphia was only a short train ride away from Manhattan, Clark was able to add a booking on his show to the national appearances new groups made while in New York City. Among stars-to-be who "visited" Clark early in their careers were Johnny Mathis, Chuck Berry, Fats Domino, and a duo called Tom and Jerry (who later changed their name to Simon and Garfunkle), as well as John Travolta and Madonna.

It should be noted that, in the days when black performers had trouble getting network exposure, "American Bandstand" was color blind.

One thing that brought Dick Clark national notoriety was his uncanny business acumen. He typically retained rights to performers' appearances on his show and today owns one of the industry's most comprehensive music archives.

Succeeding years have made Dick Clark incalculably rich through hosting and owning TV game shows, hosting and producing TV "blooper" specials, owning broadcasting licenses and, of course, ringing in the New Year. But there are three decades of rock musicians who can thank him for important early career exposure on his teen dance parties.

Alan Freed

If a tree falls in the forest and there's no one there to hear it, does it make a sound? If exciting new music exists but no one has yet named it rock 'n' roll, does it create a revolution? Alan Freed made all the difference.

Freed, a disc jockey on a Cleveland rhythm and blues radio station in the early 1950s, started developing a reputation for hanging out with the acts whose music he played. Among those artists whose careers he boosted were Bo Diddly and Chuck Berry (and he is credited with writing lyrics to Berry's hit "Maybelline"). When R&B began catching on among America's rapidly growing

teenage population, Freed made it explode with a pair of live shows at Brooklyn's Paramount Theatre in 1955.

At about the same time, he started using the phrase *rock 'n' roll* to describe the throbbing new amalgam of R&B and rock. The name was an obvious allusion to sexual activity, and it only added to the concern that parents already felt over their children's obsession with the sound. Freed symbolized both and therefore became the point man for a generation (the previous one) outraged over the "threat" that rock 'n' roll posed to decency.

In 1960—following investigations conducted by the House Subcommittee on Legislative Oversight—he was indicted for accepting $30,000 from six record companies to play their releases on his show. The practice came to be called "payola" (q.v.), and its taint turned the popular Freed into a pariah. His jobs dried up, clearing the field for a slightly younger (and somewhat cleaner) upstart named Dick Clark to rise to prominence. Freed died in 1965 at the age of forty-two.

Payola

At the time it was practiced, payola wasn't seen as a problem, but as a solution. In the 1950s, with rock 'n' roll on the rise, there was a concerted effort on the part of the major record labels against recording it. The freeze wasn't entirely their fault; the big labels (RCA, Decca, Columbia, Capitol, etc.) traditionally reflected the interests of the composers and authors of old-line, "pop" songs. That bias, combined with the closed shop of ASCAP (American Society of Composers, Authors and

Publishers), effectively shut young, visionary rockers out of the business. Denied access to major labels and blocked from broadcast, independent distributors resorted to bribing disc jockeys to play their songs on the air. In hindsight, the effort seems redundant; by 1958, 70 percent of the records sold in America were being bought by teenagers.

It's important to remember that until the mergers and buyouts of the 1980s raised the stakes for broadcasters, disc jockeys had a relatively free hand in choosing the music they played. That was before market research, consultants, tight playlists, and computerized tracking took the personality out of music radio. Deejays were kings of the airwaves, and when somebody like Alan Freed in Cleveland, "Cousin" Bruce Morrow in New York, or Dave Maynard in Boston spun a platter, it turned into gold.

Soon Congress wanted to know what was going on. Incensed at the 1958 television quiz show scandals, Representative Oren Harris of Arkansas held hearings before the House Subcommittee on Legislative Oversight in 1959-60 that exposed the practice of payola. At the same time, charges of "plugola"—gifts or money given to station executives in exchange for mentioning products on the air—also came to the fore.

The upshot of the quiz show, plugola, and payola revelations was that the FCC enacted rules that would force broadcasters to divulge any income they received relating to program content as well as a vague requirement to stop deceptive programming practices. (This explains the elaborate disclaimers that radio and TV stations must include when they run promotional giveaways.)

Get a Life: Puff the Magic Dragon

Question: Was the Peter, Paul and Mary song, "Puff, the Magic Dragon" about marijuana?

Answer: The code words are there if you want to look for them: "Puff" is the way grass smokers toke on a joint; the "boat with billowed sails" is hauling a shipment of contraband; Jackie watches out for narcs while "perched on Puff's gigantic tail"; "noble kings and princes" yield to drug lords; and, in the end, Jackie grows up and enters rehab,

causing Puff to "cease his fearless roar." The end.

Not hardly. Paul Stookey insists that Puff—who lived, as every flower child (especially Jackie Paper) knows, in the land of Honalee—has nothing to do with any kind of drug. To make his point, he even debunked the rumor by showing how any song could be seen as containing drug symbolism and used "The Star-Spangled Banner" as an example. As Freud said (but probably didn't), "Sometimes a cigar is just a cigar."

"Top 40"

There are, obviously, far more than forty worthwhile songs in circulation at any given time. But that didn't stop Omaha, Nebraska, radio programmers Bill Stewart and Tom Storz from inventing the "Top 40" format in 1955. Its function was to take the guesswork out of spinning platters by reducing the choices that could be played. But its real purpose, many insist, was to keep troublesome (read: creative) deejays from exercising too much freedom. Also called "More Music Radio," it restricted a rock station's playlist to the forty top-ranked songs according to their popularity on the record charts and then specified which of them was to be played at any given point during a broadcast hour. By the end of a typical four-hour DJ shift, all forty songs would have been played, many more than once.

For example, the number one hit was to be played at the top of the hour, followed by an older one (but not too old), followed by the number four song, followed by a commercial. At the bottom of the hour, the number two song could be played. Songs were groped in clusters of three, with a seamless transition (called a *segue*) between them. The DJ was allowed to speak into an open mike while a song's instrumental intro was playing (a process called a *talk-up*) so as to give the impression of continuous programming. At no time would more than one song separate a "familiar" and a "hit" song. When a song fell from the charts (say, as a result of being played to death), the others moved up. As long as there was a constant flow of new songs, but not too many, the "Top 40" remained fresh.

"Top 40" was soon perfected by programmer Bill Drake in Los Angeles and seized as gospel by pop stations nationwide. It was just what hungry record companies wanted in the '50s to sell albums, and it survived well into the '60s until FM "free form" radio and longer songs slowed the pace down.

The lure of the "all the hits, all the time" format is that it enables people to listen to exactly the kind of music they want without being bothered hearing music they don't want. As long as the DJ plays the right songs (generally planned by a program director rather than by the actual announcer), it encourages audiences to stay tuned. So rigid are the categories, however, that before long, clever artists and record producers began structuring their albums to contain at least one song that could be programmed by any station format. The result was that people who bought a twelve-song album on the strength of one song often discovered that they hated the other eleven.

Although "Top 40" faded slightly during the '70s, it was revived at the decade's end as "Top 50" or "Contemporary Hit Radio"; the names were as varied as the consultants who copyrighted and licensed them (*AOR: Album Oriented Rock; Softrock; Adult Contemporary; The Zoo; Kiss; The Beat*, etc.). But whatever the name, "Top 40" and its clones all served the same purpose: Give the public what they want rather than expose them to what they need.

Answers

Bop Till You Drop (Answers)

1. Janis Joplin—overdose, 1970
2. Jimi Hendrix—overdose, 1970
3. Jim Croce—plane crash, 1973
4. Phil Ochs—suicide, 1976
5. Keith Moon—overdose, 1978
6. Elvis Presley—probable overdose, 1977
7. Richie Valens—plane crash, 1959
8. Buddy Holly—same plane crash, 1959
9. J. P. "Big Bopper" Richardson—same plane crash, 1959
10. Otis Redding—plane crash, 1967
11. Spinal Tap drummers—explosion, choking on vomit, etc.
12. Sid Vicious—overdose, 1979
13. Brian Jones—drowning, 1969
14. Dennis Wilson—drowning, 1983
15. Jim Morrison—heart attack/stroke, 1971
16. Bob Marley—cancer, 1981
17. "Mama" Cass Elliott—heart attack, 1974 (not by choking on a ham sandwich)
18. Sam Cooke—shot, 1964
19. Kurt Cobain—suicide, 1994
20. John Lennon—assassination, 1980

Paul Is Dead (Answers)

Answers 6, 8, and 10 were invented for this book. The others were circulating before. Of course, they are all false: Paul McCartney is very much alive and well and probably frustrated that Michael Jackson bought the rights to all the Beatles songs.

Commercial Music (Answers)

1. Sunkist citrus products
2. Trans World Airlines
3. Mazda automobiles
4. Heinz ketchup
5. Sirocco automobiles

Sing Me a Story (Answers)

1. "Deck of Cards" (Tex Ritter)
2. "Teen Angel" (Mark Dinning)
3. "Dead Man's Curve" (Jan and Dean)
4. "The Leader of the Pack" (Shangri-Las)
5. "The Legend of Tom Dooley" (Kingston Trio)
6. "Ode to Billy Joe" (Bobbie Gentry)
7. "American Pie" (Don MacLean)
8. "Maxwell's Silver Hammer" (The Beatles)
9. "Eleanor Rigby" (The Beatles)
10. "Found a Peanut" (traditional)

Odd Person Out (Answers)

1. Stuart Sutcliff (The Beatles)
2. Al Kooper (Blood, Sweat and Tears)
3. Al Jardine (The Beach Boys, temporarily)
4. Pete Best (The Beatles)
5. Eric Clapton (The Yardbirds)
6. Signe Anderson (Jefferson Airplane/Starship)
7. Tory Crimes (The Clash)
8. Jeremy Spencer (Fleetwood Mac)
9. Doug Sanden (The Who)
10. Vinne Lopez (E Street Band)

Question and Answer Songs (Answers)

1. "Ballad of the Green Berets" (Sgt. Barry Sadler)
2. "Maybellene" (Chuck Berry)
3. "Get a Job" (The Silhouettes)
4. "A Married Man" (Richard Burton)
5. "My Guy" (Mary Wells; both question and answer written by Smokey Robinson)
6. "Man, Oh Man" (Rosemary Clooney)
7. "My Generation" (The Who)
8. "Battle of New Orleans" (Johnny Horton)
9. "Day-O" (a.k.a. "Banana Boat Song") (Harry Bellafonte)
10. "Ballad of Davy Crockett" (Bill Hayes)

Pips, etc. (Answers)

1. As The Crickets, they backed Buddy Holly.
2. Before they changed their name to The Band and backed Bob Dylan, they also backed Ronnie Hawkins.
3. Neil Young's bar-band-plus
4. They helped James Brown feel good; woo!
5. Bob Dylan's Rolling Thunder Revue compatriots
6. Bob Seger's survivors
7. Assembled by Leon Russell for front man Joe Cocker
8. Backed the other Elvis (Costello)
9. As if anyone has forgotten, Janis Joplin sang for them (or, if you believe the remix after her death, they sang for her).
10. Stevie Wonder's wunderkinder

Who's Who in Music (Answers)

1. p
2. q
3. n
4. m
5. r
6. l
7. u

Answers

8. j
9. w
10. h
11. x
12. e
13. c
14. b
15. g
16. d
17. k
18. i
19. o
20. v
21. f
22. t
23. s
24. a

Note: And for the last time, already, Alice Cooper is *not* Eddie Haskell (Ken Osmond).

Dances (Answer)

They all were.

Musical Bios (Answers)

1. i
2. c
3. k
4. j
5. f
6. l
7. a
8. d/g (Yes, Chopin had *two* biographies, and he isn't even on MTV.)
9. e
10. b
11. d/g
12. h

Chapter 4

Twentieth Century History

Georges Santayana had it wrong: Those who do not learn from history are not necessarily condemned to repeat it. They are condemned to smack themselves on the head when they see how much the stuff is now worth.

The fact that everyone's mother threw away his/her comic books is only one of the three corollaries of Santayana's First Rule of Nostalgia (if we may call it that). The other two are that if you hold onto something hoping it will become valuable later, it won't, and that the moment you give up on something becoming valuable and throw it away, it will.

Society at large has a curious regard for its past. It's sort of like the way college kids treat the stuff they grew up with once they go away to school: They store it at home where Mom and Dad will take care of it. Then one day Mom and Dad are gone, the kid goes to look at his stuff and it's gone.

The public at large treats its history the same way. We depend on the Library of Congress to save one of everything (books, newspapers, magazines, pamphlets, stock reports, yearbooks, movies, recordings, TV shows, plays, etc.), but they don't, because they can't. The ephemeral nature of creativity in the twentieth century makes traditional archival techniques impossible and new ones prohibitively expensive. As a result, it is believed that, for example, 90 percent of the American movies made before 1950 have vanished forever; the first ten years of *The Tonight Show Starring Johnny Carson* were erased by NBC in a routine housecleaning; the family of Martin Luther King, Jr., had to sue Boston University, charging improper custodianship of his original papers; and there exists no complete copy of both text and score of the modern musical theatre's first masterpiece, *Showboat*.

Mothers didn't destroy these things. We did. Here's why.

The twentieth century spawned a culture that was more interested in exploring the future than in preserving the past. Newer is better. Don't look back. Planned obsolescence. Fast food, one-time-use carbon paper, disposable diapers, and so forth. What can you say for a culture that invents frozen rice that you can boil in the bag in fifteen minutes as opposed to making on the stove from scratch in, um, fifteen minutes (am I missing something here?).

So it shouldn't be too surprising that a few things slip through the cracks. That's why we have museums, libraries, and archives, right?

So who is preserving our culture? At the beginning of the 1980s, some forty-eight large media companies produced movies, owned TV networks, and published books, newspapers, and magazines. By the end of the century, the power will be concentrated in the hands of perhaps nine or ten, even fewer, given the mergers, joint ventures, and cross-ownership between and among them. Untangling intellectual property rights has become a legal specialty; with all the mergers and buyouts, it's hard to know who owns the rights to what anymore or, more importantly, who's saving the stuff for posterity. Small wonder, then, that individuals have taken it upon themselves to become the archivists of culture. On any weekend in a major city, you can find at least one "collectors show," where people will come to buy, sell, and swap everything from old postcards, movie memorabilia, magazines, and books to campaign buttons, historic documents, and, of course, comics. Profit is seldom the motive; the only thing these passionate, well-informed fans have in mind is to maintain a chunk of the past so that future generations will see the way we were.

Museums don't really care about matchbooks from Bugsy Siegel's Flamingo Hotel or Rootie Kazootie comics in 3-D or postcards of the 1939 World's fair or an original six-sheet poster from *King Kong.* They were made to be tossed away, and that's why they're so rare nowadays. But, in their own way, they say more about America than a dozen scholarly history books.

Will the twentieth century be the first disposable century? Will progress be so powerful a mandate that it will nullify the past, even rewrite it, as George Orwell predicted in *1984*? You've heard the maxim, "History is written by the winners." As an example, ask any high school student (or any adult under forty, for that matter) who John L. Lewis was. Or Allen Dulles, or Emmeline Pankhurst, or J. William Fulbright. Some people never even heard of Rosa Parks. All of these people shaped the 1900s yet, despite their importance, may be found in the wake of history. (For the record: John L. Lewis founded the Congress

of Industrial Organization, which later merged with the American Federation of Labor to become the AFL-CIO; Allen Dulles ran the CIA in the '50s, while his brother, John Foster Dulles, ran the State Department; Emmeline Pankhurst fought for women's suffrage at the turn of the last century; J. William Fulbright was one of the first U.S. Senators to strongly oppose American involvement in Vietnam; and Rosa Parks is the black woman who refused to yield her bus seat to a white woman, as the law in Montgomery, Alabama, demanded.)

How important is it for one generation to know the achievements of the preceding generation? That question haunted Henry Hampton, executive producer of the multi-award-winning television series *Eyes on the Prize,* about America's civil rights struggle. On one hand, Hampton offered, it was important for children who benefited from those events to know about them; on the other, the fact that they took the rights for granted was proof of their success.

If there is one pervasive, unifying factor in the history of the century, it is, for better or worse, the availability of information. Much of that

comes from broadcasting. Another chapter explores television, but this chapter pays respect to the miracle of the simultaneous witnessing of events that occur nowhere near the people who observe them. From the rise of radio networks in the '30s to the supremacy of television networks in the '70s—roughly the middle half of the twentieth century—no other era in human existence has seen disparate people drawn together in times of national need. Be it the tragedy of a presidential funeral or the exhilaration of the first moon landing, broadcasting permitted people the instantaneous sharing of emotion. Now that radio is mostly rock or talk (not news) and cable television has splintered the viewing audience—except for the occasional police car chase—that national sense of community is gone, probably forever.

There is irony in that people today can gain access to more information than ever before, yet take interest in so little of it. Newspaper readership is dropping, sales of self-help books surpass that of research volumes, and once-prestigious television news programs are turning more and more often to tabloid and fluff just to keep people watching.

At the same time, the 1900s have seen two global wars and several massive regional ones; the reconfiguration of the Middle East, Africa, and eastern Europe; the eradication of smallpox; the birth and proliferation of computers; physicians go from making house calls to forming HMOs; and at least three new images apiece for Madonna, Michael Jackson, and Bob Dylan.

People are still alive today who watched manned flight progress from Kitty Hawk to the moon; who lost friends to influenza in 1918 but can now get a heart replacement; who grew up fearing Communism and now can retire in freedom; who saw *Citizen Kane* when it was new and Strom Thurmond when he was young.

It's been quite a century. Especially when you remember the good parts.

Get a Life: Make War, Not Prayer

Question: Name the two United States presidents who administered wars, despite having been raised by parents whose strict religious beliefs made them pacifists.

Answer: Dwight D. Eisenhower and Richard M. Nixon

Quiz: Average Citizens Who Changed History

You don't have to be an elected official to make a difference. Sometimes average citizens can effect social change by just doing what they think is right. Here are ten who did things that altered American history in widely differing ways. Can you identify them?

1. Rosa Parks
2. Frank Wills
3. John Henry Faulk
4. Allan Bakke
5. Marybeth Tinker
6. Renee Chen and Myca Le
7. John T. Scopes
8. N. G. Slater
9. Gary Dahl
10. Francis Xavier McNamara

Quiz: First Pets

Not counting interns, match the White House pets to the presidential administration that owned them:

1.	Fala	a.	Kennedy
2.	Macaroni	b.	Johnson
3.	Socks	c.	Bush
4.	Checkers	d.	Roosevelt
5.	Millie	e.	Clinton
6.	Him, Her, and Yuki	f.	Nixon
7.	Rex	g.	Carter
8.	Old Whiskers	h.	Reagan
9.	Misty Malarky Ying Ying	i.	Harrison
10.	Buddy	j.	Clinton

Quiz: Where Were You When . . .

It's probably only an urban myth, but it involves a teenager questioning her teacher about the 1960s. "You've talked about Jack Kennedy and John Kennedy," she asks. "Were they related?" (Ah, the generation gap.) They're in chronological order, so swallow hard and draw your line in the sands of time. Cite the dates if you can, and add where you were when these events occurred:

FDR died.

V-E Day—Germany surrendered.

The first A-Bomb was dropped on Hiroshima.

V-J Day—the Japanese signed the official surrender.

Sputnik was shot into orbit.

Alan Shepard went up into space.

John Glenn went around the earth.

JFK was shot.

LBJ announced he wouldn't run again.

Martin Luther King was shot.

RFK was shot.

Neil Armstrong walked on the moon.

Kent State students were shot.

Peace was declared in Vietnam.

Nixon announced he would resign.

Rhoda got married.

John Lennon was shot.

The "Challenger" space shuttle exploded.

The World Trade Center was bombed.

The Oklahoma City bombing of the Alfred P. Murrah Building took place.

Princess Diana died.

Quiz: Who Shot Whom?

Before the twentieth century, political assassination was a rare occurrence. Now it seems like the second most popular method of changing leadership (elections remain number one). In this quiz, match the victim with his/her assassin—attempted or successful, lone or multiple (which is another whole story). Dates are given as reference.

	Victim		Assassin	Date
1.	Archduke Ferdinand	a.	Gavriolo Princip	6/28/14
2.	Czar Nicholas II	b.	Arthur Bremer	7/12/18
3.	Michael Collins	c.	Bolsheviks	8/22/22
4.	"Pancho" Villa	d.	Ramon del Rio	7/20/23
5.	Huey Long	e.	Marcos gunmen	9/8/35
6.	Leon Trotsky	f.	Unknown	8/20/40
7.	Mohandas K. Gandhi	g.	Unknown	9/17/48
8.	Medgar Evers	h.	Byron De La Beckwith	6/12/63
9.	Ngo Dinh Diem	i.	Lee Harvey Oswald	11/2/63
10.	John F. Kennedy	j.	NLF coup	11/22/63
11.	George Wallace	k.	Commandos	5/15/72
12.	Anwar El-Sadat	l.	Sikh bodyguards	10/6/81
13.	Benigno Aquino, Jr.	m.	Carl Austin Weiss	8/21/83
14.	Indira Gandhi	n.	Nathuram V. Godse	10/31/84

Quiz: Rumors

Nothing travels faster than bad news, unless it's a rumor. Match the following '50s, '60s, and/or '70s rumors to the subject they were about:

1. Paul McCartney
2. Lee Harvey Oswald
3. James Dean
4. Marilyn Monroe
5. Elvis
6. President Kennedy
7. Walt Disney
8. Alice Cooper
9. John Dillinger
10. Louie, Louie
11. Quarter to 3
12. Number Nine
13. Tobacco companies
14. Smoking banana skins
15. Coca-Cola and aspirin
16. Coca-Cola
17. Ritz crackers
18. Bubble-Yum
19. New York sewers
20. McDonalds burgers

a. Copyrighted names of dope for when it's legalized
b. Is being kept alive
c. Contains spider eggs
d. Eats at McDonald's
e. Has his penis preserved in the Smithsonian
f. Is really Eddie Haskell
g. Is dead, plus he's the walrus
h. Have worms as filler
i. Was killed by CIA
j. Gets you high
k. Is "Turn Me on Dead Man" played backward
l. Gets you high
m. Are inhabited by alligators
n. Has filthy lyrics
o. Is frozen
p. Is being kept alive
q. Acted alone
r. Contains cocaine
s. Have "sex" written on them
t. Has filthy lyrics

"Star Wars"

Star Wars didn't set out to change history. Like most great inventions, it just seemed like the best way to get the job done. In this instance, the job that George Lucas wanted to do was tell an epic action story that had been gestating in his mind for three years and was in production for two. But when it finally opened in theatres on Wednesday, May 25, 1977, it was no longer a product; it altered history in ways that few movies have ever done.

By now the *Star Wars* saga, its reissues, special editions, prequels, sequels, and multimedia spin-offs have generated untold billions of dollars—all from a "space opera" modestly described in its earliest (and long-forgotten) preopening advertisements as "a story about a boy, a girl and a universe."

But the effects of *Star Wars* and its brilliant creator, George Lucas, are anything but modest. Beyond the immense financial impact that is had on the film industry and pop culture, *Star Wars* nearly single-handedly changed the consciousness of Hollywood. Here's how:

1. How films are released: Before *Star Wars*, Hollywood held Christmas to be its most lucrative box office season. After *Star Wars*, the summertime, with its millions of vacationing young ticket buyers, dominated the year's marketing schedules.

2. The youth market: Before *Star Wars*, the sixteen- to twenty-one-year-old audience was seen as a small but intense group who consumed low-budget horror and action films that could be quickly made and cheaply sold, usually by independent companies. After *Star Wars*, the big studios recognized that this teen audience could make or break a film, and they began gearing their productions almost entirely toward its less sophisticated tastes.

3. The star system: Two days before *Star Wars* opened, the marquee read "Alec Guinness in *Star Wars*." After opening day, it was clear that the star was the special effects, not Sir Alec.

4. Symphonic music returned: Before *Star Wars*, composers of the 1960–70 "film generation" had switched to rock, jazz, and experimental. John Williams's full-out symphonic score for *Star Wars* was magnificent. Ironically, postproduction had taken so long that the original preview trailers went out not with John Williams's rousing theme but with a canned background from Vivaldi's *The Four Seasons*.

5. Special visual effects: Brought into the computer age by Stanley Kubrick's *2001: A Space Odyssey* in 1968 (Douglas Trumbull, Con Pederson, Wally Veevers, and Tom Howard), the techniques were expanded for *Star Wars* by John Dykstra and Richard Edlund. Since then the "special effects film" has become its own Hollywood genre.

6. Good guys and bad guys: Before *Star Wars*, war pictures had fallen out of favor, thanks to Vietnam. After *Star Wars*—with its clear-cut heroes and villains—audiences once again cheered movies that killed the right people.

7. Religious pictures: Before *Star Wars*, religion was something tucked away in churches or biblical spectacles. After *Star Wars* and its generic "Force," the evangelical subculture in American films woke up.

8. Merchandising: Before *Star Wars,* the licensing of products was limited to a couple of coloring books, a sound-track album, and maybe a stuffed animal. After *Star Wars,* producers began to place promotable elements in their movies, few of which attracted a fraction of the following of George Lucas's huggable (and wonderfully guileless) heroes.

In short, an escapist fantasy about a rebellion in outer space caused an equal upheaval in that other cosmos, Hollywood. It also brought a dark side. The success of Lucas's *Star Wars* and *Indiana Jones* trilogies consolidated the belief that audiences preferred high tech to depth of character. The short attention spans and cultural naivete of those coveted young audiences have confined Hollywood to a blockbuster mentality. The sixteen- to twenty-one-year-old audience now dictates what films get made, usually to the exclusion of grown-up fare.

Today the stakes are higher than ever. The original *Star Wars* cost $8 million to make and a half a million to market; twenty years later, budgets for similar films had risen by 2,000 percent. Yet somehow Lucas has remained above it all.

"Space is the final frontier, as someone famous once said," he has explained with that mixture of insight and self-effacing humor that made his films so endearing. "Anybody who looks up into the stars—it's been a fascination of Mankind ever since we could think. When I was young I looked up and said, 'What's up there, and what does it mean to me?'"

Star Wars was the answer. And Lucas figured out how to share it with the rest of the world.

Press Cover-ups

Usually the press exposes scandals, but on occasion they have been known to cover them up. This was true even before the 1980s when corporate mergers raised doubts about who "controls" what the media covers and how they cover it.

"The men with the muckrakes are often indispensable to the well-being of society," President Theodore Roosevelt told the Gridiron Club in 1906, "but only if they know when to stop raking the muck and to look upward . . . to the crown of worthy endeavor."

Not every news story is a Watergate, Iran-Contra, or Teapot Dome—so big it can't be hidden. In an era of tabloid news, however, the emphasis has been changed from "What Sells," sometimes to the exclusion of "What's Important." The notion of journalists covering up the news rather than covering it is not new. In the past, some major stories were buried by the people who were sworn to expose them. Were the reasons valid? You decide:

1. **FDR's infantile paralysis**. Although the public knew that Franklin Delano Roosevelt had developed polio in 1921, newspaper photo editors honored White House requests not to publish pictures

of the president in leg braces or on crutches, his wheelchair, or his being carried about by aides. In general, reporters covering Washington, D.C., politics through the 1950s systematically refused to report which elected officials drank, philandered, or got arrested, unless (as one correspondent said), "it affected his ability to carry out his job."

2. **Woodrow Wilson's stroke**. In September of 1919 President Woodrow Wilson suffered a severe stroke that left him partially paralyzed. Rather than allow Vice President Thomas R. Marshall to be sworn in as chief executive, Wilson continued in office, allowing his second wife, Edith Bolling Galt, to assume many of his duties, in violation of the U.S. Constitution. The extent of her activities was not reported.

3. **The savings and loan crisis**. In the late 1980s the rise of "junk" bonds allowed more Americans to invest, and more banks to lend, than at any time since the Great Depression. And, shades of the stock market crash, the chickens came home to roost in 1987. The market "adjusted," yuppies were wiped out, and the savings and loan corporations behind the funny money shifted the burden to the American people. The press covered it until it got boring, then stopped; the Resolution Trust Corporation, set up to manage the huge losses, quietly faded away in 1997; meanwhile, the taxpayers are still paying for it.

4. **Conglomeritization of the press itself**. Prior to 1981, the FCC (Federal Communications Commission) limited to five the number of TV stations that a single owner could possess. Under the Reagan-Bush FCC that number was increased to twelve, greatly increasing the attractiveness of such ownership to a prospective corporate buyer. The so-called "twelves" rule passed—according to some, because the then-powerful networks (NBC, CBS, and ABC) suppressed news stories that might embarrass the administration. Since the change, all three have been sold at handsome profits.

5. **JFK's Addison's disease**. In addition to the World War II back injury that occasionally flared up, President John Fitzgerald Kennedy suffered from Addison's disease, a disorder of the adrenal system that affects digestion and imparts a brownish coloration to the skin. It is not fatal, but it is uncomfortable, and the fact that JFK had it was not reported. On the other hand, neither were his alleged affairs.

6. **Ronald Reagan's senility**. Reporters who covered the Reagan White House were invariably charmed by the garrulous and charismatic chief executive, chalking up his occasional *gaffes* to his busy schedule and his studied persona of being a manager rather than a detail man. If they noticed the encroachment of his Alzheimer's Disease, they said nothing.

7. **Noriega the instant drug lord**. The 1989 United States invasion of Panama and the kidnapping/arrest of General Manuel Noriega—an act whose legality remains hotly debated among constitutional scholars—was preceded by a program of demonization of Noriega by President George Bush. The mass media happily complied, possibly remembering how they were barred by a secretive Reagan administration from covering the 1983 U.S. invasion of Grenada.

Quiz: Famous Firings

Who fired these people, and why?

1. Archibald Cox
2. Douglas MacArthur
3. Julius LaRosa
4. Thomas Eagleton
5. Air traffic controllers
6. George Cukor
7. George III
8. Billy Martin
9. Jackie Mason
10. Pete Best

Quiz: Presidents and Scandals

Match the president to the scandal for which he is best remembered:

1. Warren G. Harding		a.	Supreme Court packing
2. Richard M. Nixon		b.	Blacklisting
3. Ronald Reagan		c.	Iran hostages
4. Bill Clinton		d.	Watergate
5. John F. Kennedy		e.	Monicagate
6. Lyndon Baines Johnson		f.	U-2 spy mission
7. Jimmy Carter		g.	Iran-Contra
8. Harry Truman		h.	Teapot Dome
9. Dwight D. Eisenhower		i.	Bobby Baker
10. Franklin D. Roosevelt		j.	Bay of Pigs

Quiz: The Draft

Section 3(a) of the Military Service Act specifies that "it shall be the duty of every male citizen of the United States, and every other male person residing in the United States, who . . . is between the ages of 18 and 26, to present himself for and submit to registration . . ." for the draft. At the same time, the Nuremberg Trials established that a soldier should disobey immoral orders. For many, the orders issued during war are considered immoral.

Courts martial exist to divine the difference only after the fact, but during the bitterly divisive Vietnam War years, many young Americans chose to make that distinction for themselves by resisting conscription into the military. In other words (depending where you stood/stand politically), they either *evaded* the draft or *dodged* it. Time has done little to heal the wounds caused by such decisions, but it may have done something to blur the memory about what the major draft classifications were. Explain the following. (No fair looking in the wallet you carried to the Moratorium march to the Pentagon.)

1. 1-A
2. 1-A-O
3. 1-D
4. 1-H
5. 2-A
6. 2-D
7. 2-S
8. 3-A
9. 4-C
10. 4-F

Get a Life: Kent State

Question: Name the four students who were killed at Kent State.

Answer: On May 4, 1970, Ohio National Guardsmen opened fire on a group of one thousand unarmed students who were protesting the American military invasion of Cambodia. Those killed were Jeffrey Miller, Allison Krause, William Schroeder, and Sandra Scheuer. Miller and Krause had been demonstrators; Schroeder and Scheuer had been walking to classes. Between eight and eleven others were wounded.

Presidential Buns

When President Kennedy addressed an adoring West German crowd on June 26, 1963, he said, "All free men, wherever they may live, are citizens of Berlin. And therefore, as a free man, I take pride in the words, *ich bin ein Berliner*."

Technically, although a *Berliner* is, indeed, one who is a citizen of Berlin, it is also slang for a sweet, doughy breakfast bread, much as "Danish" can mean either "citizen of Denmark" or a flaky baked good. In effect, what JFK was telling everybody was, "I am a pastry."

Get a Life: The Turtles

Question: Are you a Turtle?

Answer #1: "You bet your sweet ass I am!"

Explanation—Sometime in the early 1960s (social movements are always tough to pin down), there was an informal organization called the Turtles. No one knows who started it, but anyone with enough gall and gumption to have membership cards printed up could open his/her own chapter.

You joined by answering four apparently dirty, but in reality very clean, riddles:

1. What, on a man, is hard and hairy and sticks so far out of his pajamas that you can hang a hat on it?
2. What four letter word ending in *K* means the same as intercourse?
3. What's hard and dry going in and soft and sticky coming out?
4. What does a man do standing up, a woman sitting down, and a dog on three legs?

But wait, there's more. According to the lore of Turtledom, it was believed that all Turtles must own a donkey, and therefore if you are asked, "Are you a Turtle?" your only correct response must be, "You bet your sweet ass I am." If you were unable to answer in that manner (for embarrassment or some other reason), you had to buy the other person a beverage of his choice.

Throughout the '60s it was rumored that people as disparate as astronaut (and senator-to-be) John Glenn and TV genius Steve Allen were Turtles, and it became something of a contest to ask them in as public a forum as possible (Steve Allen invariably laughed and said "Smok, smok!" For the record, John Glenn's office acknowledged the rumor but would neither confirm nor deny it, and Steve Allen, through his spokeswoman, professed to have heard of the Turtles, but denied membership therein.)

The days when a person could be embarrassed by saying *ass* have long passed, so there must be a lot of very thirsty Turtles out there.

Answers #2
1. His head
2. *Talk*
3. Chewing gum
4. Shake hands

Quiz: Mythtory (sic)

History, they say, is written by the winners. Of the following persistent myths, pick out those that are true. (There are no "trick" questions, but be sure to assess the overall statement.)

1. Abner Doubleday invented baseball, which is a wholly American sport, in Cooperstown, New York, in 1839.
2. The Battle of Bunker Hill in the American Revolutionary War was actually fought at Breed's Hill.
3. King Canute of England sought to prove that he was not divine by ordering his bearers to carry him to the sea, at which point he ordered the tide to recede. It didn't, proving that he was mortal.
4. Unlike his contemporaries, Christopher Columbus knew the world was round.
5. The German sinking of the Lusitania in 1915 brought America into World War I.
6. The United States stood alone in refusing to sign the Geneva Accords at the 1954 Geneva Conference on Vietnam.
7. Paul Revere never made it to Concord on his famous midnight ride that began American history.
8. Betsy Ross sewed the first American flag.
9. Pocahontas saved Captain John Smith from execution by Powahatan's tribe.
10. Typhoid Mary never came down with the disease that she so liberally spread to others.

Quiz: Icon Identification

As often happens with cultural innovators and newsmakers, event often obscures the person responsible for it. Identify the discovery, device, moment, or movement for which the following people achieved fame:

1. Mrs. Ruth Colhoun
2. Ed "Big Daddy" Roth
3. Robert Crumb
4. Francis Gary Powers
5. Frank Costello
6. G. David Schine
7. Fred Fisher

Quiz: Don't Quote Me

Match the quotes with the historical figure who said them, and note the occasion:

1. "Radioactive poisoning of the atmosphere and, hence, annihilation of any life on earth has been brought within the range of technical possibility."
2. "We will bury you."
3. "I am prepared to wait until Hell freezes over."
4. "I stand before you today the happiest guy on the face of the earth."
5. "There have been so many lovely things said about me, and I'm just glad that I had the opportunity to thank everyone."
6. "I remembered a line from the Hindu scripture, the *Bhagavad Gita*: 'I have become Death, the destroyer of worlds.'"
7. "A sex symbol becomes a thing. I just hate being a thing."
8. "If I am stopped, this movement will not stop, because God is with the movement."
9. "The only people for me are the mad ones, the ones who are mad to live, mad to talk, mad to be saved."
10. "I am waiting . . ."

a. J. Robert Oppenheimer
b. Dr. Martin Luther King
c. Lou Gehrig
d. Adlai Stevenson
e. Jack Kerouac
f. Lawrence Ferlinghetti
g. Albert Einstein
h. Nikita Khrushchev
i. Marilyn Monroe
j. Babe Ruth

Terms of Endurance

Like the phrase in *Corinthians*: "When I was a child, I spake as a child . . . but when I became a man I put away childish things," the same holds true for fads. In one year they swept the country and the next year were swept into the attic. Not to judge these once-hot-now-not items, but, sorry, folks, they're over:

Afro hair style
Air guitar contests
"Baby on board" signs
Banana clips
Barney
Bean bag chairs
Beatlemania (not the Beatles, but an incredible simulation)
Biological clock, talk shows dwelling upon ticking of
Biorhythms
Bohemian Rhapsody (Queen)
Boom boxes (replaced by Walkmen so people go deaf alone)
Boone's Farm Strawberry Wine
Casual sex
Chinese fire drills
Cigars (behind every smoker's back, people think they're jerks)
Clam-diggers (calf-length pants)
Clogs
Colorizing B&W movies
Cowboy clothing (except by cowboys)
Designer labels
"Dungeons and Dragons"
Elvis impersonators (he's dead, Jim)
Erasable typing paper
EST (Erhard Seminar Training)
Eve or Keane paintings (the kids with the big eyes)
Farrah posters
Fondue parties
Friendship bracelets
Fur (except on animals)
Garfield anything

Goldfish swallowing
G-spot, discussions of
Guillain-Barret Syndrome, magazine articles about
Hair, ironing straight
Hair, pony tails, on men over thirty
Hair, real short, on men over thirty
Hair, real short, on women
Hereford cow (sweetened flavored cream liquor)
Hot pants
In-a-Gadda-da-Vida (Iron Butterfly)
Jell-o or mud wrestling
Jonathan Livingston Seagull
Just Say "No" (never worked, never will)
Karaoke (actually, it was never "in," just tolerated)
Knack, the first album
Leisure suite
Macrame
Mateus wine
Menudo
Metric system (America resists! So there!)
Mood rings
Mooning
Mother-of-pearl bumper stickers
Mutton chops (wide sideburns)
Nehru jackets
Neiman, Leroy paintings
O.J. books
Omelette parties
On acid, use of phrase, to describe anything
Phone booth stuffing

"Piña Colada Song," the (by Rupert Holmes)
Playboy bunny logo air fresheners dangling in cars
POGs
Quiche
Rainbows
Roller boogie
Screaming Yellow Zonkers
Scream therapy (Victor Janov)
Shoulder purses for men
Sideburns-moustache combo on same person
Spice Girls, the
Streaking
Strobe candles
Studio 54
Tanning salons
"Trivial Pursuit"
Ubby-Dubby ("Zoom" talk)
Unicorns
Val speak
Van, paintings on the sides of
Velvet Elvi
Warhol, Andy
Wet look, the
Wet T-shirt contests
Whip-its (breathing nitrous oxide from aerosol whipped cream)
Whiskey sours (and whiskey sour parties)
Wide lapels
Wide ties

Caution: If you haven't heard of some of these, beware; they may be a retro waiting to happen!

Quiz: Real or Fake?

Seeing is believing—or is it? If you think it is, just try matching a cooked frozen pizza with the way it looked on the box. The same holds true for the public trust that was once guarded by television.

The 1990s were chronicled by countless TV talk shows that raided trailer parks and sideshows to collect people that nobody would want to bring home to supper. Just when they insisted they never booked fakes, some faker would surface to detail how he or she had scammed this or that talk show. In the end, only the truly gullible believed any of it, so what else is new? This true-false quiz is not about how television news covers reality. It's about the way the far more lenient entertainment programs have crossed the line—or maybe not. Are/were the following entertainment programs legit?

1. *That's Incredible!*
2. *Twenty-One*
3. *Candid Camera*
4. *Totally Hidden Video*
5. *America's Funniest Home Videos*
6. *Ripley's Believe It or Not*
7. *You Asked for It*
8. *Real People*

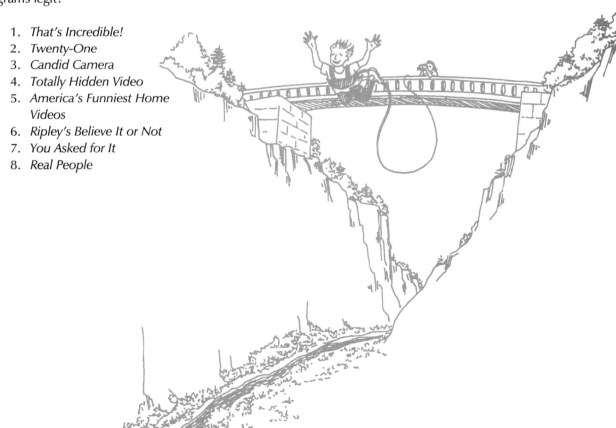

The Youth Market

The most highly sought-after commercial market in America today is the "youth market": that ephemeral group of young people between the ages of twelve and twenty-one who buy most of the records, see most of the movies, wear most of the clothes, and call all the trends, yet don't always show up on surveys. They are unsophisticated, mercurial, passionate—and rich.

It wasn't until 1955 that the so-called youth market became defined as a separate (and highly sought-after) group; that was when the controversial film *The Blackboard Jungle* was released. Although writer-director Richard Brooks didn't plan it that way, his drama about juvenile delinquency in public schools simultaneously touched two kinds of nerves: raw ones for adults, sympathetic ones for teenagers. Until this time, motion pictures had always been aimed toward general audiences. But as the opening titles appeared with the energizing accompaniment of Bill Haley and the Comets singing "Rock Around the Clock," the "youth exploitation movie" was born. It had been thought that rock 'n' roll was just another passing fad, but when Hollywood hopped aboard the bandstand, a marriage was made.

It could only have happened in the '50s. But it began in the late '40s.

When the GIs returned from the war, they found that their wives had gotten used to independence. Come peacetime, "Rosie the Riveter" wasn't content to go back into the kitchen. She wanted some freedom—perhaps not to work full time but certainly more leisure around the house. Fortunately, manufacturers were eager to help, and such blessings as Kelvinator, Fridgidaire, and Amana refrigerators; Maytag washers and dryers; Westinghouse and Hotpoint ranges; and Hoover and Bissel vacuum cleaners found their way into the Levitown and other "starter" houses. Thanks to the GI Bill, a veteran and his wife could actually buy a home for $4,000. It may have been only 20 feet away from the one next door, but it was home, sweet home, circa 1946.

It was also time to leave the cities. The interstate highway system expanded during the Eisenhower administration and reached into what had hitherto been undeveloped land, much of it agricultural, all of it cheap. What developers built was not the cramped, high-rise culture of the big city but a contiguous system of bedroom communities close enough for commuting but far enough for safety. They were called suburbs.

Kids raised in suburbia didn't learn how to be street smart; consequently, there quickly developed an "us" and "them" rivalry between city and suburb. If you lived in the 'burbs, you needed a second car to get around and came to loathe fighting the traffic and parking in town. Department stores, supermarkets, entertainment, transportation, and manufacture took the hint. The shopping malls that opened with fecundity throughout the '60s did more than follow the money into suburbia, they inadvertently depleted the tax base of the cities.

Yet, by the '80s, the cities were reborn as yuppies (as "young, urban professionals" came to be known) dominated the real estate and securities market, bought Volvos and Mercedes, had 1.3 children, and started voting Republican. As former Chicago 7 defendant Jerry Rubin said, "While we were in the streets demonstrating, the conservatives went out and got all the good jobs." Little has changed since then. Although the baby boomers dictate overall trends in the American economy, it is still young people between twelve and twenty-one who make most of the consumable purchases. We have become the first culture in history to create the concept of adolescence, milk it for all it's worth, and then criticize adolescents for being, well, so *adolescent*.

Average Citizens Who Changed History (Answers)

1. Rosa Parks is the black seamstress who, in 1955, refused to yield her seat on a Montgomery, Alabama, bus to a white man. This sparked the bus boycott that began the civil rights movement.

2. Frank Wills was the janitor at the Watergate complex in Washington, D.C., who noticed a piece of masking tape holding an office door open on June 17, 1972. He then called the police.

3. Radio commentator John Henry Faulk, in 1957, was accused of leftist leanings by a right-wing hate group called Aware. Six years later, Faulk successfully sued Aware out of business and began the erosion of the infamous blacklist.

4. In 1978 the U.S. Supreme Court ruled that Allan Bakke, a white man, had been unfairly denied admission to a medical school—the school had accepted black applicants with weaker academic credentials. This decision established "reverse discrimination," while, at the same time, it allowed that race could be considered in school admissions.

5. Teenage Marybeth Tinker was suspended in 1965 for wearing a black armband to her Des Moines, Iowa, junior high school class as a protest against the Vietnam War. The ACLU (American Civil Liberties Union) lawsuit that followed won, in the U.S. Supreme Court, all students a victory for free speech, directly enabling the antiwar protests of the Vietnam era.

6. On July 23, 1982, an accident on the set of *Twilight Zone: The Movie* killed actor Vic Morrow and two young children, who, according to later charges, had been hired illegally as extras. The press kept referring to the victims as "Vic Morrow and two Asian children." Their names were Renee Chen and Myca Le, and their deaths led to a tightening of safety codes on Hollywood movie sets.

7. Tennessee school teacher John T. Scopes was arrested in 1925 for teaching evolution in a state that permitted the teaching of only the biblical version of Genesis. The resulting trial, argued by Clarence Darrow and William Jennings Bryan, articulated the conflict between religion and science as well as the separation of church and state. On appeal, the Tennessee Supreme Court upheld the law but reversed Scopes's conviction.

8. N. G. Slater was a New York manufacturer of pin-on buttons. Around 1969, he started making and marketing "smile" buttons. The design may not have originated with Slater, but it soon turned up in the artwork of underground comic artist R. (Robert) Crumb, who intended it as a joke, not a movement. It went on to become both.

9. In 1975 advertising man Gary Dahl invented—but, more importantly, marketed—the Pet Rock. Thus began America's modern infatuation with useless fads.

10. Caught short for cash to pay a meal tab in 1950, Francis Xavier McNamara started Diners Club, popularizing the use of credit cards in restaurants.

First Pets (Answers)

1. d
2. a
3. e/j
4. f
5. c
6. b
7. h
8. i
9. g
10. j/e

Where Were You When . . . (Answers)

Franklin Delano Roosevelt died on April 12, 1945.

Germany surrendered on May 7, 1945.

America dropped the first A-Bomb on Hiroshima on August 6, 1945.

Japan surrendered on September 2, 1945.

The USSR launched Sputnik into orbit on October 4, 1957.

Astronaut Alan Shepard flew his suborbital flight on May 5, 1961.

Astronaut John Glenn went around the earth three times on February 20, 1962.

John Fitzgerald Kennedy was shot on November 22, 1963.

President Lyndon Johnson announced he wouldn't seek re-election on March 31, 1968.

Dr. Martin Luther King was shot on April 4, 1968.

Robert F. Kennedy was shot on June 5, 1968.

Astronaut Neil Armstrong walked on the moon on July 20, 1969.

Four Kent State students were shot by Ohio National Guardsmen on May 4, 1970.

Peace was declared in Vietnam (in theory, anyway) on January 27, 1973.

Richard M. Nixon announced he would resign on August 8, 1974.

Rhoda got married on October 28, 1974.

John Lennon was shot on December 8, 1980.

The Challenger space shuttle blew up on January 28, 1986.

The World Trade Center bombing occurred on February 6, 1993.

Answers

The Oklahoma City bombing of the Alfred P. Murrah Building occurred on April 19, 1995.

Princess Diana died on August 30, 1997.

Who Shot Whom? (Answers)

1. a
2. c
3. f/g
4. f/g
5. m
6. d
7. n
8. h
9. j
10. i
11. b
12. k
13. e
14. l

Rumors (Answers)

1. g
2. q
3. b/p
4. i
5. d
6. b/p
7. o
8. f
9. e
10. n/t
11. n/t
12. k
13. a
14. j/l
15. j/l
16. r
17. s
18. c
19. m
20. h

Note: All these rumors are FALSE. Well, maybe Oswald . . .

Famous Firings (Answers)

1. Richard Nixon fired Attorney General Archibald Cox ("The Saturday Night Massacre") for refusing to fire Justice Department officials who were investigating Watergate.
2. President Harry S. Truman fired General Douglas MacArthur for publicly differing with the White House over Asian policy.
3. Radio talkmaster Arthur Godfrey fired singer Julius LaRosa on the air for not being "humble" enough.
4. Democratic presidential nominee George McGovern asked Senator Thomas Eagleton to resign the vice presidential nomination when it was disclosed that Eagleton once suffered from manic depression.
5. President Ronald Reagan fired the air traffic controllers when they went on strike for better working conditions. (In a move that redefines *irony*, in 1998, Congress renamed Washington's National Airport in honor of Ronald Reagan.)
6. Producer David O. Selznick fired director George Cukor from *Gone with the Wind* when star Clark Gable felt Cukor was giving too much attention to the actresses.
7. Oh, come on. The Continental Congress "fired" King George III of England by writing the Declaration of Independence.
8. George Steinbrenner, owner of the New York Yankees, fired Billy Martin. A lot.
9. TV emcee Ed Sullivan fired comedian/prophet Jackie Mason for supposedly flipping him the finger, although the exact gesture remains in dispute.
10. Whether drummer Pete Best was "fired" from the Beatles by George Martin is a continuing topic for debate.

Presidents and Scandals (Answers)

1. h
2. d
3. g
4. e
5. j
6. i
7. c
8. b
9. f
10. a

The Draft (Answers)

1. 1-A   Available for military service
2. 1-A-O   Conscientious objector available for noncombatant duty
3. 1-D   Taking ROTC (Reserve Officer Training Corps)
4. 1-H   Not subject to processing
5. 2-A   Deferment for civilian occupation (nonagricultural)
6. 2-D   Deferment for study of ministry

7. 2-S Student deferment
8. 3-A Deferment for extreme hardship to dependents
9. 4-C Alien not liable for service
10. 4-F Unfit for military service

Additionally, in 1969 the Nixon administration instituted a yearly draft lottery whereby a nineteen-year-old's birthday was paired with numbers 1–366 (to include Leap Year). The purpose was to let registrants know how likely they were to be called for active service; for example, numbers 1–125 were a dead certainty, numbers 126–250 were iffy, and numbers 251–366 were home free. Its covert purpose, however, was to neatly turn a generation against itself. If you were "safe" from the draft, that bus ride to Washington became just a little too long to bother with, and the rally at the student union building was just a little too far to walk. It was a brilliant, if cynical, way to defuse the antiwar movement. Until Kent State, that is.

Mythtory (Answers)

1. False. Doubleday's invention of baseball was determined in 1908 by fiat of a commission appointed by the A. G. Spalding sporting goods company, which also admitted that all records of the game's origins had been lost. The British game of "Rounders," for example, easily predates baseball. Oh, sure, and next we'll hear that apple pie is French, as in *apple tatin*.
2. True. The report of the battle was never formally corrected. The Colonials suffered nearly four hundred killed, but it demonstrated for the first time that British troops could be successfully opposed and provided an enormous emotional boost for the Continental Army.
3. True, according to English legend. By asserting that he was not a god, Canute paved the way for England and the Holy Roman Empire to grow closer.
4. Both true and false. The key phrase is "unlike his contemporaries." Since the days of Greek scholarship, everybody realized that the world was round. Columbus's reason for setting sail was to find a shortcut to the spices of the Far East. (Please note how this answer neatly sidesteps the issue of who discovered America.)
5. False. It may have become a battle cry, but since America didn't enter the war until 1917, it couldn't have mattered that much. The Lusitania was not an American ship, she was British; she was carrying munitions that the Germans considered to be contraband, and they warned her that she was entering a war zone. The German U-boat that torpedoed her just happened to-be there after the Lusitania changed

course, but the public relations damage to Germany was handily exploited by the Allies.
6. False. None of the other parties present (Cambodia, France, Laos, China, USSR, the UK, and "north" and "south" Vietnam) signed the "Final Declaration" either.
7. True. After warning "every Middlesex village and town" (per Longfellow's poem), he got off his horse and into a boat that took him up the Charles River to warn John Hancock and Sam Adams in Lexington, then headed for Concord, where he was recognized and captured by British troops.
8. False (until proven otherwise). Miss Ross was, indeed, living in Philadelphia at the time of the Revolutionary War, and she was, through her husband, related to General George Ross, one of the signers of the Declaration of Independence. But as to whether George Washington (or anybody else) asked her to sew the first "Old Glory" is unproven by documentation. The story did not even enter the public record until 1870, forty-four years after her death, when it was presented as a scholarly paper by her grandson.
9. Probably true, although John Smith apparently exaggerated more about the story than Disney did in their animated cartoon. The real Pocahontas was eleven years old at the time she saved Smith. She went to England in 1616 with her husband, John Rolfe, and became quite the celebrity until she died there in 1617.
10. False. Mary Mallon was a carrier of the typhus bacteria who may have had a mild case of the disease, but recovered. She was able to spread it because she worked as a cook and domestic in New York City and refused to stay out of circulation. Although the New York City Health Department eventually had her committed to an isolation center on North Island, she may have been responsible only for fifty-one cases and three deaths—something that history (and epidemiology) ignores.

Icon Identification (Answers)

1. Mrs. Ruth Colhoun built an elaborate underground bomb shelter in Los Angeles in 1951, an upscale ($1,995) version of the back yard and basement bomb and fallout shelters that would come to define nuclear fear over the next twenty years. Of course, all would be useless.
2. Ed "Big Daddy" Roth created (with pen and airbrush) elaborate, brightly colored artwork featuring burly, toothy, slack-jawed monsters drag-racing in souped-up hot rods. The artwork graced T-shirts, vans, and posters until the flower era of the late '60s.

Answers

3. Robert Crumb is the spiritual father of American "underground" comics of the '60s, having created Fritz the Cat, Mr. Natural (as in "keep on truckin'"), and various anthropomorphic large-breasted female animals. His unusual life and controversial work are profiled in the 1994 documentary *Crumb*.

4. Francis Gary Powers flew U-2 spy planes and was shot down over Russian soil on May 1, 1960. Powers was taken prisoner by the Soviets (and later returned to the U.S. after being traded for a Russian prisoner held here), but his mission was used by Nikita Khrushchev as an excuse to walk out of an important US-USSR summit meeting.

5. Frank Costello was the "star" of the 1950 Kefauver Crime Commission hearings. A self-confessed mobster (and self-possessed witness), Costello appeared on the televised hearings (a first), but, on his lawyer's insistence, only his hands were allowed to be seen on camera.

6. G. David Schine was an army private who was accorded special favors (and wartime safety) thanks to the intervention of Roy Cohn, special aide to Senator Joseph R. McCarthy. He later became one of the producers of the movie *The French Connection*.

7. Fred Fisher, a young lawyer working in the office of Joseph Welch, was smeared by Senator Joseph R. McCarthy during the 1954 Army-McCarthy hearings. In response, Welch upbraided McCarthy, "You have done enough, senator. Have you no sense of decency, sir? At long last, have you no sense of decency?" It was the beginning of the end for McCarthy (but not McCarthyism).

Don't Quote Me (Answers)

1. g (television address on A-bomb)
2. h (threat made to America)
3. d (spoken to Russian ambassador during Cuban Missile Crisis)
4. c (speech to fans on his retirement on account of ALS [amyotrophic lateral sclerosis])
5. j (speech to fans honoring him as he was dying of cancer)
6. a (commenting on his reaction to first A-bomb test)
7. i (comment to reporter)
8. b (comment to followers)
9. e (in *On the Road*)
10. f (title/mantra of poem in *A Coney Island of the Mind*)

Real or Fake? (Answers)

1. *That's Incredible!* (1980–1989): Some stunts were rigged, but many were just normal, albeit esoteric, talents that were hyped for dramatic purposes. Some daredevils purposely put themselves in jeopardy trying to get on the show.

2. *Twenty-One* (1956–1958): In this show—which caught the most flack during the quiz show scandals of the late 1950s—contestants who proved more popular with audiences were slipped advance answers with the tacit approval of the sponsors, producers, and network brass.

3. *Candid Camera* (1948–1990): This venerable "gotcha!" series was created by and cohosted by Allen Funt. As are most things involving honest reactions by average people, *Candid Camera* was always the genuine thing.

4. *Totally Hidden Video* (1989–1991): This blatant rip-off of *Candid Camera* was criticized when it was revealed that some contestants were actors and some gags had been staged.

5. *America's Funniest Home Videos* (1990–present): Questionable, but harmless. Some of the videos (except, presumably, for those in which people get hit in the crotch) are obviously staged. The question is why the producers don't just acknowledge it.

6. *Ripley's Believe It or Not* (1949–1986; not continuous): Originally hosted by Bob Ripley himself and later by Jack Palance (would *you* ask Jack Palance if he's telling the truth?), this show never purported to be real; *viz* the title. Some things were; some things weren't; believe it or not!

7. *You Asked for It* (1950–1959; 1972–1977; 1981–1983; 1991): The ultimate in wish fulfillment, this series tried to meet viewer requests for unusual sights, events, people, and places. Apparently only those things that were real or worked got on the air.

8. *Real People* (1979–1984): Building on the viewer mail aspect of *You Asked for It* and employing the field production freedom of *P.M. Magazine,* this chatty curiosity show offered profiles of actual people doing unusual things, as well as less visual oddities (letters, newspaper goofs, etc.). It was as real as what was submitted.

Television   Movies   Music

Twentieth Century History   Sayings & Common Sense

Chapter 5
Stuff You Learned In School but Forgot

Religion   Science & Geography

Home Frontier   Celebrity   Minutiae

There's a bumper sticker that says it all, and maybe more: "If you can read this, thank a teacher." The problem with the message is not that a teacher taught you how to read but that a teacher apparently didn't teach you that any argument that can fit on a bumper sticker isn't an argument, it's a premise. The distinction is important: An *argument* implies an exchange of information; a *premise* is a one-sided assertion.

Most people forget what they were taught in school; namely, to listen to all the information before making up their minds. On the other hand, a lot of what is taught in school is just plain hogwash. Facts change, and who has time to learn the new ones? Besides, isn't it on the Internet? We want results, not process; we want the end, not the means. Why memorize dates in American history when you can look them up any time you need them? Why learn to titrate reagents in chemistry; isn't that what they have lab technicians for? Excuse me, but Christopher Columbus was five hundred years ago. And who says he really discovered America, anyway?

America is returning to traditional education; the irony is that the people who are teaching it are the product of '60s relevance, and they've come around to discovering that the best schooling is schooling that makes what kids *need* to know as interesting as what kids *want* to know. The way to do this is not fast-paced CD-ROM electronic tutoring but something that has been there all along: the alliance between teacher and pupil. Humans learn from other humans; the excuse "I don't know where he got it; he certainly didn't learn it from me" shouldn't be a disclaimer. Mother birds teach their fledglings how to fly, and mother bobcats teacher their cubs how to hunt. What on earth should be so wrong with adult people teaching their children how to study?

School is more than a place to collect information; it is a community where peers discover how to interact with one another in ways that will prepare them for a vastly more challenging world than that of the schoolhouse. (This is why home schooling is so controversial.) It is also a place where young people learn from older people, who have to pass along a selection of experience broader than what is available in the home. It is, most importantly, a protected milieu. The reality is that school is an environment designed to reward achievement; the world-at-large is a place that often crushes achievement. The only way to survive the latter is by excelling at the former.

Which brings us to what happens the day you graduate: You forget everything. Your locker combination is the first to go (or did they change it over the summer?). Then you forget how to diagram a sentence—assuming you ever learned it in the first place. Next goes how to compute the area of a trapezoid; oh wait, what's a trapezoid? And forget about balancing $C_{12}H_{22}O_{11}+NaCl \rightarrow H_2O+X$.

And that's only when you graduate high school. When you graduate college, you have much, much more "useful" information to forget.

The key to retention is reinforcement. Once you leave school and focus on a career, however, the only knowledge that gets reinforced is the specific knowledge you need to perform your job. Oh, there's the occasional insurance salesman who moonlights as a particle physicist, but the principle of atrophy applies pretty much the same to the brain as it does to the biceps.

Oddly enough, one phenomenon that seems to have encouraged people to go back and resume their studies is the TV show *Jeopardy*. Begun in 1974, the syndicated television quiz—first hosted by Art Fleming, then by Alex Trebek—prides itself on the difficulty of its questions or, rather, its answers. But while *Jeopardy* tests its contestants' instant recall, it does not challenge their ability to apply those facts, compose a persuasive argument, or place them within historical context. Knowledge is about connecting one fact with another, and sometimes more. It is less important, for example, to know that the Spanish Armada was defeated by Sir Francis Drake in 1588 (and also, ahem, by Lord High Admiral William Howard and Sir John Hawkins) than to realize that the naval victory allowed England to embark on its program of world colonization. Hearing that yellow printing ink was perfected in 1896 by the *New York Journal* seems like a pleasant bit of technology—until you also recall that the publisher of the *New York Journal* was William Randolph Hearst, and you realize that that's how "yellow journalism" got its name.

This chapter is the one that will make the most light bulbs go off above your head. Whether you finished college or high school or went out before it was time to toss your mortar board in the air, get ready to recognize things that you thought you left in the classroom—as well as the cloakroom, the playground, the tree fort, and, most likely, the principal's office.

Slavery (Part 1)

When President Abraham Lincoln issued the Emancipation Proclamation in 1863, he didn't exactly free the slaves as he intended—or perhaps he did exactly as he intended.

The Emancipation Proclamation said that all slaves under the Confederacy were "forever free." The only catch was that Lincoln wasn't president of the Confederacy during the War Between the States—Jefferson Davis was. Therefore, Lincoln had absolutely no jurisdiction over the South. It was, however, a shrewd political move on Honest Abe's part. Not until the passage of the Thirteenth Amendment in 1865 was slavery officially outlawed in the re-United States of America. Even then, slavery and involuntary servitude remained permissible for persons duly convicted by jury verdict.

Incidentally, the Thirteenth Amendment was successfully used by actress Olivia DeHavilland against Warner Bros. studios to break her personal service contract (q.v.). The Court held the studio to be acting illegally whenever they extended the star's seven-year contract every time they placed her on suspension for refusing to accept an assignment. The same argument was also used in the establishment of free agency in baseball.

Slavery (Part 2)

Years before Abraham Lincoln "freed the slaves" (q.v.) by issuing the Emancipation Proclamation in 1863, the Founding Fathers had tried the same thing—and were just as unsuccessful.

In his original 1776 draft of the Declaration of Independence, Thomas Jefferson wrote of King George III:

He has waged cruel war against human nature itself, violating its most sacred rights of life and liberty in the persons of a distant people who never offended him, captivating and carrying them into slavery in another hemisphere, or to incur miserable death in their transportation hither. This piratical warfare, the opprobrium of [infidel] powers, is the warfare of the [Christian] king of Great Britain. Determined to keep open a market where [men] should be bought and sold, he has prostituted his negative for suppressing every legislative attempt to prohibit or restrain this execrable commerce.

The fact that Jefferson, himself, owned slaves did not diminish his fervor to free them. Predictably, the slavery passage was opposed by the Southern colonies, who withheld their votes for independence until it was removed from the Declaration.

The deletion was not performed without rancor or, astonishingly, prescience. Although Benjamin Franklin, ever the pragmatist, consented to its elimination, he was chastised by Samuel Adams (John Adams's cousin), who cautioned, "Mark me, Franklin, if we give in on this issue, there will be trouble a hundred years hence; posterity will never forgive us"—in essence, predicting the American Civil War.

But the saddest irony is that of Jefferson, who once argued against slavery with the words "nothing is more certainly written in the Book of Fate than that this people shall be free." What Jefferson abhorred in the abstract, he apparently approved of in the specific, because he never did get around to releasing his own slaves.

Get a Life: Slam Books

Question: What is a Slam Book?

Answer: A Slam Book is a book in which your friends anonymously write the worst things they can think of about you and then let you read it. In that wonderfully solipsistic way that peers have of treating each other like trash, the idea is to "improve" the recipient by pointing out his/her physical, behavioral, tonsorial, and genetic "shortcomings." Needless to say, when school administrators intercept Slam Books, they are not amused. Nevertheless, the practice continues.

Quiz: Historical Who's Who

Identify these people, who have become part of the folklore of early America:

1. Crispus Attucks
2. Johnny Appleseed
3. Elizabeth Foster Goose
4. John Brown
5. Frederick W. Douglass
6. Cotton Mather
7. Thomas Paine
8. Oliver Hazard Perry
9. John Hancock
10. John Henry

Quiz: Familiar Expressions

When Paul McCartney plays music "by ear," does that mean he does it by placing his lobes on the keys? And when someone "pulls strings," are they really making a pass at Pinocchio? Sometimes we use expressions without knowing what they really mean. If you think you know, then give the definition and origin of these common phrases:

1. "Have an albatross around your neck"
2. An "apocryphal" story
3. "Untie the Gordian knot"
4. "Dog in the manger"
5. "Far from the madding crowd"
6. "Blow us to kingdom come"
7. "Most unkindest cut of all"
8. "Open, Sesame"
9. "Pearls before swine"
10. "To the manner born"

Quiz: Fiddle-Dee-Dee

There's an old joke that has a man in the Middle Ages leaving home and telling his wife, "Good-bye, dear, I'm off to fight the Hundred Years' War." Match the war to the belligerents that fought it. (For extra credit, give details.)

1.	Napoleonic Wars	a.	Normans vs. Saxons
2.	French Revolution	b.	England vs. France
3.	Spanish Armada	c.	Rome vs. Carthage
4.	Crusades	d.	Church vs. Heretics
5.	Hundred Years' War	e.	Lancasters vs. Yorks
6.	Russian Revolution	f.	Spain vs. England
7.	Battle of Hastings	g.	Christians vs. Moslems
8.	Punic Wars	h.	Czarists vs. Bolsheviks
9.	Wars of the Roses	i.	France vs. Russia
10.	Inquisition	j.	Louis XVI vs. Robespierre

Quiz: Who Led Whom?

Some people are born great, some achieve greatness, and others have greatness thrust upon them. Match these leaders (but not necessarily rulers) to their respective lands. (For extra credit, give details.)

1.	Joan of Arc	a.	Huns (pre-Germany)
2.	Charlemagne	b.	France
3.	Alexander the Great	c.	Carthage
4.	Genghis Khan	d.	Jacobins—France
5.	Cleopatra	e.	Rome
6.	Augustus Caesar	f.	England
7.	Attila the Hun	g.	Greece
8.	Hannibal	h.	France
9.	Richard the Lion-Hearted	i.	Egypt
10.	Jean-Paul Marat	j.	Mongolia

Quiz: Peer Pressure

No one ever said growing up is pretty. For every school rule, kids themselves invented others that were worse. Sociologists called it peer pressure, but kids knew the difference between fitting in and being shunned. Here are some things you just had to know if you grew up in the '50s and '60s. What did they mean?

1. Wearing green and yellow on Thursday
2. "Safety"
3. Fruit loops/fink rings
4. Class ring turned around
5. Buckle on the back of pants unbuckled
6. When should one wear a slide rule/pocket protector?
7. Applause in school cafeteria
8. What do you do with used Dixie Cup® lids?
9. Vicks Vap-o-Rub in somebody's jock strap
10. "No matter how you wiggle and how you dance, the last drop always goes on your pants."

Quiz: Pen Names

Match these famous authors to the names they used, which were not the ones their parents gave them:

Pseudonym		**Name Given**	
1.	Charlotte Bronte	a.	Mary Ann Evans
2.	O. Henry	b.	Hector Hugh Munro
3.	Saki	c.	Currer Bell
4.	Voltaire	d.	David Cornwell
5.	Mary Westmacott	e.	William Sydney Porter
6.	George Sand	f.	Françoise-Marie Arouet
7.	John le Carré	g.	Eric Blair
8.	Lewis Carroll	h.	Agatha Cristie
9.	George Eliot	i.	Charles Lutwidge Dodgson
10.	George Orwell	j.	Amandine Dupin

Bell Science Films

From 1956 to the early 1960s, the American Telephone and Telegraph Company, in association with N. W. Ayer and Son, sponsored an unprecedented series of hour-long educational science programs on network television. Conceived by Oscar®-winning director Frank Capra (*Mr. Smith Goes to Washington, Lost Horizon*) and produced under the personal supervision of Jack L. Warner (cofounder of Warner Bros.), these highly praised documentaries quickly became the most eagerly anticipated TV specials for the generation of Americans growing up in the Sputnik era. Teachers assigned their students to watch TV when they first aired, and—in the days before home video—schools eagerly borrowed 16mm prints for classroom use and ran them *with the commercials.* Each program began with the same promise: "The Bell Telephone System brings you another of its series of programs on science—Man's effort to understand Nature's Laws."

Every one became a classic.

According to Frank Capra in his acclaimed autobiography *The Name Above the Title,* the Bell Science Films came about when he got a call from Don Jones of the N. W. Ayer Agency in New York asking him to advise Mr. Cleo F. Craig, president of AT&T, about a new television program on science that the Bell Telephone System was contemplating. Capra met with Craig, Harry Batten (president of Ayer), and Jim Hanna, the head of Ayer's TV and Radio Division. They explained that they had chosen Capra because he was the only director they knew who combined science with entertainment. As a film-maker he was peerless; what most people didn't know (but AT&T did) was that he also held a physicist's degree from Cal Tech.

Craig wanted to do science documentaries but knew that they were all dull, and since Ayer wanted to get the biggest audience for Bell's buck, they wanted Capra. Initially, Capra asked scientist-designer Willy Ley and writer-critic Aldous Huxley to submit treatments for "The Sun," which would be the subject for the pilot show. Capra also wrote his own version, obtaining Harvard astronomer Donald Menzel's book *Our Mr. Sun* and adapting it as a play in which "Dr. Research" and a "Fiction Writer" hash out truth and myth, supported by characters "Mr. Sun," "Father Time," "Thermo the Magician," and "Chloro Phyll." He sent all three proposals to Ayer, and Ayer chose his.

But Capra balked when they asked him to direct it, explaining that "a physical fact is boring, unless it is illuminated by a touch of the Eternal," and that "science, in essence, is just another facet of man's quest for God." That is exactly what Bell and Ayer wanted: a bridge between scientists and other human beings.

The Bell Science Films ran on network TV for two seasons. The first group, made under Capra's scrutiny, were hosted by the genial Dr. Frank C. Baxter ("Dr. Research"), who was paired with actor Richard Carlson ("The Writer") to explore a variety of topics:

- *Our Mr. Sun:* This topic offered a scientific and historical exploration of the earth's nearest stellar neighbor.
- *Hemo the Magnificent:* The importance of blood to the human body is debated by the various organs—animated, of course.

- *The Strange Case of the Cosmic Rays:* Radiation's effect on life, presented in a non-alarmist way, was the focus of this mystery.
- *Meteora, the Unchained Goddess:* Science and imagination navigate weather—with its majesty and its mysteries.

    The first series, which debuted on CBS, proved so popular that AT&T reran it the following year on NBC. They also embarked on a second series, this time with Dr. Baxter—who had emerged as an unlikely media star—exploring his topics alone.

- *The Alphabet Conspiracy:* A young girl's frustration over the complexity of language is soothed by understanding the joy of speech and writing.
- *The Thread of Life:* The science of genetics is unraveled in ways that people of all strains can grasp.

- *About Time:* The ruler of a new planet is given a lesson in how to set his clock—and what it means.

    The Bell Science Films ceased production in the mid-'60s, the victim of a shift from prime-time family television to the more commercially attractive adolescent and young adult market. In the 1970s the Public Broadcasting Service (PBS) introduced the popular *Cosmos, Life on Earth, Nova,* and other fact-based programming, such as nature shows. At first considered a joke, the nature genre rose sharply in popularity with the advent of cable television—so much so that they rekindled the market for informational shows. Now there are entire networks devoted to nature, history, discovery, and learning.

    Frank Capra and Dr. Frank Baxter would be proud.

Quiz: Decisions, Decisions

Sometimes school is just memorization, such as *gazintas* ("2 gazinta 4 twice, 2 gazinta 6 three times," etc.). Other times it's landmark legal decisions such as *Plessy* vs. *Ferguson*. Who's Ferguson? What's a Plessy? Or the Dred Scott decision: Who was Dred Scott, and what did he decide? Identify each famous case where the name may be more familiar than the principle:

1. *Brown* vs. *Board of Education*
2. *Plessy* vs. *Ferguson*
3. The Missouri Compromise
4. Dred Scott Decision
5. *Marbury* vs. *Madison*
6. *Roe* vs. *Wade* (Hint: This is *not* two ways to get across a lake.)
7. *Gideon* vs. *Wainwright*
8. Sherman Anti-Trust Act
9. *Miranda* vs. *Arizona*
10. *Furman* vs. *Georgia*

Quiz: Plot Capsules

Mark Twain (Quick: What was his real name?) once said that a "classic" is a book that people praise and don't read. See if you can identify these classics from their glib plot descriptions. No fair using *Cliff's Notes*.

1. The Martians are coming! The Martians are coming!
2. A mousy girl becomes the second wife of a brooding aristocrat.
3. A mousy girl becomes the young wife of a brooding aristocrat.
4. Hijinx in England in the Middle Ages. You can't tell the players without a can opener.
5. Fiddle-dee-dee; Boom!
6. Napoleon is no *Tovarich*!
7. Recalled to life; Boom!
8. Good morning. I'm a cockroach.
9. I had caught a fish this big, but sharks got him.
10. Leave the blue light on and let's party!

Quiz: (Easy): Hip Books

No bookshelf of the '60s, '70s, and early '80s could be without these books. Who wrote them?

1. *Been Down So Long It Looks Like Up to Me*
2. *Jonathan Livingston Seagull*
3. *Steal This Book*
4. *Love Story*
5. *Gravity's Rainbow*
6. *Trout Fishing in America*
7. *Where the Buffalo Roam*
8. *The Electric Kool-Aid Acid Test*
9. *One Flew Over the Cuckoo's Nest*
10. *The Psychedelic Reader*
11. *You and I*
12. *Do It!*
13. *Zen and the Art of Motorcycle Maintenance*
14. *Dutchman*
15. *The Fire Next Time*
16. *In Someone's Shadow*
17. *A Confederacy of Dunces*
18. *The Confessions of Nat Turner*
19. *Yes I Can*
20. *The Autobiography of Malcolm X*

Quiz: Wise Science

It's often been said that fantasy/science fiction writers can address contemporary issues more honestly than other writers because their ideas have the appearance of whimsy. Be that as it may, who wrote the following works and what were they about?

1. *I Have No Mouth, and I Must Scream*
2. *Stranger in a Strange Land*
3. *The Time Machine*
4. *The Wizard of Oz*
5. *Gulliver's Travels*
6. *Spider-Man*
7. *Invasion of the Body Snatchers*
8. *Alice's Adventures in Wonderland*
9. *Monkey Planet*
10. *The Incredible Shrinking Man*

Quiz: Inventions

Who is generally credited with the following inventions or innovations?

1. The bifocal
2. Contained stove for heating rooms
3. Lightning rod
4. The post office
5. Daily newspaper
6. Public library
7. Interstate highway system

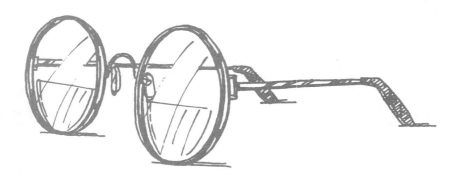

Quiz: Food Facts

True or false:

1. The tomato is a vegetable.
2. Saffron is the stamen of a flower.
3. Peanuts aren't really nuts.
4. Artichokes are related to cabbages.
5. Cranberry juice cocktail is less than half actual juice.
6. You can't buy fresh tomatoes in supermarkets.
7. There is glue in nondairy whipped dessert toppings.
8. Brussels sprouts are young cabbages.
9. "The two things you must never actually see being made are sausage and legislation."
10. Wonder Bread has more vitamins than homemade bread.

School Cafeteria

Few social systems in American life are as rigid as the school cafeteria. Time may have changed the styles, but the peer pressure remains the same.

It starts in the first grade. Here the child's selection of his/her lunchbox (Roy Rogers *si!*, Heckel and Jeckel *no!*; Barbie *si!*, Raggedy Ann, *no!*) marks him/her as a worthy dining companion—or not.

By the third grade the group sensibilities have spread from what's outside the box to what's in it: PBJ (peanut butter and jelly) is okay, ham is better, but tuna salad is yucky because it soaks through the white bread. The trading of food is introduced and quickly replaces baseball cards as currency: Packaged chips and cookies outrank the exact same foods wrapped by mom in a baggie (in the '50s it was waxed paper). Hostess® Twinkies and Cupcakes rule, as did Hydrox® (until they changed their recipe) and Oreos®. Candy bars trump anything else.

At this time, mores begin to take shape. Bullies shaking down younger classmates for their milk money is suffered in silence (this was before students brought guns to school), but even the biggest and baddest bully never dares steal dessert from a calorically challenged kid.

Junior high school finds the emergence of fashion sense. This is never on public view more than when entering the lunchroom. Long before the days of gang garb—when denims and T-shirts were prohibited by school boards—young people know what to wear and what not to wear. Guys wear pegged black pants (they were the hoods) or loose khakis with light-colored shirts, often buttoned at the top (if you're a nerd) or open-collared (if you're not). Girls wear dresses that come to their calves, sweaters or blouses that cover their necks, and absolutely no patent leather shoes (Hint: nuns). Makeup must also be minimal, except for a quick eyeliner in the girl's lavatory between third period and lunch.

Boys who carry brief cases are advised to hide them in their lockers, but girls are allowed to balance their textbooks from the previous class on their trays (unless they can get a goony guy to carry it for them). Trouser cuffs cannot be rolled up, white socks are not allowed, and no Keds (Running shoes? In the early '60s? Haw!).

Group behavior toward others invariably runs to the negative. In the certain event that a hapless kid accidentally drops his tray, the entire room bursts into a spontaneous round of applause. If, by some chance, his Sloppy Joe heroically skitters across the floor and lands on the faculty monitor's shoes, nothing less than a standing ovation will do.

Junior high schoolers practice their gross-outs with zeal. One method is a game called "garbage," in which, after everybody has finished eating, a tablespoon is passed around the table and dipped into as disgusting a combination of food as possible. Then someone is chosen to eat it.

"Lookie" was another middle-school gross-out prank. It is almost exclusively a guy game. Here's how it was done: John sits at one end of the lunchroom cramming food into his mouth while his friend Scottie sits at the other end. On signal, Scottie calls out, attracting as much attention as possible, "Hey, John, what are you eating?" Taking the bait, everybody in the lunchroom looks over at John. So John opens his messy mouth and says, "Lookie!"

But high school is where the customs become calcified for the rest of life—not just school life, but forever. For the first year, girls sit with girls and guys sit with guys; naturally, they talk about each other. By second semester they change their routes to "accidentally on purpose" walk past each other's tables, hoping against hope to be invited to sit down. By the second year (including one summer), couples going steady will sit with each other if they have the same lunch period or will pine away for each other if they do not.

Students in cliques will rush straight to where their friends are seated. The most charismatic person of the group will sit in the center of the table, not at the end; as with seating at Buckingham Palace, the farther one is from the leader, the less favor one is in at the moment. Status changes, and so do lunch seats.

Any high school student who makes more than one lap of the lunchroom risks social ridicule; obviously he/she doesn't recognize any friends, and no one has caught his/her attention. If you don't see someone you know on the first lap, you are going to have to settle for someone you don't know on the second. But if you sit next to someone you don't know, the chances are terribly high that they will have finished their lunch and leave as soon as you sit down, and you'll be A-L-O-N-E. What to do?

- Remember you have an orthodontist appointment and leave.
- Get your period and go to the school nurse.
- Leave your tray and walk over to ask a friend about homework; he/she may say, "Bring your tray over."

- Announce, "Hey, who wants my ice cream? It gives me gas."
- On no occasion should an upperclassman ever sit with an underclassman.
- When in doubt, punt: Drop your tray, go for the standing ovation, and leave.

And now a word about wombats.

Cafeteria jobs are not exactly fulfilling. They combine the tedium of the assembly line with the frustration of dealing with the public on a daily basis. To make matters worse, the public are adolescents who are used to home cooking, not institutional food, and definitely not institutional food whose blandness has been decreed by a nutritionist working on a budget. Since kids are hardly going to march down to the school board's office to grouse about soggy fries, it's the cafeteria workers who bear the brunt of it.

These workers are not diplomats. They are not paid to be. Many are part-timers, some are retirees, but a large number are from hospitals and special needs schools that cater to men and women who have diminished learning ability. Political correctness calls them "special," but kids—in that endearing way they have of being cruel to people they don't understand—call them *wombats*.

Has cafeteria changed since the baby boomers left high school? Just visit any country club, office commissary, or executive dining room. No wonder people prefer lunch counters. The food may be greasy, but at least you don't have to dodge the football team, pray for a friend, or protect your cookies.

Although you *do* have to tip the wombats.

Quiz: New Math

The end of life as we know it began sometime around 1959. That was when People Who Know These Things invented New Math and insisted on having it taught in schools.

New Math was supposed to help students grasp the concepts behind the way numbers do their job. So far so good. The problem was that the people who designed it already knew how to use numbers, whereas the people they were teaching it to didn't. Think of it as trying to invent a French-German dictionary for people who don't yet speak either language.

Or, put another way (in the words of satirist Tom Lehrer, who, as it happens, is also a math teacher): "In New Math the important thing is to know what you are doing rather than to get the right answer."[1]

Here's a pop quiz on New Math. (No fair checking the answers at the end of the section.)

1. What are Venn diagrams?
2. What are prime numbers?
3. What is Base 8?
4. Describe and demonstrate the commutative theory of addition and multiplication.
5. What is the binary system?
6. What are natural numbers?
7. What is the distributive property of multiplication over addition?

---

[1] Tom Lehrer's *That Was the Year That Was* is available on Reprise CD.

Get a Life: Hopefully

Hopefully, alot of yous know that due to the fact of grammar, this ain't good writing to put up with.

Question: Find and annotate six errors of form or style in the previous sentence.

Answer: Hopefully[1], alot[2] of yous[3] know that due to the fact[4] of grammar, this ain't[5] good writing to put up with[6].

1. *Hopefully* is perhaps the most frequently misused word in conversational English. Strictly speaking, it means "full of hope," not "I hope that . . . "

2. Very simply, *alot* is not a word. The expression *a lot* means "many," and *allot* means "allocate."
3. The plural of *you* is, and always has been, *you*.
4. The expression *due to the fact* is redundant. *Due to* implies that the reason follows, as in *due to rain, the game has been canceled.*
5. Despite decades of education, people still think that *ain't* is a word. It ain't.
6. "A preposition at the end of a sentence," Winston Churchill supposedly joked, "is something up with which I will not put."

Quiz: Patriotic Sayings

Match the saying with the person generally credited with uttering it. (Hint: Go with legend, not accuracy.)

1. "I regret that I have but one life to lose for my country."
2. "I cannot tell a lie."
3. "I am not a crook."
4. "Don't fire until you see the whites of their eyes."
5. "Give me liberty or give me death."
6. "Go west, young man."
7. "Shoot if you must this old gray head, but spare your country's flag."
8. "A house divided against itself cannot stand."
9. "I have not yet begun to fight."
10. "The summer soldier and the sunshine patriot may, in this crisis, shrink from the service of his country."

a. Abraham Lincoln
b. John Paul Jones
c. Horace Greeley
d. Patrick Henry
e. George Washington
f. Thomas Paine
g. William Prescott
h. Barbara Frietchie
i. Nathan Hale
j. Richard Nixon

Quiz: Schoolroom Myths

Despite what the playground know-it-all said, which of the following childhood myths are true?

1. If you swallow chewing gum, it sticks to your heart.
2. You have to be married in order to get pregnant.
3. A girl in Mrs. Blumberg's class never washed her hair, and one day they found cockroaches living inside her head.
4. Even identical twins never have the same fingerprints.
5. The skin is the body's largest organ.
6. It's true what they say about men who have big feet.
7. The human body is worth around $4.98.
8. If you hold in your wind, you'll explode.
9. It is impossible to keep your eyes open when you sneeze.
10. If you shave off hair, it grows back even thicker.

Quiz: Gangsters

Everybody knows that Al Capone was sent to prison on income tax charges and that he died there of syphilis, and that John Dillinger walked into an FBI trap as he left a movie theatre. So much American gangster history is fable that it's hard to tell what's true. Are these true or false?

1. G-man Melvin Purvis shot John Dillinger first.
2. When Patty Hearst was captured by the FBI, she wet her pants.
3. Nathan "Babe" Leopold and Richard "Dickie" Loeb were executed for killing little Bobbie Franks in 1924.
4. John Noland got the nickname "Legs Diamond" because he dated leggy chorus girls.
5. Meyer Lansky was just a modest businessman, not a syndicate kingpin.
6. Ma Barker was forced into crime by her wayward sons Herman, Lloyd, Arthur ("Doc"), and Freddy.
7. Although they were killers, Bonnie and Clyde were just petty thieves.
8. J. Edgar Hoover never actually caught anybody himself.
9. A lawyer with a briefcase can steal more than ten men with machine guns.
10. Murderess Ruth Snyder holds the distinction of being the only person photographed at the moment of execution.

Quiz: Are You Sure?

Gertrude Stein once said, "You know what you know, you know?" Do you really know these multiple choice questions?

1. What's the windiest city in the United States?
   a) Boston, Massachusetts
   b) Chicago, Illinois
   c) Great Falls, Montana
2. Which demographic group votes most often in elections?
   a) 18–21
   b) 55–64
   c) 65–74
3. What is the average person's biggest fear in life?
   a) Speaking in public
   b) Going to the dentist
   c) Wedding night
4. What is the geographic center of the forty-eight contiguous United States?
   a) Oklahoma City, OK
   b) Butte County, SD
   c) Smith County, KS
5. How many dog years actually equal one human year?
   a) 7
   b) 5.5
   c) 8

6. Other than praying mantises, which of these insects kill their mates?
   a) Cockroaches
   b) Houseflies
   c) Black widow spiders
7. How much wood could a woodchuck chuck if a woodchuck could chuck wood?
   a) 2-foot tree
   b) 18-inch tree
   c) 6-inch tree
8. What is the natural home of the Tasmanian Devil?
   a) Southern Australia
   b) New Zealand
   c) Warner Bros.
9. What food was *not* on the menu of the first Thanksgiving?
   a) Venison
   b) Eel
   c) Turkey
10. What's the difference between a boat and a ship?
   a) A Naval commission
   b) Anything over 50 feet is a ship
   c) A boat can be hauled aboard a ship

Quiz: Seven Wonders of the World

Which of the following are the Seven Wonders of the World (as listed by Antipater of Sidon in the second century BC)?

1. Hanging Gardens of Babylon
2. Radio City Music Hall
3. Temple of Artemis at Ephesus
4. Skywalker Ranch
5. Mall America
6. Statue of Zeus at Olympia
7. Statue of Heffner at Playboy Mansion
8. Pyramids of Egypt
9. Milli Vanilli's career
10. Lighthouse at Alexandria
11. Headlights of Kitten Natividad
12. Colossus of Rhodes
13. Colossus of Stryker
14. Mausoleum at Halicarnassus
15. Head dress of Carnac the Magnificent

Quiz: Formulas

The ever-quotable *Mad* magazine once said that "the area of a square is measured by his height, weight and suit size." *Mad* also reported that "the shortest distance between two points is a taxi." Other than Alfred E. Neuman, however, mathematicians worry about matching the following formulas with their geometric goals. Can you?

1. Area of a square	a.	a^3
2. Area of a circle	b.	$2\pi r$ (radius) or πd (diameter)
3. Surface of a sphere	c.	1/3 of (base area x height)
4. Volume of a cylinder	d.	$4\pi r^2$
5. Volume of a pyramid	e.	πr^2
6. Volume of a cube	f.	height x width
7. Perimeter of a circle	g.	$\pi r^2 h$

Speed-Reading

Speed-reading is the equivalent of fast-forwarding a videotape and thinking you've watched it. Popularized during the Kennedy years (when JFK revealed he could "scan" a book in a matter of minutes), speed-reading became the domain of the Evelyn Wood Reading Dynamics. Its adherents conceded that you sometimes lost the flavor of the book, but you developed remarkable retention of the content. The trick was not to read each word individually but, rather, to take in blocks of words, usually assisted by running one's finger down the side of the page.

Whether speed-reading actually works or was just a way to call attention to America's declining reading habits remains controversial (this author, for example, who was originally taught to read by the preferred phonetic method, was actually slowed down by a speed-reading course, which uses the now-discredited "word recognition" method).

The truth is that some material is probably easier to "scan" than other material—news reports versus literature, for example. In any event, the fad has passed, and nobody reads anything except self-help and diet books anyway.

And another thing: The word *scan* doesn't mean "glance at quickly." It means "examine minutely." Did Evelyn Wood ever scan a dictionary?

Get a Life: One Hen

Question: Before Johnny Carson replaced Steve Allen on NBC's *Tonight* show in 1962, there was a succession of guest hosts, one of whom was Jerry Lewis. In the course of Lewis's frantic week, he insisted on teaching Hugh Downs—who preceded Ed McMahon as announcer—a memory test. By Friday, not only did the unflappable Downs know it by heart, so did every kid in America. Did you? It begins "one hen . . ."

Answer: One hen; **Two** ducks; **Three** squawking geese; **Four** corpulent porpoises; **Five** limerick oysters; **Six** pairs of Don Alvarado's favorite tweezers; **Seven** thousand Macedonians in full battle array; **Eight** brass monkeys from the ancient, sacred crypts of Egypt; **Nine** apathetic, sympathetic, diabetic old men on roller skates with a marked propensity toward procrastination and sloth; **Ten** lyrical, spherical, diabolical denizens of the deep who quiver and quake and shiver and shake around a corner all at the same time.

Answers

Historical Who's Who (Answers)

1. A sailor of mixed race, Crispus Attucks was one of five colonists killed by British troops in the Boston Massacre in 1770 and thus was among the first men to die in the Revolutionary War.
2. Johnny Appleseed (Real name: John Chapman) built an apple tree nursery in Pennsylvania and traveled the countryside planting apple trees in the 1700s.
3. Elizabeth Foster Goose is better known as "Mother Goose," a Boston resident of the late 1600s who collected folk rhymes.
4. A leading abolitionist, Brown and his band of revolutionaries rode the countryside freeing slaves. In 1859 he took over a federal arsenal in Harper's Ferry, Virginia, was captured, tried for treason, and hanged.
5. An escaped slave who became a forceful abolitionist speaker, Frederick W. Douglass bought his freedom with money earned on the speaking circuit in the late 1800s.
6. Cotton Mather, a Puritan and scholar, dwelled in the Massachusetts Colony in the late 1600s and helped support the Salem witch trials that led to the execution of some twenty innocent people.
7. Thomas Paine was the Colonial patriot and author of *Common Sense*, the anonymously published pamphlet that urged revolutionary war against England in the 1770s.
8. Naval Commander Oliver Hazard Perry, in a message sent from the battle of Lake Erie in the war of 1812, wrote, "We have met the enemy and they are ours." This is not to be confused with Walt Kelley's comic strip character Pogo who said, "We have met the enemy and they are us."
9. John Hancock was president of the Continental Congress and guided debate on American independence. He is most famous for his large signature on the Declaration of Independence, supposedly written "so fat George in London can see it without his glasses."
10. John Henry is a legendary black railroad worker who lost a heroic contest with a steam-driven stake driver in the 1800s and thereafter died of exhaustion. He is often confused with John Hancock (president of the Continental Congress) by people who say "Put your John Henry on the dotted line" in reference to one's signature.

Familiar Expressions (Answers)

1. The albatross is the reminder of a personal burden. In Samuel Taylor Coleridge's epic poem *The Rime of the Ancient Mariner*, the central character kills an albatross (a bird not unlike a sea gull) that has been flying alongside their ship, bringing the crew terrible luck. As punishment, his mates force him to hang the dead bird around his neck ("instead of a cross / the albatross / around my neck was hung").
2. Among the books of the Bible is the Apocrypha, whose veracity is doubted but whose writing nevertheless holds apparent truth. An apocryphal story is one that may or may not be true but whose lesson remains valid.
3. Gordius, king of ancient Phrygia, constructed an immensely complex knot and vowed that whoever untied the Gordian Knot would rightwise rule all Asia. Alexander the Great, rather than untie it, merely cut it with his sword and proceeded to conquer the East. The saying refers to ingenuous problem solving.
4. A dog in the manger has nothing to do with the nativity but, rather, is from an Aesop fable in which a dog, lying in a box of hay, bit an ox that tried to eat some of it, despite the hay being of no use to the dog. The phrase refers to one who does a spiteful deed solely for the mere joy of it.
5. When one is physically distant from civilization, one is "far from the madding crowd." The phrase popularized as the title of Thomas Hardy's romantic novel. Incidentally, the phrase is *not* "far from the *maddening* crowd," as some people insist.
6. "Kingdom come" is found in the Lord's Prayer and refers to Heaven. To be blown, dragged, beaten, or otherwise sent to kingdom come refers to being dispatched to the embrace of God.
7. When Brutus stabbed Julius Caesar, it not only killed him, but it was the betrayal by a friend. "The most unkindest cut of all" is drawn from Shakespeare's play *Julius Caesar* and refers to a grievously hurtful deed. The double superlative is accurate, by the way, even if it is currently out of fashion linguistically.
8. "Open, Sesame" is the command that is given by the Forty Thieves to open their cave of treasures and that Ali Baba overhears. In the mouth of Popeye in the Max and Dave Fleischer cartoon, the phrase became "Open, sez me," which, frankly, makes a lot more sense.
9. Jesus told his followers from the mount, "Give not that which is holy unto the dogs, neither cast ye your pearls before swine." The idea is not to waste your efforts on someone who cannot appreciate them. There's a funny story in which writer/diplomat Clare Boothe Luce held a door open for poet/wit Dorothy Parker to enter first, saying with a smile, "Age before beauty." Smiling back, Miss Parker replied dryly, "Pearls before swine."

10. One who is raised in the lap of luxury is said to be "to the manner born." The phrase is from Shakespeare's *Hamlet*. It has nothing to do with the incorrect spelling "to the *manor* born," which probably means that the person inherited a mansion.

Fiddle-Dee-Dee (Answers)

1. i
2. j
3. f
4. g
5. b
6. h
7. a
8. c
9. e
10. d

Fiddle-Dee-Dee (Extra Credit)

1. Napoleonic Wars: Emperor Napoleon Bonaparte—he crowned himself in 1804—conquered much of Europe but lost most of his armies trying to invade Russia. He then took on the British and the Prussians in Belgium but met his Waterloo—quite literally—in 1815.
2. French Revolution: The 1789 revolution ended ten centuries of rule by kings (the last of which was Louis XVI and his queen, Marie Antoinette) and ushered in the Republic. Unfortunately, under Robespierre, the Reign of Terror executed most nobles and created such havoc that Napoleon was able to emerge as dictator and, eventually, emperor.
3. Spanish Armada: King Philip II of Spain ruled the seas with the one hundred ships of the Armada. His goal was to conquer England, but Sir Francis Drake—with help from Holland's navy and bad weather—turned the decks on the Spaniards, sinking half their ships. With the British in control of the seas, they could begin exploring the New World and did.
4. Crusades: The late eleventh through thirteenth centuries saw the forces of Christianity fighting the Moslems for control of Jerusalem and the Holy Land. Ignited by religious fervor, European rulers thus gained a taste for new lands and experiences.
5. Hundred Years' War: England invaded France in the mid-1400s and was eventually driven off by the French, many of whom rallied behind Joan of Arc.
6. Russian Revolution: The October 1917 Russian Revolution pitted the Bolsheviks under Lenin against Czar Nicholas II. Inspired by privations during World War I, the revolution formally lasted until 1918,

although it continued informally throughout the existence of the USSR.
7. Battle of Hastings: William the Conqueror crossed from France with his Norman army and subdued the Saxons of England, who were fighting under King Harold, in 1066.
8. Punic Wars: Rome and Carthage were in constant battle, and the three wars that occurred during the second and third centuries BC are the Punic Wars. The third and final war destroyed Carthage.
9. Wars of the Roses: The families of the House of York (white rose symbol) and House of Lancaster (red rose symbol) fought bitterly for thirty years, from 1455, for control of England. In 1486 Henry Tudor (Lancaster/red) married Princess Elizabeth (York/white) and took the throne, thus ending the hostilities.
10. Inquisition: The Roman Catholic Church in the thirteenth century established a court to try cases of heresy, then turned its victims over to civil authorities (who were controlled by the church anyway) for harsh punishment.

Who Led Whom? (Answers)

1. b
2. e/b
3. g
4. j
5. i
6. e
7. a
8. c
9. f
10. d

Who Led Whom? (Extra Credit)

1. Joan of Arc: She rallied the French people behind her to battle the invading English armies in the mid-1500s, bringing about the end of the dreaded Hundred Years' War and establishing the rightful king to the French throne. Then she was burned at the stake by a grateful Catholic Church.
2. Charlemagne: Crowned first emperor of the Holy Roman Empire in AD 800, he was King of France in the late eighth and early ninth centuries and is known for his greatness. The Holy Roman Empire stood into the sixteenth century, albeit gradually withering.
3. Alexander the Great: He ruled Greece in the fourth century BC and conquered the known world east to India.

4. Genghis Khan: In the late 1100s to early 1200s, Khan, the emperor of Mongolia, conquered much of northern China and southwest Asia.

5. Cleopatra: First Century AD Egyptian queen who seduced Julius Caesar and, after Caesar's assassination, lived with Marc Antony. She died, legend has it, from the bite of an asp.

6. Augustus Caesar: The first emperor of Rome (and Julius's adopted son) from 44 BC to AD 14, he brought peace to the empire and was ruler when Jesus was born.

7. Attila the Hun: He was the fifth-century king of the Huns (pre-Germans), who overran, killing and pillaging, much of central and eastern Europe.

8. Hannibal: He was the Carthaginian general who crossed the Alps from Spain into Italy with one hundred thousand men and numerous elephants during the second Punic War. His objective—not achieved—was to conquer Rome.

9. Richard the Lion-Hearted: Son of Henry II, Richard was the English King who fought in the Crusades. When captured and held for ransom, he inspired the rise of Robin Hood, who held off King John until Richard could return. (Robin and Richard were both legends, albeit different kinds.)

10. Jean-Paul Marat: This eighteenth-century revolutionary French writer and leader of the Jacobins was a radical offshoot of the French Revolution founded by Robespierre. He was stabbed to death by Charlotte Corday while bathing.

Peer Pressure (Answers)

1. Wearing green and yellow on Thursday meant you were gay (in some regions, it was green only).

2. If you passed wind and didn't say "safety" to warn your friends nearby, they could slug you.

3. They were little tabs on the back of dress shirts that could be used to hang them in your gym locker, but really served no purpose.

4. You turned your class ring around to face the other direction once you had been graduated.

5. Boys' fashions in the '60s included slacks with useless buckles in the back. An open buckle meant that you were available for dating; a closed buckle meant you were seeing somebody. A class pin or ring worn as a necklace, of course, meant you were going steady.

6. Never. Slide rules and pocket protectors are worn only by nerds. (Note to current generation: Slide rules were a low-tech computing device that didn't require batteries, only a brain.)

7. Applause in the school cafeteria was always given anybody who dropped his/her tray, preferably while leaving the lunch line, full of food.

8. You slap them sticky side up underneath the lunch table, of course.

9. This punishment was reserved only for guys who had committed some gross impropriety in phys ed. Be warned.

10. Be careful tidying up after using the lavatory.

Pen Names (Answers)

1. c
2. e
3. b
4. f
5. h
6. j
7. d
8. i
9. a
10. g

Decisions, Decisions (Answers)

1. *Brown* vs. *Board of Education of Topeka* (1954): The U.S. Supreme Court held that "separate but equal is now equal" and struck down school desegregation.

2. *Plessy* vs. *Fergusson* (1896): Racial segregation was constitutional as long as accommodations were equal. It was overturned by *Brown* (q.v.).

3. The Missouri Compromise (1819): This act of Congress admitted Missouri to the Union as a slave state in exchange for admitting Maine as a free state, but only if slavery was abolished in the rest of the Louisiana Purchase territory. It was overturned by *Scott* (q.v.)

4. Dred Scott Decision (1857): It was also known as *Dred Scott* vs. *Sanford,* in which Scott, a runaway slave, was ordered returned to his owner because he was property, not a citizen. This ruled the Missouri Compromise (q.v.) unconstitutional.

5. *Marbury* vs. *Madison* (1803): This was the first time the U.S. Supreme Court overturned an act of Congress. The decision established the principle of judicial review of American laws.

6. *Roe* vs. *Wade* (1973): This decision upheld a woman's right to privacy in deciding whether to have an abortion.

7. *Gideon* vs. *Wainwright* (1963): This decision saw to it that poor defendants in criminal trials have an attorney provided for them at state cost.

Answers

8. Sherman Anti-Trust Act (1890): This act of Congress curtailed the powers of U.S. business monopolies. It didn't do squat, however, until the passage of the Clayton Anti-Trust Act in 1914, which empowered the government to actually enforce such laws.

9. *Miranda* vs. *Arizona* (1966): This decision provided for police to apprise suspects of their "Miranda" rights before questioning them (it has been somewhat eroded in recent years).

10. *Furman* vs. *Georgia* (1972): This decision overturned the death penalty unless the states rewrote their statutes to make them more objective. By 1977, many did.

Plot Capsules (Answers)

1. *The War of the Worlds* by H.G. Wells
2. *Rebecca* by Daphne du Maurier
3. *Jane Eyre* by Charlotte Bronte
4. *Ivanhoe* by Sir Walter Scott
5. *Gone with the Wind* by Margaret Mitchell (via *Mad* magazine)
6. *War and Peace* by Leo Tolstoy
7. *A Tale of Two Cities* by Charles Dickens
8. *The Metamorphosis* by Franz Kafka
9. *The Old Man and the Sea* by Ernest Hemingway
10. *The Great Gatsby* by F. Scott Fitzgerald

. . . And Mark Twain's real name was Samuel Langhorn Clemmons.

Hip Books (Answers)

1. Richard Fariña
2. Richard Bach
3. Abbie Hoffman
4. Erich Segal
5. Thomas Pynchon
6. Richard Brautigan
7. Hunter S. Thompson
8. Thomas Wolfe
9. Ken Kesey
10. Timothy Leary (Who else?)
11. Leonard Nimoy
12. Jerry Rubin
13. Ronald L. Disanto and Thomas J. Steele
14. LeRoi Jones (Amiri Baraka)
15. James Baldwin
16. Rod McKuen
17. John Kennedy Toole
18. William Styron
19. Sammy Davis, Jr.
20. Rod McKuen

Wise Science (Answers)

1. Harlan Ellison; computers absorb humanity, literally
2. Robert A. Heinlein; cautionary tale of messianism
3. H.G. Wells; dangers in capitalist versus socialist ideologies
4. L. Frank Baum; gold versus silver financial standards
5. Jonathan Swift; satire on English government in the 1700s
6. Stan Lee; with great power there must also come great responsibility
7. Jack Finney; depersonalization by Communist-like take-over
8. Lewis Carroll; foolish bureaucracy in Queen Victoria's court
9. Pierre Boulle; fascism impedes progress despite evolution throwing a monkey wrench (source for *Planet of the Apes*)
10. Richard Matheson; all living things have value in the universe

Inventions (Answers)

1. Benjamin Franklin
2. Benjamin Franklin
3. Benjamin Franklin
4. Benjamin Franklin
5. Benjamin Franklin
6. Benjamin Franklin
7. Benjamin Franklin

Food Facts (Answers)

1. False. Technically, the tomato is a berry, but it is also a fruit that is eaten like a vegetable.
2. True. Saffron is the dried stamen of the cultivated crocus.
3. True. Peanuts are legumes, or vegetables.
4. False. Artichokes are related to thistles.
5. True. The amount of juice is about 27 percent. The rest is sugar water.
6. True. Most tomatoes are picked miles away while still green and are gassed with ethylene to make them look ripe. An accidental byproduct is that they also taste like tennis balls.
7. False, but only on a technicality. Nondairy toppings include sodium caseinate, which is a substance derived from milk protein (just like Elmer's glue).
8. False. They are buds from the stem of a plant.
9. True (according to Otto von Bismark)
10. True, but they are artificially added.

New Math (Answers)

1. Venn diagrams are circles, each representing a "set" or category (numbers, vegetables, people, etc.). The extent to which the circles overlap represents the number of attributes that the sets have in common (even numbers, green vegetables, people with brown eyes, etc.). It's a symbolic thing.

2. Prime numbers are numbers that can be divided only by themselves and by the number 1 (1, 3, 5, 53, 343, etc.).

3. Base 8 is a system of numeration in which sets are made of 8, not the standard 10. Where the normal Base 10 (decimal) system goes "ones, tens, hundreds, thousands," etc., a Base 8 system goes "ones, eights, sixty-fours, five-hundred-and-twelves," etc. Doesn't make any more sense now than it did then, does it? Again, Tom Lehrer: "Base 8 is just like Base 10, really. If you're missing two fingers."

4. The commutative system of addition and multiplication reveals that no matter what order you add or multiply numbers, the result will be the same. Whether you add 2+4+6+8 or 8+6+4+2 you will still get 20. The same holds true for 2x4x6x8 and 8x6x4x2 equaling 2304 (but just to make it harder, New Math replaced the "x" multiplication sign with a "•"—raised dot).

5. The binary system is the basis of all computer language. Just as Base 8 was built on sets of 8, the binary language is built on sets of "0" and "1." This corresponds to electronic circuitry being either "on" or "off," the myriad combination of which form the digital systems we have come to embrace everywhere.

6. Natural numbers are numbers invented by humankind to be used in counting—one ox, two pigs, three oranges, etc.

7. The distributive property of multiplication over addition specifies that, in an equation, you perform the addition before you perform the multiplication. Let's take **(2+3)•(4+5)=x,** which involves adding and multiplying numbers in the same equation. But which action do you do first? The distributive property dictates that you enclose the addition in parentheses: (2+3)•(4+5)=x and perform the addition first: (5)•(9)=x. Only then do you multiply their sums: 5 times 9 equals 44. See? Well, it really equals 45, but, as Lehrer says, "It's the thought that counts."

Patriotic Sayings (Answers)

1. i
2. e
3. j
4. g
5. d
6. c
7. h
8. a
9. b
10. f

Schoolroom Myths (Answers)

1. False. It goes through your digestive system.
2. False. All it takes is sex.
3. False. Lice, maybe, but not cockroaches.
4. True. There are also many more subtle differences.
5. True. The human body has about 14 to 18 square feet of skin.
6. True: Men who have big feet wear big shoes.
7. True, but from purely a chemical standpoint. If each organ plus blood is sold *ala carte*, however, it can fetch much more. (Reminder: This is illegal.)
8. False, but you'll have more friends.
9. True. I have no idea why.
10. False. It just *feels* thicker because it's stubble.

Gangsters (Answers)

1. False. Purvis led the 1934 ambush and never shot Dillinger. He did, however, commit suicide years later with the same pistol.
2. True.
3. False. Leopold was paroled in 1958 and Loeb was knifed to death in prison in 1936 for making a pass at a fellow inmate (or, as one newspaper wryly put it, "He ended his sentence with a proposition").
4. False. He won the sobriquet because he was good at dodging police as a kid thief.
5. False. Yeah, and Vito Corleone just sold olive oil.
6. False. She actually planned their robberies and wound up dying with Freddy in an FBI shootout.
7. True. Bonnie Parker and Clyde Barrow knocked over gas stations and small banks, rarely getting more than $1,000 per job.
8. False. He personally captured gangster Alvin Karpis, who had dared the FBI chief to come and get him.
9. True, according to author Mario Puzo, who was never able to get his famous line into any of the three *Godfather* movies.
10. True. Thomas Howard, a reporter for the *New York Daily News* (naturally), sneaked a camera strapped to his ankle into the electrocution chamber and snapped the gruesome results.

Answers

Are You Sure? (Answers)

1. c
2. b
3. a
4. b
5. b
6. c (duh)
7. b
8. a
9. c
10. c

Seven Wonders of the World (Answers)

Answers: 1-3-6-8-10-12-14. Of the seven, only the pyramids survive.

Formulas (Answers)

1. f
2. e
3. d
4. g
5. c
6. a
7. b

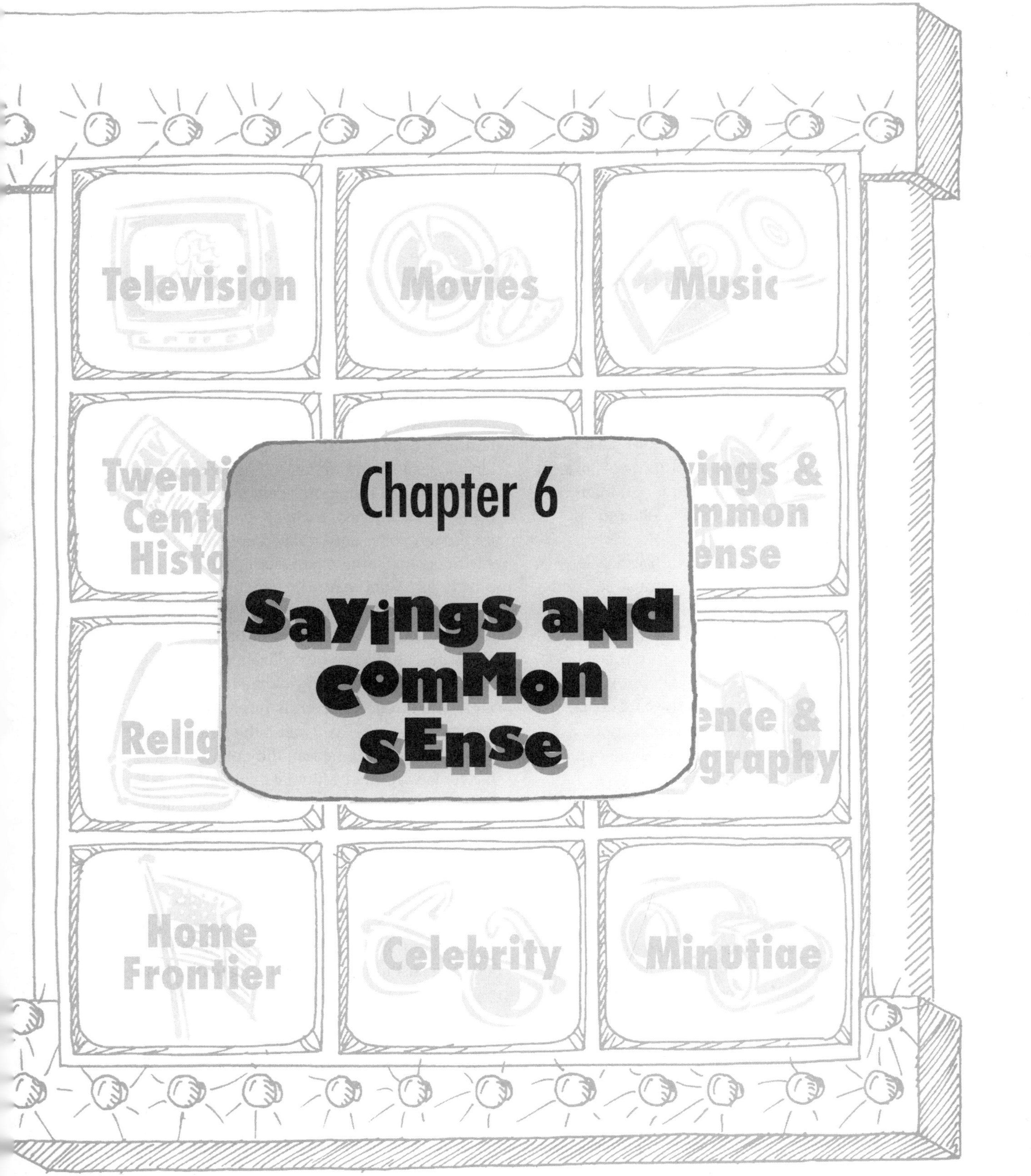

Chapter 6

Sayings and comMon sEnse

Television

Movies

Music

Twentieth Century History

Sayings & Common Sense

Religion

Science & Geography

Home Frontier

Celebrity

Minutiae

There is no greater proclamation of humanity than humankind's ability to pass along culture from one generation to the next. Salmon return to their birthplace to spawn; wolves train in packs to pick off caribou; even the microscopic planarian worm has been discovered to pass along conditioned responses. But these are all instincts that are triggered by biological catalysts. Only human beings seek to expand their knowledge, adapt to new situations, and then both represent it and interpret it so that their offspring can benefit and, beyond that, grow.

Culture is handed down in a variety of ways. On a mechanical level, it must be fixed in a tangible form such as writing, diagram, numerals, audio tape, film, video, or digital storage/retrieval system. But culture truly reveals the human condition when it is expressed on a less concrete basis. People even use a separate lexicon for this: poetry, fiction, fine art, dance, music, and the oral storytelling tradition of drama.

Caught somewhere in the middle—that is, the bastard offspring of technology and aesthetics—are the mass media. Today, more than ever, the mass media are assigned the tasks both of recording humankind's chronicles and interpreting its soul. The heady job is not without its liabilities; history is strewn with the bodies of messengers who lost their lives because the recipient didn't cotton to the news they brought.

This is why it is not just the passing along of culture that is important but the *accurate* passing along of culture. Just as the fires of war have been fanned by rumor, so have whole populations been crushed by ignorance. This responsibility falls upon everybody who has ever told a racist or an ethnic joke, made a sexist or homophobic comment, repeated an unfounded personal rumor, or, in general, allowed stupidity to go unchallenged.

And nowhere does that risk run greater than in the area of human experience that we benignly call "common sense." "Common sense is not so common," ventured Voltaire in his 1764 *Dictionnaire Philosophique*. Were the French writer alive today, he would probably make the same observation, even though, as Matthew Arnold ventured, a century after Voltaire, "The free-thinking of one age is the common sense of the next."

Is it? The history of civilization is the process of old doctrines yielding to new ones. The torch, however, is rarely passed voluntarily. Whether you call it the generation gap or a political upheaval, the cold truth is that society advances funeral by funeral. Revolutions—whether in government, morality, or science—always start at the bottom, and they are never without casualties. Change is constant, seldom forgiving, always frightening. People do not surrender their convictions without a fight.

How is that possible? Why do human beings persist in holding onto long-outmoded ways of thinking? We acknowledge this with a glossary of words, all of which describe beliefs that we're not all that sure about: *aphorism, adage, catchphrase, saying, slogan, motto, maxim, prevailing wisdom, popular belief, platitude, verity, truism, old wives' tale, rule of thumb, myth,* and *parable.*

On the other hand, there's only one word for *truth,* and that was it.

The battle is fought in the arena of popular culture with a variety of weapons. Sometimes the instrument can be as gentle as a fable that tries to teach a moral point. At other times it can be an insidious stereotype. On occasion, it can embody both at once, such as the now-discredited children's tale *Little Black Sambo,* where our affection for one value can blind us to the harmfulness of the other.

This chapter is about the stories and myths that illustrate the human condition, from comic books to commercials and mottos to "Mommy Mommy" jokes. It's a wide selection that asks the question, "How do we learn about ourselves?" and raises one more: "Is it the truth?"

The answers are made more complicated by the growing relationship between culture and commerce. Put another way, there's money to be made by selling things to people who are, shall we say, not encouraged to learn much about the product. Whether it's the government trying to silence Daniel Ellsberg for releasing the *Pentagon Papers* in 1971 or Texas beef producers suing Oprah Winfrey for dissing hamburger in 1998, the establishment has a way of discouraging open discussion of its activities. What's so absurd is that the bottom line isn't truth, it's money.

Popular culture and commerce are driven by humankind's desire to protect its beliefs. Relinquishing them is tantamount to admitting error for having chosen them in the first place. Ask any advertising expert to name the toughest part of his/her job and he'll/she'll admit that it's getting consumers to switch brands. Funny how people can be loyal to a cigarette but not each other. Perhaps that's why the 1985 fiasco over "New Coke" replacing "Classic Coke" drew such attention; at least it explains why America refused to embrace the metric system.

Popular myths die an even less willing death. To this day there are folks who insist that Elvis is alive, that Walt Disney is frozen, that the moon landing was a hoax, that Nixon didn't know about Watergate, or that OJ is innocent. And those are just urban legends; religious dogmas die even harder, when they die at all.

Why do fables endure? At their most benign, there is comfort to be found in oft-told tales. What's the harm in telling a child that Santa Claus is real or that it's the Tooth Fairy who leaves a quarter under the pillow? On the other hand, when uncorrected myths lead to discrimination, accusation, lynching, or genocide (as they have in the past), it's time to intervene.

Trivia is neutral about such things. For as much as knowledge expanded during the twentieth century and however much it corrected misconceptions held during the nineteenth, Trivia served as a nonjudgmental signpost along the way. The morality associated with getting a sexually transmitted disease, for example, is open to debate, but not the fact that you don't catch it from toilet seats. Whether Stan Lee or Steve Ditko should be called "Spider-Man's daddy" is an ongoing discussion among comic book fans, but none of them can say that the first time Spidey appeared wasn't in *Amazing Fantasy* magazine in August 1962. No one really knows why females were considered bad luck aboard a ship, but no one can argue that women suffered for years because of this superstition.

Besides, folklore is a reflection of the times. Before kings grasped the principle that the earth revolves around the sun, astronomers who asserted as much were made to suffer. Before medical researchers discovered that germs cause disease, doctors thought the body's own "ill humours" created sickness spontaneously. The Trivia behind such events is less about the science than the scientist (Galileo and Pasteur, respectively).

What distinguishes the homey maxims and mottos in this chapter is not that they are so entertaining but that for years many of them were taken seriously enough to raise issues of life or death. Be warned: Today's wisecrack may have been yesterday's ethic. As Composer John Cage says, "I can't understand why people are frightened of new ideas. I'm frightened of old ones."

The ideas in this chapter are both old and new, but they represent a palette of human thought. Most reside in that repository of societal wisdom called "popular culture," whether the first lines of classic books or the last word on Spider-Man. There are light bulb jokes, age-old falsehoods, and superstitions—all of them forming a snapshot of a society that loves holding onto its dreams, even after waking up.

Get a Life: Joel Chandler Harris

Question: Who was Joel Chandler Harris, and what is his contribution to American folklore?

Answer: Although he is not well known now, Joel Chandler Harris became famous in the late nineteenth century through his literary creation, Uncle Remus. Harris was also a pioneer in what has come to be known as "the oral tradition," particularly stories told by African-American slaves.

Harris is said to have based the fictitious Uncle Remus on a man called Harbert, a slave on the Turnwold plantation, owned by Joseph Addison Turner, a Georgia newspaper publisher for whom Harris worked as an apprentice printer in the years before the Civil War. He became so enamored of Harbert's fables about Brer Rabbit, Brer Fox, Brer Bear, and tar babies—all of which described ways in which black slaves subtly outwitted their white owners—that he wrote them down. His tales were first seen in the pages of Turner's The Countryman newspaper, then in the Atlanta Constitution, where he went to work in 1876. His first collection was called Uncle Remus: His Songs and Sayings and was published in 1881.

From his tidy Atlanta home, "The Wren's Nest" (located at 1050 Gordon Street, S.W. Atlanta, Georgia), Chandler continued recording the folk narratives of Southern blacks, presenting them through the eyes of a naive white child who encounters them during visits to the plantation slave quarters. Despite challenges, Harris always insisted that he didn't make them up but only preserved what he actually heard in the rich dialects of the storytellers.

Remus's lovable "creatures" charmed many a reader, including a young Walt Disney, who encountered them as a boy growing up in Marceline, Missouri. It was through Disney's efforts that Remus was immortalized by actor James Baskett in the 1946 film, Song of the South. The film—a moving combination of song, animation, and live action—is seldom screened (and is not available on home video in America) because of its tolerant depiction of antebellum slave life.

Ironically, Harris, who appropriated Harbert's stories, was himself eclipsed by Disney.

Quiz: I Christen Thee . . .

People who discover comets are permitted to name them after themselves, but when it comes to inventions or political movements, the naming is often done without the consent of the one who kicked it off. Identify the actual person behind the following:

1. Crapper
2. Frisbee®
3. Bowdlerize
4. Sandwich
5. McCarthyism
6. Reaganomics
7. Polaroid® Land Camera
8. Hobson's Choice
9. Guillotine
10. Oscar®

Quiz: Opening Lines

"Start at the beginning," the Cheshire cat said to Alice, "and when you get to the end, stop." Good advice, too. Name the novels that began with these lines and the authors who wrote them:

1. When Gregor Samsa woke up one morning from unsettling dreams, he found himself changed in his bed into a monstrous vermin.
2. On top of everything, the cancer wing was Number 13.
3. You better not never tell nobody but God.
4. Though I haven't ever been on the screen I was brought up in pictures.
5. In my younger and more vulnerable years my father gave me some advice that I've been turning over in my mind ever since.
6. "What's it going to be then, eh?"
7. It was love at first sight.
8. It was a bright, cold day in April and the clocks were striking thirteen.
9. You don't know about me without you have read a book by the name of *The Adventures of Tom Sawyer*; but that ain't no matter.
10. I went back to the Devon School not long ago, and found it looking oddly newer than when I was a student there fifteen years before.
11. I heard this story from one who had no business to tell it to me, or to any other.
12. It was the best of times, it was the worst of times . . .

Stan Freberg

If you laughed (on purpose) at a TV commercial in the '70s and '80s, chances are it was made by Stan Freberg. The multitalented, mega-award-winning Freberg is the comic genius behind such memorable ad campaigns as these:

- The Lone Ranger and Tonto for Jeno's Pizza Rolls
- Ann Miller in a full Hollywood tap-dance number for Heinz Great American Soups
- Grocer Survival Kits for Kaiser Quilted Aluminum Foil
- "Eight Great Tomatoes in that Little Bitty Can" (Contadina Tomato Paste)
- "Today the Pits—Tomorrow the Wrinkles" (Sunsweet Prunes)
- "Who Listens to Radio?" (Bekins Movers)

Freberg is also the master humorist behind the bestselling comedy records "St. George and the Dragonet," "Little Blue Riding Hood," "Sh-Boom," "Day-O/Banana Boat Song," "The Flackman and Reagan," and the all-time classic comedy album "Stan Freberg Presents the United States of America," all for Capital Records.

He has performed voices for numerous Warner Bros. cartoons and countless radio shows, was the original "Cecil" in Bob Clampett's landmark children's TV series *The Adventures of Beany and Cecil,* has been a network commentator for CBS radio, and is the author of such books as *A Child's Garden of Freberg* and the half-autobiography *It Only Hurts When I Laugh.* His radio commentaries are heard on over 130 stations.

Born in Los Angeles in 1926 to the Reverend Victor Freberg, a Baptist minister, and the former Evelyn Dorothy Twyla Conner, Freberg early in life developed a passion for entertaining others, usually in the form of self-produced satires. He performed one-man shows in public school and at home and, in his teen years, ventured into Hollywood (from Pasadena, where the family had moved) to break into acting. Almost by accident he stumbled into a born-again talent agency that set him up with an audition for Warner Bros. cartoons. Relying on what he calls "on the job training"—basically lying about his skills in order to land the job and then hurriedly practicing them—he quickly provided character voices, accents, and animal noises for the best and brightest animators. Working alongside Mel Blanc, June Foray, Daws Butler, Paul Frees, and others, Freberg—or, rather, his vocal cords—left their impressions on scores of cartoons and radio shows beginning in the 1940s.

At about the same time, he joined a traveling orchestra as a combination guitarist and comedian. That he couldn't play the guitar didn't faze him (more "on the job training"); the fact that he was a terrific comedian made up for it.

Settling back in LA, it was cartoon director Robert Clampett who invited Freberg and voice actor Daws Butler to try their hands—rather, four hands—at television, with *Beany and Cecil,* on KTLA-TV in Los Angeles. The chaos grew as Freberg wrote and performed the nascent children's TV show and continued to do voice work to make financial ends meet.

A series of immensely popular comedy records followed (an outgrowth of a soap opera parody he created for one of his orchestra comedy spots), which naturally led him into movie roles and television guest appearances. A regular network show, however, proved tougher. The problem? He was irreverent, something a satirist is supposed to be by definition but also something that drives corporate brass up the flagpole, so to speak.

So there's no accounting, therefore, for why the advertising agency for Contadina Tomato Paste called on the iconoclastic Freberg to design a campaign for their product, whose sales were slipping. But they did, and the overwhelming success of his catchy "Eight Great Tomatoes in that Little Bitty Can" approach opened a new era in America for funny commercials.

Freberg describes his philosophy as "more truth than the client had in mind." When Kaiser Quilted Aluminum Foil brought him aboard, he learned that the reason their figures were down was because grocery stores didn't stock the product. So he designed a "grocer's survival kit" and sent the public into stores across the country to ask why they couldn't find this great product on their grocers' shelves. As a result, Kaiser picked up thousands of new outlets.

He once made sure that everybody in America knew that the H. J. Heinz company had a product called "Great American Soups" by filming a gala production number with tap-dancing star Ann Miller and dozens of chorus girls on a Hollywood sound stage. And he established Jeno's Pizza Rolls as one of the most popular party appetizers with a series of inventive TV spots ranging from the Lone Ranger and Tonto (Clayton Moore and Jay Silverheels) munching on them, to a fiery Italian actress fighting with the cameraman to focus on her instead of the package ("Eef you show the box, I keel you!").

Today Stan Freberg and his company, Freberg, Ltd., continue to design advertising campaigns that challenge industry ideas. He starred his son, Donavan, in a series of long-form TV spots for Encyclopedia Britannica that makes fun of long-form TV spots ("Now you're gonna flash the 800 number, aren't you? Yup, there it is."). Through it all, Freberg continues to call life as he sees it, which is usually from an angle nobody else has ever considered. Or will think of any other way, afterward.

Married (Donna) with two children (Donavan and Donna Jean), Freberg creates in and dwells in Beverly Hills.

Manners vs. Superstition

- In the Middle Ages it was believed that demons would jump down our throats when we yawned to take possession of our souls, and for this reason we cover our mouths—not out of politeness (although it has come to mean that) but out of superstition.
- We "knock on wood" before making a wish or hopeful statement because, in the past, it was believed that harmful spirits dwelled in hollow trees and would wreck our plans if they overheard them. Knocking on the wood supposedly scared them away.
- We shake hands upon meeting one another to demonstrate that we are not carrying weapons in them.
- The word *good-bye* is a contraction, over the centuries, of the expression *God be with ye.*

PTM: Stan Lee

As editor and chief writer for Marvel Comics, Stan Lee was the cocreator (with artists including Jack Kirby, Steve Ditko, John Romita, and John Buscema) of Spider-Man®, The Incredible Hulk®, The Fantastic Four®, *the* X-Men®, *the* Silver Surfer®, *and their colleagues who inhabit the Marvel™ Universe. Since inspiring the "Silver Age" of comics, Stan has continued to grow; he now heads Marvel Films and has expanded into the Internet. Although comic books have undergone numerous challenges and changes since they were introduced in the early 1930s, they only acquired respect in the years that Stan was at the helm . . . and the typewriter. Here he reveals the rarefied process.*

By Stan Lee

Creating a comic character is either a very simple thing or a very complex thing. A writer might have an idea for a character, contact an artist and develop it, and then present it to an editor. Or the editor may have the idea for the character, call the writer or perhaps call the artist, and have them design the character. If you're doing superhero books, you have to create the character's powers and have an origin for them.

The design is primarily the artist's job, but very often the writer will say, "This is what I want the character to look like, specifically," or the writer may say, as I did in many cases, "This is the kind of character I have in mind; now you go and draw whatever it suggests to you." With someone like a Jack Kirby, Steve Ditko, John Buscema, or John Romita, these people are so brilliant that I would never deign to tell them how to design a character. I would just say what type of character I was looking for and what the personality was, and then turn the artist loose, and I'd get something much better than I ever dreamed of.

When it came to writing and drawing the actual pages, I devised the so-called "Marvel Method" in the 1960s, out of desperation. In those days I was writing all the stories. I might have been writing for Jack Kirby when Steve Ditko came by the offices and needed a story. Since these men were all freelancers and got paid by the page, if they weren't drawing, they weren't earning a salary. So I couldn't say to Steve, "You'll have to wait till I finish Jack's story," because that might have taken another day. So I would say, "Look, Steve, I don't have a script for you, but this is what I'd like the story to be." I wouldn't give him a complete story; I'd give him a quick synopsis of a plot. Steve and Jack and most of our other artists were so talented that all they needed was just a suggestion of what the story should be, and they would draw it themselves and put in more detail than I could have thought up. Then they would bring the boards to me, and I could see the action and the expression on the person's face and write the dialogue to suit. Nine times out of ten, the way the artist visualizes a story is better than what could be scripted. So by going back and forth, I could juggle several stories at once, and that became known as the "Marvel Method." It started out just as an expediency, but turned out to be a superior method, and it is still in use today.

Spider-Man came out of a desire I had held to do a strip that would break all the rules: a strip that would feature a teenager as the star, a strip in which the main character would lose as often as he would win, a strip in which none of the relationships would go according to formula.

I remembered a pulp magazine hero from my preteen years called *The Spider—Master of Men*. The Spider wore a slouch hat and a finger ring which, when he punched a foe in the face, would leave an impression of an arachnid. As far as I can remember, The Spider had no super powers, but his name intrigued me, and that was enough.

I told Marvel's publisher, Martin Goodman, that I wanted to try a tongue-in-cheek strip about a spider-man. Martin's reaction was natural enough; he thought I'd lost my marbles. People didn't like spiders, he said, but he eventually gave in and allowed us to introduce Spider-Man in the final issue of *Amazing Fantasy*, a magazine that had just been canceled.

I invented Peter Parker, a high school student beset with typical teenage problems, whose life was turned upside down when he was bitten by a radioactive spider during a class field trip and became "Spider-Man." The tone of the strip came out of Peter acquiring the abilities of an arachnid without losing any of the liabilities of being a kid.

Spidey was probably the first superhero to wear his neuroses on his sleeve. We gave him a superpower, but we let him have all the worries and problems that any normal teenager would have. He'd have dandruff, acne, ingrown toenails; he'd worry about dates with girls, making a living, family problems—which could encompass everything and anything.

The only thing he would never have would be a teenage sidekick. You know, there's probably nothing wrong with teenage sidekicks, but I've always hated them. I used to feel that if I were a superhero and had a superpower, why would I want to hang around with some teenage kid all day? I mean, at the very least, people might talk. Besides, Peter himself was a teenager!

The strip was a one-time gambit, and that was supposed to be that. Well, within a few months the sales department reported that Spider-Man was a sales sensation, so we gave him his own book, *The Amazing Spider-Man*, as soon as we could create it.

Having any sort of sales sensation was rare in those days. Before our books really began to sell, I must say neither I nor any of the artists or writers thought we were accomplishing anything really significant or that we were reviving a dying field or anything like that. When we heard that the books sold well, we thought we were pretty lucky and let it go at that.

Our very first big hit was *The Fantastic Four*. One of the funny things that happened when we started publishing *The Fantastic Four*, followed by *Spider-Man* and then *The Incredible Hulk*, was that, up until that time, we rarely, if ever, got any fan mail at Marvel. If we did, we would take that letter and hang it on the bulletin board, excitedly exclaiming, "Hey, look, we got a letter from somebody!" But right after *The Fantastic Four* was published, we actually began to get fan letters, and it was the most exciting thing. After *Spider-Man* and *The Incredible Hulk*, the trickle became a torrent.

Says You

Is there truth in the old adages repeated by farmers, sailors, and other professions prone to superstition? Apparently there's more to them than meets the skeptical ear.

1. "Red Sky at morning, sailor take warning; red sky at night, sailor's delight." The morning sun glows red because the atmosphere refracts its rays toward the red end of the spectrum. But if it's a cloudy day, we can't see the light, which means that there may be bad weather coming from the east. A red glow at sunset, however, suggests clear weather coming from the east for the next day. Or so they say.

2. "Dog Days of Summer." Those last few hot days before autumn (in the northern hemisphere) have nothing to do with canines. They have to do with the ancient Romans who noticed that Sirius, the "dog star," glowed brightly overhead whenever such weather occurred.

3. "It's going to be a harsh winter; squirrels are gathering nuts and animals are growing fur as never before." The astonishing *Farmer's Almanac* notwithstanding, there is no way to predict weather patterns more than a week into the future. Meteorologists can sketch general trends based upon past data, but nothing more specific. As for the *Farmer's Almanac*, its folk value surpasses its scientific usefulness.

4. "Women are bad luck aboard a ship." If this was the case, the Love Boat would be in dry dock. Supposedly—in an earlier maritime era—it was thought that women would distract all-male crews from their duties. In such a circumstance, it seems that the bad luck would probably affect the women more than the ship. If the argument seems a little familiar, that may be because it is still used by the military today.

5. "Chicken soup is a cure for the common cold." There are two schools of thought on this tradition. One is that chicken soup may trigger an enzyme in the body that fights off the cold infection. The other explanation is that when you have a cold, you stay home in bed and your mother stands over you while you finish the soup. It's the rest and personal attention more than the chicken soup that does the job.

Actor Superstitions

Perhaps because nobody knows what creates fame or how to preserve it, actors tend to be extraordinarily superstitious. Whether big star or bit player, most are prone to the same rituals. Here are some of them:

1. "The Scottish Play." Whether by tradition or affectation, actors will seldom refer to Shakespeare's *MacBeth* by its real name. They will always call it "the Scottish play," because of the unlucky history of flops and mishaps associated over the years with productions of the drama.

2. "Merde." Scatological references are said to bring good luck before a performance. The only thing that brings bad luck is saying "good luck."

3. "Break a leg." Since wishing somebody good luck is considered bad luck, wishing somebody bad luck is tantamount to wishing them the best. Therefore, telling somebody to break a leg (while hoping that he/she really won't) is doing him/her a favor. For obvious reasons, this does not apply when said by an understudy.

4. "No whistling in the dressing room." If this is done accidentally, the only cure is to run out of the dressing room, turn around three times, say "merde," and return to the dressing room.

5. "Don't tell me who's in the audience." Although actors may sneak a look at the audience through a peephole in the curtain (there's one in every theatre), it makes them nervous if they are told when friends or important people are waiting to watch them perform.

6. "Don't look at me backstage before a show." Apparently this only applies to Diana Ross.

7. "It's magic time." This line is spoken by Jack Lemmon to himself before he goes on stage or does a "take" on film. Rituals can be comforting (and, in Lemmon's case, frequently inspiring).

8. "Darling, you were wonderful!" If you go to see a friend in a play, you are obligated to go backstage afterward. If you go backstage afterward, you are obligated to say how much you liked the performance. If you didn't like the performance, you are obligated to lie.

9. "There are no small parts, only small actors." True enough, but according to the late Laurence Olivier, "Being a small-part actor is not a bad thing, but after a while they think of you in terms of a small-part actor's *salary*, and *that* is a bad thing."

10. "No dogs or actors allowed." Yes, well, times have changed since the days when this sign was posted on boarding houses and restaurants. Not only was it rude, but the billing was terrible.

Quiz: Famous (Mis)Quotes

Even though everyone knows that Bogart never said *exactly*, "Play it again, Sam" in *Casablanca* (q.v. Chapter 2), few people are aware of how many other so-called well-known quotes we routinely screw up. What's wrong with the following?

1. "Alas, poor Yorick. I knew him well, Horatio." (Shakespeare, *Hamlet*)
2. "Under the spreading chestnut tree the village smithy stands. The smith, a mighty man is he, with large and brawny hands." (Longfellow, *The Village Blacksmith*)
3. "The unkindest cut of all." (Shakespeare, *Julius Caesar*)
4. "Music hath charms to soothe the savage beast." (Congreve, *The Mourning Bride*)
5. "I have nothing to offer but blood, sweat and tears." (Churchill, speech to House of Commons)
6. "Elementary, my dear Watson." (Sherlock Holmes)
7. "That's one small step for man, one giant leap for Mankind." (Armstrong, moon landing)
8. "God rest you, merry gentlemen." (Traditional Christmas carol)
9. "Methinks the lady doth protest too much." (Shakespeare, *Hamlet*)

Quiz: Word Origins

Who put the *bop* in the bop-she-bop-bop? More importantly, who put the *arch* in *architect*? Modern language is a fascinating amalgam of ancient words whose form and meaning have changed over the centuries. Try to deduce the origins of these commonplace words. (By the way, *architect* is a combination of the Greek *archos* for "primary" and *tekton* for "builder," making "primary builder.")

1. Pusillanimous
2. Confident
3. Aspic
4. Delegate
5. Tantalize
6. Utopia
7. Aggravate
8. Blindfold
9. Gymnastics
10. Golf

Quiz: Aphorisms

"A stitch in time saves nine." "The apple doesn't fall far from the tree." "One good turn deserves another." "As ye sew so shall ye reap." Yadda yadda. Aphorisms are just observations that are true more often than not, but—to quote one that happens to be wrong—"it's the exception that proves the rule." (Think about it: If there's an exception, then the rule is *disproved*.) Mottos come from folk tales, scripture, fortune cookies, and other reliable sources. Many of those we cherish today come from Aesop. Match the following durable maxims with the Aesop's fable that coined them:

1. "I can't help myself—it's my nature."
2. "Appearances can be deceiving"
3. "Slow and steady wins the race."
4. "Don't count your chickens until they are hatched."
5. "No act of kindness, however small, is ever wasted."
6. "Familiarity breeds contempt."
7. "A crust eaten in peace is better than a banquet eaten in anxiety."
8. "Any excuse will serve a tyrant."
9. "God helps those who help themselves."
10. "In unity there is strength."

a. "The Tortoise and the Hare"
b. "The Fox and the Lion"
c. "The Milkmaid and Her Pail"
d. "The City Mouse and the Country Mouse"
e. "The Bundle of Sticks"
f. "Hercules and the Wagoner"
g. "The Wolf and the Lamb"
h. "The Lion and the Mouse"
i. "The Wolf in Sheep's Clothing"
j. "The Scorpion and the Frog"

Mommy Mommy Jokes

No one knows where "Mommy Mommy" jokes came from (or cares, but that's neither here nor there). They appeared sometime in the mid-1950s and, surprisingly, have not reappeared in the way that elephant jokes, light bulb jokes, and assorted ethnic slurs have. Most "Mommy Mommy" jokes have the cadence of advertising lines ("More Park's Sausages, Mom!"), which may help explain their origins. They are of sociological interest because they presume that Mommy is home tending the household. Oh, and they are also sick. Do any of these ring bells?

1. Kid: "Mommy, Mommy, it spells my name."
   Mommy: "Shut up and flush the toilet."

2. Kid: "Mommy, Mommy, I don't want to run around in circles."
   Mommy: "Shut up or I'll nail the other foot to the floor."

3. Kid: "Mommy, Mommy, Daddy's on fire!"
   Mommy: "Shut up and pass the marshmallows."

4. Kid: "Mommy, Mommy, can I play with Grandma?"
   Mommy: "No, Junior, you've already dug her up twice this week."

5. Kid: "Mommy, Mommy, I don't want to go to Europe."
   Mommy: "Shut up and row the boat."

6. Kid: "Mommy, Mommy, Daddy just got run over by a steam roller."
   Mommy: "Don't bother carrying him in, dear, just slide him under the door."

Quiz: Moron Jokes

Until America's anonymous humor mill started targeting people of ethnic extraction for defamation, children of a more innocent time told "moron" jokes. "Moron" jokes were merely updates of "fool" or "simpleton" jokes going back centuries, albeit with the dubious charm of backhanding people with learning disabilities. They survive as examples of preteen humor. In the interest of being politically correct, *dufus* will be substituted for *moron, fool, simpleton*, etc.

1. Why did the dufus tiptoe past the medicine cabinet?
2. Why did the dufus close her eyes when she opened the medicine cabinet?
3. Why did the dufus throw the clock out the window?
4. Why couldn't the dufus make ice cubes?
5. What happened after the dufus locked his keys in the car?

Quiz: Light Bulb Jokes

Light bulb jokes may be the perfect joke. They ingeniously nudge the foibles of a particular group without skewing an individual member of that group; everybody knows what a light bulb is and how to change one; and the majority are clean. Fill in the punch lines of these:

1. How many Teamsters does it take to change a light bulb?
2. How many New York cab drivers does it take to change a light bulb?
3. How many feminists does it take to change a light bulb?
4. How many psychiatrists does it take to change a light bulb?
5. How many film studio executives does it take to change a light bulb?
6. How many pre-law students does it take to change a light bulb?
7. How many surrealists does it take to change a light bulb?
8. How many Jewish mothers does it take to change a light bulb?
9. How many northern Californians does it take to change a light bulb?
10. How many Zen masters does it take to change a light bulb?
11. How many college girls does it take to change a light bulb?
12. How many WASPs does it take to change a light bulb?

Quiz: Hey Myth-ter

When the Firesign Theatre recorded an album in the 1970s titled *Everything You Know Is Wrong,* how were they to know that certain myths would turn out to be remarkably persistent? Which of the following commonly held beliefs are true?

1. The female praying mantis must bite the head off her male mate in order to complete the pro-creative process.
2. There is no chalk in blackboard chalk.
3. The expression "drink like a fish" is inaccurate because fish don't drink.
4. You can burn the American flag in protest but cannot sew a torn one to save it.
5. No two snowflakes are alike.
6. Despite their reputation, bulls can't see the color red.
7. Eve fed an apple to Adam in the Garden of Eden.
8. After Prohibition was repealed in 1933, distillers introduced the "fifth" and sold it at the same price as pre-Prohibition quarts in order to distract customers from the increase.
9. More people commit suicide during the holiday season.

Get a Life: Fredric Wertham

Question: Who was Fredric Wertham, and what did he accomplish in the 1950s that no mother could match?

Answer: In 1954 Fredric Wertham, a psychiatrist with the New York City Department of Hospitals, published *Seduction of the Innocent*, a book by which he sought to prove that comic books corrupted young minds and would lead to the destruction of America.

Wertham's theories were based upon observation rather than reputable science and led him to erroneously link comic books with the incidence of young men being sent to reform school. His logic may have been flawed, but his timing wasn't; coming in the wake of the '50s Red scare, the public was primed to "do something" about their wayward children.

The resultant uproar inspired hearings in April of 1954 before the Senate Subcommittee to Investigate Juvenile Delinquency and, thereafter, the implementation of the self-regulatory "Comics Code" by fearful publishers. What is less often reported is that the uproar was inspired, in part, by mainstream comic book publishers in a concerted effort to force maverick *Entertaining Comics* publisher William Gaines out of business (and they did, too, right into inventing *Mad* magazine).

"It was a very easy thing to sell to parents who couldn't control their kids," explains writer/historian Mark Evanier. "Well, parents are *never* able to control their kids. So we had the banning of horror comics and crime comics, then we had the laundering of what was left. And, of course, we all know that there was no juvenile delinquency after that."

Wertham, in his later years, recanted his observations, but, by then, the Golden Age of comics had been well and truly destroyed. As for the reference to mothers, didn't every boy's mother toss out his comic book collections when he went away to school?

I Christen Thee . . . (Answers)

1. Thomas Crapper (yes, it's true) actually invented the flush toilet. In the 1800s Crapper was a Royal plumbing engineer who devised a way to run water through a commode to rinse away waste and then (this is the important part) cut off the water flow once the job was done.
2. In the 1870s Bridgeport, Connecticut, baker William Russell Frisbee produced a pie tin that Yale students in the 1940s discovered they could sail through the air. Since then, Frisbee® has become the aggressively protected trademark toy of the Wham-O Manufacturing Corp.
3. Thomas Bowdler was a self-appointed censor of the 1800s who cut the "naughty bits" out of works of literature he deemed offensive.
4. The Earl of Sandwich popularized placing slices of bread around a piece of meat, thereby preventing the soiling of one's hands with grease.
5. Senator Joseph R. McCarthy (R-Wisconsin) had his name applied to any hysterical accusation, usually false, that damages someone by innuendo rather than fact. McCarthy was America's most strident anti-Communist in the 1950s; he insisted on pursuing suspected Reds at a time when Communism was perfectly legal.
6. It was Ronald Reagan whose name was applied to his peculiar economic philosophy, which complained about high taxes while exponentially increasing taxpayers' national debt (this was also called "Voodoo Economics").
7. Dr. Edwin Land developed the self-developing camera, which works equally well on the sea, in the air, and, of course, on the land.
8. A Hobson's choice—in effect, a choice that has no favorable outcome—is named in honor of Thomas Hobson, a horse trader with the habit of not offering his customers a choice at all.
9. The French beheading device was not invented by Dr. Joseph Ignace Guillotin, as is often thought, but was named after him when he campaigned so fiercely for its use as an alternative to the, er, "hit and miss" approach then popular in France. It was adopted as the official capital punisher in 1792.
10. The Academy Award statuette was designed in 1927 by Cedric Gibbons, MGM's art director, as an award of merit, but it was cast in a more informal light when an employee saw it and remarked, "Oh, it looks just like my Uncle Oscar."

Opening Lines (Answers)

1. Franz Kafka, *The Metamorphosis*
2. Alexander Solzhenitsyn, *The Cancer Ward*
3. Alice Walker, *The Color Purple*
4. F. Scott Fitzgerald, *The Last Tycoon*
5. F. Scott Fitzgerald, *The Great Gatsby*
6. Anthony Burgess, *A Clockwork Orange*
7. Joseph Heller, *Catch-22*
8. George Orwell, *1984*
9. Mark Twain, *The Adventures of Huckleberry Finn*
10. John Knowles, *A Separate Peace*
11. Edgar Rice Burroughs, *Tarzan of the Apes*
12. Charles Dickens, *A Tale of Two Cities*

Famous (Mis)Quotes (Answers)

1. There is no *well* before *Horatio*.
2. The correct word is *sinewy*. *Brawny* comes in the next sentence, "And the muscles on his brawny arms . . ."
3. Mark Antony said Brutus administered the *most* unkindest cut of all to Caesar.
4. It should be a *savage breast*.
5. When Sir Winston Churchill first spoke the phrase in 1940, he said, "I have nothing to offer but blood and toil, tears and sweat." He later misquoted himself, reasoning that "blood, sweat and tears" sounded better. Either way, he got it from Henry James's novel *The Bostonians* (and not the horn-heavy 1960s rock group!).
6. Believe it or not, Sherlock Holmes never says "Elementary, my dear Watson" in any of Sir Arthur Conan Doyle's stories. It was invented for the movie series starring Basil Rathbone.
7. Neil Armstrong actually said "for a man," but the syllable was garbled in transmission from the lunar surface, and he has been misquoted since 1969.
8. The comma is in the wrong place. It should be "God rest you merry, gentlemen," meaning "take it easy." And *you* is sometimes written *ye*.
9. It's "The lady doth protest too much, methinks." And *protest* doesn't mean "complain," it means "assert," as in "she's being really pushy about this point, I think."

Word Origins (Answers)

1. *Pusillanimous*: *Pusillus* means small; *animus* is the mind. Together they mean small of mind, or timid.
2. *Confident* means "assured." It combines *con*, meaning "with," and *fides*, meaning "faith."
3. The English word *aspic* takes its name from *aspis*, the Latin name for the snake (asp) that took the life of Egyptian Queen Cleopatra. What does a snake have to do with a cold mean jelly? Go ask the French.

4. Most often connected with politics, a *delegate* is one who is sent by the voters to represent them. It is drawn from *delegatus,* meaning "do," to go away from, and "lego," which means to "assign with a purpose."

5. The mythical god Tantalus offended the gods and was condemned to spend his days chin deep in a tree-shrouded lake whose water receded when he bent down to drink, and whose fruit-laden branches lifted out of his reach whenever he tried to eat. Tanualus became *tantalize.*

6. Long before it was applied to Shangri-La, *Utopia* was coined by Sir Thomas More in 1551 in his novel about an imaginary island of perfection. The Greek words *ou* for "not" and *topos* for "place" combine into "land of nowhere."

7. Although *aggravate* means to inflame or bother, it is historically formed from the Latin *ad* ("to") and *gravis* ("heavy"), meaning, more properly, "to burden." Nowadays it just means to bother somebody.

8. A *blindfold* is a mask tied around the eyes, and it derives from the Middle English word *blindfellen,* meaning "strike blind."

9. Believe it or not, the Olympic-level competition of *gymnastics* comes from the Greek word *gymnazo,* or "train naked," and its derivative *gymnos,* meaning solely "naked." Since ancient Olympic games were often run in the nude (as many TV Olympics-watchers wish they still were), it stuck.

10. The popular Scottish game of *golf* seems to have drawn its name from the Dutch *kolf,* Holland's name for the peculiar bent club that was used to goad the balls into the cup. As is known by those who don't appreciate its popularity, golf is also known as "a good walk spoiled."

Aphorisms (Answers)

1. j
2. i
3. a
4. c
5. h
6. b
7. d
8. g
9. f
10. e

Moron Jokes (Answers)

1. He didn't want to wake the sleeping pills.
2. She didn't want to see the Bayer Aspirin.

3. He wanted to see time fly.
4. He lost the recipe.
5. It took him two hours to get his family out.

Light Bulb Jokes (Answers)

1. Fifteen. You got a problem with that?
2. None of your friggin' business.
3. That's not funny.
4. One, but the bulb has to really want to change.
5. Does it have to be a light bulb?
6. Five: one to change it and four to pull the ladder out from under him.
7. The fish.
8. Don't bother; I'm fine sitting here in the dark.
9. Three: one to do it and two more to share the experience.
10. Two: one to change it and one *not* to change it.
11. That's *women,* and it's not funny, either.
12. Three: one to mix martinis, one to fix prices, and one to hire a member of a minority group to do the actual hands-on work.

Hey Myth-ter (Answers)

1. False. But she sometimes gets hungry *after* sex and, well, whatever's handy . . .
2. True. These days it's plaster of paris or a mixture of P.O.P. and gypsum.
3. True—the statement is inaccurate. Fish don't swallow water; they retain it from their food and from what passes through their mouths and gills. But water does not enter a fish's body through its stomach.
4. True and false, in that order. The First Amendment to the U.S. Constitution has been interpreted by the U.S. Supreme Court as allowing the burning of the American flag as an expression of free speech. The Flag Code (not codified until 1976) indeed allows for the mending, washing, and ironing of a torn flag.
5. False, from a statistical point of view, but who's going to prove it?
6. True. Like many animals, bulls see monochromatically. They react to the movement of the matador's cape, not its color.
7. False. According to Genesis 3:6, Eve fed Adam the fruit of the forbidden tree. Nothing specifies the type of fruit.
8. True
9. False. They just *want* to. According to the National Center for Health Statistics, April is the killer month, not December.

Chapter 7

ReliGiOn

Television

Movies

Music

Twentieth Century History

Sayings & Common Sense

Religion

Science & Geography

Home Frontier

Celebrity

Minutiae

Nothing is more sure to break up a dinner party than discussing politics or religion. This chapter is about the latter.

Even though most of the world's religions now believe in a single God, there is no shortage of wars fought over how to practice that belief. The current armageddon between fundamentalists (of all faiths) and secular humanists differs only in temporal context from those that have been fought in the past between pagans and Christians, infidels and crusaders, pluralists and monists, Pantheists and Atheists, and, who knows, hill people and plains people. (The larger question—why God would allow such blood to be shed in His name—is seldom discussed.)

This chapter won't deal with any of that. What do you think, we're crazy? Instead, this chapter will celebrate the names, dates, factoids, and symbols that define the indefinable: Faith. If people can't agree on religion, maybe they can agree on the names of the apostles; if the exact date of Christ's birth is not known, the dates of the more recent Kwanzaa are; if nobody has the last word on God, there are still some famous last words spoken by people before meeting Him.

Religion is more than a belief in a higher power. To billions of people, it is a way of life, a meaningful schemata for daily existence set down in holy writings meant to guide every activity from waking to sleeping. Some religions accord their adherents more freedom than do others; on the other hand, members of the more draconian sects insist that once

the element of choice is removed, they are more free to explore other things. Is the idle brain really the Devil's playground?

It does not demean religion to explore its trivia. After all, every house of worship is built of stone, wood, metal, and glass; the mortar is the people who come there to pray. And what does every child learn in parochial school as the foundation of faith but the names of the men (and, occasionally, the women) among the faithful. The Ten Commandments are God's laws revealed to humankind, but what are they? What are the books of the Bible, the *suras* of the Qur'an, or the gods of Ancient Rome?

The fascinating thing about religion is the way people believe theirs to be the only one that's valid, and throughout history they have demonstrated this passion by offering their lives. The fact that there are so many different religions around the world ought to raise the question of whose is right and whose is wrong. Fortunately, God doesn't take sides. Unfortunately, no general has ever fought a battle without insisting that God was riding with him—at least in theory.

Why does religion raise such ungodly fury in mortals? Has it inspired the confidence of correctness or the fear of doubt? Is there any reason "why bad things happen to good people" or does God merely "work in strange and mysterious ways"?—in other words, no matter what, people will never be able to understand.

That raises as important point (and one often cited by the anti-fundamentalists): Why would God create a human being who is capable of learning, then allow religions to inhibit that process? And that brings us to the atheists.

At its most basic, atheism commemorates the triumph of reason over religion, of fact over faith. The existence of atheism stands as an ongoing challenge that confounds some people and angers others. The quandary is best expressed in the parable about the two goldfish who, one day, were discussing the existence of the Almighty. Finally, one of the goldfish shrugged his fin and said to the other, "Oh yeah? Well, if there's no God, who changes the water?"

Say It Ain't So, Santa

Like Elvis, UFOs, and J. D. Salinger (all of whom seem to appear to everybody except reliable witnesses), Santa Claus has grown greater in legend than in reality. Now it's time to clear up a few misconceptions.

For starters, there's nothing about Santa Claus in the Holy Bible. In fact, the Bible is not even clear as to the exact birth date of Christ (many scholars estimate April 3, 6 BC) or when the Christmas celebration itself occurs.

Tradition holds that it is variously observed anywhere from December 25 to January 7. Not until AD 354 was the present December 25 formally adopted by Bishop Liberius of Rome, possibly to take advantage of the concurrent pagan celebration of winter solstice as a means of easing the transition to Christianity.

Saint Nicholas—or "Santa Claus" (mistranslated from his Dutch name, "Sint Nikolaus")—probably owes his origins not to an actual canonized saint but to a combination of pagan harvest rites and early Christian deeds. The man we now consider St. Nicholas was a fourth-century Bishop of Myra, in Asia Minor, who was a legendary gift-giver. (His bequest of three bags of gold to a nobleman in Parara is said to be the derivation of the sign of the pawnbroker.) Years later the bishop became associated with a December 6 children's holiday in Holland. The Dutch colonization of New York in the 1700s brought the tradition to America, and by the time Washington Irving wrote of it in 1809 (under his pseudonym Diedrich Knickerbocker), Saint Nicholas was firmly established.

Our modern notion of Santa as "chubby and plump, a right jolly old elf" comes from Clement C. Moore's description in his 1822 poem, *A Visit from St. Nicholas*, more popularly known as *The Night Before Christmas* (in which, incidentally, the name *Santa Claus* is never mentioned). Ironically, it was not Moore's writing but an 1863 drawing by cartoonist Thomas Nast that fixed the image in our minds. The red-and-white costume has nothing to do with Moore but is, instead, the remnant of an advertising campaign devised by the Coca-Cola company in the 1930s to link Christmas with their corporate colors and urging children to leave a Coke out where Santa could enjoy "the pause that refreshes" during chimney duty.

Finally, there really *was* a Virginia (as in "Yes, Virginia, there is a Santa Claus"). In 1897 young Virginia O'Hanlon wrote to journalist Francis Pharcellus Church asking if her friends were right to insist that St. Nick was imaginary. Church replied (in a *New York Sun* editorial) that Santa did, indeed, exist, adding that "ten times ten thousand years from now, he will continue to make glad the heart of childhood."

Quiz: Ye Gods

At the 1997 funeral of Princess Diana, her brother, Earl Spencer, noted with irony that she shared a name with Diana, Roman Goddess of the hunt, and, in the end, was hunted to death. How many of these other gods and goddesses (courtesy of pantheistic cultures) can you name?

1. War
2. Love
3. Wine
4. Son of Chief God
5. Messenger of the Gods
6. Sleep
7. Moon
8. Death
9. Oceans
10. Chief God of Olympus

Quiz: Banned Books

Which of the following books have been banned, at various times, from public libraries, schools, and stores, by local conservative religious groups?

1. *The Color Purple* by Alice Walker
2. *Go Ask Alice* by Anonymous
3. *Huckleberry Finn* by Mark Twain
4. *Of Mice and Men* by John Steinbeck
5. *Slaughterhouse-Five* by Kurt Vonnegut, Jr.
6. *I Know Why the Caged Bird Sings* by Maya Angelou
7. *Mein Kampf* by Adolf Hitler
8. *Ulysses* by James Joyce
9. *Our Bodies, Ourselves* by the Boston Women's Health Collective
10. *The Bell Jar* by Sylvia Plath

Quiz: Bible Details

1. "Blessed are the meek, for they shall inherit the earth" appears in which Gospel?
2. Who promised, "Your eyes shall be opened and ye shall be as gods, knowing good and evil?"
3. What happened to Lot's wife?
4. What alternate sacrifice saved Abraham's son?
5. Who was Nebuchadnezzar?
6. Where did John the Baptist baptize Jesus?
7. Who was married to Abram/Abraham?
8. Was Jonah swallowed by a whale?
9. What did Moses do to thirty Israelites for worshipping the golden calf?
10. Genesis says that Cain knew his wife. Where did Mrs. Cain come from?

Quiz: Who Slew Whom?

Match the biblical killer (either acting directly or by giving the command) with the biblical victim:

Killer	**Victim**
1. Cain	a. King Agag of the Amalekites
2. David	b. Abel
3. Samuel	c. Isaac
4. Israelites	d. Goliath
5. Moses	e. Six thousand Philistines
6. Samson	f. Judas
7. Pilate	g. John the Baptist
8. Salome	h. Thirty Israelites
9. Judas	i. Jesus
10. Abraham	j. Canaanites

Quiz: Famous Last Words

According to Shakespeare in *Macbeth*, the Thane of Cawdor was praised upon his execution with the compliment, "Nothing in his life became him like the leaving it." Others have thoughtfully offered their own famous last words. Identify the decedent:

1. "It is finished."
2. "Assist me up, and in my coming down I will shift for myself."
3. "I've just drunk eighteen straight whiskeys. Nobody's ever done that."
4. "I shall hear in heaven."
5. "What is the answer? In that case, what is the question?"
6. "Nonsense, they couldn't hit an elephant at this dist—"
7. "Don't mourn—organize!"
8. "It is well, I die hard, but I am not afraid to go."
9. "Thomas—Jefferson—still surv—"
10. "This is the Fourth?"
11. "I still live."
12. "You should."

Get a Life: Sign of the Fish

Question: What does the sign of the fish mean in Christianity?

Answer: Born-again Christians often sport a silhouette of a fish to designate their beliefs. The sign not only acknowledges the apostles as "fishers of men" but also acknowledges that letters that spell the Greek word for fish, *ichthus*, mysteriously form the acronym for the Greek expression *Jesous Christos Theou Uios Soter*. The English translation is "Jesus Christ, Son of God, Savior."

Quiz: Origins of Religions

The difference between a *cult* and a *religion* usually depends on who's doing the defining, but it's safe to say that the older a spiritual belief system is, the better the chance it has of being respected. Among the world's major sects, match the religion to its (highly encapsulated) origin:

1. Christianity
2. Buddhism
3. Confucianism
4. Islam
5. Judaism
6. Taoism
7. Shinto
8. Sikhism

a. Philosopher K'ung Fu-tzu contained his sayings in books called the *Analects*.

b. Collected by philosopher Lao-tze from ancient teachings, this contemplative religion follows *The Classic of the Way and Its Virtue*.

c. The chieftain Abraham taught his people to worship one God.

d. Prince Siddhartha Guatama became the Enlightened One; his teachings are in sacred books.

e. Jesus, the son of God, came to earth in human form; his teachings appear as Scripture.

f. Founded in India by Guru Nanak, its teachings are in the *Adi Granth*.

g. The Prophet Muhammad taught holy Scripture, written by Arab scholars, as the *Qur'an*.

h. A folk religion with no holy book, this belief system draws from other religions and holds the emperor as divine.

Kwanzaa

Although it is not a religious festival *per se*, Kwanzaa (*Nguzo Saba*) has become an event of spiritual significance to African-Americans since it was initiated by Dr. Maulana Ron Karenga on December 26, 1966. Kwanzaa—which is based on a cultural belief system called Kawaida—is a week of remembering black history and rejoicing at its strengths.

It was Dr. Karenga who came to realize, during the politically active 1960s, that black Americans did not share the same religious heritage as white Americans, and certainly nothing that reflected the changes that were coming about through the civil rights struggle. Dr. Karenga thereby constructed a seven-day celebration, each day of which would stress one of the primary symbols of Kwanzaa:

1. MKEKA: Symbolically, the *mkeka* (em-kay-cah) is a straw mat which serves as a basis, or tradition, upon which all things rest.

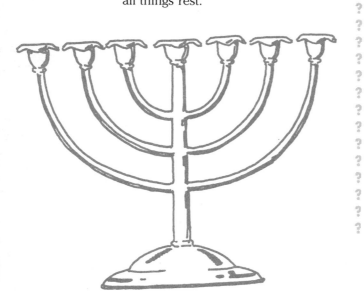

2. KINARA: The *kinara* (kee-na-ra) is a seven-candle holder symbolic of the common well from which African-Americans came, much as a stalk of corn produces ears of corn.

3. MSHUMAA: The seven candles of the *kinara* represent the seven principles (*mshumaa*; em-shu-ma) of society flowing from the firstborn. They are *Umoja* (unity), *Kujichagulia* (self-determination), *Ujima* (collective effort and responsibility), *Ujamaa* (cooperative economics), *Nia* (purpose), *Kuumba* (creativity), and *Imani* (faith).

4. MUHINDI: Ears of corn represent the promise (children) born of the stalk. So every house uses one ear of corn (*muhindi*; moo-hin-dee) for each child present. Houses without children use at least one ear to signify potential.

5. KIKOMBE CHA UMOJA: The *kikombe cha umoja* (kee-coom-bay cha oo-moe-juh) is the unity cup that is passed among family members, who drink from it in praise of ancestors and the struggle they began.

6. ZAWADI: Gifts (*zawadi*; zuh-wah-dee) are given to children in promise of commitment to do good deeds not only for themselves but also for the community, throughout the coming year.

7. KARAMU: The feast of *karamu* (ka-rah-moo) symbolizes the unity of the community to give thanks to the creator for the previous year. It is held on December 31.

Quiz: Bible Maxims

True/False: Which of the following quotations can be found in the Bible?

1. "Fools rush in where angels fear to tread."
2. "Pride goeth before destruction, and a haughty spirit before a fall."
3. "God helps those who help themselves."
4. "Cleanliness is next to Godliness."
5. "There were giants in those days."
6. "The imagination of Man's heart is evil from his youth."
7. "And the Jews ordered the crucifixion of Jesus."
8. "And Jonah lived three days in the belly of the whale."
9. "Joshua fought the battle of Jericho and the walls came tumbling down."
10. "There came three wise men from the east to Jerusalem."

Quiz: Noah's Ark

According to Genesis, Noah was a just man and found grace in the eyes of the Lord at a time when the Lord was sorry that he had made Man on earth and vowed to destroy him.

But He spared Noah and his three sons, Shem, Ham, and Japeth, and his wife <u>A</u> and directed Noah (who was 500 years old at the time) to build an ark.

It was made of <u>B</u> wood and measured <u>C</u> cubits in length, <u>D</u> cubits in width, and <u>E</u> cubits in height. It shall have <u>F</u> decks, a window near the top and a door. Its inside and outside walls should be sealed with <u>G</u>.

The human guest list for the ark included <u>H</u> people and <u>I</u> of each sort of animal, including <u>J</u> and <u>K</u>.

By the time the flood waters were on earth, Noah was <u>L</u> years old. It had rained for <u>M</u> days when the Noah party went into the ark, and then it rained for <u>N</u> days and <u>O</u> nights, after which the earth was covered with water for <u>P</u> days.

When the ark finally settled on dry land, it rested on <u>Q</u>. And the Lord gave Noah a <u>R</u> as his covenant that he would never destroy life on earth again (at least not by flooding).

Religious Sacrifice

The literature of many religions is filled with stories of people and animals who were ritually killed or tortured at the behest—or the fallacious orders—of a deity. Here is a small sample. (Warning: some readers may find these descriptions disturbingly vivid.)

1. The dry Yucatan peninsula was the site of the city of *Chichen Itza*, one of the last Mayan cities. Two wells, fed by underwater rivers, supported the city in different ways: One provided drinking water and the other was a place of sacrifice. In hard times, a maiden was tossed down the 60-foot sacrificial well. On the off chance that she survived a few hours, priests lifted her out to hear what, if anything, the gods had told her.

2. The aforementioned Aztecs also sacrificed some fifteen thousand men each year to *Huitzilopochtly*, their sun god, whom they feared died every night and needed human blood in order to rise again the next morning.

3. In the Book of Joshua in the Old Testament, God commanded Moses to lead the Israelites to slaughter the Canaanites in order to prevent them from contaminating the race. This has been used by some to justify the Holocaust as retribution.

4. The deceased pharaohs in ancient Egypt were entombed with enough material goods (much of it plundered in subsequent centuries) to support them in the afterlife. Many were also entombed with a cadre of servants to meet their any wish. Unfortunately (for the servants), they were alive at the time their pharaoh's tomb was sealed for the ages.

5. Dishonored Japanese *samurai* warriors atone for dishonor by the act of *harakiri*, or "belly cutting," during a ritual known as *seppuku*. The victim first disembowels himself with a dagger or sword, after which a trusted friend beheads him. This momentous self-sacrifice pleases the emperor, and that pleases the gods.

6. In autumn of 1978, Jim Jones, who insisted that he was, if not *the* God, at least *a* god, inspired 913 of his followers to drink a cyanide-laced soft drink believing in his promise of an afterlife more pleasant than the existence they had built out of the jungle in Guyana, South America. Many of his worshippers fed the poison to their children; others murdered visitors—including Congressman Leo Ryan—who were trying to get help.

7. The Spanish Inquisition—in which Tomás de Torquemada led investigations of heresy against the Catholic Church in the thirteenth century—would encourage confessions by foot roasting and the toca. In foot roasting, the feet of suspects were covered with lard and slowly cooked over an open fire. The toca involved strapping subjects to a board that was then tilted so that their heads were lower than their feet. Their noses were clamped shut and a rag was stuffed into their mouths. Water was then dripped onto the rag, which

slowly suffocated the subjects or got them to confess, whichever came first.

8. In Roman antiquity, in honor of Vesta, goddess of the hearth, six vestal virgins maintained a fire in the tabernacle. Drawn from noble families when they were six to ten years old and kept in service for thirty years, they swore to remain intact (although they could leave the order and marry at any time). If any of them did break her vow of chastity, however, she would be sealed in an underground room at the edge of the city and left there to die (unless, of course, she was rescued by her family or boyfriend).

9. Crucifixion, though iconographic of Christianity, was a pagan punishment that had been established well before it was used on Jesus. Its cruelty is seldom understood, for most people believe that its victims bleed to death after they are nailed hands and feet to a wooden cross. In fact, death comes through exposure and suffocation as the diaphragm and stomach muscles gradually weaken and cramp from the uncomfortable semi-supported position that the sufferer is forced to assume.

10. Before the movie *Braveheart,* the procedure of drawing and quartering could only be imagined or witnessed in person by those who dared doubt the supremacy of the King of England (or whatever). There are two versions: In one (favored by czars), the victim's arms and legs are tethered to four horses that are simultaneously slapped and sent in four separate directions. If this didn't do the trick, the remaining torso was decapitated. In the more showy English version, the victim was dragged behind a horse to his gallows, hanged by the neck until he was almost, but not quite, dead, and then disemboweled, his intestines burned in a fire while he watched. Then he was decapitated and cut into pieces.

Creation Theory

One of the most discredited, yet persistent, beliefs about the earth is the creation theory. This precept insists that the Bible is to be taken literally and that all information contained in its pages is absolute truth.

A key to dismissing the creation theory (which its adherents erroneously refer to as "Creation Science") is the work of James Ussher, archbishop of Armagh. In 1650 Ussher used the ages of the holy men and women of the Christian Bible to calculate the age of the earth. More interested in the Rock of Ages than the age of rocks, he determined that the moment of creation was October 26, 4004 BC at 10 AM.

It is not known what time zone he was using, whether he used the current or the Roman calendar, or if the first three days of creation were twenty-four hours long (remember that there was no sun, and thus no night and day, until the fourth day).

Science dates the age of the earth at 4.6 billion years.

Get a Life: The Ten Commandments

Question: When Hollywood producer-director Cecil B. DeMille said he was going to make *The Ten Commandments,* he was talking about a movie. When churches talk about the Ten Commandments, they mean several different assortments of "thou shall's and "thou shall not's according to pertinent scripture. Here is a list of commandments. Place the right ones with the world's leading Judeo-Christian religions that observe them (compare the wording carefully):

Commandments

1. I am the Lord your God who delivered you out of slavery.
2. You shall have no other God before me, or make a carved image of me for yourself.
3. Do not use the name of the Lord thy God in vain.
4. Remember the Sabbath day and keep it holy.
5. Honor thy father and thy mother.
6. Thou shalt not commit murder.
7. Thou shalt not commit adultery.
8. Thou shalt not steal.
9. Thou shalt not bear false witness against thy neighbor.
10. Do not covet thy neighbor's wife, or covet his house or anything that belongs to him.
11. You shall not have another God before me and you shall not make a carved image of me for yourself.
12. You shall not covet your neighbor's wife.
13. You shall not covet your neighbor's house or anything that belongs to him.
14. You shall have no other god before me.
15. You shall not make a carved image of me for yourself.

Jewish: 1-10
Christian and Eastern Orthodox: 3-10, 14, 15
Roman Catholic and Lutheran: 2-13

Quiz: Saints

The Roman Catholic Church confers sainthood upon those men and women who have met certain established criteria. They must have died as martyrs for the faith, have been credited with provable miracles, and have withstood the test of time, which explains why Mother Teresa won't have her canonization for a while yet. Patron saints watch over the welfare of people in various professions or personal situations. Some—St. Jude (desperate situations), St. Christopher (travellers), and St. John (sick people)—are universally known. Match the following lesser known Catholic saints with the domain for which they are protector:

1.	Genesius	a.	Cab drivers
2.	Joseph of Cupertino	b.	Midwives/falsely accused
3.	Sebastian	c.	Television
4.	Thomas More	d.	Altar boys
5.	Francis de Sales	e.	Athletes
6.	Aloysius Gonzaga	f.	Air travelers
7.	Anne	g.	Lawyers
8.	Clare of Assisi	h.	Writers
9.	Raymund Nonnatus	i.	Women in labor
10.	Vitus	j.	Skaters
11.	Fiacre	k.	Dancers
12.	Gabriel	l.	Actors/secretaries
13.	Lidwana	m.	Radio workers
14.	John Berchmans	n.	Plasterers
15.	Bartholomew	o.	Youths

Quiz: Here's Yiddish

Yiddish is one of the most expressive languages on earth, and also one of the most mongrelized. A blend of Rhenish, High German, Aramaic, and Hebrew, with bits of Slavic dialect thrown in (mostly consonants, it seems), it transcends national borders and forms the basis for an entire cultural subculture, both Jewish and non. Thanks to its use in show business, most people are familiar with such basic Yiddish as *shtick* (one's act; literally a piece of something), *shlep* (carry), and *meshugah* (crazy), there are many, many more that lend color to everyday conversations. Match the Yiddish with the meaning. (Note: none of these are vulgar.)

1.	Farblondjet	a.	Gentile male
2.	Schnorrer	b.	Shrewish woman
3.	Chozzerai	c.	Human being (affectionately)
4.	Tummler	d.	Dishonest person
5.	Gonif	e.	A rabble-rouser
6.	Pisher	f.	Rash; lousy food
7.	Schmaltz	g.	Meaningful conversation
8.	Trayf	h.	To offer unwanted advice
9.	Chutzpa	i.	Young, naive person
10.	Mensch	j.	Corny (literally: chicken fat)
11.	Yenta	k.	Unclean; not Kosher
12.	Shaygets	l.	Gall; nerviness
13.	Schmooz	m.	Rag piece of cloth
14.	Kibitz	n.	Lost; mixed-up
15.	Shmatte	o.	A moocher

Quiz: Holy Books

Match the Holy Book with the religion that follows its teachings:

1.	Bhagavad Gita	a.	Taoism
2.	Qur'an	b.	Confucianism
3.	Torah/Prophets/Writings	c.	Islam
4.	Analects/Five Classics	d.	Judaism
5.	New Testament	e.	Hinduism
6.	Tao-teChing	f.	Christianity

Note: This list is not meant to represent all the books embraced by the religions shown.

Pilgrimage to Mecca

Mecca—the holy city in Saudi Arabia, where the prophet Muhammad was born in the sixth century—was a place of worship long before the time of the leader of Islam. It is believed to trace back to pre-Islamic times—to the Hebrew patriarch Abraham. Muhammad, who received the Qur'an (the holy scriptures of Islam) from Allah in AD 600, was believed to be the last in a line of prophets—flowing back to Adam, Abraham, Moses, and Jesus.

Every Moslem is expected to make a pilgrimage, or *hajj*, to Mecca at least once in his/her lifetime to pray at, touch, and kiss the Black Stone in the Kaaba shrine. The *hajj* is a major event in a Moslem's life and involves sacrifice and devotion. Followers of Islam (the Arabic word for "submission to God") pray in the direction of Mecca five times each day. Because Mecca symbolizes both piety and a destination, its name has been used by non-Moslems to represent any fervently desired goal (as in "Hollywood is a mecca for film fans"). Strictly speaking, this shows disrespect for the importance that the real Mecca holds to Islam.

Get a Life: Plagues

Question: Name the ten plagues visited upon the people of Egypt by the Lord in order to compel Pharaoh to release the Hebrews from bondage. (Random order is okay for all but the last one.)

Answer: The answers may be found in Exodus, chapters 7–12, in this order:

1. Waters turned to blood
2. Frogs
3. Lice
4. Swarms of flies
5. The pestilence that killed only Egyptian livestock
6. Boils
7. Hail, thunder, and fire
8. Locusts
9. Darkness
10. Death of firstborn

Note: According to Exodus 9:14-16, the Lord's purpose in these plagues was not people's destruction but their conversion. Ultimately, the last plague so softened Pharaoh's heart (or at least scared it sufficiently) that he released the Children of Israel from slavery.

PTM: Rosalyn Bruyere

"If not God, then who?" is a question frequently asked by people of faith when they challenge people whose faith is in question. Yet the varied spiritual movement in America has transcended such specifics in an effort to bring people closer to the source of their faith, be it God, a higher power, or, ultimately, something that does not even have an equivalent in human language. Reverend Rosalyn L. Bruyere is a healer—not an evangelical, Chautauqua tent, faith healer but an ordained minister who has helped people achieve inner peace, whether during their life or as they approach the end of it. These comments were made to the author at the time of the release of the film Resurrection *in 1980.*

I studied parapsychology because my children were thought to be, at that time, gifted children, and I wanted to raise them responsibly. Healing was part of the psychic development course I took, and during it I was able to help my teacher who had a bad case of ulcerated colitis that had not responded to treatment, and she was healed. Then a close friend was healed, and after that other people started calling me, and I was in business and didn't intend to be. It was frightening.

You have to be an ordained minister to practice healing, and I continued studying and was ordained three years later. I was ordained in an order in which the normal church movement is not terribly involved, and my center is a nondenominational one.

We function very much as a clinic and an institution of learning; we make a devotional statement about wanting to serve God by serving our fellow human beings.

[It is not "faith healing"]. Over and over again I've been asked whether or not the patient has to believe. It doesn't have anything to do with the patient's belief. I think it has to do with what I believe and what I believe is possible. It's the patient who is the sick person, and I think we do a great disservice to the sick when we insist that they believe a certain way before we attend to their needs.

We get mostly what medicine isn't effective with; we get rare diseases, terminal patients, or people that have not responded to regular medical care—not that there isn't care, but just that they have not responded.

As a healer and a minister, sometimes my job is to sit with someone as they pass graciously, as they live as painlessly up to those last moments as possible. I am willing to be their pain-relief mechanism. I may not be there to save their life; I may be there to be with them as they continue their life in the next form. I don't necessarily rush in there to save everyone. There is a time when we're through. I'm not sure that individual people always know that time, but, as a healer, there is some insight, and I am always very clear with the patients that what we are doing is not saving their lives, and, "Do you want me to continue?"

Bruyere practices Chakra healing, a holistic system, which she presents on Psychic and Institutional Healing, *the 1997 audiotape she cowrote with Judith Orloff.*

Ye Gods (answers)

	Realm	Roman	Greek
1.	War	Mars	Aries
2.	Love	Cupid	Eros
3.	Wine	Bacchus	Dionysus
4.	Son of Chief God	Hercules	Heracles
5.	Messenger of the Gods[1]	Mercury	Hermes
6.	Sleep	Somnus	Hypmus
7.	Moon	Luna	Selene
8.	Death	Mors	Thanatos
9.	Oceans	Neptune	Poseidon
10.	Chief God of Olympus	Jupiter/Jove	Zeus

Banned Books (Answers)

All of them except *Mein Kampf* by Adolf Hitler.

Bible Details (Answers)

1. Matthew
2. The serpent in the Garden of Eden
3. She was turned into a pillar of salt for watching the destruction of Sodom and Gomorrah.
4. A goat
5. King of ancient Babylon
6. In the river Jordan, although technically Jesus didn't need baptizing
7. Sarah
8. He was swallowed by a great fish; whales are mammals.
9. He ordered them slaughtered.
10. Good question!

Who Slew Whom? (Answers)

1. b
2. d
3. a
4. j
5. h
6. e
7. i
8. g
9. f (suicide)
10. c[2]

Famous Last Words (Answers)

1. Jesus Christ
2. Sir Thomas More, about to be beheaded at Henry VIII's behest
3. Dylan Thomas (supposedly)
4. Ludwig van Beethoven
5. Gertrude Stein
6. General John Sedgwick, commander of the Union Army
7. Union activist Joe Hill
8. George Washington
9. John Adams[3]
10. Thomas Jefferson
11. Daniel Webster
12. Charles MacArthur[4]

Origins of Religions (Answers)

1. e
2. d
3. a
4. g
5. c
6. b
7. h
8. f

Bible Maxims (Answers)

1. False; Alexander Pope, *An Essay on Criticism*
2. True; Proverbs
3. False; Aesop
4. False; Rabbi Phinehas ben-Yair, old Hebrew prophet
5. True; Genesis
6. True; Genesis
7. False; Do we have to keep going over this?
8. False; As stated previously, the Bible mentions "a great fish." Whales are mammals.
9. False; The phrase is from an American spiritual song.
10. True; Matthew does not say "three kings," as in the hymn.

Noah's Ark (Answers)

This is from the King James translation of the Bible:
A: Mrs. Noah is not named.
B: Gopher wood

---

[1] It is not true that alternate messengers of the gods are Faxus and FedExus.
[2] Trick question. When Abraham prepared to kill his son, Isaac, to prove his devotion to God, God then provided him with a ram for sacrifice instead.
[3] In history's most haunting coincidence, Founding Fathers John Adams and Thomas Jefferson both died on July 4, 1826, each believing that the other was attending the fiftieth anniversary celebration of the Declaration of Independence.
[4] No one will get this, but I had to put it in because I love it. Writer Charles MacArthur (*The Front Page*) lay on his deathbed slipping in and out of coma, as his wife, actress Helen Hayes, sat beside him. At one point she leaned toward him and whispered, "Charlie, I love you." He came out of coma, smiled, and said, "You should." Those were his last words.

Answers

C: 300
D: 50
E: 30
F: Three
G: Pitch (tar)
H: Eight—Noah, Shem, Ham, and Japeth and their unnamed wives
I: Two (male and female) (Genesis 6:20), although Noah is also told to bring along "seven each of every clean animal, a male and his female; two each of animals that are unclean, a male and his female; also seven each of birds of the air, male and female" (Genesis 7:2–3). Depending on how many species existed before the flood, this could have meant anywhere from three hundred thousand to one million critters.
J-K: Ravens and doves are the only animals specifically named in the story of Noah.
L: 600 (by now)
M: 7
N-O: 40
P: 150
Q: The mountains of Ararat
R: Rainbow

Saints (Answers)

1. l
2. f
3. e
4. g
5. h
6. o
7. i
8. c
9. b
10. k
11. a
12. m
13. j
14. d
15. n

Here's Yiddish (Answers)

1. n
2. o
3. f
4. e
5. d
6. i
7. j
8. k
9. l
10. c
11. b
12. a
13. g
14. h
15. m

Holy Books (Answers)

1. e
2. c
3. d
4. b
5. f
6. a

Chapter 8

Politics and Law

Whoever said, "I never vote—That only encourages them" meant it as a joke, but over the years an alarming number of Americans have been taking it seriously. From 1960 when 63 percent of eligible voters went to the polls to chose between Nixon and Kennedy, the rate has steadily dropped to where barely 49 percent cast ballots in 1996 for the Clinton-Dole race. (Source: Committee for the Study of the American Electorate) And that's just for Presidency; voter turn-out for off-year elections is even lower, so much so that the head of one right-wing Christian group once boasted, "In any local election only about 30 percent actually vote, so all we need to win is 15 percent—plus one."

Millions of people around the world would give their lives (and have) to secure the very right which half the American population routinely ignores. Why? Maybe it's who's running.

"It is intolerable to be confronted every four years with the choice between the bad and the worse," offered consumer advocate Ralph Nader in 1996—the year he, himself, broke a long-standing promise and stood for electoral office. Granted, the reason behind Nader's candidacy was more educational than political, but it begs the question of why people have become so turned off.

"It's the politicians, stupid!" is as good a reason as any. After all, nobody trusts them to keep campaign promises; political action committees (PACs) countermand the wishes of the voters anyway; Congress refuses to pass meaningful campaign reform; politicians introduce legislation they know to be unconstitutional just to grandstand for their constituents; and no matter who you call at City Hall, the street in front of your house never gets fixed.

We blame the politicians, but they're just the ones who make noise. In fact, the system they serve is more dependable, less mercurial, and definitely here to stay. The labyrinthine genius of the United States government is that it relies on law, not caprice, and throughout two centuries has shaped up into the "greatest hits" of every other form of government that Mankind has ever devised. Yet just as former Speaker of the House Thomas "Tip" O'Neill once said that "all politics is local," so will this chapter delve into the trivia of the American system.

That doesn't mean that politics is trivial. Despite choleric news reports that suggest otherwise, the country remains built on good, Constitutional bedrock. For every Monica Lewinsky, Linda Tripp, Newt Gingrich, Kenneth Starr or James Carvelle who becomes *bete-noir*-of-the-month, and for every White House scandal, legislative pork barrel or judicial surprise, the system has never derailed.

The major reason for this is, astonishingly, the one that's usually vilified as the cause: the media. Now hold on. It was the media in the Twentieth Century that actually brought the public closer to politicians, and vice-versa. The first political campaigns of the 1900s were held in town halls, town squares and torchlight rallies, without microphones, to a limited number of people. Word was only spread by newspapers who frequently bent stories to serve their publishers' biases—just as politicians tweaked their speeches to suit the crowd they were addressing. The introduction of radio in the 1920s changed everything: now politicians could take their case directly to the people, and it had better be consistent.

If they weren't good talkers, however, they were at a disadvantage; it wasn't only the Great Depression that kept Herbert Hoover from being re-elected in 1932, it was that he couldn't top the oratorical skills of Franklin Roosevelt. By the time television entered the equation in 1960, it was virtually assured that John F. Kennedy would edge out the less telegenic Richard M. Nixon; to this day, people who listened to their "great debates" on radio insist that Nixon won the polemic, while those who watched them on television report a Kennedy victory.

With so much to report, however, the mass media slipped back into their role as middlemen. Where once such press barons as Hearst and Pulitzer twisted their reporting to support their own agendas, so has television subtly burnished its coverage by reducing it to sound bites. You can't discuss issues in the seven-seconds accorded by the average news broadcast. Unless somebody is accused of marital infidelity, of course, in which case the issue plays like a telethon.

The amazing thing is that America tends to work, and that has less to do with politics than with the way the system itself is constructed.

The Twentieth Century has been one of phenomenal legislative and judicial progress. For example, the Bill of Rights was passed in 1789 but it was barely enforced until the 1900s. One of our most cherished beliefs, freedom of speech, didn't even prevail until 1918 when the U.S. Supreme Court (in *Abrams v. United States*) allowed the publication of a controversial political pamphlet by holding that truth is best "reached by free trade in ideas."

Unfortunately, the system also works slowly, which frustrates a generation raised with short attention spans and a reactionary temperament. It also demands compromise; Otto von Bismarck's admonition is as true today as when he said it in the mid-1800s: "The two things you must never actually see being made, if you like either, are sausage and legislation."

Yet the 1900s have seen Civil Rights legislation (albeit eroded in the 1990s), women's suffrage, reproductive freedom, bank regulation, food and drug standards, and the preservation of religious freedom. This, despite fighting wars abroad, a Depression at home, Watergate, the rise of hate groups and a constant immigration into America of people from other cultures. Whether the country advances *because of* or *in spite of* these forces is anybody's guess.

This chapter is about the way the nation affects our daily lives, often in ways that we don't recognize. It highlights individuals who have made a difference, laws that changed our lives, and details that make life better—or at least more interesting.

It Seemed Like a Good Idea at the Time

Just as "kill for peace" and "make love for chastity" are examples of political slogans gone awry, so are the following sound bites from people who thought they were making sense at the time:

1. "Let's get one thing straight. The police aren't here to create disorder. The police are here to *preserve* disorder."
    —Mayor Richard J. Daley (D-Chicago), during 1968 riots

2. Ketchup is to "be counted as one of the two vegetables required as part of the school lunch program."
    —U.S. Department of Agriculture, 1981

3. "Capital punishment is our society's recognition of the sanctity of human life."—Senator Orrin Hatch (R-Utah), 1988

4. "We do not have censorship. What we have is a limitation on what newspapers can report."
    —South Africa Ministry of Information, 1988

5. Instead of lying to Congress, he said he was offering "a different version from the facts."
    —Lt. Col. Oliver North, 1987

6. "I don't feel we did wrong in taking this great country away from [the Indians]. There were great numbers of people who needed new land and the Indians were selfishly trying to keep it for themselves."
    —John Wayne, *Playboy* interview

7. "When I sell liquor it's called bootlegging. When my customers serve it on silver trays on Lake Shore Drive, it's called hospitality."
    —Al Capone during Prohibition

8. "The most important thing in acting is honesty. And if you can fake that, you've got it made."
    —George Burns

9. "The trouble with the rat race is that even if you win it, you're still a rat."
    —Lily Tomlin

10. "The great question, which I have not been able to answer, despite my thirty years in research into the feminine soul, is, "'What do women want?'"

    —Sigmund Freud

Quiz: Letter of the Law

The dictionary makes a distinction between the following pairs of terms, even though conversational speech may not. What are the fine points?

1. Assault and battery
2. Forgery and uttering
3. Burglary and robbery
4. Abdication and abrogation
5. Prostate and prostrate
6. Slander and libel
7. Inalienable and unalienable
8. Habeas corpus and corpus delicti
9. Malfeasance, misfeasance, and nonfeasance
10. Pardon versus parole

Get a Life: The Chicago Seven

Question: Name the Chicago 7—the radicals who were tried for conspiracy to obstruct the 1968 Democratic National Convention in Chicago.

Answer: Rennie Davis, David Dellinger, John R. Froins, Tom Hayden, Abbie Hoffman, Jerry Rubin, and Lee Weiner. Black Panther leader Bobby Seale was also indicted for conspiracy but was tried separately after he protested in court and was cited for contempt by Judge Julius Hoffman, who then ordered Seale bound and gagged. William Kuntsler served as defense lawyer in the 1969 trial and was himself cited for contempt. All were found innocent of conspiracy, although Seale served four years on the contempt charges.

Essential Rights

Everybody knows that the Bill of Rights protects such things as freedom of the press, freedom of religion, the right against self-incrimination, etc. Most people also know that these rights were not in the original U.S. Constitution when it was adopted in 1787 but were added in the form of amendments in 1789. But very few people are aware that even the venerated First Amendment was not upheld in court until 1920. Following are eight important Bill of Rights cases:

1. The Palmer raids (1920): Attorney General A. Mitchell Palmer ordered the detention and deportation of foreign-looking Americans for expressing interest in trade unions, antiwar sentiments, or other views considered "radical." Hundreds were imprisoned and sentenced without representation by a lawyer. The ACLU (under founder Roger Baldwin), in its first year of existence, successfully fought this violation of the First Amendment.

2. James Joyce's *Ulysses* (1933): Federal Judge John M. Woolsey of New York upheld the right of American people to read *Ulysses,* by overturning an import ban on the acclaimed book.

3. Internment of Japanese-Americans (1942): President Roosevelt issued Executive Order 9066 calling for the imprisonment of anyone of Japanese ancestry. Thousands of Japanese–Americans—two-thirds of whom were American citizens—were detained in concentration camps on American soil. Not until the late 1990s did the government issue a formal policy against such actions and make reparations.

4. Abortion rights upheld (1973): In *Roe* vs. *Wade* and *Doe* vs. *Bolton* the privacy right of a pregnant woman to continue her pregnancy was upheld when the U.S. Supreme Court—in a decision that remains their most controversial—decriminalized the procedure.

5. Creationism declared a religion (1981): Although religious radicals insist on offering Creationism as an alternative to evolution, a U.S. District Court judge ruled that it is, instead, a religion and has no place in schools.

6. Voting Rights Act (1965/1982): The act guaranteeing all Americans over eighteen the right to vote was passed in 1965, during the civil rights struggle, by a Congress fueled by the changing morality of the times. It was renewed by Congress in 1982, only after a long and bitter grassroots fight that was also fueled by the changing sensibility of the times.

7. *Sullivan* vs. *New York Times* (1964): An important freedom of the press case was decided in favor of, well, freedom of the press. An Alabama public official sued the *New York Times* for libel, but the U.S. Supreme Court said that three things had to be present for there to be libel: injury to the person or his reputation; reckless disregard for the facts; actual malice.

8. The *Lovers* decision (1964): An Ohio theatre manager, Nico Jacobellis, was arrested for showing the critically acclaimed Louis Malle film *The Lovers,* on grounds of obscenity. The U.S. Supreme Court overturned the

conviction, with Justice Potter Stewart offering his definition of obscenity: "I know it when I see it." Yet it wouldn't be till the 1970s (in *Roth* vs. *U.S.*), when Justice William Brennan handed down a more elaborate (if no clearer) definition: The work, taken as a whole, violates community standards; has no redeeming social or artistic value; and appeals primarily to prurient interest. Jacobellis, by the way, later served with distinction as a film company executive.

Miranda

It's become so much a part of the vernacular that TV cop shows now use the same shorthand as the cops themselves use when arresting a suspect: "Read him his rights."

Okay, *what* rights? Why, *Miranda* rights (paraphrased):

1. You have the right to remain silent; if you choose to speak, anything you say can be used against you in legal proceedings.
2. You have the right to know the crime with which you are charged.
3. You have a right to the presence of a lawyer immediately at any questioning. If you cannot afford a lawyer, one will be appointed to you free.
4. You have the right to make a phone call.

Background. On March 13, 1963, Ernesto Miranda was arrested by Phoenix, Arizona police on suspicion of stealing $8 from a bank employee. After two hours of interrogation, he confessed to kidnapping and raping a young woman eleven days previously. Miranda, twenty-two and unemployed, was not offered a lawyer at his questioning and his confession was used to convict him at trial. He received a twenty-year sentence and, from jail, petitioned the Supreme Court to overturn his conviction because his rights had been violated. In 1966 the Court agreed, granted Miranda a new trial, this time without admitting the confession as evidence, and establishing the *Miranda* rights of the accused.

Two previous cases paved the way for *Miranda*. In 1961, in *Mapp* vs. *Ohio*, Cleveland police broke into the home of Dollie Mapp looking for someone else. When they didn't find him, they arrested Ms. Mapp for having obscene literature. When the police couldn't produce a warrant for the literature, Mapp's conviction was thrown out. The *Mapp* case supports the rule that illegally seized evidence cannot be admitted at trial.

Three years later, in 1964's *Escobedo* vs. *Illinois*, the Court ruled that Danny Escobedo's murder confession had to be excluded because he was denied a lawyer after he changed his mind during the interrogation and asked for one. In that case, police textbooks were produced to show that police were trained to ignore a suspect's rights.

So the *Miranda* decision (which was handed down in 1966) established the rights of the accused. It has also ignited a slew of test cases bent on overturning it ever since. For example, the Court has said that evidence seized with a faulty warrant may still be admitted at trial *if the arresting officer thought he was acting in good faith at the time*. It is also possible to use a suspect's words against him if he keeps talking even after demanding a lawyer; although the confession may be invalid, it can still be introduced to establish a suspect's character.

Incidentally, even with the exclusion of his confession, Ernesto Miranda was again convicted of rape and kidnapping at his retrial.

FOIA

When the Nixon administration's "White House enemies list" was uncovered during the Watergate hearings, it stunned Americans: A president was actually going after private citizens who had voiced opinions that differed from his. Some people who had considered themselves anti-Nixon were further stunned to learn that their names were *not* on his list!

Nevertheless, in 1974 the Congress overrode President Ford's veto to pass the Freedom of Information Act (FOIA), permitting individuals to gain access to their government records to see what, if anything, was "on file" about them. The results were often frustrating: Extensive deletions were routinely made from documents because of "national security," a notation that usually meant "if this got out, boy, would we be embarrassed."

Today the FBI—which, if nothing else, knows how to keep files—actually sells public figures' FOIA files for 10¢ a page. Here's a partial list of the inventory. (Note: Appearance on this list is not an accusation.)

Name and Profession	Pages
Louis Armstrong (musician)	25
Lucille Ball (comedienne)	142
Kate "Ma" Barker (gangster)	5
Irving Berlin (composer, "God Bless America")	19
Hugo Black (Supreme Court justice)	156
Leonard Bernstein (composer/conductor)	720
Al Capone (efficiency expert)	2,397
Caesar Chavez and United Farm Workers	2,021
Clergy and Laity Concerned About Vietnam	1,699
Communist Party USA (Cointelpro file)	30,743
Bobby Darin (singer: "Mack the Knife")	43
Daughters of Bilitis (lesbian activists)	248
Walt Disney (Mickey's dad)	474
Duke Ellington (musician)	30
William Faulkner (author)	18
Clark Gable (actor)	181
Greta Garbo (enigma)	8
Lorne Greene (Ponderosa landlord)	23
Woody Guthrie (troubadour)	109
John W. Hinckley, Jr. (bad shot)	801
Danny Kaye (entertainer/humanitarian)	92
Joseph P. Kennedy (founding father)	1,054
Rev. Martin Luther King, Jr. (leader)	16,659
Peter Lorre (person who stole letters of transit)	180
Audie Murphy (most decorated U.S. soldier)	427
Ezra Pound (author)	1,512
George Lincoln Rockwell (American Über-Nazi)	674
Clyde Tolson (Mrs. J. Edgar Hoover)	2,141
UFOs	1,600
Waco (Branch Davidian compound)	21,819

FOIA request forms and files may be obtained under Title 5 USC, Sec. 552, the Freedom of Information Act and Title 5 USC, Sec. 552a, the Privacy Act. Write:

Federal Bureau of Investigation
Freedom of Information Act Office
935 Pennsylvania Avenue, NW
Washington, DC 10535-0001

Quiz: Dumb Laws

The law is a funny thing. At the turn of the century it was mandated that an automobile had to be preceded by a man on horseback to warn others that an automobile was coming. How many of these laws actually existed (per Stephen J. Spignesi's book, *The Odd Index*)? True or false:

1. Harrisburg, PA: You can't have sex with a truck driver in a toll booth.
2. Monterey, CA: You must vacate your bed and breakfast by 11 AM.
3. Newcastle, WY: You can't have sex in a butcher's freezer.
4. Tremonton, UT: You can't have sex in an ambulance.
5. Manchester, NH: You can't have sex in a movie theater.
6. Willowdale, OR: A husband can't talk dirty to his wife during sex.
7. Bay Shore, NY: You can't have suggestive bumper stickers on cars.
8. Washington, DC: Sex is allowed in missionary position only.
9. Boston, MA: You can have only one drink at a time (and no boilermakers) in bars.
10. Sewickley, PA: You can't have sex with a corpse.

Quiz: Elections

1. What was the only state carried by George McGovern in 1972?
2. Who are the only presidents who were impeached?
3. What Democratic presidential nominee twice went against Ike?
4. Who was the first vice president to die in office?
5. Who was William Miller (1964)?
6. What Massachusetts politician was re-elected from jail?
7. What elective office has the Reverend Jesse Jackson held?
8. Name a priest who served in the U.S. Congress.
9. Who was described as "the little man on the wedding cake"?
10. Who said "the vice presidency isn't worth a pitcher of warm spit"?

PTM: Judge Wapner

Judge Joseph A. Wapner sat on the California bench for over twenty years, but after retiring—and spending twelve seasons on The People's Court—*he became a national figure. In a world growing increasingly litigious, Wapner offered a voice of reason—and an explanation. He also had some helpful hints on how to avoid disputes in the first place.*

Nat Segaloff: Why have we become such a litigious society?

Judge Joseph A. Wapner: Generally what happens is that people's feelings are hurt. They feel that they have been wronged by somebody, and, come hell or high water, they are going to get their day in court and see to it that they win. They haven't been taught the art of compromise and that settlement is better than lawsuits. My specialty on the court when I sat was settling lawsuits. But people don't know one another; their next door neighbor is someone they may say hello to over the fence, but they don't know who they are. Most of the time, people could settle disputes if they would just be polite and understanding.

Segaloff: How could it be prevented?

Wapner: First, in order to prevent things from happening, what you have to do is the simple thing of getting it in writing. If you have a workman who's going to work for you, decide what it's going to cost and when it's going to be done and what materials are going into the job. Write these things out in simple language, rather than after the work is done and it's your word against my word and you go to the judge. Second, once you've done something, try and get together with the person and evaluate your position, and his or her position, and try to reach some common ground to settle it. If they just say, "sue me," then you are dealing with an individual who doesn't have any scruples. People like that think that the longer they keep the money in the bank earning interest, let the other guy wait for it. I've met people like that, and, as a lawyer, I remember suing people like that. It's hard to collect when you're just dealing with human beings who need to be taught a lesson and who are not going to pay unless they are sued.

PTM: Meegan Lee Ochs

Meegan Lee Ochs is the daughter of Phil Ochs (1940–1976), the singer-songwriter who could well be called the troubadour of the antiwar generation. Between 1964 and 1975 he recorded a legacy that reflected the anguish, but also the unfettered spirit, of his turbulent times. His music formed the voice of the '60s and '70s: "I Ain't Marching Anymore," "Here's to the State of Mississippi," "Outside of a Small Circle of Friends," and dozens more. Meegan has dedicated much of her adult life to supporting progressive social causes, many of which she learned about from Phil—remembering and extending the optimism that her father, toward the end, tragically forgot. Here she recalls one of the more pleasant events of the otherwise turbulent 1968 Democratic Convention in Chicago. She was 5, her father was 28, and America was 192.

By Meegan Lee Ochs

Phil Ochs' songs were an anthem to the times, and the times informed his soul. 1968 was one of those times. It was the Year of the Pig—at least in Chicago. Everybody in the antiwar movement expected the Democratic National Convention to be a sham, which is why they all met there to protest, in the streets, what was happening in the suites. After all, LBJ was in the White House, he was escalating the war, peace candidates didn't stand a chance, and yet the American people were overwhelmingly against what Washington was doing to Vietnam in their name.

At that time, activists called policeman "pigs," and since Mayor Daley of Chicago was using them to stifle protest, Abbie Hoffman, Jerry Rubin, and my father conspired to go out and get a real pig and run him for office. In the way that Abbie Hoffman and the others had of using humor to educate people, running a pig for public office seemed like a logical thing to do. They bought a pig, named it "Pigasus," and his campaign slogan was "Why take half a hog when you can have the whole thing?"

The pig announced his candidacy at a rally in Grant Park on August 23, 1968. Of course, Mayor Daley's cops arrested everybody—even the pig. It sounds funny now, but at the time they were terrified; the city was in the grip of a police riot, and there was the real chance that they would all be beaten in jail.

As they were led into the holding cell, a very grim cop came up to them. He was deadly serious, and he stared them squarely in the face.

"You guys are in a lot of trouble," he said. Then he paused, and then said, "The pig squealed."

That's when my father and everybody realized that things might not be all that bad, at least this time.

Four days later, on August 27, the Yippies held a demonstration at the Chicago Coliseum. It was called as a un-birthday party for Lyndon Johnson as well as a show of strength to urge Eugene McCarthy, Robert Kennedy, and other presidential hopefuls to force a peace plank onto the Democratic Party platform. That night my father appeared with Tom Hayden, Dick Gregory, William S. Burroughs, Jean Genet, Abbie Hoffman, Paul Krassner, David Dellinger, and five thousand of their closest friends. It was also the gathering of a new coalition: old faces from the Left, new faces from the schools, and bloody faces from the streets. My father sang "The War is Over"—and of course it wasn't. Then he sang "I Ain't Marching Anymore." The crowd sang along. When he got to the line "Even treason might be worth a try / The country is too young to die," somebody in the crowd lit a friendly match. Then somebody else did, too. Soon there were hundreds of people raising lighted matches—and then there were hundreds more raising lighted draft cards.

Paul Krassner called it "a patriotic display of spontaneous combustion." My father called it the most exciting moment of his career.

Quiz: Ideologies

Identify the person who espoused the following philosophies that have guided, at various times, the world's governments, commerce, and morality (these are indirect quotes):

1. Retaining power is more important than being liked. The end justifies the means.
2. Governments can best serve nations by a laissez-faire attitude toward economies.
3. Population increases geometrically while the world's resources increase arithmetically; so we'd better keep the population down.
4. Beware of all enterprises that requires new clothes.
5. Religion is the opiate of the masses.
6. Government is a necessary evil.
7. If there were left to me a choice between government without newspapers or newspapers without government, I would prefer the latter.
8. All propaganda has to be popular and must adapt its perception level to the least intelligent of those it intends to reach.
9. That government is best which governs least.
10. Nobody ever went broke underestimating the intelligence of the masses.

Quiz: CIA and USA

The Central Intelligence Agency (CIA) was formed after World War II in order to protect the security of America from without (as opposed to within, which was the FBI's ken). Over the years, the CIA has applied that mandate in a number of ways. Because of their ethic of secrecy, however, the CIA is often blamed for/credited with things they didn't do. Which of the following operations have been publicly linked with the CIA?

1. Gave LSD to people without telling them first
2. Despite inside sources, failed to predict fall of the Berlin Wall
3. Ran Bay of Pigs invasion
4. Spied domestically on Americans protesting Vietnam War
5. Supported/trained foreign groups that tortured people
6. Involved with groups trading drugs for arms in Iran/Contra
7. Carried out first recovery of man-made space object
8. Helped overthrow elected Chilean President Salvador Allende
9. Hired Nazi war criminals to spy on Russia after World War II
10. Backed coup attempt against Saddam Hussein by Iraqi exiles

Quiz: Abdications and Ascensions

The years following World War II were revolutionary for world politics. Match the ruler on the left (no pun intended) with his/her/its successor/spin-off on the right (pun sometimes intended). For extra credit, name the country involved. Where no human predecessor is named, it's because the successor was the first independent leader.

1.	George VI	a.	Itzhak Ben-Zvi
2.	Mao Tse-tung	b.	Gen. Mohammed Neguib
3.	President Prio Socarras	c.	Josip Broz (Tito)
4.	Farouk I	d.	Norodom Sihanouk
5.	Talal	e.	Nikita Khruschev
6.	Harry S. Truman	f.	Dwight D. Eisenhower
7.	Chaim Weizmann	g.	Chiang Kai-shek
8.	Josef Stalin	h.	Gen. Fulgencio Batista
9.	The Comintern	i.	Hussein
10.	France	j.	Elizabeth II

Quiz: Mass Murderers

In his black comedy *Monsieur Verdoux,* Charles Chaplin said of war, "One murder makes a villain, millions a hero. Numbers sanctify." The grizzly exception to that logic is mass murder—not by despots, but by individuals. Match the mass murderer or serial killer with his/her crimes:

1.	David Berkowitz	a.	28 black children, 1979–81
2.	Charles Starkweather	b.	33 boys and men, 1972–78
3.	Richard F. Speck	c.	3 to 17 (?) lonelyhearts, 1940s
4.	Charles Manson	d.	Unknown, 1929–1934
5.	Martha Beck	e.	8 student nurses, 1966
6.	Ted Bundy	f.	7 cult murders, 1969
7.	Howard Unruh	g.	18 friends and strangers, 1957–58
8.	"Baby Face" Nelson	h.	13 neighbors, 1949
9.	Wayne Williams	i.	6 car passengers, 1976–77
10.	John Wayne Gacy	j.	30 women, 1970s

Quiz: Are You Now or Have You Ever Been?

In 1947 the House Un-American Activities Committee (HUAC) held hearings to determine the extent of Communist influence in the movies, first in Los Angeles, and then in Washington, D.C. HUAC's chairman was Congressman J. Parnell Thomas (R-NJ); one of his associates was Congressman Richard M. Nixon (R-CA).

In 1950 Sen. Joseph R. Mccarthy (R-WI), after alluding to having a list of "known Communists" employed by the State Department, began a similar inquiry by his Senate Foreign Relations Committee. By the mid-1950s hundreds, possibly thousands, of Americans were blacklisted for their political beliefs. It was a time of fear. With half a century of hindsight, answer these questions:

1. What happened to Rep. J. Parnell Thomas?
2. What happened to Sen. Joseph R. McCarthy?
3. How much Communist material was found in Hollywood movies?
4. How many names did Joe McCarthy actually have on his list?
5. Name the "Hollywood Ten."
6. How long did the blacklist last?
7. What was *Red Channels*?
8. Who was Philip Loeb?
9. What was the legality of being a Communist?
10. What part did Robert F. Kennedy play in the era?

Quiz: People of the '60s

Match the people with what made them famous—or infamous—in the 1960s:

1. Lester Maddox
2. Kitty Genovese
3. Caesar Chavez
4. James Meredith
5. Albert Shanker
6. H. A. R. Philby
7. Betty Friedan
8. Otto Kerner
9. Paul Ehrlich
10. Bill Baird

a. Formed Zero Population Growth, Inc., to stabilize population
b. Authored *The Feminine Mystique*, which inspired the feminist movement
c. Closed his Pickrick restaurant rather than serve black customers
d. Journalist who defected to USSR in major spy scandal
e. Supervised controversial report on racial division in America
f. Confrontational birth control advocate
g. Founded United Federation of Teachers in New York
h. California community leader who organized United Farm Workers
i. Black student who enrolled in all-white Ole Miss
j. New Yorker stabbed to death while neighbors watched

Quiz: Seminatural Acts

Sometimes laws are passed that are so sweeping that they acquire a mystique and an identity all their own. Match these laws with their impact:

1. Blue Skies Laws
2. Mann Act
3. Holdberg Technicality
4. Sunset Laws
5. Blue Laws
6. Insanity Defense
7. Dyer Act
8. Unwritten Law
9. Three Strikes
10. Jury Nullification

a. Protects insane or incompetent people from prosecution for their crimes, but demands rigorous proof
b. Allows FBI to investigate auto theft
c. Curbs fraudulent investment schemes
d. Prescribes life behind bars without parole for three-time losers
e. Provides for a judge to throw out a jury verdict if he/she deems it was not based on the evidence
f. Outlaws transport of women across state lines for immoral purposes
g. Anti-farm-theft laws passed during Reconstruction to forbid transactions after sundown
h. Puritan-based regulation of business on Sunday
i. Famous conviction that was overturned because the defendant's name was misspelled
j. Outlawed legendary (and non-statutory) practice of a jury acquitting a husband for murdering a nagging wife

Quiz: Act of Succession

Comedians Peter Cook and Dudley Moore were once asked to explain the British Act of Succession to the crown. Without batting an eye, Cook said, "If fifty million people die tomorrow, Dudley is Queen." Apart from the throne, place these titles in order of British peerage, from highest to lowest:

1. Viscount/Viscountess
2. Earl/Countess
3. Baron/Baroness
4. Duke/Duchess
5. Marquis/Marchioness

COINTEL-PRO

As demoralizing as Watergate was to America, a policy called COINTEL-PRO served an even more sinister purpose. Begun without ceremony by FBI director J. Edgar Hoover under the Eisenhower administration and formalized in 1967 during the Johnson presidency, the FBI's "Counter-Intelligence Program" was nothing less than the systematic destruction of any political or social opposition to the *status quo*. COINTEL-PRO targeted such groups as Students for a Democratic Society (SDS), Congress of Racial Equality (CORE), Southern Christian Leadership Conference (SCLC), Socialist Workers Party (SWP), Student Non-Violent Coordinating Committee (SNCC), the American Nazi Party, and dozens of other legal and above-ground organizations. They did it through a combination of domestic spying activities including wiretaps, infiltration, breaking and entering, disinformation, and, in some cases, assassination. Although COINTEL-PRO's energy focused more strongly on left-wingers, the occasional archconservative was also hit; what made a group culpable was not its politics but how far it veered from the mainstream.

But Hoover saved his real venom for high-profile black trendsetters, chiefly individuals such as the Rev. Dr. Martin Luther King, Jr., and organizations such as the Black Panther Party.

Although, at its height in the late 1960s, the Panthers boasted fewer than a thousand members in the U.S., they had gained enormous—and enormously favorable—visibility through their free breakfast programs in Chicago schools and their efforts in forming a "rainbow coalition" among a spectrum of social reformers. That ended on December 5, 1969, when the FBI—acting on information provided by informant William O'Neal—raided Panther headquarters and shot Panther leaders Fred Hampton and Mark Clark in cold blood. O'Neal's credibility and the presence of Panther weapons have been disputed for three decades, but the effect on fringe organizing was striking. Combined with the Nixon draft lottery and the Kent State shootings, COINTEL-PRO went a long way toward scattering and demoralizing political protest in America.

More Dumb Laws

These days—when people seem more interested in the affairs of states*men* than in the Affairs of State—one is reminded that America is, after all, a nation of laws, and nobody is above them. Okay, buster, take a gander at *these* laws, all of which got on the books.

Hooray for Father Spaulding: In Alabama it is illegal to wear a fake moustache that causes laughter in church.

Hello, my name is Bullwinkle, and I'm an alcoholic: Fairbanks, Alaska, has a law against feeding alcohol to a moose.

Waiting for the Moon: In Nogales, Arizona, suspenders are illegal.

But it's okay to do it in the Governor's mansion?: In Arkansas, flirtation on the streets of Little Rock between men and women may result in a thirty-day jail term.

But, Officer, she looked over twenty-one hours old: Pacific Grove, California, has made it illegal to "molest" butterflies (actually, there's a famous Monarch Butterfly sanctuary in Pacific Grove).

And your little dog, too: People who make "ugly faces" at dogs in Oklahoma may be fined and/or jailed.

The only good dandelion is a dead dandelion: In Pueblo, Colorado, it's illegal to let a dandelion grow within city limits.

To get to the other side, your Honor: Quitman, Georgia, passed a law against letting a chicken cross a road.

What, Me Worry?: Baltimore, Maryland, passed a law banning Randy Newman's song, "Short People," on the radio.

No, but Lucca Brazzi can sleep with them: You can't fish in your pajamas in Chicago.

Golly, Toto, tell your mother we're not in Kansas any more: Wichita, Kansas, does not allow a man's mistreatment of his mother-in-law to be used as grounds for divorce.

Third time's the charm, but fourth time's an indictment: A woman can't remarry the same man four times in Kentucky.

Particularly nasty weather?: In Portland, Maine, it is illegal for a man to tickle a woman under her chin with a feather duster.

Belch "Amen!" somebody: Parents may be arrested if their child burps during a church service in Omaha, Nebraska.

I brake for sparrows: Birds have the right of way on all highways in Utah.

Tough room: Clergy in Nicholas County, West Virginia, are forbidden to tell jokes or humorous stories from the pulpit during church services.

How many surrealists does it take . . . : Tennessee banned the use of a lasso to catch fish.

PTM: John Randolph

In 1997, half a century after the implementation of the infamous Hollywood blacklist, the film community offered its victims an apology. One of those victims was actor John Randolph. Now known as Roseanne's father on the hit Roseanne *TV series, other credits include* Touched by an Angel, Seinfeld, *and PBS's* A Foreign Field, *as well as key roles in* Serpico, The Front, Prizzi's Honor, All the President's Men, *and the miniseries* Blind Ambition. *First seen on Broadway in the Federal Theatre's production of* Medicine Show, *Randolph, while struggling as a young actor, wrote an article entitled "Americans All" for the magazine* New Masses. *The article was considered radical, and so was he.*

"How could you not *become radicalized during the Depression?" he said later. "You'd have to be an idiot not to be a radical with seventeen million unemployed!" By 1952, Randolph, himself, joined the ranks of the unemployed. Blacklisted until his role in* Seconds *in 1968, Randolph was not allowed to work in movies or TV. That didn't mean he had to be silent about it, however; indeed, he was (and is) an outspoken critic of repression. (From an interview with the author.)*

By John Randolph

In 1955 I was in a play called *Much Ado about Nothing* at the Brattle Theatre in Cambridge, Massachusetts. I was in the company of some very elite actors; they all seemed very strange to me. I had done *Guys and Dolls* in New York, playing one of the leading parts, Nathan Detroit, and then I went right into *Much Ado about Nothing.*

I also had just signed a contract to do [a play called] *Wooden Dish,* with Louis Calhern [after *Much Ado* finished its run]. Louis Calhern was a Hollywood actor, so far as I knew; I didn't know anything else about him.

I told my wife, "You take care of the contract, Sarah." In our business we have a "five day" clause which says that they have five days to fire you, or you can give them notice in five days, and be out of the show. But if it was a run-of-the-play contract, if they fired you, they had to pay you all the rest of the time the show was running. Well, my wife told them, "John doesn't want to be stuck with a run-of-the-play contract." If ever I'd wanted to be stuck, it was then, because that's when my name appeared as being subpoenaed by the House Un-American Activities Committee. [The Committee was holding hearings in New York City in August of 1955 under committee counsel Frank Tavenner].

When I got my subpoena, there's a difference between saying "Well, screw them, they can't do anything to me" and realizing that it's still the United States government that says you have to appear. I was scheduled to appear in the afternoon [in New York], but I had to be on the stage of the Brattle Theatre [in Massachusetts] that night. Now, I'm brave and I know how to fight, but on the train I was writing pamphlets, leaflets, and damn it, at the same time I know there's a telegram waiting for me at the Brattle Theatre to fire me.

So, when I came in to the Brattle, there was the stage manager with a telegram in his hand. Now, I want to tell you, it's terrible when you know that's your end in the business; you can't work on stage, on radio or television—I could not work anywhere by that time. But I opened the telegram and it said, "I just want you to know that we're going to have a wonderful run together," signed Louis Calhern.

I said to myself, "Well, I can fight now. I've got the star behind me. But what about these other actors I'm working with?" I could see getting support from the cast of *Guys and Dolls,* but here was a group of actors doing *Much Ado about Nothing* and putting on their makeup and feathered hats and dancing.

But I went into the dressing room, and as soon as I walked in they looked at me and began to sing the union organizing song, "Which Side Are You On?" and then they began singing "Solidarity Forever!" and I knew, Jesus Christ, I'm with friends.

Get a Life: Great Catherine

Question: The joke used to go, "By day she was Catherine of Russia, but by night she was Catherine the Great." You knew this was coming, so here it is: How did Catherine the Great die?

Answer: Alone. The Russian Empress—who succeeded to the throne in 1762, when she had her husband, the feeble-minded Peter III, killed—died on November 17, 1796, most likely of a stroke. The sixty-seven-year-old Catherine had spent the night with her twenty-seven-year-old lover, and, after he left, she retired to her dressing room to refresh herself. When she failed to emerge, her servants entered and found her semiconscious on the floor. Contrary to persistent schoolyard legend, a horse, ropes, and scaffolding had nothing to do with it.

Letter of the Law (Answers)

1. *Assault* is a threat or attempt of violence; *battery* is actually doing it.
2. *Forgery* is creating a false signature with intent to defraud; *uttering* is putting the forged item to use.
3. *Burglary* is unlawful presence, with the intention of taking; *robbery* is taking something using violence or intimidation.
4. These words are often confused: *Abdication* means to relinquish something, such as elective office; *abrogation* is a formal cancellation, such as of a contract.
5. The *prostate* is a gland; *prostrate* means laying face down on the ground. Try not to confuse these.
6. *Slander* is a spoken statement that damages someone's reputation; *libel* is a written statement. Both are properly called *defamation*.
7. Both *inalienable* and *unalienable* mean the same thing: irrevocable. Despite over two hundred years of confusion, the Declaration of Independence uses *unalienable*.
8. *Habeas corpus* is a judge's order to bring the prisoner forth to determine the legality of his imprisonment; *corpus delicti* is the evidence that proves a crime has been committed. It can be a dead body, but it can also be stolen diamonds, a hot stereo, etc.
9. *Malfeasance* is an improper act by a public official; *misfeasance* is screwing up a proper act; *nonfeasance* is the failure to perform a proper act at all.
10. A *pardon* is the complete forgiveness for a crime (usually without wiping out the record of the conviction); *parole* is the release from prison of a convicted felon, usually with additional requirements. *Exempli gratia*: Nixon was pardoned, but G. Gordon Liddy got paroled.

Dumb Laws (Answers)

1. True
2. False
3. True
4. True
5. False
6. True
7. False
8. True
9. True
10. True

Elections (Answers)

1. Massachusetts
2. Andrew Johnson and Bill Clinton
3. Adlai Stevenson
4. George Clinton (under President James Madison)
5. Barry Goldwater's vice presidential running mate
6. James Michael Curley
7. None
8. Fr. Robert F. Drinan, S.J. (Massachusetts)
9. Thomas E. Dewey (who opposed Truman in 1948)
10. John Nance Garner (FDR's last vice president)

Ideologies (Answers)

1. Niccolo Machiavelli, *The Prince*
2. Adam Smith, *The Wealth of Nations*
3. Thomas Malthus, *Essay on the Principle of Population*
4. Henry David Thoreau, *Walden*
5. Karl Marx, *Critique of Hegelian Philosophy of Right*
6. Thomas Paine, *Common Sense*
7. Thomas Jefferson, letter to Col. Edward Carrington
8. Adolf Hitler, *Mein Kampf*
9. Unknown—usually attributed to Thomas Jefferson; quoted by Thoreau in *Civil Disobedience*
10. H. L. Mencken, *Chicago Tribune* column

CIA and USA (Answers)

The CIA has been publicly linked with all of them.

Abdications and Ascensions (Answers)

1. j (England)
2. g (Taiwan)
3. h (Cuba)
4. b (Egypt)
5. i (Jordan)
6. f (USA)
7. a (Israel)
8. e (USSR)
9. c (Yugoslavia)
10. d (Cambodia)

Mass Murderers (Answers)

1. i
2. g
3. e
4. f
5. c
6. j
7. h
8. d
9. a
10. b

Answers

Are You Now or Have You Ever Been? (Answers)

1. J. Parnell Thomas was convicted of padding his expense account and sentenced to jail in Danbury, Connecticut. Among his fellow inmates were two of the "Hollywood Ten" (q.v.).
2. After being censured by the Senate, Joseph R. McCarthy died an alcoholic.
3. No Communist material was ever found in Hollywood movies.
4. The number of names Joe McCarthy had on his list was never known, since he refused to substantiate it. His aide, Roy Cohn, suggested that "57" might be a good number to settle on, after consulting the label on a ketchup bottle.
5. The "Hollywood Ten"—ten writers, producers, and directors who were cited for contempt of Congress for refusing to "name names" to HUAC—were (alphabetically) Alvah Bessie, Herbert Biberman, Lester Cole, Edward Dmytryk, Ring Lardner, Jr., John Howard Lawson, Albert Maltz, Samuel Ornitz, Adrian Scott, and Dalton Trumbo.
6. The Hollywood blacklist started to crumble in 1960, when Dalton Trumbo was given screen credit by producer-director Otto Preminger for *Exodus* and by producer-actor Kirk Douglas for *Spartacus*. Fifty years later, Hollywood is still trying to restore correct credits to films "fronted" by others.
7. Published (anonymously) by formal U.S. Naval Intelligence officer Vincent Hartnett, *Red Channels* was a paperback booklet that accused people of left-leaning activities, without proof and with no recourse.
8. When he was unable to get work, blacklisted actor Philip Loeb—costar of early television's popular series *The Rise of the Goldbergs*—committed suicide.
9. It has never been against the law in the United States of America to be a Communist.
10. As a young man seeking experience in Washington, Robert F. Kennedy served for a short time as an investigator for Senator Joseph R. McCarthy.

People of the '60s (Answers)

1. c
2. j
3. h
4. i
5. g
6. d
7. b
8. e
9. a
10. f

Semi-Natural Acts (Answers)

1. c
2. f
3. i
4. g
5. h
6. a
7. b
8. j
9. d
10. e

Act of Succession (Answers)

4, 5, 2, 1, 3

Chapter 9

Science and Geography

What good does it do to study science or geography? When will it come up in later life that you need to know the difference between an *isthmus* and a *peninsula*, or why H_2O_2 is an isotope and H_2O isn't?

The irony is that the second half of the twentieth century saw the most profound progress in science and geography since human curiosity was rekindled during the Renaissance. From the Wright Brothers' take-off in 1903 to Neil Armstrong's landing in 1969, humankind fulfilled a species-long ambition. Likewise, from Jules Verne's fictitious circumnavigation of the globe in eighty days in 1872 to John Glenn's orbiting it in eighty minutes in 1962, the earth became more intimate, its secrets less remote. In 1944 nobody could see an atom; in 1945 the atomic bomb had split one.

To a society in which education has been bifurcated into *pure* and *applied*—with emphasis on applied—it's hard to make a case for studying subjects that don't put groceries on the table. Math has a clear purpose; so does chemistry; so do foreign languages (if only to ask your illegal nanny not to testify against you if you ever get that cabinet nomination). But science and geography? Might as well be art history.

And so, with such values, begins the devolution of the human mind. The secret of humankind's dominance on the planet has been not only how one wins the day but also how one builds the future. The most difficult thing about studying science is keeping track of it. Quite literally, given the speed of discoveries nowadays, by the time a textbook gets into print, it is already out of date. As for geography, now that we know where everything is on earth, we can take the time to go back for a closer examination. In so doing, we may discover connections between disparate locales and clues to the creation of the planets. After we've measured the highest, lowest, longest, shortest, hottest, and coldest places, we can start unraveling a mystery that is even more provocative: *Why?*

To know science is to know the foundation of life on earth. To study humankind's relationship with the universe is to take control of one's self rather than to be buffeted by the forces of fear and ignorance. Knowledge will always be threatening to people who don't have it. The one thing that separates human beings from other animals is that we can ask questions and find answers.

In 1957 the United States was shocked into learning about science. That was the year that the Soviet Union placed Sputnik into orbit around the earth. Both the US and the USSR had been working toward just such a feat, and it stunned Americans to realize that the Russians did it first. An explanation was offered by a frustrated National Aeronautics and Space Administration (NASA) official: "Their German scientists were better than our German scientists." Immediately, President Eisenhower declared the IGY—the International

Geophysical Year—and launched an ambitious plan to gear the nation's schools toward the study of science. At the same time, however, scientists were persecuted for stepping outside the lab: It was okay for them to build H-Bombs, for example, but it was deemed unpatriotic for them to sign petitions banning them.

But, then, scientists had been encountering discrimination since the turn of the century. The "Golden Era" of discovery from roughly 1880 to the World War I saw the introduction of the automobile, heavier-than-air flight, electric lights, the phonograph, movies, telephones, and a myriad other inventions. At the same time, the promise of these devices had become sullied by the reality of their use: Motor cars clogged city streets; electric lines insulted the skyline; the telephone interrupted quiet evenings at home; and movies were not fit for family viewing. The last straw may have been the 1912 sinking of the unsinkable Titanic, a ship that epitomized people's arrogance. Of course, scientists were to blame. Not only that, they were agnostic, or worse, blasphemers who dared to challenge the miracle of creation. "I am more interested in the Rock of Ages than the age of rocks," said William Jennings Bryan at the Scopes "Monkey Trial" in 1925, denying not only the legitimacy of science but the possibility of truth.

Even as science solves problems, it raises others. There's the old joke—a man discovered a cure for which there was no known disease—that pokes fun at scientists' penchant for doing research for its own sake without heed to what they might turn up. Such ethical dilemmas haunt the men and women who must make them, as well as deeply trouble society at large. Has curiosity gotten out of hand? Has science "gone too far"? Or are these thorny moral issues the price we pay for being human? In the final analysis, science is not the villain. The villain is what the misguided human mind does with it. The trick is to inspire the human heart to guide the way.

A Ralph by Any Other Name

George Bernard Shaw supposedly said that the Americans and the British are two nations separated by a common language. The same might be said of Americans from different regions of the country. Here are some examples of how geography can change the name of familiar items and activities:

1. Soda fountain drink in which ice cream, flavoring, and milk are whipped together: frappe/cabinet/milk shake
2. Long sandwich: hoagie/hero/sub/grinder
3. Sausage made of beef, pork, and filler: frank/frankfurter/hot dog/wiener/steamer/red hot
4. Cod fish: scrod/schrod/codfish/whitefish (Note: In New England, *scrod* is a young cod; *schrod*, spelled with an *h,* is a young haddock.)
5. Shellfish peculiar to Gulf region: crayfish/crawfish/crawdad/crawdaddy
6. Kitchen appliances used to keep food cold: ice box/refrigerator/fridge[1]
7. Kitchen appliance for heating/cooking food: stove/range
8. Torso covering: pants/trousers/slacks; dungarees/jeans/levis[2]

9. Container: bucket/pail ?
10. Diagonal positioning: cattycorner/kitty-corner/catercorner ?
11. Work clothes: overalls/coveralls/bibs ?
12. Arachnic's trap: spider web/cobweb ?
13. 55 mph road: freeway/turnpike/highway/throughway ?
14. Circular intersection: rotary/round-about/circle ?
15. Carbonated drink: soda/pop/tonic/soft drink ?
16. Carbonated drink made from hops: beer/brew/brewskie/cervesa
17. Best place to get rid of carbonated drink made from hops: loo/head/crapper/bathroom/toilet/lavatory/gents/necessary/latrine/throne/commode/visiting Mrs. Murphy
20. What Jed Clampett found: bubblin' crude/oil, that is/black gold/Texas tea

---

[1] Nickname derived from Fridgidaire®

[2] Levi's® Levi-Strauss Co.

Get a Life: Mercury 7

Question: Name the *Mercury 7*.

Answer: Seven military test pilots were selected by NASA in April of 1959 to participate in Project Mercury. Here are their names and the dates of their flights:

Lt. L. M. Scott Carpenter, USN
Capt. L. Gordon Cooper, Jr., USAF
Lt. Col. John H. Glenn, Jr., USMC
Virgil I. "Gus" Grissom, USAF
Lt. Cmdr. Walter M. "Wally" Shirra, Jr., USN
Lt. Cmdr. Alan B. Shepard, Jr., USN
Capt. Donald K. "Deke" Slayton, USAF

Aurora 7: May 24, 1962
Faith 7: May 15–16, 1963
Friendship 7: February 20, 1962
Liberty Bell y: July 21, 1961
Sigma 7: October 3, 1962
Freedom 7: May 5, 1961
Apollo-Soyuz Docking Pilot: 1975

Quiz: Far Out

Name the farthest geographical points of the fifty states:

1. East
2. West
3. North
4. South
5. Highest
6. Lowest
7. Exact Center

Quiz: Science Myths

Before Copernicus, everybody thought the sun revolved around the earth; it took a while (and several inquisitions) to catch on, but nowadays most people know better. Here are a couple of persistent scientific myths. Or maybe not. Which are true?

1. Water swirls down the drain the other way in Australia.
2. You can catch a bird if you put salt on its tail.
3. You can't stare too long at the sun.
4. There is no such fish as a sardine.
5. Hair and fingernails keep growing after death.
6. Mixing milk and meat is dangerous.
7. Owls see perfectly well during the day.
8. It's okay to mix alcoholic drinks.
9. When you freeze food, it kills the bacteria.
10. Saltpeter is useful in suppressing sexual urges.

Quiz: Weather or Not

Here's a weather question for you: If Dorothy Gale, in the movie *The Wizard of Oz* had been carried off by a tornado instead of a cyclone, would she still have been able to play Twister? How much meteorology do you remember from school? Match the spinning wind to the name for it:

1.	Cyclone	a.	Rotating storm greater than 75 mph
2.	Tornado	b.	Small dusty tornado that precedes a bigger tornado
3.	Hurricane	c.	Small atmospheric vortex that comes from surface heating, not thunderstorms
4.	Waterspout	d.	Rotating column of air occurring over water
5.	Dust devil	e.	Violent vortex rotating in the same direction as the earth
6.	Gustnado	f.	Violently rotating air column, beneath a thunderstorm, that touches the ground

Quiz: Real or Contrived

Truth may be stranger than fiction, especially if you're a writer trying to find a name for something. Below are planets, elements, institutions, and characters. Which were named from scratch and which draw their name from real life?

1. Vulcan
2. Kryptonite
3. Cavorite
4. Zirconium
5. Quark
6. Nanosecond
7. Platformate
8. Kodak
9. E. J. Korvette's
10. Oz

Space Aliens

Why do the tabloids call them "space aliens"? Is it to distinguish them from, what, illegal aliens? Resident aliens? Enemy Aliens? Aliens who own tabloid newspapers? And who believes they've really landed, anyway? Just in case, here are some telltale signs. (The cast of *Men in Black* or *Third Rock from the Sun* need not apply.) You know your coworker is a space alien if he/she evinces (that means "shows") several of the following characteristics:

1. Has strange eating or dressing habits. If they wear mismatched clothes or eat French fries with a spoon, that means that they don't have the knack of earth living.
2. Has a bizarre sense of humor. This is particularly true at supermarket checkout lines, where they try to make conversation with the bagger, and he doesn't get it.
3. Is unfamiliar with national holidays. Anybody who doesn't know what Thanksgiving or Fourth of July are about is obviously "not from here" (hint hint).
4. Acts strangely around microwave ovens. This is because the radiation may be altering his/her alien's perception of reality.
5. Talks to himself/herself. This is a clue that the "person" is trying to get a grip and has no one else to trust.
6. Makes fun of *Star Trek* or *Babylon 5* but fully understands *2001*. When you think about it, this is logical. Since space aliens are familiar with the real thing, why should they bother with mere speculation?

7. Becomes impatient with simple tools. Because space aliens have highly sophisticated equipment at their disposal, they can become irritated that simple hammers, screwdrivers, computers, and CAT-scan machines perform more slowly than they are used to.
8. Receives high-quality cable TV. No one on earth gets cable TV worth a damn, so anybody who does has *got* to be a space alien.
9. Has seen Elvis recently. No explanation needed.

Sharks!

Jaws in 1975 was only the dorsal fin in the water of the public's obsession with sharks. Nowadays it's hard to find an aquarium, bookstore, or cable channel that doesn't scream "shark" in a crowded marketplace. Author/broadcaster Paul Erickson—who probably encounters more sharks in business suits than in the ocean—has a take on the phenomenon.

By Paul Erickson

Not long after the release of Steven Spielberg's *Jaws*, while I was lecturing to an audience about sharks at Boston's New

England Aquarium, a young man with a troubled look on his face asked me if it was safe to go in the water. I gave him my standard spiel about how sharks in the waters off New England savored fish, not people, and that he should just listen to the lifeguard and not worry about sharks when he went swimming in the ocean.

"I'm not talking about the ocean," he said. "I'm talking about swimming in a lake."

That's when I began to realize the full extent to which *Jaws* had stirred up fear. After I convinced the youngster that running into a shark in Walden Pond was right up there with his spending Christmas on the planet Neptune, I recalled some of my own fears as a kid who spent summers on the New Jersey shore.

Back then, in the '60s, every once in a while we'd hear about shark scares and something terrible having to do with sharks "long ago." But, aside from the little spiny dogfish sharks that washed up dead from time to time, I gave little thought to sharks; we were far more concerned with lightning, because a boy had died after being struck during a midsummer thunderstorm that swept through Long Beach Island.

It wasn't until years later that I learned of something horrible that *did* happen along the New Jersey shore. During the summer of 1916, within a roughly two-week period, one or more sharks killed four people and left a survivor with an impressive scar on his leg.

Yes, some sharks can mangle you pretty effectively. Just ask some of the surfers who've been shredded by sharks off California's mid-coast. Most sharks, however, want nothing to do with the odd primates in bathing suits or scuba gear who wade or sink into their watery world. But if we're talking about the rare case when a shark noshes on a human, what fascinates us is the fact that a shark is one of the few things that will actually eat you. Unlike, say, a grizzly bear or a crocodile that you find in some distant wilderness, most predators don't visit major population centers. Yet it *is* possible for potentially deadly sharks to swim the inner harbors of New York, Boston, San Francisco, and other coastal cities.

But the reason I like sharks is the same reason I like airplanes: There are enough different kinds to fascinate you for a lifetime. For example, there are some 375 species of sharks. At a length of 45 feet or more, the whale shark is Mr. Big. Then (in the category of famous predators) there are tiger sharks, bull sharks, and great whites. There's also no shortage of oddballs; we've all seen pictures of those bizarre hammerheads. And the miniature 18-inch-long deep-sea "cookie cutter" shark is bold enough to even attack submarines!

All in all, sharks are just plain fascinating, occasionally lethal, and have a lot more charisma than some of the other things that can kill you, like a virus or a beer truck.

©1998 Paul Erickson. Paul Erickson is a marine biologist as well as an award-winning author, broadcaster, and producer with the New England Aquarium. He has explored and photographed Loch Ness, the Red Sea, the Caribbean, the Solomon Islands, Boston Harbor, and Baja, California.

Museums

Comedian Steven Wright says he once went to a children's museum where all the artwork was hung on refrigerators. Most museums don't have a sense of humor, however, as anyone who's ever been to a presidential library can attest.

Here are some museums with which you might not be familiar. Surely not all of them wear a straight face. But which?

1. Museum of Jurassic Technology (9341 Venice Boulevard, Los Angeles, CA 90034). This museum contains carefully researched and preserved relics establishing the scientific advancements of the best known dinosaur period. The staff is extremely helpful, and the exhibits are astonishing. That's if you don't get it. If you do catch on, it becomes a giddy experience in performance art.

2. U.S. National Tick Collection (Institute of Anthropodology and Parasitology, Georgia Southern University, Statesboro, GA 30460). The government funded this stash of 120,000 vials containing over a million dead ticks. Given the human diseases associated with the tiny critters (Rocky Mountain Spotted Fever and Lyme disease being the best known), the collection is useful for diagnostic purposes. At last count, it contained 760 of 850 known species from pinhead-sized to over an inch. And, no, there isn't a tick museum somewhere else.

3. First Century Museum (off the I-90 at the 14th Street exit, in a shopping mall west of Rochester, MN). Whatever the owners may call it, this is the Spam® Museum. It's built by Hormel, the meat products producer and traces their history—which is, of course, the history of American consumer mass-marketing. They make Dinty Moore®, Cure 81 hams, Little Sizzlers® and, of course, Spam®, Spam®, Spam®, Spam®, and Spam®.

4. Museum of Questionable Medical Devices (291 S.E. Main Street, Minneapolis, MN 55414). Looking to grow back amputated fingers? Exercise your eyes aerobically? Grow hair where you want it and stop growing it where you don't want it? Heal rheumatism? Build your breasts or giganticize your johnson? This museum preserves over 250 items that were sold as patent remedies, chiefly in the early twentieth century, when charlatans of the marvels of technology held promise for all but cures for none.

5. Barbie® Hall of Fame (460 Waverly Street, Palo Alto, CA 94301). Mattel's trend-setting doll is immortalized in all her trendy, fashion-conscious glory. Since her introduction in 1959, she has almost done better than the little girls for whom she was designed: astronaut, doctor, soldier, executive, chef, and rock star. At least one of each (and sixteen thousand more) live in this lovingly kept human-sized doll house—with Ken, of course.

6. Crayola Hall of Fame (1100 Church Lane, Easton, PA 18044). If there is anywhere in America that people can still use the word *colored*, this is it. Built by Binney and Smith, makers of the beloved green-and-yellow-boxed Crayola crayons, this site was built in reaction (atonement?) to the company's highly controversial dropping of eight outdated colors and the umbrage (or was it raw umbrage) that resulted. The Hall of Fame offers playbacks of people reminiscing about what Crayolas and colors mean to them.

7. International Checkers Hall of Fame (220 Lynn Ray Road, Petal, MS 39465). President Nixon wasn't the only one who did well with Checkers; Petal, Mississippi, does pretty well every couple of years, when they host international tournaments of this time-honored game (which began a thousand years ago in India). In addition to a floor-sized checkerboard with throw pillows for markers, the museum features a collection of boards, checkers, and living quarters for visiting pros.

8. Buford Pusser Home and Museum (342 Pusser Street, Adamsville, TN 38310). Sheriff Buford Pusser was a celebrated sheriff of McNairy County whose courage against organized crime inspired the *Walking Tall* films as well as a violent assassination attempt that took the life of his wife, Pauline. To some, Pusser, who died in 1974, was Andy of Mayberry; to others, he was a thug with a badge. Only the former will enjoy this shrine to his life and career that exists just as he left it.

Nobel Prizes

"Inherited wealth is a misfortune which merely serves to dull a man's faculties," declared Alfred B. Nobel in his will in 1895, when he established his $9.2 million endowment for the prizes that would bear his name. Nobel, who got rich from inventing dynamite in 1866, willed that his fortune should be invested "in safe securities . . . the interest accruing from which shall be annually awarded in prizes."

Among the first awards were those to W. C. Roentgen for his discovery of X rays and Emil von Behring for his diphtheria vaccine.

Quiz: Inventions

Who invented, developed, or popularized the following items:

1. Yo-yo
2. Typewriter
3. Parking meter
4. Bunsen burner
5. Zipper
6. Escalator
7. Steamboat
8. Vacuum tube
9. Sewing machine
10. Electric razor

Get a Life: Laika

Question: Who was Laika?

Answer: In November of 1957, after the USSR had launched *Sputnik* and President Eisenhower declared the space race open, the Soviets launched *Sputnik 2*. Sealed inside *Sputnik 2* and shot into space was a female husky dog named Laika. Since, at the time, there was no way to retrieve satellites from their orbit, Laika became, by design, the first orbital casualty of humankind's exploration of the stars. In August of 1960, the Soviets launched two more dogs, Strelka and Belka, on a twenty-four-hour flight and recovered them.

Fun Food Facts

1. The lollypop was named after a race horse, Lolly Pop, of the early 1900s.
2. The Baby Ruth candy bar was not named after baseball player Babe Ruth but, rather, in honor of President and Mrs. Grover Cleveland's daughter.
3. You know those wonderful Junior Mints and other candies made by Welch's? Robert O. Welch, who founded the company (it's since been sold), was also founder of the John Birch Society.
4. M&Ms are named after Frank Mars, the candy maker, and his business associate, Bruce Murrie.
5. It's true: Wintergreen LifeSavers® emit sparks when chewed in the dark (and, presumably, when chewed in the light, only you can't see them). The reason is triboluminescence.
6. The reason you don't see people drinking beer in the TV commercials is that the foam is usually made of detergent suds.
7. An ostrich egg will feed twenty-four people, but it takes three apples to make a glass of cider.
8. There is no such person as Betty Crocker. She was invented in 1921 by the Washburn Crosby Company, a miller, to answer customer baking questions.
9. One in ten TV commercials is for fast food.
10. Caesar salad is named after Tijuana restaurant owner Caesar Cardini. Originally, the romaine lettuce leaves were uncut and eaten whole, using the fingers.

Human Extremes

- Tallest man: Robert Pershing Wadlow; 8 feet 11.1 inches
- Tallest woman: Zeng Jinlian; 8 feet 1.75 inches
- Tallest living man: Haji Mohammad Channa; 7 feet 7.25 inches
- Tallest living woman: Sandy Allen; 7 feet 7.25 inches
- Shortest man: Calvin Phillips; 26.4 inches
- Shortest woman: Pauline Musters; 23.2 inches
- Oldest person: Jeanne Louise Calment; 121 years old, from Arles, France (died as this book was being written)
- Heaviest living woman: Rosalie Bradford; once 1,200 pounds
- Heaviest living man: Walter Hudson; once 1,197 pounds

Our Bodies, Our Trivia

- Tooth enamel is the hardest substance in the human body.
- The stirrup bone in the ear is the smallest bone in the body.
- Fingernails and toenails take six months to grow from base to tip. Contrary to rumor, they do not keep growing after death; instead, the cuticles shrink.
- The human heart beats more than 2.8 billion times during the average life (except during Wes Craven films).

- The male pulse rate is 72 times a minute; the female pulse is 75, although when they're together, they can be faster.
- The body's largest organ is the skin.
- Four groups of bacteria live on the human body; saliva contains six.
- A dog's mouth is cleaner than a human's mouth in the sense that the spaces between a dog's teeth harbor less bacteria; on the other hand, dogs *do* eat their own poo.
- A human sneeze shoots stuff out at 100 mph.

Get a Life: Phlogiston

Question: What is phlogiston?

Answer: In ancient Greece, Aristotle taught that there were four substances—earth, air, fire, and water (not to be confused with Earth, Wind, and Fire, the '70s pop music group)—from which sprang all things on earth. They also came to believe in a fifth element called "phlogiston," which was supposed to be a chemical that was created when fire burned. In fact, just the opposite is true: Fire is the *result* of the combustion of matter in the presence of oxygen, giving off light, heat, and flame.

Quiz: Medical Saviors

Match the doctor/researcher with the medical discovery:

1.	Thomas H. Weller	a.	Nitrous oxide as anesthetic
2.	John F. Enders	b.	X rays
3.	Louis Pasteur	c.	Measels vaccine
4.	von Behring and Kitazato	d.	Ether as anesthetic
5.	Edward Jenner	e.	Diphtheria vaccine
6.	Jonas Salk	f.	Stethoscope
7.	Horace Wells	g.	Smallpox vaccine
8.	William Morton	h.	Cholera vaccine
9.	Wilhelm Konrad Roentgen	i.	German measels vaccine
10.	Rene Laennec	j.	Polio vaccine

Quiz: Additives

A helpful maxim regarding food additives is, "If you can't pronounce it, don't eat it." Identify the purpose of the following:

1.	Sodium ascorbate	a.	Color fixative; also burning agent
2.	Sodium carbonate	b.	Thickener and firming agent
3.	Nitrate	c.	Levening agent; also fireproofing
4.	Benzoic acid	d.	Anti-oxidant; retards spoiling
5.	Ammonium phosfate	e.	Synthetic flavor; nail polish remover
6.	Hydrolyzed vegetable protetin	f.	Emulsifier/gelling agent; cosmetics
7.	Butyl acetate	g.	Soda ash; antacid and neutralizer
8.	Furfural	h.	Antifungal agent; candy flavoring
9.	Guar gum	i.	Synthetic flavor and insecticide
10.	Gum arabic	j.	Flavor enhancer; high salt content

Four Laws of Thermodynamics

Energy flows from the greater to the lesser until both sides are equal; this is an aspect of *entropy*, which measures energy in a given system. Put another way, this means that if you douse a hot poker into a bucket of water, the heat from the poker will raise the temperature of the water until they are both the same. Scientists believe that, eventually, the universe will arrive at a, well, universal temperature, too (but not before your student loans have to be paid back).

This is an extension of the four laws of thermodynamics. Beginning in the nineteenth century, scientists formulated the four laws. However, they didn't formulate them in order; after they had agreed on three, a fourth one made itself apparent with such logic and clarity that they went back and made it number zero (or the zeroth law of thermodynamics):

0. No heat will flow between any two bodies that are the same temperature.
1. Energy can be neither created nor destroyed (a body gains or loses energy by taking it or passing it to its environment or another body).
2. Heat will not pass spontaneously from a cold body to a hotter one. (So when you put ice cubes in your drink, it's not the ice that cools the drink but, rather, the heat that flows into the ice, giving the *relative* sensation of making the drink cooler.)
3. It is impossible to cool a body to absolute zero (the state at which there is no movement of matter; that is, -273.16°C) because to do so would require a still cooler object.

Priestley Cola

The carbonated drink owes its existence to the man who co-discovered oxygen. Joseph Priestley, who, with Karl Wilhelm Scheele, discovered the presence of oxygen in the 1770s, lived near a brewery in Leeds, England. Because of the fermentation, the brewery could supply Priestley with plenty of CO_2, otherwise known as carbon dioxide. In 1772 Priestley devised a way of impregnating liquid with the gas and tried to market his discovery as "Pyrmont water," a fizzy version of a local mineral water. It didn't sell as a curative, but the secret has kept the world burping ever since.

Deserts Hot and Cold

Quick, think of a desert. The Sahara, right? Lots of sand and heat? You'd only be half right. Strictly speaking, a desert is a barren area that has too little rainfall (less than 10 inches a year) to support life. By this definition, Antarctica is as much of a desert as the Sahara. Although some life can survive in desert conditions (insects, small reptiles, and sparse plants in heat; seabirds and some fungi in cold), most are merely visitors, such as camels, seals, and humans.

Approximately one-tenth of the earth's surface is covered with a permanent ice cap. If Antarctica and Greenland were to melt, the earth's oceans would rise 200 feet and engulf New York and Tokyo, among other large cities. The salinity of the world's oceans would also be greatly diluted, since the ice caps comprise roughly 30 percent of the world's fresh water.

Another kind of desert is called an *edaphic* desert, where, despite rainfall, the soil is too poor to grow anything. Edaphic deserts can be found on volcanic Iceland and in some areas of Colorado that were volcanic in the past (and where dinosaur fossils are now found). These three types of deserts account for 34 percent of the earth's surface.

What a Body

There are lots of things to know about the human body. Some things we discover for ourselves; others are brought to our attention by education. Here are ten tidbits that you might have missed:

1. By the age of two, a normal child has attained roughly half his/her adult height. So when your child turns two and you mark his/her height behind the bedroom door, double it to see what he/she will be when fully grown.
2. There is no truth to the old maxim that "we only use 10 percent of our brain." But if it were true, wouldn't it be nice if we could defrag ourselves every couple of years?
3. The heart beats more than 2.8 billion times during the course of an average human's life. An adult man's average resting pulse rate is 72 beats per minute, a woman's is 75, and an athlete's of either gender can be 20 to 30 beats per minute less.
4. If the 300,000 *alveoli*, or air sacs, in the lungs were flattened out, they would equal 1,000 square feet; if two

feet were flattened out, however, they would not equal 300 million *alveoli*.
5. 65 percent of a person's weight is water.
6. Each night we grow 0.3 inches but shrink back during the day because gravity re-compresses the cartilage discs in our spine. This is why astronauts can grow by as much as two inches during a long space flight.
7. The average adult sleeps in ninety-minute cycles that range from light to deep to light sleep. If we are awakened while in deep sleep, we remain groggy. This is why three hours of sleep can be more refreshing than four.
8. A baby has 300 bones at birth; an adult has 206. No, you don't lose 94 bones when you pass puberty; some of them fuse during the normal growth process.

Body Rebellion

1. The longest sneezing fit on record is that of twelve-year-old Donna Griffiths of England, who started in January of 1981 and stopped in September of 1983. It lasted 978 days.

2. Charles Osborne of Indiana is believed to hold the world hiccup record. A hiccup happens when the diaphragm and the muscles between the ribs suddenly contract, causing an inhalation of air that does not reach the lungs, because the windpipe has been closed by a muscle spasm. Mr. Osborne went through seven million hiccups a year from 1922 until February 1990. He died in 1991.

3. People think that *neurofibromatosis*, also known as "the Elephant Man's disease," is the same as *elephantiasis*. It is not. *Neurofibromatosis* is a genetic disorder in which numerous nonmalignant tumors grow on skin, bone, and sometimes internal organs. In some cases, they can progress to the point of deformity, although it is often correctable surgically. *Elephantiasis*, on the other hand, is a blockage of the lymph system that prevents drainage from the surrounding areas. This leads to inflammation and thickening of the vessel walls, most frequently affecting the legs but also the breasts and scrotum. Elephantiasis is caused by a parasitic worm.

4. *Steatopygia*, sometimes called "Hottentot Bustle," after the African tribe in which it was first noticed by outsiders, is the storage of exceedingly large and pronounced amounts of fat in the buttocks.

5. According to *The Guinness Book of Records*, the heaviest object ever removed from a human stomach was a 5-pound 3-ounce hairball taken from a twenty-year-old compulsive swallower at the South Devon and East Cornwall Hospital, England, in March 1895.

6. *Gynecomastia* is the name given to enlarged breasts in males. Extra breasts or nipples is called *polymastia* or *pleomastia*.

7. The human brain registers pain for the entire body yet has no pain sensors for itself. It also produces its own painkillers, called endorphins and enkephalins, that block pain without producing side effects associated with pharmacological drugs. Athletes, soldiers, and parents report that they feel no pain while under the stress of a crisis or tense moment.

Quiz: Booga Booga

Match the shrink with the (glibly summarized) theory:

1.	Alfred Adler	a.	Behaviorism counts
2.	Alfred Binet	b.	Used scientific method on psychology
3.	Eric Erickson	c.	Gestalt psychology leads to insight
4.	B. F. Skinner	d.	Frightened child=neurotic adult
5.	Anna Freud	e.	Devised intelligence quotient (IQ)
6.	Sigmund Freud	f.	Individuality and inferiority complex
7.	Carl Jung	g.	Developmental stages
8.	Wolfgang Kohler	h.	Personality=collective unconscious
9.	Ivan Pavlov	i.	Id, ego, superego, and Mom
10.	John Watson	j.	Behavioral therapy and reinforcement
11.	Wilhelm Wundt	k.	Ding-a-ling=mmmmmm

Get a Life: Cubit

Question: How big is a cubit?

Answer: One cubit equals 18 inches, or about the length from the elbow to the fingertips (excepting Shaquille O'Neal's). For example, Noah's ark, as described in Genesis 6:15, was 300 by 50 by 30 cubits, or 450'x75'x45'. (Note: Some scholars believe that ancient cubits were 22 inches, which puts Shaq back in the running).

Dam It

Few man-made structures are more impressive than the giant dams that harness the energy of mighty rivers and create new real estate opportunities. Here is some dam good information about the dam things:

1. The Grand Coulee Dam across the Columbia River in Washington State, which opened in 1942, became the structure whose volume finally dwarfed the Great Pyramid of Cheops. Its volume is more than 10.6 million cubic yards, and it generates more energy—2 million kilowatts—than the pyramid (not counting psychic power).

2. Egypt's Aswan High Dam—364 feet high and nearly 2.5 miles long—altered the flow of the Nile River, when it was built in the 1960s. For centuries the Nile delta had been flooded annually and the silt that was deposited there provided nutrients for agriculture. The Aswan Dam, however, while creating Lake Nasser, also stopped the floods and has allowed the desert to reclaim parts of the delta.

3. In the second century, Roman engineers built two dams in Merida, Spain, that are still in use. The only repair they have needed in eighteen hundred years was a little stone work in the 1930s.

4. The world's highest dam is the Rogun Dam in Vakhsh, Tajikistan (which also has the world's second-highest dam, the Nurek). Their heights are 1,066 and 984 feet, respectively, and they were completed in 1985 and 1980, also respectively.

5. The world's largest dam is the New Cornelia Tailings Dam on Ten-Mile Wash in Arizona. Completed in 1973, it contains 274,015 cubic yards of earth-fill.

6. The landmark Hoover Dam is only the world's nineteenth tallest dam. Completed in 1936, its imposing 726-foot-high face tames the Colorado River between Arizona and Nevada. The reservoir formed behind it, Lake Mead, can hold 1,241,445 million cubic feet.

Get a Life: Periodic Chart

Question: By what logic are elements listed on the periodic chart?

Answer: The 103 known elements are listed on the periodic chart vertically, according to the similarity of the structure of their atoms, and horizontally, in order of their increasing atomic number.

Biggest Man-Made

Here is the long and the short of it, world geography-wise.

1. Longest big-ship canal: The Suez Canal links the Red Sea with the Mediterranean. Its length is 100.8 miles from the Port Said lighthouse to Suez Roads, and its width is 984 to 1,198 feet.
2. Tallest free-standing tower: The CN Tower, in Toronto, Ontario, Canada, is 1,815 feet 5 inches high.
3. Longest commerce tunnel: Seikan Rail Tunnel, between Tappi Saki, Honshu, and Fukushima, Hokkaido, Japan, runs 33.4 miles 328 feet beneath the Tsugaru Strait sea bed. (In case you were wondering, the Channel Tunnel, between Folkestone, England, and Calais, France, is 31.03 miles.)
4. Longest bridge-tunnel experience: The Chesapeake Bay Bridge and Tunnel, between the eastern shore of the Virginia peninsula and Virginia Beach, Virginia, is 17.65 miles long.
5. Tallest bridge towers: The twin towers of the Golden Gate Bridge, between San Francisco and Marin County, rise 745 feet above the water. Unfortunately, this also means that the water is 745 feet below, as the suicide records will attest.
6. Tallest monument: The Gateway Arch, in St. Louis, Missouri, spans 630 feet and also rises 630 feet.
7. Longest wall: To no one's surprise, the Great Wall of China is the longest wall. At 2,150 miles, it varies between 15 and 39 feet high and up to 32 feet thick. Despite rumors, it is not "the only man-made structure visible from outer space."

A Bridge Too Far

Are there limits to what a bridge can do? The Tacoma Narrows Bridge, across Puget Sound in Washington State, raised the question only four months after it opened in 1940 by literally twisting itself to death on November 7, 1940.

Built to withstand winds up to 120 miles an hour, the 2,800-foot structure collapsed under winds of only 42 miles per hour. Newsreels have preserved the horrifying action: After three hours of moderate winds crossing the narrow structure, the bridge deck began to move back and forth in wavelike contortions. The roadway itself torqued up to 90 degrees, first breaking the suspension cables and then sending sections of roadway into Puget Sound like so many pencils rolling off the edge of a table. Fortunately, the bridge had been closed in time, so no lives were lost.

Pangaea

Two hundred million years ago the entire surface land mass of the earth was collected in
a single immense continent that geologists
today call Pangaea (from the Greek words for
"all earth").

Around 180 million years ago, Pangaea
began to split apart into two separate masses:
Gondwanaland—which contained Africa, South
America, India, Antarctica, and Australia—and
Laurasia—which contained North America,
Europe, and Asia. This theorized "continental
drift" can be explained by the similarity of the
fossil and mineral records despite thousands
of miles of separation across the oceans, as
well as by a visual inspection of the jigsaw
"fit" of the coastlines.

As the continents continued to float apart
on their giant tectonic plates, they assumed
their present (yet still-shifting) positions. The
Middle East shifted toward Asia from the
west; India crunched into it from the south to
push up the wrinkle known as the Himalayas;
and North and South America appeared to
connect across the isthmus of Panama.

Only one part of the puzzle remains
missing: a giant-sized piece that would have
been smack dab in the center of everything
and would have remained stable while the
other land masses were drifting away. Some
people insist that this could only have been
the fabled Lost Continent of Atlantis.

Windy the Poo

In addition to their usefulness in the food
chain, cows offer another service to
humankind: methane gas. Methane is a flam-
mable substance that can replace fuel oil in
generators and boilers. Cows—whose vegetarian diet creates methane in their digestive
systems—generate it in two significant ways.
One is directly into the atmosphere through
flatulence and the other is as a byproduct of
the fermenting of their dung.

Hey, look, a herd of a thousand cows
can make 450 gallons of a new kind of fuel
oil every day, as anybody who has ever
driven past a dairy herd with the car windows open can attest to. Cow dung can be
sealed within giant fermenting containers. As
it decomposes, it gives off methane. Not only
that, but what's left afterward is handy-dandy,
odor-free fertilizer.

Quiz: Eureka!

Match the scientist with his/her discovery:

1. Archimedes
2. Niels Bohr
3. Nicolaus Copernicus
4. Marie Curie
5. Albert Einstein
6. Euclid
7. Galileo Galilei
8. Robert H. Goddard
9. Edwin Hubble
10. Isaac Newton

a. That objects with different masses fall at the same velocity
b. Special and general theories of relativity
c. That there are galaxies beyond our Milky Way (led to the big bang theory)
d. Plane geometry
e. Quantum mechanics and the electron configuration of the atom
f. That an object's density can be measured by its displacement of water
g. Sun-centered model of the Solar System
h. Laws of motion and gravity
i. Radium
j. Tested first successful liquid-fueled rocket

Quiz: Sun Days

Match the solar event with its definition:

1. Summer solstice
2. Winter solstice
3. Spring equinox
4. Autumn equinox
5. Lunar eclipse
6. Solar eclipse
7. Transit
8. Sunspots

a. Earth's shadow blocks moon
b. Longest day of the year
c. Moon's shadow falls on earth
d. Shortest day of the year
e. Sun crosses equator; day=night
f. Inner planet passes between sun and earth
g. Magnetic storms
h. Sun crosses equator; day=night

UFOs

It may be significant that *The Guinness Book of Records*, which sees fit to chronicle everything from the fastest selling debut album (*Cracked Rear View* by Hootie and the Blowfish) to the largest fungus (1,500 acres of *Armillaria ostoyae* in Washington State), has no listing under UFO.

On June 24, 1947, a private pilot, Kenneth Arnold, told the Civil Aeronautics Administration (CAA) that he saw nine shiny, pulsating objects flying over the Cascade Mountains at speeds of up to 1,700 mph. The CAA doubted his claim—which did nothing to dispel it.

Ten days later, on July 4, the UFO phenomenon (as we now recognize it) began in Roswell, New Mexico, when an alien spacecraft supposedly crash-landed in the desert. Although early reports described the site as containing surviving life forms amid the wreckage of an astonishingly light metal vessel, within hours all information ceased. Later it was all denied and ascribed to a test flight that failed.

Beginning in about 1952, the CIA got involved in reports of sightings but concluded that whatever they were, they weren't UFOs and, anyway, posed no threat to national security. Another rash of UFO sightings was reported in 1973–1974. When Stephen Spielberg made the optimistic *Close Encounters of the Third Kind* in 1977, it was hard to say that the general public wasn't along for the ride. On the other hand, skepticism continued from the scientific community, with Carl Sagan pointing out, in his 1995 book, *The Demon-Haunted World*, the flawed logic in UFO proponents' argument that "absence of evidence is not evidence of absence."

By the 1960s, Project Bluebook had been established by the Air Force. Insiders called it project grudge. Commissioned to investigate unidentified flying objects, it was more often used to excuse sightings than to explain them. Fifty years later, the government admitted to a cover-up—not of real UFOs, but of their own incompetence in handling the details.

Some UFO sightings were undeniably fallout from cold war paranoia. In the 1950s, the Air Force used weather balloons not only to explore the atmosphere but also to spy on the Soviets. Moby Dick, Skyhook, Mogul, Grandson, and Gentrix were code names for some of these missions, some of which were mistaken from the ground as UFOs. None of these missions, of course, was ever admitted to by the government. And it was almost a certainty that if America was sending things over Russia, Russia was also sending things over America, and the problem compounded.

In addition, as nations began sending satellites into space, the re-entry trails and burn-up of the launching rockets could be construed as UFOs.

Then there is the practice—often reported but never confirmed—of visitations and abductions. In the old days, Sagan reports (*ibid*), aliens merely talked to earthlings and urged them to support world peace; more recently, they have taken to sexually molesting them. In no instance have aliens ever given humans any factual knowledge that would prove alien superiority. (Sagan also asks why a race capable of traveling light years to earth would always make contact with people whose credibility is suspect and not simply take over the TV networks, for efficiency's sake.)

Despite such arguments, some 50 percent of Americans are said to believe that UFOs exist. And the supermarket tabloids eagerly exploit this wish by inventing stories to support it: If there really *are* aliens, do they hate the *paparazi* too? And if they do, do they have death rays?

That doesn't stop people from believing in them or hoping that they exist. As a scientist once said, "Sometimes I think we're alone in the universe and sometimes I think we're not. Either way, the prospect is quite frightening."

Something to Sneeze At

Kleenex® was a byproduct of World War I. According to history, the Kimberly-Clark Corporation invented a product they called Cellucotton as a replacement for the cotton used in bandages at the front during the war to end all wars. Soldiers discovered that it could be used not only to dress wounds but also as a good air filter for their gas masks.

After the armistice, however, Kimberly-Clark had warehouses full of the Cellucotton, so they decided to market it to women as a soft cloth for removing makeup. They called it Kleenex Kerchiefs, and, unlike linen towels and face cloths of the era, it was completely disposable. Not long afterward, women consumers began to notice that their husbands were stealing their Kleenex Kerchiefs to use in the place of cloth handkerchiefs. By the 1920s, Kimberly-Clark had devised the one-at-a-time pop-up box that became so familiar, and 60 percent of the public had accepted the product, not as a face cloth, but as a nose rag.

Kleenex® remains a registered trademark of the Kimberly-Clark Corporation, which has to constantly guard against generic use of the name of their "facial tissue."

Quiz: Moon and Six

Does the moon really affect human behavior? Are more crimes committed under a full moon than a new moon? Does it do any good to get moon faced and moon the moon? Inquiring minds want to know. Paul Katzeff, in his book *Full Moons* (NJ: Citadel Press, 1981), runs the lunar gamut from tides to werewolves and comes to some fascinating conclusions about our nearest neighbor in space (not counting Shelley Winters). According to Katzeff, which of these age-old moon myths are true?

1. The moon is made of green cheese and once a month is eaten by the sun.
2. *Lunacy* is drawn from *luna*, the Roman word for moon, and refers to people (*lunatics*) who go crazy as a result of moonlight.
3. The moon's gravity pulls on the water in people's bodies just as it pulls on the oceans to create tides.
4. People turn into werewolves by the light of the full moon.
5. The moon brings on seizures in people who have epilepsy.
6. The moon causes earthquakes.

Get a Life: U.S.S. George Washington

Question: What was the scientific scandal surrounding the *U.S.S. George Washington?*

Answer: The scandal surrounding America's first nuclear powered submarine wasn't about the sub itself; it was about the fact that the Russians learned about its design not from the KGB but from going to a hobby shop and buying the plastic model.

Apparently, while one branch of the U.S. Navy was going to great lengths to protect the secret of atomic power, another branch had routinely filed blueprints with the government. When the Aurora manufacturing company was adding the *George Washington* to its patriotic line of aircraft, destroyers, and other combat items, they simply based their scale model on the public domain plans, "and then the fun really started." All of which continues to show that there are some things that should be classified but aren't and some things that shouldn't be classified but are.

Earth Daze

In case you're ever in a geography bee, here are some world records that are, literally, records about the world:

1. There are seven continents:
   a) Africa
   b) Antarctica
   c) Asia
   d) Australia
   e) Europe
   f) North America
   g) South America
   (Some people combine Europe and Asia into a single Eurasia; the North Pole arctic region is an ice cap.)

2. Following are the five largest lakes (water surrounded by land):
   a) Kaspiyskoye More (Caspian Sea; USSR/Iran)
   b) Superior (US/Canada)
   c) Victoria (Tanzania/Uganda/Kenya)
   d) Aralskoye More (Aral Sea; USSR)
   e) Huron (US/Canada)

3. There are four oceans (all the rest are seas):
   a) Atlantic
   b) Pacific
   c) Indian
   d) Arctic

4. The deepest point on earth (ocean) is Marianas Trench, at 35,808 feet below sea level.

5. The lowest point in the United States (land) is Death Valley, California at 282 feet below sea level.

6. The highest point on earth is the top of Mt. Everest (Nepal/Tibet), at 29,029 feet.

7. Because of continental drift, each year North America and Europe move 1.2 inches farther away from each other. So you weren't just imagining it.

8. Is there a place on the earth's surface where, quite literally, "the sun don't shine"? Yes: the Arctic and Antarctic Circles. Within the Arctic Circle at 66°30' north latitude, on or about the December 22 winter solstice, and within 66°30' south latitude, on or about the June 22 summer solstice, the sun is not seen to rise for a full twenty-four-hour period.

9. What is the "Pole of Inaccessibility"? It is the point on Antarctica that is farthest in all directions from the seas that surround it. Located on the polar plateau, it is the site of a Russian weather research station, and it is, without a doubt, in the exact middle of nowhere. Even Domino's doesn't deliver there.

10. The coastline of the Continental United States is 12,383 miles long.

Far Out (Answers)

1.	East	West Quoddy Head, Maine
2.	West	Cape Wrangell, Attu, Alaska
3.	North	Point Barrow, Alaska
4.	South	South Cape, Hawaii
5.	Highest	Mount McKinley, Alaska
6.	Lowest	Death Valley, California
7.	Exact Center	Castle Rock, South Dakota

Science Myths (Answers)

1. False. The Coriolis force (caused by the earth's rotation) may affect large swirls, such as hurricanes and whirlpools, but not something as small as a bathroom drain.
2. False. Think about it: If you're close enough to a bird to put salt on its tail, why not just grab it?
3. True and False. Never stare into the sun—*or* use vague language.
4. True. A "sardine" is whatever fish the sardine-packer wants to put in the can, usually small herring.
5. False. It is the shrinkage of the skin that makes hair and fingernails *appear* to grow slightly after demise.
6. False. As my scoutmaster, reminded finicky eaters, "It all goes to the same place, anyway." Religious teachings may prohibit combining certain foods, but there is no current scientific basis for doing so.
7. True. It's just that their prey (rodents) are night creatures, so owls have to work the lobster shift, so to speak.
8. True, if your intention is to get drunk. Alcohol is alcohol regardless of what other flavors accompany it.
9. False. Bacteria freezes, too, and is just as alive when it is thawed. The only way to kill bacteria in food is to cook it completely.
10. False. Despite rumors in every army barracks or high school, saltpeter (KNO_3) is a diuretic, which means that it makes the body get rid of water. The other, saltpeter ($NaNO_3$; calcium nitrate), is used in gunpowder. Try not to confuse them.

Weather or Not (Answers)

1. e
2. f
3. a
4. d
5. c
6. b

Real or Contrived (Answers)

1. Created. Until this century it was believed that there existed a planet named Vulcan that orbited between Mercury and the sun. By the way, the earliest publicity materials for *Star Trek* indicated that Mr. Spock came from the planet Vulcania. It was later shorted to Vulcan.
2. Real. Krypton is a gaseous element (number36 on the periodic chart).
3. Created. Cavorite is the fictitious antigravity material devised by the character named Cavor in H. G. Wells's novel *The First Men in the Moon*.
4. Real. Zirconium is real (element number 40) and occurs naturally, as a crystal that is often used as a gemstone, usually an ersatz diamond.
5. Real. A quark is a subatomic particle that physicists believe to comprise all matter; they cannot be seen, only discerned mathematically. The word is in James Joyce's *Finnegans Wake*. (It is also the name of the cunning Ferengi, played by actor Armin Shimerman, in *Star Trek: Deep Space Nine*®.)
6. Real. Although it sounds like a Robin Williams word, a nanosecond is one billionth of a second.
7. Created. A 1960s gasoline additive that supposedly made one's car travel farther, platformate was a "nonce" word—that is, it was invented for a single occasion, in this case an advertising campaign.
8. Created. Inventor/businessman George Eastman devised the brand name *Kodak* because he thought the letter *K* sounded forceful, and he wanted a unique word that couldn't be easily misspelled but could be registered as a trademark. Some people believe that *Kodak* is onomatopoeic for the sound a camera shutter makes.
9. Created. According to legend, the discount store was founded by *Eight Jewish Korean War Veterans*.
10. Created. Author L. Frank Baum needed a name for the Emerald City, where the Wizard dwelled, and got it by glancing at the bottom drawer of the filing cabinet in his office that held O-Z.

Inventions (Answers)

1. Don Duncan
2. Christopher Latham Sholes
3. Carl Magee
4. Robert W. Bunsen (duh)
5. Whitcomb Judson
6. Charles Seeberger and Jesse Reno
7. Robert Fulton
8. Lee deForrest
9. Merrit Singer
10. Jacob Schick

Answers

Answers

Medical Saviors (Answers)

1. i
2. c
3. h
4. e
5. g
6. j
7. a
8. d
9. b
10. f

Additives (Answers)

1. d
2. g
3. a
4. h
5. c
6. j
7. e
8. i
9. b
10. f

Booga Booga (Answers)

1. f
2. e
3. g
4. j
5. d
6. i
7. h
8. c
9. k
10. a
11. b

Eureka! (Answers)

1. f
2. e
3. g
4. i
5. b
6. d
7. a
8. j
9. c
10. h

Sun Days (Answers)

1. b
2. d
3. e/h
4. h/e
5. a
6. c
7. f
8. g

Moon and Six (Answers)

1. False, of course. *Green*, in this sense, refers to "un-aged" cheese, not its actual color.
2. The etymology is true, but moonlight does not cause insanity, although people who are already mentally disturbed may over-react to the moon as a result of their illness.
3. True, but so does the sun, and nobody blames the sun for things like moodiness, crime, and bizarre behavior. Besides, the moon's (or sun's) effect on our bodies is negligible, as opposed to the tens of feet that some tides can change.
4. True. Surprisingly, there is an actual disease whose symptoms include leathery skin, red teeth, and long hair. But it is not *lycanthropy* as in the werewolf legends; it is called *porphyria*. Among its more precisely defined symptoms are skin rashes and lesions, progressive distortion of the cartilage of the nose and ears, and reddening of the teeth. As the skin becomes acutely sensitive, the victim is unlikely to shave or encourage contact. In less informed times, this could easily have been thought to be a demonic condition.
5. False. The term *moonstruck* (which, in ever-dependable Latin, is *lunaticus*) has been applied to epilepsy victims who supposedly suffer the effects of the brain affliction when the moon is full. There is no cause-and-effect relationship.
6. True. An MIT study focusing on earthquakes that occurred between 1913 and 1970 concluded that "when the moon exerts its greatest pull on the surfaces of an earthquake fault," tremors were twice as likely to occur as at other times. The greatest exertion comes at new and at full moons.

Chapter 10

HoMe FrontieR

Television

Movies

Music

Twentieth Century History

Sayings & Common Sense

Religion

Science & Geography

Home Frontier

Celebrity

Minutiae

When the expected post-war depression never happened after V-J Day, America found itself—to quote Winston Churchill—"at the summit of the world." As a result, the atomic bomb wasn't the only thing that went "boom" in 1945; so did the population. By the mid-1950s, America not only had more mouths to feed, it had a burgeoning economy that was rapidly taking advantage of a generation of new consumers.

Unlike their parents, who had been hardened by the economic catastrophe of 1929, the baby boomers knew only prosperity. By the time they started hitting their teen years, they had become defined as a separate—and enormously attractive—demographic group. In other words, they were spenders.

The baby boomers still call the turns. They are, as they have been cynically described, "the goat going through the belly of a snake," a kind of amorphous human juggernaut that commands attention. Their interests matured as their bodies did. In the '60s they dictated the fate of the movie and record industries; in the '70s they vexed the automobile and electronics markets; in the '80s they hit Wall Street and real estate; throughout the '90s they shaped legislation with voting that contradicted the '60s; in the next century they will certainly rewrite the rules for health care, pension plans, and gerontology. Put another way, it's time to invest in Depends®.

A verbal roller-coaster ride through the last fifty years shows how fads have become trends and trends have become history. Hold onto your lexicon. Remember when **The Authorities** wouldn't let you wear jeans or **sneakers** to school? For that matter, do you remember when they were just called sneakers or **tennis shoes** (a.k.a. "**tennies**"). The sole (*sic*) choice of brands was between **Keds** and **P.F. Flyers**—none of these **Adidas, Nikes, Reeboks,** or **Air Jordans**. Oh, and they cost maybe $3.98/pair when **penny loafers** cost $9.98 ($10.00 including the pennies, and the salesman gave you a free, **promotional-sized comic book**). The sneakers were good for playing **Tag, Duck-Duck-Duck-Goose, Red Rover, Capture the Flag, Red Light/Green Light, Freeze Tag,** and the venerable **Hide 'n' Seek** (*Ready or not, here I come, anyone around my base is "it."*). **All-y, all-y in free**!

Sneakers were for outside; toys were for inside, especially dolls. Gone were **Raggedy Ann** and **Raggedy Andy,** that the previous generation held dear; the newer, more life-like-looking brood included **Chatty Cathy, Barbie** (q.v.), **Betsy Wetsy, Patty Play Pal, Tiny Tears,** and that studly newcomer, **Ken** (for girls). While boys—for whom dolls were renamed "action figures"—had **G.I. Joe, Billy Blastoff, Great Garloo, King Zor,** and the ever-popular **Mr. Machine** (by the time of Vietnam, war toys fell from favor, only to return with the war frenzy of the Middle East).

Many parents, inspired by Dr. Spock, raised their kids to make love, not war—but only so far. Instead of playing doctor with each other, boys and girls could examine **The Visible Man** and **The Visible Woman** (neither of which, alas, was anatomically correct enough for a ten-year-old's curiosity). After that, if they could play together without fighting, they could share custody of **Mr. and Mrs. Potatohead**.

Dolls and action figures were recognized means of exercising a child's imagination long before the principle of play therapy came into being; sometimes a cigar is just a cigar and a Betsy Wetsy is just a Betsy Wetsy. Besides, dolls are not designed to be competitive; that's what board games and plastic ordinance are for.

Somewhere around first grade we learn that life isn't all **Chutes and Ladders** and **Candyland**. It's also **Careers, Parcheesi, Nine Men Morris, Monopoly, Clue, Operation,** and **Life** itself. And this is without getting near games that were based on TV game shows, such as **Password, Concentration, Jeopardy,** and even drama and comedy series like **Hardy Boys, Nancy Drew, Brady Bunch,** and **Happy Days**.

For loners there was **Etch-a-Sketch, Colorforms, Tinker Toys, Silly Putty, Slinky, View-Master, Lincoln Logs, Legos,** and **Erector Set** (**Play-Doh** was in a class by itself). **Frisbees®** were the only sport you could play in public with either friends or a dog, and **Hacky Sack** could likewise be a singular or plural game. Adventurous types could explore the paranormal with **Ouija Boards** and the **Magic 8-Ball**, although a lot of parents drew the line at anything more occult than a **cootie-catcher. Twister**? Not over the age of twelve, you don't.

Kids who took their imagination into combat could play with **Tommy-Burst Detective, Dick Tracy 2-Way Wrist Radio, Jimmy Jet, Battle Wagon, Big Shot, Roy Rogers's Quick Shooter Hat, Shootin' Shell Pistols (with Greenie Stick'em Caps),** and, if they were really good for Christmas, a **Daisy** air rifle ("Be careful with that thing or you'll put your eye out!"). And let's not forget **slot cars, Hot Wheels, Super Ball,** and **Lionel Trains**.

Hula Hoops were in a class by themselves, unless you tried them indoors and broke something, after which you were sent to your room by yourself. And **Boomerangs** never worked unless you were Australian (as in "**Tie Me Kangaroo Down, Sport**").

Computers ruined everything. Just when it seemed that minds would be saved by **Rubik's Cube** (a frustrating update of those flat puzzles that had fifteen sliding squares and sixteen spaces), the electronic toy arrived. For the first time in history, there could be something on television besides television. With the introduction of **Simon**, a random-sequencing unit that made you play back an ever-growing series of colors and notes (and razzed you when you didn't), the power shifted. It was as though the toy was playing with you rather than the other way around. Not long afterward came **Pong** (so costly and cumbersome that only barrooms could afford them). Not for long. Miniaturization enabled the arrival of **Atari**, followed by **Game Boy** and **Nintendo**, with contests from the merely silly **Donkey Kong** to the infamous **Custer's Revenge**, with characters from **Pac-Man** to **The Borg** and **Doom** (and every contrivance in between, most of them violent). Some devices could be held in the palm of the hand; others needed expensive joy sticks and playback units to function. From the days when moms warned "Don't sit too close to the TV set or you'll go blind," kids now spend three hours at a stretch hovering twelve inches away from the monitor. Has anybody else noticed this?

The home was invaded by grossly conflicting signals as the century rounded the fifty-yard line. In the '50s the fanciest thing a hostess could serve her guests were **Nabisco Brown-Edged Wafers** or tiny crackers called **Sociables** that were shaped like the suits of playing cards. Beginning in the '80s, anything less than **Famous Amos** or **Mrs. Fields** cookies was considered rude.

When company stayed over in the Eisenhower years, they were offered a **Castro Convertible** sofa bed or an old army cot. By the Carter era, nothing less than a **Charles Webb** bed or a **Futon** would do—as long as the guest removed his or her **Top Siders** or **Earth Shoes** before retiring, that is.

When home ice boxes—oops, sorry, refrigerators—were improved to the point where they could freeze food, ice cream was liberated from soda fountains and "ice cream parlor" to become a standard item. When it did, **Breyer's/Dreyer's** was good enough for anybody. Not so by the late '70s; that's when **Haagen-Dazs** started fighting it out with **Ben and Jerry's** for the Hippie-turned-Yuppie "I've paid my dues and now I can afford it" market. By the time the fat had cleared, **Dove Bars** had won.

On the **halitosis** side, **Clorets** yielded to **Tic-Tac** and **Certs** fell to **Binaca**; somewhere along the way the **electric toothbrush** tried, and failed, to replace elbow grease.

Americans continued to crave candy; it just cost more than a nickel. Way more. **Good 'n' Plenty, Juicyfruits, Jujubes, Red Devils, Root Beer Barrels,** and **Mary Janes** just don't hit the same spot as **gourmet jelly beans, Godiva chocolate,** and **Gummi Bears**. Despite that, **Snickers** and **Tootsie Roll Pops** are still the biggest sellers nationwide, so maybe there's still hope.

In fact, there's more than hope; there's something called *Retro*. Retro is best summarized by the Peter Allen song "Everything Old Is New Again." All of a sudden **Granny Dresses** are back, people are returning to the simple joys of **Maxwell House Coffee** (forsaking **Starbucks**), and even **French's Yellow Mustard** is pushing **Grey Poupon** off of hot dogs (which, themselves, are replacing **Basil-Fennel Chicken Sausages with White Wine**).

The good news is that in the name of "family values," we seem to have returned to products that have survived the test of time rather than the lure of marketing. Not only that but we have mercifully leap-frogged over **cartridge pens, CB radios, mother-of-pearl "Aquarius" signs, unicorns, Pop-it beads, rainbows, eight-tracks,** and those darn **clocks with flipping numbers that kept you awake counting the seconds between turns**.

The bad news is that now it all costs ten times as much.

Quiz: Toy Slogans

Toy, games, and recreational product manufacturers went to great lengths to distinguish themselves from each other in the '50s and '60s, even if their toys all seemed to fall into similar categories: space, war, cowboys, and home economics. Fill in the following blanks with the name of the company that used the catch phrase:

1. ___ comics are good comics!
2. Hooray! It's a ___ toy!
3. It's a wonderful toy—it's ___ !
4. Gee, Dad, it's a ___ !
5. You can tell it's ___ , it's swell!
6. Every boy wants a ___ toy—and so do girls!
7. It's ___ —it's fun!

Quiz: Spokescreatures

Decades before Joe Camel personified a product, advertising agencies knew that nothing sells something like a celebrity—even if they had to make one up. Match the following spokescreatures with the product they hawked:

1.	Bucky Beaver	a.	Chocolate cereal
2.	Silly Rabbit	b.	Ipana toothpaste
3.	Fresh-up Freddie	c.	Rice Krispies cereal
4.	Speedy Alka-Seltzer	d.	Trix cereal
5.	Count Chocula	e.	Borden evaporated milk
6.	Frankenberry	f.	Seven-Up
7.	Cap'n Crunch	g.	Elmer's Glue
8.	Cuckoo Bird	h.	Alka-Seltzer
9.	Buster Brown and his dog, Tige	i.	Buster Brown Shoes
10.	Snap, Crackle and Pop	j.	Berry flavored cereal
11.	Elsie the Cow	k.	Crunchy cereal
12.	Elmer the Calf	l.	Cocoa-flavored cereal

Things That Didn't Last

When you're a kid, you assume that whatever is in your life is going to stay there forever, because, darn it, that's the way things are *supposed* to be. This explains why growing up is a succession of closed restaurants, widened streets, changed car designs, thrown-away comic books, and discontinued products. And speaking of that, here are some childhood things that used to be better than they are today or aren't here any more but should be:

1. **Hydrox chocolate cookies**. Admit it: They were better than Oreos, but when they changed the formula for their white icing, they lost it.

2. **Nabisco sugar wafers** were great in the days when they were made of sugar, not that slimy-tasting corn syrup substitute.

3. **Fizzies**. They look like Alka-Seltzer, but when you dropped them in a glass of water, they fizzed and exploded in taste. Or if you put one right in your mouth, you could really gross out your mother.

4. **TV Time Popcorn**. It came in a two-pocket pouch: In one was the yellow, coagulated grease, and in the other was the corn and salt. Okay, so it was a heart attack in a packet. But you couldn't watch *Davy Crockett* with anything else.

5. **Bonomo's Turkish Taffy**. You could hold it in your hand till it got soft and then stretch it into strands, or you could whack it on the counter

and break it into bite-sized pieces. It also pulled every filling out of your head. It came in vanilla, banana, and strawberry, but the vanilla was best.

6. **Forever Yours®** candy bar. The Mars Candy Company made Forever Yours, which they billed "a vanilla Milky Way." If ever the sharp chocolate taste of a Milky Way® got to you, you could fall back on a Forever Yours for a break. No more.

7. Remember when Mars candy advertised that you could share a nickel **Three Musketeers®** bar with two friends? Now you can only afford to do that if their names happen to be Spielberg or Gates.

8. Whatever happened to **Popsicles®** that had real fruit flavor in them? Orange was the last holdout, wasn't it?

9. Whoever invented **Lik-M-Ade** knew how to give a kid a good time. Lik-M-Ade was fruit flavored sugar that was sold in packages of five paper envelopes containing cherry, orange, grape, lemon-lime, and strawberry. You tore them open and shook a little into your mouth. You could also mix them in a glass of water, but that was for wimps. The best thing about them was that they turned your tongue colors (see "Fizzies").

10. Once upon a time, either **Nabisco Vanilla Wafers** were actually made out of real vanilla or the FDA (Food and Drug Administration) changed their rules to make Nabisco come clean. And while we're on the subject, whatever happened to those sweet and nutty **Brown-Edged Wafers**?

TV Dinners

Few food products are more symbolic of the '50s than the TV dinner. There it was, everything you needed for a balanced meal, and all in one place, too. Come to think of it, TV dinners looked just like what you got in the school cafeteria, only made right at home.

Frozen TV dinners had their origin not in TV but in the Arctic. In 1915 Clarence Birdseye (yep, that's his real name) was hunting in Labrador when, quite naturally, the fish and meat he bagged managed to freeze rock-hard on the way back to his shelter. Birdseye was astonished to discover that when food was quick-frozen and then defrosted and cooked, it remained edible. By 1923 he had perfected nature's process in his laboratory and founded Birdseye Seafoods. He expanded his menu until General Foods made him a buyout offer in 1929.

Swanson Foods is credited with inventing the TV dinner in 1953. Carl Swanson had been selling his popular frozen chicken pot pie since 1951, when his sons suggested the family business might do well with a product that provided a full-course meal. He wasn't interested until Crawford Pollock, who was in Swanson's marketing department, suggested packaging it as an item that busy families could eat while watching TV. The next year Swanson's turkey TV dinner went on the market.

It consisted of turkey, corn bread, peas, gravy, and potatoes, presented in a compartmentalized aluminum tray that was heated and—this was the important part—served straight from the oven to the table—the TV tray table, that is.

Pringles and Toilet Paper

It was in 1971 that Proctor and Gamble introduced a snack that would redefine the industry: Pringles. Technically speaking, Pringles are not potato chips. Rather, they are crisps that have been reconstituted from dehydrated potatoes, salt, water, and, where so designated, flavorings (barbecue, salt and vinegar, ranch, etc.). A decision by the FDA, however, allows Proctor and Gamble to call their product "chips" anyway, and as such they have come to claim a formidable share of the market.

The culinary merits of Pringles have always engendered debate: Lacking the texture, crunch, and flavor (they once introduced a line that had "more potato flavor," whatever that is) of potato chips, they have come to assume their own niche. Just as there are hamburgers and then there are McDonald's, so there are potato chips and then there are Pringles.

What remains most intriguing about Pringles, however, is their shape: all the same. Unlike real potato chips—which were invented in 1853 by chef George Crum at Moon Lake Lodge in Saratoga Springs, New York—Pringles aren't just cooked, they're processed. They are made from a potato dough that is stamped by machine and then fried on a molded screen that gives them their uniform shape and allows them to be stacked, packed, and shipped uncracked.

"Sweet" Potatoes

Although food and snack manufacturers go to great lengths to differentiate their product from the competition, most of them have four things in common: fat, salt, sugar, and expense. Sugar is easily the most seductive ingredient. It even turns up in fast-food French fries.

Because the popular shoestring side dish served by burger chains cooks so quickly (and is often precooked prior to being frozen, bagged, and shipped to restaurants), the slender cuts may be sprayed with sugar water. When dropped in boiling oil, the sugar coating caramelizes to create an appetizing light brown "cooked" color. Lacking the sugar, the thin potatoes would otherwise appear to be raw.

Supermarkets

The origin of the supermarket is about as clear as mud. The grocery store, however, is another matter.

Originally, Americans bought their household goods at a variety of local specialty stores, if they lived in a city, or one consolidated general store, if they were rural dwellers. Putting everything under one roof nationwide began in 1861 in lower Manhattan in the area of what is now, ironically, the World Trade Center. George Hartford and George Gilman opened The Great American Tea Company with the intention of lowering the price of tea by eliminating the middlemen and importing it directly from the growers. By 1865 the idea caught on, and the two Georges had five stores. Ever the tireless self-promoters, they changed their chain's name in 1869 to The Great Atlantic and Pacific Tea Company, and not long afterward their satisfied customers nicknamed them the A&P. By 1927 there were fifteen thousand of them across the country.

The expansion of grocery stores into supermarkets—that is, a retail store that carries nonfood items—remains less certain. Some credit King Kullen in Queens, New York; others favor the Triangle Cash Market in Pomona, California; still others cite their own home towns as the founding site.

According to Vince Staten in *Can You Trust a Tomato in January?* the father of the supermarket was Clarence Saunders, whose Piggly Wiggly Store in Memphis, Tennessee, opened its doors in 1916 and promptly cleared $114,000 in its first six months.

But what really established supermarkets was the invention of the shopping cart in 1937. That was when Sylvan Goldman, a store owner in Oklahoma City, Oklahoma, noticed that his customers stopped shopping when their hand-carried baskets filled up. Goldman had an employee, Fred Young, construct rolling baskets. Ironically, Staten reports, the newfangled shopping carts caught on with store owners but not shoppers. It was only after employees' wives were hired to demonstrate the carts in stores that other shoppers got the picture.

The 4-D Club

Comedian/painter Martin Mull once created commercials for a fictitious fast-food restaurant called Bun and Run, whose slogan was "Where *Food* is a four-letter word." Unfortunately, in one real instance, that would have made a joke as sick as the truth.

Not too many years ago a fast-food chain in the U.S. was discovered to have been selling hamburgers made not of ground beef but of ground kangaroo meat that they had imported from Australia. The marsupial meat was sent to the U.S. as ground beef through port-of-entry Los Angeles. A meat inspector dutifully reported the wrong color of the meat (green???). But since his manager was on a two-week vacation, nothing got done about it. Fortunately, he saved a sample in the freezer for future analysis.

Kangaroo is an accepted foodstuff down under, but usually for dog, not human, victuals. When the Aussies discovered that it was, indeed, used to feed Yanks, they had some fun singing "Tie me 'amhurger down, sport," a twist on the old standard, "Tie me Kangaroo down." But that's not the best—er, worst—part of the story.

The USDA (United State Department of Agriculture), which is responsible for inspecting all meat sold for consumption in the U.S., has a designation called "4-D"—in other words, Diseased, Dying, Dead, or Decayed. Apparently the kangaroo meat that was making it into people's pouches was of the 4-D variety. When the restaurant chain was eventually cited for the infraction, their management was hopping mad at what their provision buyers had done. (Note: This incident was not connected with the e-coli deaths the same chain weathered years later.)

Barbie

Even though she's middle aged, Barbie® has kept her girlish teenage figure. No, she doesn't keep a portrait hidden in the attic—but she does keep a patent in Washington, D.C., and the affection of tens of millions of Americans of all ages. Barbie is, simply and indisputably, the number one doll ever made.

The eleven-and-one-half-inch-tall fashion doll that went from toy to icon in the space of two years was born on March 1, 1959. Her creator, Ruth Handler of Mattel Toys, named her after her own daughter—a wise decision, it turned out, given that Barbie's prototype was a German doll that, Mrs. Handler did not realize, had been based upon a comic strip prostitute named Lilli.

Barbie—two inches shorter than the motion picture Academy's equally celebrated Oscar®—was conceived as "the only anatomically perfect doll manufactured today" when she was offered at the 1959 Toy Fair, a pitch that both offended retailers and puzzled industry wags. Sears-Roebuck and Company, for example, deemed the teenage fashion doll too sexy to stock. Male buyers eschewed her with comments ranging from "fashion dolls are dead" to "mothers won't buy a doll with breasts." Her enthusiasm dampened by rejection, Handler reduced her initial order.

Soon after Barbie's March 1, 1959, "coming out," however, Mattel found themselves with a craze on their hands and no inventory to meet it. The attraction was not only the well-built Barbie herself but also the stylish wardrobe and accessories that came with her—all sold separately, of course. It took three years for Mattel and their Japanese manufacturer to catch up with the back orders.

Barbie continues to be the world's top-selling doll. Her clothes change with the times (to every parent's continuing frustration), and she has acquired countless other possessions: houses, campers, furniture, cars, and, of course, Ken.

There are off-the-rack fashions for Barbie as well as designer clothes, with some fans even designing their own trousseaux. There are even Star Trek® fashions (Beam me up, Ken?).

And there was also a backlash. In 1964, the *Saturday Evening Post* dubbed her "the ultimate material girl," and she continues to be a target for outraged feminists, who cite her as the unattainable goal against which all American females are unrealistically compared.

But Barbie is laughing all the way to her life-sized bank. The original $3 doll from 1959 is now worth $1,000 on the collectors market. In 1976 she was included in the American bicentennial Time Capsule. If that isn't longevity, nothing is.

Get a Life: Aunt Jemima

Question: Is there really an Aunt Jemima?

Answer: "Aunt Jemima," a black woman whose likeness is still used to sell pancake mixes and syrup, was, indeed, a real person, although the real Aunt Jemima had nothing to do with the Aunt Jemima created by the food industry as an advertising fantasy. Yes, there were two Aunt Jemimas. Clarification follows.

Histories vary, but Aunt Jemima seems to have been taken from a vaudeville routine performed in the late nineteenth century by two male troupers. When the Aunt Jemima Company decided to personify their symbol for the 1893 Chicago World's Fair, they hired a local cook, Nancy Green, to play the part. Miss Green continued to serve as a spokeswoman until her death in 1923.

At about the same time, "Aunt Jemima" was taken as a stage name by actress-singer Tess Gardella, a hefty white woman who performed in blackface. Her most notable role was in the original 1927 production of *Showboat,* in which she played the key role of Queenie. Oddly enough, the program listed Queenie as being played by Aunt Jemima, not Tess Gardella. A scrap of Miss Gardella's rousing performance is preserved in an early sound film prologue to the otherwise-silent 1929 movie version of the musical.

Aunt Jemima's closest "competitor" was Betty Crocker, who was created as a generic homemaker in 1936 by artist Neysa McMein for the Home Services Department of the Washburn Crosby Milling Company of Minneapolis (now General Mills).

Quiz: The Name Is Unfamiliar

The French have a word for it, but does English? Match the name with the object it identifies. These are common items, things you see around the house every day but never knew what they were. (Note: These are not Rich Hall's "sniglets.")

Thingy

1. Punt
2. Harp
3. Berm
4. Brassard
5. Aglet
6. Sprocket
7. Columella nasi
8. Ferrule
9. Snorkel box
10. Jarns

Name Thereof

a. Metal band around pencil eraser
b. Tip at end of shoelace
c. Hoop on lamp that holds the shade
d. Dent on bottom of wine bottle
e. Armband
f. #@!+#!
g. Mailbox chute for drive-by mailings
h. Cement "bumper" or curbstone
i. Groove on upper lip beneath nose
j. Toothed wheel in movie projector

Quiz: Product Slogans I

Match the slogan with the product it sold:

1. You'll wonder where the yellow went
2. From the land of sky-blue waters
3. Mother, please, I'd rather do it myself!
4. A little dab'll do ya.
5. Look for the red, yellow, and blue balloons on the wrapper
6. The pause that refreshes
7. While you're up, get me a ___.
8. Takes the worry out of being close.
9. Aren't you glad you used ___? Don't you wish everybody did?
10. Next to myself, I like ___.

a. BVDs
b. Wonder Bread
c. Grant's Scotch
d. Ban deodorant
e. Dial soap
f. Anacin
g. Coca-Cola
h. Hamm's Beer
i. Brylcreem
j. Pepsodent

Quiz: Product Slogans II

Match the slogan with the product it sold:

1. Breakfast of champions
2. Fresh as the breeze
3. LS/MFT
4. Silly Rabbit, ___ are for kids!
5. They're Greeeeeeaaaaaaat!
6. Good to the last drop
7. Bet ya can't eat just one.
8. 99 and 44/100% pure
9. I may not use my deodorant today.
10. I'd rather fight than switch.

a. Mitchum
b. Tarryton
c. Lay's Potato Chips
d. Lucky Strike
e. Wheaties
f. Old Spice
g. Ivory Soap
h. Frosted Flakes
i. Maxwell House Coffee
j. Trix cereal

Get a Life: Lava Lamps

Question: What made lava lamps work?

Answer: Lava lamps were a tear-drop shaped glass container sitting atop a base containing a light bulb and a heating coil. The container conducted the light into a glow, and the heat from the coil made a wad of . . . well, of *something* (okay, wax) . . . writhe around in the fluid.

How they worked: The colored stuff was an oil-based mixture that got more liquidy as the water around it warmed up; it moved because of convection currents. Oil and water don't mix, but they do homogenize, which is why one should never shake up a lava lamp. Lava lites were invented by Craven Walker in England and presented in 1965. They were marketed in America by Adolf Wertheimer.

Glad You Asked?

1. Toothbrushes with nylon bristles were first marketed in 1938 by DuPont, taking the place of natural bristles, which were, at one point, culled from the hair of hogs, horses, and beavers.
2. Gelatin is a substance found in the bones and sinews of animals.
3. Rennet, a substance used as a thickener in some custards, comes from the lining of the fourth stomach of cows (remember Elmer's Glue®?).
4. That soft *chamois* ("shammy") cloth you use for fine cleaning is—if it's real—the skin of the Alpine chamois. A cheaper version is a specially tanned sheepskin.
5. According to the authoritative French cookbook *Larousse Gastronomique*, cats should be cooked in much the same way as rabbits. They taste best when braised or *fricasséed*, and it is better to choose a young one (they're less stringy).

Fat and Sodium

In manufacturing they use a drawing of a triangle whose points are labeled "good," "fast," and "cheap." Whenever a customer asks for a price quote, he/she is shown the diagram and told, "You can have any two."

It seems that the same brutal choice has become the quandary of people who are trying to control their diets. A plethora of low-fat foods have been introduced since the mid-'90s. Most of them taste like the inside of a potholder, but those that taste pretty good have a dirty secret: salt.

"Fat" is a carrier. It enables those molecules that our tongue detects as "flavor" get through to the little taste buds and thrill them into ecstasy. When you remove the fat from food, you also remove the flavor. So manufacturers add salt—as much as 50 percent more—to compensate.

Just because something is "low fat" doesn't necessarily make it healthful. True, some people can handle salt better than they can handle fat, but that's a medical decision.

And remember that "no cholesterol" doesn't always mean "no fat." *Cholesterol* is the name given to a fatty substance produced by animals. Vegetables such as avocado, peanuts, coconuts, and palm have tons of saturated fat, even though none of it is called cholesterol.

Supermarket Strategy

Here are ten things you probably suspected about supermarkets but never had confirmed until now:

1. Supermarkets don't make money selling turkeys for 49¢ a pound at Thanksgiving. They are a "loss leader"; that is, they use advertising to lure customers into the store so that they can buy the trimmings, which are sold at an advanced price. The belief is that shoppers will pay a little extra money to stay at one store rather than leave and drive to another one.

2. Foods that appeal to children are placed at an adult's knee level, which happens to be a child's eye level.

3. Items displayed at the end of the aisle are no bargain. The manufacturers pay the supermarket to let them use that prominent position.

4. Meats and dairy are located at the back of the supermarket because they are staples. In getting to them, the customer must pass everything else.

5. Bakeries and delis are placed at the entrance of the supermarket to entice shoppers with food aromas when they are just starting their spending adventure.

6. Never shop while hungry. Always make a list of what you need *before* going to the store, and stick to it.

7. Many supermarket chains are giving out free "shopping club cards." They will use these to track their customer's buying habits (and to compile mailing lists, which they can sell). To convince people to join the shopping clubs, they will artificially raise the prices of various foods so as to make club membership look like a bargain (state attorneys general please note).

8. Supermarkets make only a tiny profit per item, sometimes no more than a few cents. They make their money on volume, which is why spoilage and pilferage are such problems.

9. It's a tragic irony that community-minded supermarkets that would otherwise give away food to homeless people are prevented from doing so because of their insurance liability. Fortunately, church and civic groups are interceding as middlemen.

10. Once upon a time, checkout clerks knew their produce without having to have it labeled with those little stickers.

11. There is no reason for the checkout clerk to summon a store manager to okay a check. This is an archaic labor practice designed to make checkers (usually female) subservient to managers (usually male). Computers are changing this.

12. On the bottom of a paper shopping bag, you will often find the name of the person who made it. This is for company morale and public relations.

13. In the days when homes had milk boxes and milkmen made house calls, competing dairies would sabotage each other's shipments by using a hypodermic needle to inject lemon juice through the cardboard lids of their rival's milk bottles. The milk inside would curdle, and the customer would invariably switch dairies.

14. Say, if competition among supermarket chains is so fierce, how come you never see two supermarkets across the street from each other?

15. Has any supermarket ever run out of cream of tartar?

Quiz: Whence Come Convenience?

Some modern convenience foods are older than we think. Match the popular product to the year of its discovery:

1. Jell-O®
2. Pringles®
3. Tang®
4. Kool-Aid®
5. Minute® Rice
6. Ritz®
7. Life Savers®
8. Jif®
9. Hershey's Kisses®
10. Cool Whip®

a. 1934
b. 1966
c. 1968
d. 1912
e. 1956
f. 1907
g. 1927
h. 1958
i. 1946
j. 1897

Quiz: I Dare You

True or false: Can you really do these things with these products?

1. Make an apple pie out of Ritz Crackers?
2. Improve your fingernails with Jell-O?
3. Keep silverware from tarnishing with blackboard chalk?
4. Deodorize a refrigerator with baking soda?
5. Fuel the space program with Tang?
6. Practice satanism with Proctor and Gamble products?
7. Support the John Birch Society with Welch's candies?
8. Give body massages with Wesson Oil?
9. Ripen tomatoes with an apple?
10. Cook a pie shell with raw beans?

Quiz: Flesh or Fantasy?

Match the huckster to the product he/she hawked. (Extra credit: Which of them were real and which were an advertising creation?)

1. Colonel Harlan Sanders
2. Clara Peller
3. Jimmy Dean
4. Orville Redenbacher
5. Sara Lee
6. Duncan Hines
7. Chef Boyardee
8. Mrs. Paul
9. Ronald McDonald
10. Ed McMahon

a. Magazines
b. Fish sticks
c. Fried chicken
d. Dessert
e. Canned pasta
f. Pork sausage
g. Hamburgers
h. Cake mixes
i. Popcorn
j. Hamburgers

Quiz: Food and Zeal

The following people began as health faddists whose zeal led to changes in diet and the introduction of foods, some of which carry their names. As history would have it, most of them migrated to Battle Creek, Michigan, allowing their cereals—if not always their names—to live on. Identity them and their legacies.

1. Dr. James H. Salisbury
2. Sylvester Graham
3. Dr. John Harvey Kellogg
4. Charles W. Post
5. Henry D. Perky
6. James C. Jackson
7. Alexander P. Anderson

Quiz: Culinary Buggy Whips

Have you gone into an electronics store lately and asked to see a hi-fi? Or, for that matter, have you gone into a record store and asked to see a *record*? Times change, and sometimes language doesn't. As proof, here are some kitchen terms that, like the iceman, wenteth. Identify them:

1. Top of the milk
2. Oleo
3. SOS
4. Flapjacks
5. Johnnycakes
6. Scrapple
7. Soya flour
8. Fool

Quiz: Homemade Soft Drinks

During the 1950s, fluoride and Strontium-90 apparently weren't good enough to be the only additives added to Americans' water and milk. Identify the following commercial products from descriptions of what they did:

1. You dropped one into a glass of water and stood back for the bubbles to stop. If you were really thirsty, you waited until it floated to the top and then drank around it.
2. You either dropped one of these five-to-the-pack flavored sugar packets in a glass of water or tore open the top of the envelope and poured it straight down your throat.
3. These chips of milk-soluble flavor were wedged inside soda straws, which you dunked in milk until the liquid turned beige (supposedly chocolate) or pink (strawberry).
4. These crystals of an indeterminate flavor could be dissolved easily in hot milk and less easily in cold milk.
5. This rich, super-sweet chocolate syrup mixed easily in milk.
6. This rich, less sweet chocolate syrup, strangely enough, was sold more for ice cream sundae application than for use in milk.
7. This powdered chocolate (and, later, strawberry) flavoring actually dissolved in cold, as well as hot, milk.
8. This orange-flavored sugar got a sales boost from rumors that it was developed for NASA and a playground boost when kids realized that its name was a vulgarism in Spanish.
9. A packet of this makes two quarts of a flavorful soft drink, especially when you add a cup and a half of sugar. It tastes best when served from a smiling, spherical frosted pitcher.
10. This product added the *je ne sais quoi* of New York City to any glass of milk.

Fashion Arrest

Each person has his/her own idea of what hell might be, but one way to get a spine tingling preview of it is by looking at old photographs that show not just how you looked when you were a teenager *but how you dressed.*

When you're a teenager, you think that the worse thing that can happen is for your face to break out. But the true horror that really awaits you is when you open that old box in the closet and find those snapshots of you wearing (as may be gender-applicable) bell-bottoms, sack dresses, love beads, clogs, and whatever else made you the fashion plate of 19—ugh—72.

Here's a checklist of things in your past that doubtlessly lurk in your future:

1950s
Moo-moo dress
Sack dress
Davy Crocket raccoon hat
Velveteen pants
Poodle skirt
Neck scarf
Ankle bracelet
White bucks
Saddle shoes
Duck tail (a.k.a. DA)
Teased hair
Rolled-up blue jean cuffs
Dirndls
Cigarette pack rolled up in
    T-shirt sleeve
Red James Dean jacket
Plaid skirt
Pegged pants

1960s
Pillbox hat
Bouffant (beehive) hairdo
Wrap-around sunglasses
Nehru jacket

? Paisley tie
? Peace medallion
? Bell-bottom pants
? Headbands
? Peter Max posters
? Love poster
? Love beads
? Hendrix poster (day-glo)
? Long, mutton-chop sideburns
? Wide-lapel jackets
? Ensemble: peacoat,
? Bolshevik hat, and wire-
    rimmed eye glasses
? Tie-dyed anything
? Go-go boots
? Miniskirt
? Granny dress
? Ben Franklin specs (square,
    wire-rimmed glasses)
? Amazing Adventures comics
    (Spider-Man #1)

? 1970s
? Mood ring
? Platform shoes

? Earth shoes
? Hot pants
? Elton John rose-colored
    eye glasses
? Polyester anything
? Leisure suit
? White disco suit
    (ala Travolta)
? Tank tops
? Denim anything
? Wide lapels
? Designer jeans
? Frosted hair
? Western wear (while riding
    mechanical bull)
? Toga (as in "Toga Party")
? "Smile" button
?
?   P.S. If, on the other
? hand, you had saved the
? actual items instead of only
? the *pictures* of those items,
? you could sell them as col-
? lectibles today and be Rich
? RICH *RICH!*

Quiz: Restaurant Argot

Everyone knows that "cuppa java" means "coffee" in diner jargon or that "Adam and Eve on a raft" means "two poached eggs on toast." But there's more to restaurant lingo than meets the ear—or stomach—as this partial list suggests. Translate, please:

1. Deuce
2. Three-top
3. Camper
4. 86
5. Deep 6
6. With legs
7. Setup
8. Prep
9. Stiff
10. Runners

Quiz: New and Improved

Until *additive* became a dirty word, manufacturers would proudly advertise the device (real or invented) that separated their product from the competition. Which consumer product (food or otherwise) was distinguished by these gimmicks?

1. Platformate
2. AT-7
3. Floristan
4. Schweppervescence
5. Solium
6. Guardal
7. Micronite filter
8. GL-70
9. Electronic moduflow
10. Sunshine suds

Quiz: Product Slogans III

Identify the product from its advertising slogan:

1. "Anticipaaaaaaation"
2. "The quicker picker-upper"
3. "Finger lickin' good"
4. "Gives me iron and sunshine vitamin D"
5. "Gets rid of dirt and grime and grease in just a minute"
6. Don't buy this product "unless you're fussy, terribly fussy, unbearably fussy about flavor."
7. "Do you know me?"
8. "When you're number two, you have to try harder. Or else."
9. "Only her hairdresser knows for sure."
10. "Even your best friends won't tell you."

Quiz: Pitchmen

What product did these creatures (human and otherwise) try to sell us?

1. Big green guy in the garden
2. Big bald guy with an earring and wearing a white T-shirt
3. Tiger in the gas tank
4. Handsome, greying man with an eye patch
5. Knight on white horse
6. Businessman flying into the driver's seat of a moving car
7. Avuncular man cupping his hands
8. Sea captain
9. Old British man unfolding a camera
10. Perky female plumber in overalls

Diet or Die

You know how to get to Carnegie Hall, don't you? Practice, practice, practice! Okay, then, how do you lose weight? Will power, will power, will power! Nevertheless, many diet devices—from stomach stapling to butt-bouncing machines—have been proffered over the years, and especially over the counter. Here are some (sans judgment) that were actually manufactured in the past (c. 1955). Dig the names.

> Looz
> Pounds-Off
> Ayds Diet Candy
> Slix
> Junex
> Slenderettes
> Trimitt
> Model-Etts
> Thinz

Household Hints

Everyone has tricks for kitchen success. Here are some from professional chefs:

1. Crispen wilted lettuce by soaking the leaves in a bowl of water in the refrigerator.
2. Never use a food processor to dice onions for frying; the blades will pulverize the onion, causing it to boil in its own juices rather than sautéing.
3. Food won't stick if you heat the frying pan before adding the oil.

4. To skim the fat off soup or juices, drop a whole, iced lettuce leaf on the surface of the liquid. It absorbs grease.
5. Don't store bananas in the fridge; they blacken.
6. To clean and freshen a stained pot, fill it with water and boil half a lemon until the metal is visibly brighter.
7. Prevent a skin from forming on the top of pudding and custard by covering the cups, while still warm, with tinfoil or plastic wrap.
8. To get ketchup out of the bottle, tap it on the "57" (on the neck) or rock it back and forth on a tilt. Never pound the bottom.
9. A gelatin mold can be unmolded quickly by setting it in a pan of hot water for thirty seconds.
10. To get the frozen orange juice out of the can, remove one end entirely, and then make a small hole in the other. With a little coaxing, it will slide right out.
11. You can reduce the fat content of sausages by simmering them in water for four or five minutes before frying them (in a separate pan).
12. Eggs are less likely to crack during boiling if you (a) add a few tablespoons of vinegar to the boiling pan and (b) prick a tiny hole in the large end of the egg (that's the end that has an air bubble in it).
13. If soup it too salty, add a cut-up potato; it absorbs salt (be sure to remove it before serving).
14. If you must salt meat, salt it after cooking. If you salt it before cooking,

it draws out moisture, which makes it dry.

15. You can prevent scallop shells (as in *Coquille St. Jacques*) from sliding around the plate by fixing them with a dollop of mashed potato. A wedge of melon will also sit on the plate if you cut a flat slice off the bottom.

Cleanliness in the Kitchen

With the prevailing impression that the USDA has pretty much dropped the ball as far as meat inspection, it's up to consumers to protect themselves. Here are some household tips that may make food safer:

1. Always wash off the tops of cans before opening them. You never know where they've been.
2. Always wash fruit before eating it, including lemons, oranges, and other fruit that is peeled (any germs on the outside will be transferred inside by the cutting knife).
3. Never cut meats on a wooden carving board. If you must do so, rinse the board off with hot soap and water after every use. Plastic cutting boards are even better. You should also wash off all surfaces with Windex® or another alcohol-based cleaner after cutting meat.
4. When handing somebody a knife, don't let go until the other person says thank you. If you're the other person, saying thank you is a signal that you have a good grip on the knife (this is an old Boy Scout custom).
5. Never pour grease down a drain; it congeals and blocks the pipes.
6. Never pour milk or other dairy product down a drain; the residue can turn sour and smell (if you do, pour some baking soda down the drain, and let it sit for a few minutes before rinsing it through).
7. The refrigerator is the best place to store irreplaceable papers (birth certificate, passport, etc.). Don't laugh; in case of fire or flood, the fridge is the best insulated place in the house.
8. Toothpaste is a natural, gentle polishing agent for silver.
9. A vinegar wash will get soap scum off of a glass shower door.
10. Never use old newspaper to clean windows, unless you want ink smears all over the glass. A sponge and a squeegee (separate items, not two-in-one) work best. And the best cleaning solution is still a squeeze of dish washing liquid in a bucket of water.

Un-Dirty Dozen

If you have a scratched coffee table, this is what to do until the doctor comes:

1. Cover minor wood scratches by rubbing in cigarette ash.
2. Cover minor scratches in the surface of a glass table by rubbing in a dab of Vaseline® petroleum jelly, letting it

sit for a few hours and then mopping it off. The tiny amount that remains in the scratch will refract the light to make it seem invisible.

3. Minor upholstery stains can be cleaned with shaving cream, then cleansed with soda water.

4. If you spill red wine on a tablecloth or rug, try getting it out with white wine.

5. Remove candle wax from a tablecloth by placing a brown paper bag over it and ironing it. The brown paper will absorb the wax.

6. Chewing gum can be removed from fabric by applying ice cubes until the gum becomes frozen and can be snapped off.

7. If you spill something, blot it first. If you must rub, rub inward, not outward, or you'll spread the stain.

8. It's true: Blood stains come out with meat tenderizer.

9. It's true: Club soda takes out a lot of fresh stains.

10. It's true: If you're not sure what all the funny drawings on new clothing labels say (and who does?), experiment by removing a stain on an unseen corner, say, of the tablecloth or shirttail.

11. It's true: Ballpoint pen ink comes out with hair spray.

12. White vinegar removes spots from stainless (!) steel.

Animal Problems

A dog will come when you call it, but a cat will take a message and get back to you later. In addition to that bit of knowledge, here are some other trivial notes:

1. Keep a sack of kitty litter in the trunk of your car over the winter to use for traction in getting out of snow.

2. Dogs hate baths, so try rubbing baking soda into the animal's coat and then brushing it out.

3. When a dog messes on the carpet, blot up the moisture and rub the stain with a solution of lemon juice or vinegar and warm, soapy water. Blot as dry as possible, and then use the ol' club soda trick (not sparkling designer water; you need the sodium). Blot dry. This works better if you can train the dog to do it.

4. Cat mess can be alleviated by blotting with ammonia. Blotting the stain, that is.

5. A whining puppy misses its mother. Wrap a ticking clock in a fluffy towel, and leave it in the puppy's crib; it will sound like Mama's heartbeat (Hint: Don't use an alarm clock!).

6. A barking dog is an unhappy dog. If you're not sure if your dog is barking while you're away at work, leave a voice-activated pocket tape recorder in the room.

7. If your pet has a losing encounter with a skunk, you can reduce the odor by bathing the dog in tomato juice, then shampoo. A weak ammonia rinse can also help, but be

careful of the animal's eyes, and be sure to thoroughly rinse it off afterward. Also look for bites: Skunks—especially the North American Spotted Skunk—carry rabies.

8. Cockroaches can be killed without insecticides by lightly dusting with boric acid powder. *Lightly dusting* is the secret; use an atomizer or fine strainer. The secret is to have the bugs trod through the powder, carry it into their lair, and die there.

9. Being buzzed by a wasp or bee? Don't swat it; it just makes 'em angry. Instead, spritz it with hair spray to make its wings stick together. *But be careful picking it up! (see below).*

10. Never use tweezers or fingers to pull out a bee sting—all you'll do is squeeze in more venom from the poison sac. Instead, take the edge of a credit card and "shave" the stinger out. The pain of a bee sting or ant or mosquito bite can also be reduced by rubbing a paste of meat tenderizer and water onto the welt.

Cabbage Patch Kids

One of the more bizarre fads of the '80s consumed the country in Christmas of 1983. That is when parents drove themselves into a frenzy over Cabbage Patch Kids®.

Like the smaller, brightly colored Smurfs® of 1981 (and their 1963 virtual forebears, Trolls), Cabbage Patch Kids were cuddly, passive, and clock-stopping ugly. Their popularity would have been a textbook example in how to manipulate a toy into becoming a hit had it not been a complete accident: Everybody wanted them, but the manufacturer, Coleco Industries, neglected to instruct their Hong Kong–based plant to produce enough. Consequently, riots broke out in those stores that were lucky (unlucky?) enough to receive a shipment.

Following the designs of Appalachian folk artists and embodied in the designs of sculptor Xavier Roberts, the dolls achieved a certain caché by virtue of their individuality (their features were programmed by a computer to be dissimilar) and their marketing (they were not bought and sold but, rather, "adopted," complete with certificate).

While this gimmick probably went a long way toward lessening the stigma of adoption, it raised the question of why people would trample each other to give a home to a lifeless toy while tens of thousands of lonely human orphans remained parentless. The bubble didn't burst until two years and $600 million later.

Who can predict what toy will be a hit? Most are introduced at the annual February Toy Fair in New York, but February is a long way from Christmas and the whims of tykes. In 1967, Mattel® sank a bundle into merchandise for the lugubrious *Dr. Dolittle* movie, and stuck merchants with shelves of unsold Pushmi-Pullyus. So they passed on *Star Wars* in 1977, and Kenner Toys picked up the license. Unsure of the market for a science fiction film, Kenner didn't get its act together until it was too late, and thousands of kids found redemption coupons instead of Darth Vader™ action figures under the Christmas tree.

Although product-based movies and TV shows were honed to a perverse science throughout the '80s and into the '90s (Transformers, Go-Bots, etc.), who could have predicted that a quartet of pizza-eating Teenage Mutant Ninja Turtles would be the stars of 1990? The next year it was Mighty Morphin Power Rangers. By 1996 the fad was Tickle Me, Elmo, a doll that laughed when molested.

Meat Crisis

Long before Oprah Winfrey dissed hamburger in 1997, Americans went vegetarian, in 1973. That's when hamburger went up to 99¢ a pound and porterhouse steak passed $1.69 (even at those prices, some people began hoarding meat). It looked as though the all-American meat-and-potatoes meal would be replaced by feathers and peas. Why?

Part of the reason was America's beef producers felt that they weren't getting the price they deserved for cattle and that America's farmers were charging too much for feed grain; so they cut back on produc-tion. Fewer cattle meant less meat, and soon supermarkets reported shortages. At the same time, Japanese and British cartels started investing in American livestock.

In spring of 1973, there was a week-long boycott of meat, and by the next month, sales had dropped off 60 percent. Predictably, prices began dropping, but by then people had become used to the idea of cutting back on their meat consumption. The American beef industry has been advertising ever since.

Interestingly, something else happened, although it has yet to be widely reported.

There are five main USDA grades of meat, in descending order of quality and price: prime, choice, good, commercial, and utility. Over the last decade, but starting suspiciously after the boycott, less prime meat was being sold in supermarkets.

Trash Chic

Depending on who you believe, America has 5 percent of the world's population yet pro-duces 30 percent of the world's trash. This is why landfills are starting to rival the Great Pyramids in size and why New York City loads its garbage on barges and sends it to New Jersey.

So you can imagine the relief when, in 1970, the ecologically minded folks at Whirlpool introduced home trash com-pactors to the market. Free standing or built into the kitchen counter, the device con-sisted of a deep bin that accepted anything (except pressurized cans) and squashed it into a dense mass inside a reinforced bag. Since these were the days when municipal refuse companies still hoisted cans manually, there was a certain tension that arose between homeowners and sanitation workers.

Trash compactors allowed people to side-step the need to consider recycling. In fact, they are still being used at the bottom of trash chutes in many apartment buildings.

So the problem remains, and it fell to satirist Marshall Effron to cut to the chase: "The trash compactor is an invention that takes fifty pounds of garbage and gives you back fifty pounds of garbage."

Toy Slogans (Answers)

1. Dell comics are good comics!
2. Hooray! It's a Hasbro toy!
3. It's a wonderful toy—it's Ideal!
4. Gee, Dad, it's a Schwinn!
5. You can tell it's Mattel—it's swell!
6. Every boy wants a Remco toy—and so do girls!
7. It's Kenner—it's fun!

Spokescreatures (Answers)

1. b
2. d
3. f
4. h
5. a
6. j
7. k
8. l
9. i
10. c
11. e
12. g

The Name Is Unfamiliar (Answers)

1. d
2. c
3. h
4. e
5. b
6. j
7. i
8. a
9. g
10. f

Product Slogans I (Answers)

1. j
2. h
3. f
4. i
5. b
6. g
7. c
8. d
9. e
10. a

Product Slogans II (Answers)

1. e
2. f
3. d
4. j
5. h
6. i
7. c
8. g
9. a
10. b

Whence Come Convenience? (Answers)

1. j
2. c
3. h
4. g
5. i
6. a
7. d
8. e
9. f
10. b

I Dare You (Answers)

1. True. It's called a "mock apple pie," and the recipe is on the box or can be obtained by contacting the manufacturer. No apples are harmed in baking a mock ("ersatz") apple pie.
2. True. Any gelatin—Knox unflavored, Royal, Jell-O, etc.—strengthens finger and toenails and helps keep them from chipping or breaking.
3. True. Like silicon crystals, chalk absorbs moisture in the air that would otherwise tarnish silver.
4. True. Take the top off a box of baking soda and leave it in the back of the fridge. And when it has done its job in six months, wash it down the kitchen drain to help deodorize that, too.
5. False. Tang was invented independently of NASA, although it reportedly has gone along on some of the rides. If you want to help the space program, write your congressman and senator.
6. False. This is an urban myth perpetrated by idiots.
7. False. Birch founder Robert Welch sold out his candy interests years ago.
8. True. This is especially so between consenting Wessons (any vegetable oil will work).
9. True. Place them both in a paper (not plastic) bag. The apples gives off gas that helps tomatoes ripen.
10. True. Filling a single pie shell with beans will hold it in place against the pie pan until the dough sets. The beans conduct the heat.

Flesh or Fantasy? (Answers)

1. c (Kentucky Fried Chicken)
2. g/j (Wendy's)
3. f
4. i
5. d
6. h
7. e
8. b
9. j/g (McDonald's)
10. a

Flesh or Fantasy? (Extra Credit)

1. Real
2. Real
3. Real (former country singer)
4. Real
5. Real (actual name: Sara Lee Lubin Schupf)
6. Real (former printing salesman turned restaurant critic)
7. Fake (there is no Chef Boyardee; it's an amalgam of Boyd, Art, and Dennis, the company founders)
8. Fake
9. Fake (but he's played by various actors—originally by Willard Scott)
10. Real (Hi-yo!)

Food and Zeal (Answers)

1. Dr. James H. Salisbury: Believing that fat and connective tissue interfered with the body's digestion of meat, he ground meat into a pulp and pressed it into patties, which he then broiled. Then he added butter, horseradish, and sauce to make *Salisbury Steaks*.
2. Sylvester Graham: Graham preferred whole grain flour to white flour and encouraged baking biscuits with "Graham Flour," calling the easy-to-digest results *Graham Crackers*.
3. Dr. John Harvey Kellogg: A strict vegetarian, Kellogg devised a breakfast cereal made of baked oats, wheat, and corn that was crushed into "Granula." After a lawsuit from James C. Jackson (see below), he changed the name to *Granola*. He went on to invent baked, dried corn that crumbled into *Corn Flakes*.
4. Charles W. Post: Eschewing chemicals, C. W. Post invented a non-coffee grain drink he called "Postum," after which he experimented with a granulated grain cereal so close to James C. Jackson's "Granula" (see below) that he wound up calling it *Post Grape Nuts*.

5. Henry D. Perky: Perky manufactured biscuits of steamed wheat grains that became known as *Shredded Wheat*.
6. James C. Jackson: Jackson combined Graham flour and water, baked it, crunched it, baked it again, then ground it into bits. The result resembles Grape Nuts but was known, at the time, as *Granula*.
7. Alexander P. Anderson: He sealed steamed grains in a container and exploded them; out came puffed cereals such as *Puffed Wheat* and *Puffed Rice* (cue the *1812 Overture!*).

Culinary Buggy Whips (Answers)

1. This is the layer of cream floating on top of the un-homogenized milk in a bottle.
2. Oleo, or oleomargarine, is a white, congealed nondairy edible oil developed during war rationing. Originally, homemakers had to mix a separate packet of yellow coloring into it to make it look more like butter.
3. SOS is a derogatory name for creamed, chipped beef on toast, a.k.a. "sh— on a shingle."
4. Flapjack is the rustic name for pancake/griddle cake.
5. Johnnycakes are molasses-sweetened corn bread pancakes.
6. Scrapple is a breakfast concoction of chopped, mostly hog parts bound in a spiced cornmeal mush, sliced, and fried crisp. You've heard the pork industry's famous motto "We use everything but the squeal"? Well, scrapple is the squeal.
7. Soybeans are well-known sources of protein throughout Asia, but when soy flour and soy sauce were introduced to America in the early 1940s, they were called "soya" in an effort to make them seem less Asian (Hint: It was World War II).
8. "Fool" sounds like Mr. T's favorite dessert, but it's an English concoction of cooked, crushed fruit mixed with cream or custard and served chilled (as in "Strawberry Fool").

Homemade Soft Drinks (Answers)

1. Fizzies
2. Lik-M-Ade
3. Flav-R-Straws
4. Ovaltine
5. Bosco
6. Hershey's syrup
7. Nestlé's Quik®
8. Tang®
9. Kool-Aid®
10. Powdered malt (pronounced "mawlt")

Answers

Restaurant Argot (Answers)

1. Deuce: table for two
2. Three-top: table for three (also four-top, five-top, etc.)
3. Camper: someone who stay at a table even after paying the bill
4. 86: a menu item is depleted and no further orders should be taken for it, as in "86 the veal"
5. Deep 6: throw something out
6. With legs: a take-out order
7. Setup: place setting of silverware, napkin, and glassware
8. Prep: prepare in advance of cooking, as in "prep the vegetables"
9. Stiff: to leave the restaurant without paying the bill
10. Runners: British slang ("let's do runners") for fleeing a restaurant without paying the tab (traditionally, a prank played on foreign-run curry restaurants, which is why groups of young customers are seated as far from the door as possible)

New and Improved (Answers)

1. Gasoline additive, Gulf oil
2. Deodorant additive, Dial soap
3. Fluoride variant, Crest toothpaste
4. Bubbles, Schweppes soft drinks
5. Extra whitener, Rinso bleach
6. Fluoride variant, Colgate toothpaste
7. Filter, Kent cigarettes
8. Brightener, Gleem toothpaste
9. Thermostat, Honeywell home heating system
10. Foamed yellow when it got wet, Dutch cleanser

Product Slogans III (Answers)

1. Heinz ketchup
2. Bounty brand paper towels
3. Kentucky fried chicken
4. Bosco chocolate flavoring for milk
5. Mr. Clean liquid detergent
6. Hellman's Real Mayonnaise (known as Best Foods in the west)
7. The American Express card
8. Avis rent-a-car
9. Clairol hair coloring
10. Scope mouthwash

Pitchmen (Answers)

1. Jolly Green Giant frozen and canned vegetables ("Ho ho ho")
2. Mr. Clean detergent
3. Esso (now Exxon) gasoline ("Put a tiger in your tank . . .")
4. Hathaway dress shirts
5. Ajax laundry detergent ("Stronger than dirt")
6. Hertz Rent-a-Car ("Let Hertz put you in the driver's seat.")
7. Ed Reiners insured us "You're in good hands with Allstate"
8. Old Spice after shave and cologne ("Fresh as the breeze")
9. Please! That was Lord Laurence Olivier for the Polaroid SX-70.
10. Josephine was played by Jane Withers for Comet cleanser.

Note: Advertising expert David Ogilvy states in *Ogilvy on Advertising* that using celebrity endorsements is a mistake because people tend to remember the spokesperson, not the product.

Television   Movies   Music

Twentieth Century History   Sayings & Common Sense

Chapter 11

Celebrity

Religion   Science & Geography

Home Frontier   Celebrity   Minutiae

A celebrity is somebody who is famous for being famous. It doesn't even matter that nobody remembers why.

What did Carmelita Pope ever do that was so important? Or Allen Ludden? Or the stalwarts who turned up endlessly on talk and/or game shows throughout the '50s and '60s: Arlene Francis, Zsa Zsa Gabor, Peggy Cass, Orson Bean, Kitty Carlisle, George Plimpton, Brother Theodore, Regis Philbin, Ariana Huffington, Cathie Lee Crosby, and legions of others.

The answer is that these people turned up on talk shows because they were charming and extremely bright and knew how to tell stories. Oh, they may have had other careers going for them (writer, actor, teacher), but that was less important than their, well, their personality. If some of them later made commercials, it was because their talk show exposure conferred credibility with the public. Sometimes they even made furtive attempts at film careers (remember Nina Van Pallandt—she of the Clifford Irving/Howard Hughes scandal—in *The Long Goodbye?*). Some even got their own shows, frequently proving that they were better talkers than they were listeners. But, mostly, they were all highly winning conversationalists, and, thus, lacking any other definition in a society that defines people by what they do, they were qualified only to be called *celebrities*.

Andy Warhol's supposed pronouncement that "in the future, everyone will be famous for fifteen minutes" was a comment not only upon celebrityhood but also upon the media's hunger for new faces to put on the covers of their magazines and the fronts of their broadcasts. The fact that Warhol mocked the media while exploiting it only made him more attractive to those very same editors and producers. Where else but in America could an artist of no substance draw substance from insubstantial substances?

"Celebrity" and "fame" have become pretty much the domain of the mass media. Before the invention of movies, radio, television, and photographic periodicals, a person's notoriety seldom exceeded his/her actual accomplishment. It is not in the human condition to be recognized by strangers, yet that is what is embodied by the word *ambition*. The various emperors, kings, queens, philosophers, and pontiffs who shaped world civilization were not famous *per se* so much as they were important and powerful, and the obeisance paid to them was more out of fear and respect than mere curiosity. Even presidents and other elected officials court popularity rather than familiarity; by design, fame is not only fleeting, it's illusory. It's even dangerous: Nowadays a celebrity is far more apt to be harmed by a fan than a fan is by a celebrity (the word *fan* itself is short for *fanatic*, which gives a chilling hue to the dangers strewn about the arena of public opinion).

Mass media and its handmaiden, public relations, changed the people's perception of celebrities by inviting members of the general public to see them. This greatly expanded the concept of "audience." In the time of Sophocles or Shakespeare, the actors who appeared in plays lived among the same people they entertained and were distinguished from them because they got up in public and recited lines.

Time, travel, and advances in communication changed all that. Audiences who bought tickets to Buffalo Bill's Wild West Show in the 1880s came to see celebrities they'd heard of but who lived far away and were passing through town solely as a theatrical (commercial) enterprise. They had heard about Bill's exploits as an army scout and "Indian fighter" through Ned Buntline's magazines (written—largely fabricated—by Edward Zane and Carroll Judson) not because anybody had actually *seen* William F. Cody fell a buffalo or subdue Sitting Bull but because it was in print. When Edwin Booth and Lily Langtry traipsed through the Old West, performing in saloons and town halls as well as regional theatres, they did not have to prove themselves at every stop. Instead, they were welcomed as emissaries because their arrivals (and reputations) were advertised in advance. The same advantages were enjoyed by traveling evangelists and snake oil salesmen.

It is true that all fame is fleeting, yet nobody knows when it is going to take off. Unfortunately, the expenses of celebrity linger after the *cause celeb*, if you will, evaporates. Ex-celebrities must bear the unavoidable pressure of maintaining a celebrity lifestyle without a celebrity career. Unlike Bob Hope, not everybody was prescient enough to invest in real estate. Here is where the image and the reality diverge with a vengeance. Since the public believes celebrities to be ageless and their fame timeless (a fallacy shared by some celebrities, alas), there is

the inevitable conflict between income and expenses. Child actors who had a hit TV series in the '50s have almost certainly spent what little money they earned by the time they hit their mid-twenties, which is just about the time that the nostalgia market kicks in. For the scores of stars who worked before residuals (or had theirs negotiated away by the Screen Actors Guild), it is a tough transition.

Old stars remind us of our own mortality. Nevertheless, every few months in major cities such as Los Angeles and New York there are nostalgia conventions. Here is where fans can meet their childhood heroes and heroines, sitting at long tables, outfitted for inspection, selling autographs, and reminiscing about the good old days. Some stars attend for the exposure, some do it to visit with colleagues at other tables, and some need the money (autographs, $10; with photo, $20). The convention promoters are no fools; they charge an admission fee to discourage browsers. They also provide name tags just in case the actor or actress doesn't look the same as in the reruns.

Like it or not, celebrities are us, only more so. They tend to be actors and actresses, but not always; in any event, talent is less important than personality (two of the greatest actors, Robert DeNiro and Meryl Streep, seldom show up on magazine covers and never in the tabloids). Celebrity ranks usually include sports figures, musicians (rock and rap more often than classical or folk), and the occasional business leader or politician (usually only during divorce or other crisis). The days when publicity departments manufactured stories and built stars is long gone; in fact, there's a stealth PR industry today that keeps its clients' names *out* of print.

What generally defines a celebrity today is sex. Perhaps it always did, but it's tough to sense the allure of, say, Lillian Russell through the hindsight of history. Sex is what makes famous people famous: They have it, they inspire it, they use it, they want it, they throw it off like a scent. It's what makes people look at them in a crowd, and not someone else.

Celebrities aren't the only people who have this "fame pheromone"; a motivational speaker, a gifted teacher, a charismatic minister, or a super-salesman also has it; they're just in a public enough position where outsiders notice it. Or maybe they don't want it to be noticed. Yearbooks are filled with grad-uates voted "most likely to succeed" who, for whatever reason, didn't. Don't be fooled by the hype: Nobody is a star who doesn't want to be, and nobody isn't a star who should have been.

We grow to hate celebrities—or worse, we ignore them—for the same reason we love them: They possess something we don't; they are what we secretly want to be. Make no mistake about it: The public's fascination with celebrities is a kind of love affair, and when the affair is over, little can rekindle it. But, while it lasts, it is intoxicating beyond all belief—even though, at the same time, we know it isn't very nourishing.

Get a Life: Mrs. Miller(s)

Question: Who were the two Mrs. Millers in television?

Answer: The best known Mrs. Miller was the buxom dowager who became an unlikely Capitol Records recording star with the 1965 release of her sleeper album, *Mrs. Miller's Greatest Hits*. Born Elva Connes in Joplin, Missouri, Mrs. Miller was the wife of a California rancher and recorded religious songs on the side. When somebody suggested she try her hand at contemporary music, she was a sudden smash whose covers of "Downtown," "These Boots are Made for Walkin'," and "How Gentle is the Rain" unexpectedly topped the pop charts. Her lush orchestrations and exaggerated vocal tremolo reminded many people of what Margaret Dumont (of Marx Bros. fame) might have been like with a song in her heart—or thereabouts.

The other Mrs. Miller was an elderly habitué of *The Little Theatre Off Times Square*, where Merv Griffin taped his talk show in New York in the mid-to-late-1960s. A woman in her mid-to-late-'60s herself, Mrs. Miller was considered a good luck charm and was accorded front row seats and an acknowledgement from the stage.

Quiz: What's in a Name?

Identify these well-known personalities by their names from the old country:

1. Frederick Austerlitz
2. Eunice Quedens
3. Betty Jolan Perske
4. Annemarie Italiano
5. Melvin Kaminsky
6. Doris van Kappelhoff
7. Asa Yoelson
8. William Henry Pratt
9. David Daniel Kaminsky
10. Laurence Zeiger
11. Issur Danielovitch Demsky
12. Nathan Birnbaum
13. Aaron Chwatt

14. Israel Baline
15. Joseph Kubelsky
16. Margarita Cansino
17. William Beedle
18. Roy Fitzgerald
19. Leonard Slye
20. Shirley Shrift
21. Amos Jacobs
22. Dino Crochetti
23. Virginia McMath
24. Thomas Lanier Williams
25. Monte Halparin

Quiz: Insults

If Oscar Wilde was right—that we only hurt those we love—then the following quotes describe people who are very much loved by those who spoke them. Can you identify the archer as well as the target?

1. "I have more talent in my smallest fart than you have in your entire body."
2. "Anyone can remember lines, but it takes a real artist to come on the set and not know her lines and give the performance she did."
3. "Actors like him are good, but on the whole I do not enjoy actors who seek to commune with their armpits, so to speak."
4. "She looked as though butter wouldn't melt in her mouth—or anywhere else."
5. ". . . two profiles pasted together."
6. "She is like a delicate fawn, but crossed with a Buick."
7. "I have to be nice to [him]. I still have family in the old country."
8. "[He] rolled through the film like a very belligerent barrel."
9. "I don't mean to speak ill of the dead, but he was a prick."
10. ". . . not that he would pay me that to write a script."

Quiz: Praise

Insults may be a dime a dozen, but praise has to be won, often at risk. Who handed the following kudos to whom?

1. "Oh, she's okay—if you happen to like talent."
2. "When I have talked with him, I feel like a plant that has been watered."
3. "Her career is proof of the fact that the entire history of the feature film is contained within a lifetime."
4. "[He] once played a scene in front of a cigar store, and it looked like the wooden Indian was overacting."
5. "The guy's good. There's nobody in the business who can touch him, and you're a fool to try. And the bastard knows it, so don't fall for that humble stuff."
6. "She had curves in places that other people don't even have places."
7. "She was a wonderful woman. She was the same off stage as she was on it—always the stuffy, dignified matron. The funny thing about her was she never understood the jokes."
8. "I could kill three guys and have 'em buried in the time he takes to have one of 'em hit the ground."
9. "I was lucky enough to make four pictures with her. In the first I turned her in, in the second I killed her, in the third I left her for another woman, and in the fourth I pushed her over a waterfall. The one thing all these pictures had in common was that I fell in love with [her]. And I did, too."
10. "All he had to do to dominate a scene was simply to enter it."

Heroes

There's a line in the great John Ford film *The Man Who Shot Liberty Valence* that describes the conundrum of our era: "When the legend becomes fact, print the legend." We want our heroes to be larger than life, yet we persist in tearing them down to prove they're human.

Why should this be? Ed Goodgold, coauthor of the original *Trivia* book and an avid culture wag, had this to say:

"You notice that when Paul Simon writes, 'Where have you gone, Joe DiMaggio?' he's not looking for reality, he's looking for a hero. You're looking for exemplary behavior. Not necessarily goody-goody, but you're looking for the uplifting. I managed the rock group Genesis for a little while when they had Peter Gabriel, and . . . it was like a religious service, it was like Rock 'n' Roll mass. I was always surprised that that's the way I would analyze it, and the reason is that people have this spiritual need. These aren't fed by society because it's easier to make a buck with what we call the evil inclination. It's dispiriting. Whatever is positive and healthy is often ridiculed. Sometimes people manage to do it and it's hip as well, but it's rare, it's hard."

Jim Henson and the Muppets

Like most people who create an art form, James Maury Henson didn't set out to be what he became—he just sort of backed into it. In Jim Henson's case, the art he created and came to dominate in the '70s and '80s

was The Muppets. *Muppets* is an amalgam of the words *marionette* and *puppet*, and Henson, too, was a combination of elements so complex in their simplicity that their effect on American life was profound.

Born September 24, 1936, in Greenville, Mississippi, into an agrarian society barely climbing out of the Depression, Henson moved with his parents to Hyattsville, Maryland, in the 1940s, when his father took a job with the U.S. Department of Agriculture. He began crafting puppets in high school and even joined a puppet club, but it was not until 1954—the year before he entered the University of Maryland as an art major—that he officially christened his invention. By the next year he had talked a Washington, D.C., television station into letting him write and perform *Sam and Friends* as a daily afternoon children's show. His cast included a sock with halved ping-pong balls for eyes that would later become one of Henson's most beloved creations, Kermit the Frog.

Sam and Friends ran until 1961 and gave Henson (who had married classmate Jane Nebel in 1959) access to dozens of other television and variety shows. Appearances on the Jack Paar and Jimmy Dean shows (where he introduced Rowlf) brought him wider attention.

But the praise did not dispel Henson's personal doubts about the craft he was pursuing. American television in the 1960s had a puppet glut: Burr Tillstrom's *Kukla, Fran and Ollie* (Fran Allison was live); the *Bil and Cora Baird Marionettes;* Frank Nastase's *White Fang* (who perennially haunted Soupy Sales); *Howdy Doody;* and *Captain Kangaroo's* Mr. Moose and Bunny Rabbit offered a menagerie that must have intimidated the gentle Henson.

He was able to counter with gentle humor, which, at first, was neither gentle nor subtle: An early commercial for Wilkins Coffee showed one burly creature blowing Kermit away with a cannon because Kermit didn't like the product. Still another skit had the ever-curious frog pursuing a worm only to find out—too late—that he had actually taken

the lure of a monster that gleefully swallowed him whole.

Henson admitted he treated his handheld brood more casually than they were treated by the fans. "Most of them are pulled apart as patterns for new ones," he once revealed. So much for keeping Muppets as pets.

But it was the 1969 PBS debut of *Sesame Street,* through the Children's Television Workshop, that gave Jim Henson both the legitimacy that had eluded him and the popularity that made his influence so strong. Very simply, *Sesame Street* and the Muppets shaped the viewing and learning habits of an entire generation. Big Bird, Miss Piggy, Cookie Monster, Oscar the Grouch, and their neighbors took over as role models at a time when most stations had canceled live hosts in favor of cheaper cartoons. The Muppets even appealed to adults. The duo of Bert and Ernie, for example, were named after the policeman and cab driver in Frank Capra's beloved film classic *It's a Wonderful Life.* Henson later expanded into television's *The Muppet Show* and such feature films as *The Muppet Movie, The Great Muppet Caper,* and *The Muppets Take Manhattan.*

Despite such immense popularity, Henson never abandoned his ideals. Although he licensed his creatures to selected projects, he always insisted that they be quality merchandise—an ethic shared by fellow visionary Walt Disney. And so when, in 1989, he sold the Muppets to the Disney Studios, it seemed a logical career move. After movies, TV series, specials, and myriad licenses, Henson seemed to want to move into new areas. Or perhaps he suspected that he would not be able to.

Henson died at age fifty-three on May 16, 1990, of bacterial pneumonia, the result of an untreated infection that seemed minor enough to ignore at first (which he did) but which suddenly turned deadly. He died within a matter of hours.

Almost immediately, the Henson-Disney deal—which had not been finalized—dissolved into acrimony and legal posturing. It was a legacy that the gentle Henson would neither have foreseen nor approved. Quiet and creative in an industry not known for being either, Jim Henson always considered himself a storyteller. It just so happened that he talked with his hands—through the Muppets.

PTM: Don Kopaloff

Celebrity has its privileges, and one of the things a celebrity's agent must do is secure those privileges for his/her client. Over the years, agent Don Kopaloff has come into contact with a number of requests—both normal and strange—in the course of representing top talent and hearing stories about others.

Nat Segaloff: What are some of the things that celebrities demand in their film contracts?

Don Kopaloff: Natalie Wood, for example, a complete professional and a deserving star—her contracts sometimes ran forty or fifty pages because she had so many things she required at the height of her stardom. She had to have her makeup person with her all the time, a limousine twenty-four hours a day during shooting, etc. Yul Brynner was really a special giant ego. One of the great stories about Yul Brynner was that when he was going to do *Barabbas* for producer Dino DeLaurentiis—I was representing [costar] Arthur Kennedy, that's how I knew about this—when they got through with the negotiations, he wanted a limousine. When they said okay to the limousine, he said, "Okay, but I want a limousine that has a bar, a refrigerator, the whole works." Again they agreed, when DeLaurentiis's office got another request that Brynner wanted a john built into the limousine. At that point, DeLaurentiis hired Anthony Quinn instead.

Segaloff: Was that an actor's way of getting out of the deal rather than make it look like his fault?

Kopaloff: Not really. Some have egos, but once on the set, usually they are totally pro-fessional. It's kind of idiosyncratic, and the terrible part is that the agent has to go in and ask for it. It gets ridiculous. David Janssen, at the height of his success—it was after *The Fugitive* [TV]—went to do a film in Mexico. He had to have his motor home. Do you know what it takes to get a motor home to Mexico, into the mountains? But his agent said he had to have it, "They gave it to him on the last picture." And it had to be stocked with booze, beer, whatever. This was twenty years ago before everybody had them! There was a star who had it in her contract that, every day when she came onto the set, she had to get a gift. Not flowers, not champagne, but a gift waiting for her in her dressing room.

Segaloff: What are some of the basic requirements?

Kopaloff: The women usually have more demands than the men, and this is not meant to be chauvinistic, but they will have specific requests such as hair, wardrobe, makeup, living accommodations, limousine, etc. Both men and women may request approval of the still photographers, limited visiting on the set, concern about their profiles as to which side faces the camera. But everything I stated here is from twenty years ago. Today, with the preposterous salary structures, you give them whatever they want. From all that I know, Arnold Schwartzenegger is the ultimate professional; other than his salary he has very few demands.

Don Kopaloff is a partner in the Los Angeles talent agency Soloway, Grant, Kopaloff and Associates. He now specializes in writers, producers, and directors.

Bogart Apotheosis

Humphrey Bogart died in Hollywood in 1957, but he was reborn two years later in Cambridge, Massachusetts. He died because he smoked hard, drank hard, gave people a hard time, and generally tried to be, well, Humphrey Bogart. He died of esophageal cancer, and those who were with him say he went out more bravely than he did in any of his films.

He was reborn because the owners of the Brattle Theatre, an art house in Cambridge's Harvard Square, had some screen time to fill and couldn't find anything new by Bergman, Truffaut, or Antonioni. So they dredged up some old Bogarts that had been sitting in the vaults. The rent was cheap, and the films hadn't been shown much on TV.

The films happened to be *Casablanca, The Maltese Falcon, Treasure of the Sierra Madre,* and a couple other old war horses that everybody had seen a zillion times before. Well, not exactly everybody. The Harvard students hadn't; they'd been too young. And since Harvard was in the middle of reading week before finals, there was nothing to do but hang out at the Brattle.

So Harvard went to the Brattle and Bogart went to the pantheon. The Bogart cult was born, and spread, and soon every repertory theatre in America was showing his old movies.

Bogie fought for the little guy. In 1947 when the House Un-American Activities Committee decided that the First Amendment didn't apply anymore, Bogart organized his own committee and came to Washington to lend support to reluctant witnesses. (He later recanted under pressure, however.)

When Hollywood criticized his friends for their parties, he formed the Holmby Hills Rat Pack, an informal social club, where the likes of Judy Garland, Frank Sinatra, and John Huston could complain and moan, and drink and carry on, and did.

Bogart deserved his apotheosis, but he would have been the first person to make fun of it. So why him? Why did this short, seldom-shaven, pug-faced actor with the slight speech impediment become one of America's

most enduring symbols, one of the very few movie stars whose personal legend rivals his film roles?

Obviously, he filled a need. It wasn't just that he was a tough guy, because so were John Wayne, Gary Cooper, Clark Gable, Alan Ladd, and a dozen others, and the only place you saw their old movies was on TV. Bogart films are still shown on screens.

Maybe because Bogart had, as Hemingway once described it (in another context), "a built-in bull—detector." He detested pomposity, distrusted authority, demanded loyalty as well as dispensed it, and deflated anybody who was, as he called them, "a louse." In other words, he embodied everything that young people try to emulate until they grow up and become pragmatic. Somehow Bogie stayed that way, and it made him timeless.

That's what the kids in 1959 embraced and what audiences since then have echoed while, at the same time, craving those attributes in modern movie stars, if not in themselves, seldom finding it in either.

When *Casablanca* shows at the Brattle Theatre, the audience speaks the lines along with it, and this tradition started years before *The Rocky Horror Picture Show* ever existed. They stand for "The Marseillaise," cheer at "here's looking at you, kid," hiss Major Strasser, and sing along as Doolie Wilson plays "As Time Goes By." If the reaction has occasionally waned in recent years, it isn't because Bogart's star has dimmed but because the public's sense of history has faded. Or perhaps nowadays kids get pragmatic at an earlier age.

Get a Life: D. B. Cooper

Question: Who was D. B. Cooper?

Answer: In 1971 a man named D. B. Cooper boarded a plane in Los Angeles. As soon as the aircraft was aloft, he informed the flight attendant that the briefcase he carried contained a bomb that he would detonate if he was not given $200,000 in cash and four parachutes. The flight was diverted to Seattle, where Cooper let the passengers off, collected the cash, and forced the flight crew to take off, heading east. Knowing that the FBI would be waiting for him wherever he landed, he donned the parachutes, forced the cabin door open over Arizona, and bailed out. Neither Cooper (in any form) nor the money has ever shown up. Only the newly coined word *skyjacking* marks his passing—or, if you prefer, falling.

Quiz: Scandals

Confession may be good for the soul, but it can often be bad for the reputation. Even when you don't confess, your reputation can suffer, as these public figures discovered. On the other hand, time heals a lot of wounds. As proof, do you remember why these people made headlines? The year is given as a hint.

1. John Profumo (1963)
2. Billy Sol Estes (1964)
3. Mary Jo Kopechne (1969)
4. Sir Anthony Blunt (1964/1979)
5. Janet Cooke (1981)
6. Clifford Irving (1972)
7. David Begelman (1977)
8. Checkers (1952)
9. Herb Stempel (1958)
10. Kathy Evelyn Smith (1982)

Quiz: Biographies

Whose celebrity biographies/autobiographies are these?

1. *Goodness Had Nothing to Do with It*
2. *A Book*
3. *My Autobiography*
4. *The Other Side of the Road*
5. *On the Other Hand*
6. *The Times We Had*
7. *Loitering with Intent*
8. *Yes I Can*
9. *Shooting Star*
10. *Hurricane Billy*

The James Dean Legend

There is no more an enduring symbol of American youth than James Dean. Nearly half a century after his death, his image—ever youthful, ever brooding—fuels the dreams of succeeding generations. And the film that articulates this most powerfully is 1955's *Rebel Without a Cause.*

Teenage anguish elevated to the level of tragedy is, more than anything else, what has given *Rebel Without a Cause*—and James Dean—longevity. It has all the elements: a tragic hot rod "chicken" race, furtive domestic life in an abandoned mansion, a romantic escapade at the Griffith Park Observatory, and a fatal shoot-out where innocence is murdered. These moments define this classic film and help explain its impact. They also give insight into the enigma of James Dean and begin to unravel the twisted knot of irony that has bound the man to the myth.

Born on February 8, 1931, to Winton and Mildred Dean in Marion, Indiana—a town famous solely as his birthplace—James Byron Dean moved to California with his parents when he was four, only to be shipped back to Fairmont, Indiana, by his father in 1940 when his mother died. There he was raised by his Aunt Ortense and Uncle Marcus Winslow. In Fairmont, Dean took honors in the National Forensic League's state public speaking contest and moved back to California after graduation, this time to enter Santa Monica City College and, on the side, pursue acting. He landed several bit roles in movies (*Fixed Bayonets, Sailor Beware,* etc.)

but headed for New York City in 1951 on the advice of acting teacher James Whitmore.

In New York he found work in live television, was accepted into the famed Actors Studio, and appeared briefly on Broadway in *See the Jaguar* and *The Immortalist,* before being summoned back to Hollywood by director Elia Kazan to star in *East of Eden,* John Steinbeck's retelling of the Cain and Abel legend, set in agrarian Salinas, California. *Rebel Without a Cause* was next, and after that *Giant.*

In a perverse way, James Dean's death ensured his stardom. Unlike the fans who adored him, Dean never had to grow old. He is frozen in time as a fresh-faced young man, forever hoping for a better future—a future into which his followers had to travel without him.

The last day of Dean's life was the first day of his cult. On September 30, 1955, he checked out his car—a nine-day-old $7,000 Porsche Spyder that he nicknamed "The Bastard"—at 8 AM at Competition Motors in Los Angeles. AT 10 AM he ate brunch with his father in an outdoor cafe at noisy Farmer's Market on Fairfax Avenue. And by 3:30, he had picked up his friend, auto mechanic Rolf Weutherich, and headed north for Salinas.

At 5:45 PM Dean was given a speeding ticket by the highway patrol for going 65 mph on 45 mph Grapevine Grade Ridge near Bakersfield. It did not seem to have slowed them down.

There is a bend, just over a crest, east of Paso Robles, where California Route 41 crosses U.S. 466—right to Tulare and left to Chalame. At around 7 PM—twilight—Donald Gene Turnupseed, twenty-three, was driving home to Tulare in his Ford sedan. When Dean's car sped over the hill neither man could stop or turn. They collided almost head on, the Porsche spinning 100 feet into a ditch and throwing Weutherich onto the road and breaking his leg and jaw. Turnupseed, in the Ford, sustained minor injuries.

James Dean's head was snapped backward over the seat top. He was killed instantly but was not pronounced dead until his body was taken to the War Memorial Hospital in Paso Robles. It is not known if the near-sighted Dean had been wearing his eye-glasses, but police estimated that the Porsche had been traveling 80 mph.

Within hours of the fatal crash, there arose groups of fans across the country who refused to believe that their hero had died; three thousand mourners showed up at his funeral, and within the first week, seven thousand fan letters poured into Warner Bros., for a star who could no longer receive them. To this day some people insist that Dean resides in a secret wing of some phantom hospital—presumably alongside John F. Kennedy, Marilyn Monroe, Elvis Presley, and other cultural heroes whose deaths society cannot bear to accept.

The legacy is even more ironic because his costars—Sal Mineo, Natalie Wood, and Nick Adams—also met untimely, even mysterious deaths; Mineo was stabbed, Wood drowned, and Adams overdosed on drugs, giving rise to the so-called "curse" that has haunted the "rebel without a cause" since 1955. Even now, every year on the anniversary of his death, a mysterious floral display appears at the base of the statue dedicated to him at the Griffith Park Observatory. Fans (old and new) come to pay silent tribute to a man who shaped their generation but was not able to outlive it.

Hollywood Ghost Stories

In Billy Wilder's brilliant 1950 film, *Sunset Boulevard,* Joe Gillis (played by William Holden) stumbled on a deserted-looking mansion owned by Norma Desmond (Gloria Swanson). To his surprise, Norma was still living in it. Hollywood is full of such oddities, some of them reaching from beyond the grave. Here are seven of the most famous.

1. The mysterious Lady in Black who visits Valentino's grave. When silent screen icon Rudolph Valentino died in 1926 at the age of thirty-one, his female fans went into shock. Beginning in 1931, a mysterious Lady in Black began placing flowers on his grave (wall crypt #1205 in the Hollywood Memorial Cemetery Cathedral Mausoleum Section 11). Ironically, Valentino himself had visited this crypt to pay homage to the mother of June Mathis, the screenwriter who had discovered him and guided his early career. The identity of the Lady in Black has never been revealed, despite the fact that her annual arrival was, for years, an announced publicity stunt.

2. The strange tragedies associated with *The Exorcist.* The 1973 horror classic was also a classic horror to make. During its unusually long nine-month shooting schedule, the set burned down; Jason Miller's ("Father Karras") five-year-old son was hurt in a motor-cycle accident; Jack MacGowran ("Burke Dennings") died shortly after

his scenes were shot; Max Von Sydow's ("Father Merrin") brother died; Linda Blair's ("Regan MacNeill)" grandfather died; Ellen Burstyn ("Chris MacNeill") seriously hurt her back; a crew member lost a toe in an on-set accident; and the film's budget doubled.

3. Hollywood's "Suicide Hotel." The Shelton Apartments on Wilcox Avenue in old Hollywood were the location of two of the cinema town's most notable suicides. In 1941 Jenny Dolly (of the dancing Dolly Sisters) hanged herself in her living room after years of depression following a disfiguring motor accident. And in 1962 Clara Blandick (Auntie Em in *The Wizard of Oz*) suffocated herself in a plastic bag. The Shelton was razed in 1987; another apartment building now stands on its site.

4. Ozzie Nelson's ghost. After Ozzie Nelson died in 1975, his widow, Harriet, stayed on in their 1822 Camino Palermo home near Hollywood Boulevard until 1980. The new owners almost immediately began noticing strange events: doors opening and closing, faucets and room lights turning on and off with no one nearby, strange sounds attributable to nothing but, er, Ozzie's ectoplasm. This was also the house where David and Ricky Nelson were raised (although not the one used as the setting of the popular *The Adventures of Ozzie and Harriet* TV show).

5. The cancer curse of *The Conqueror*. John Wayne played Genghis Khan in this 1956 costume epic directed by Dick Powell and produced by Howard Hughes. Although forgettable as cinema, the movie has gained a grotesque notoriety because of the enormous number of cancer deaths among those who made it. Stars John Wayne, Dick Powell, Susan Hayward, and many other cast and crew members died over the years following its release. The reason may be that the film was shot in Utah on land that had recently been used as an atomic test site, and the residual radiation probably caused the cancers—though the government has denied any connection for nearly forty years.

6. The mysterious death of George "Superman" Reeves. Those close to actor George Reeves believed that he was murdered and that he had no reason to take his own life with a gunshot in 1959 at the age of forty-five. Those who lived in his 1579 Benedict Canyon Drive home in later years reported hearing strange noises and seeing odd things inside the house, and others persist in visiting the location to hold seances in order to contact his spirit.

7. Houdini escapes the hereafter. As he lay dying, famed magician-escape artist Harry Houdini promised his wife that he would try to contact her from the spirit world every year on the anniversary of his death. He never did, although annually at the Knickerbocker Hotel (1714 Ivar Avenue), his widow held a seance for just that purpose, to no avail. His mansion (2398 Laurel Canyon Boulevard) is also supposed to be haunted, although nothing is left of it but part of a flight of cement steps.

Martinis

The martini was supposedly created by bartender Jerry Thomas at the Occidental Hotel in San Francisco in the 1860s. They quickly became the cocktail of choice for sophisticates, who came to demand a near-ritual in their preparation.

Alas, no two martini *aficionados* seem to agree. James Bond prefers his vodka variety "shaken, not stirred," while Patrick Dennis repeats his Auntie Mame's caution to "stir, don't shake; it bruises the gin." In *A Thousand Clowns,* kiddie show writer Murray Burns is asked if he wants an onion in his martini and answers, "Gosh 'n' gollies, you betcha," while in *M*A*S*H,* Trapper John McIntire specifies, "A man really can't savor his martini without an olive, you know?" Finally, in *The Thin Man,* detective Nick Charles (William Powell) sips his martini while telling his wife, Nora (Myrna Loy), who is in the next room, "I'm putting away the gin."

Try not to cringe, but the classic martini is supposed to be half gin and half dry vermouth. By the end of World War II, the proportions had changed to four to one, but bartenders soon realized that when Americans ordered a dry martini, they really meant an *extra dry* one, which is roughly eight to one. Some purists—no, make that fanatics—like to merely wet the inside of the glass with vermouth and then fill it with iced gin. Some even instruct the bartender to fill a pitcher with ice, pour in some vermouth, pour it all out, and then add the gin. There are even legends about customers who order a glass of pure gin and then whisper the word *vermouth* over it.

Chemically, the martini is no stronger, ounce for ounce, than any other mixed drink. Its reputation, however, places it at the top of the list of power-cocktails (single malt scotches head the list of un-mixed drinks).

But the last word on martinis belongs, predictably, to that wit, poet, author, and paradigm of self-destruction, Dorothy Parker:

> *I never drink martinis,*
> *One or two at the most;*
> *After three, I'm under the table;*
> *After four, I'm under the host.*

PTM: Dorothy Lamour

Dorothy Lamour—more popularly known as "the sarong girl"—was one of the most popular movie stars of the 1940s. Her chief fame came as the love interest in the Bob Hope-Bing Crosby Road *pictures that enriched Paramount Pictures and still serve as the prototype for all "buddy" movies. While she and her sarong weren't being chased by Bob and Bing, however, Lamour—who was known as "Dottie" to her friends—was a fine singer and a formidable Hollywood presence. She also appeared in one of the first disaster pictures, even though it was years before the genre was identified:* The Hurricane *(1937), a love story set in the South Seas and directed by the great John Ford.*

Dorothy Lamour: As a matter of fact, they had started to shoot *Hurricane* with another star, but then [producer Sam Goldwyn] called

Paramount to see if he could borrow me, which he did. He paid the other girl off and put me in.

Nat Segaloff: The film's harrowing storm sequence remains one of the most impressive in film history.

Lamour: During that whole thing, I was fighting an appendectomy. I was working seven days—six days on the *Hurricane* and then on the weekends I was doing the *Chase and Saborn Hour* on radio. The doctor would come on the set every day and take my blood count. When I finished it, I was in rehearsal for the radio show, and I got such a pain they had to take me into the hospital and do an emergency appendectomy. I tell you, youth has no fear!

Segaloff: Massive amounts of water were dumped on the actors time and again.

Lamour: It was like 1500 gallons at a time, in each tank, and there were four tanks. They would work on a timer or something, and they would let them go. And then there were four or five airplane machines to whip up the wind, and in the wind they would put crushed, dried leaves. When I'd go home at night in the sarong, all of my chest and shoulders and arms and legs were pitted with little bloody spots from the leaves. It was very unpleasant, especially when you were tied up there to a tree with an appendectomy and have this child [in the story] tied to your stomach. I couldn't move. But they had people standing by for emergencies. I think it took two months for just that one scene.

PTM: Robert Downey, Sr. (a Prince)

Everybody thinks that Hollywood's infatuation with youth comedy began with National Lampoon's Animal House *in 1978. In fact, the die was cast fifteen years earlier with a series of "underground" films—movies so independent that even art houses seldom booked them—by filmmaker Robert Downey.*

Better known these days as the father of Robert Downey, Jr., the senior Downey began making scathing, free-form movies with 1963's indescribable Babo 73 *and 1965's* Chafed Elbows. *He hit his stride with the 1969 satire* Putney Swope, *about a black man who was accidentally put in charge of an all-white Madison Avenue advertising agency. The spirit of rebellion that fueled Downey's work and inspired other directors (Terry Gilliam, John Landis, Ivan Reitman, etc.) backfired on Downey himself, however. In 1980 he clashed with Universal on* The Gong Show Movie *and with Warner Bros. on* Mad Magazine's Up the Academy *and has worked independently ever since (*Too Much Sun *[1991]).*

Nat Segaloff: There's irony in the freedom you gave Hollywood, but they wouldn't give to you.

Robert Downey, Sr.: There was a guy at Universal Studios who once said to me, and this is a quote, "We owe your early films a debt." And I said, "Then pay it." He didn't get it, and I was out of that office in twenty minutes.

Segaloff: Much of today's TV and movie comedy is gross and negative, as though every person who appears on screen is ripe for insult.

Downey: I've always liked my characters. I don't think of them as shocking. I just thought I was expressing myself. Half of the stuff in *Babo 73* came true. Satire in movies is tough, anyway, because film is an emotional thing, whereas satire is from the head. The best thing I ever did, which shocked them into doing something I didn't think I could do, was when David Rabe wrote a play called *Sticks and Bones* [about a highly dysfunctional American family facing the Vietnam War], which I had to do as a TV show. And Joe Papp said, "Take the laughs out. It'll be better." We did, and it wasn't funny. I liked doing that; it was fun, but why wasn't it funny—it was metaphysical satire in a way. [The trick to doing comedy is to] make sure people are in a hurry and don't let 'em sit down too much. Try not to let 'em eat or make phone calls. And move 'em to and from the camera when you can instead of left and right. There's all sorts of rules. And then the final rule is break all the rules 'case you can't do it half the time anyway.

Downey's latest film is Hugo Pool *(1997). As an actor, he was recently seen in* Boogie Nights.

Quiz: John Travolta

No star presence better embodied the spirit of the late 1970s than that of John Travolta or, ironically, suffered the same fate. At first seen widely as Vinnie Barbarino on the TV series *Welcome Back, Kotter*, Travolta was galvanizing in his first starring movie role as *Saturday Night Fever*'s Tony Manero. He was lithe, he was sensual, and he was—according to those who worked with him—one of the most genuinely nice people around. But by the early 1980s, Travolta found himself as out of fashion as the brash, polyester disco culture he had once popularized. Bruised by unwise management decisions and personal tragedy, Travolta languished for nearly a decade, until 1989's *Look Who's Talking* made him commercial again and 1994's *Pulp Fiction* made him a phenomenon.

Very few stars get second chances, but Travolta is more than a star—he is an icon. Just as America aimlessly wandered through the self-indulgent '80s, so did Travolta stumble through a string of indifferent projects. Some, like Robert Altman's 1987 *Basements,* were too obscure to score; others, like James Bridges's 1985 *Perfect,* were attacked for being too ambitious. By the 1990s—a little heavier, a little seedier, a lot more world-weary, just like his generation had become—John Travolta returned with a passion. In three years he made no fewer than twelve movies. But more than that, his resurgence restored his public's faith not only in his talent but in themselves.

In this quiz—intended to shatter once and for all the image that Travolta can only play guys from Brooklyn—identify the film by the part he plays. (Extra credit: Identify James Ubriacco.)

1. Crusading reporter who is betrayed by his own heart
2. Bumbling hit man who isn't so bumbling after all
3. Movie sound engineer who hears something he shouldn't
4. Single father on the run from the mob
5. Oil rig worker
6. Average guy who becomes a genius
7. Bomber pilot
8. Inventor turned bank robber
9. State governor
10. Mob enforcer guarding an investment

Quiz: Comic Catchphrases

The comedy album was a phenomenon of the 1960s. At a time when such brilliant comic minds as Shelley Berman, Mort Sahl, and Robert Klein were squeezed into the vanilla mold of the Ed Sullivan and other variety shows, the only way to hear their humor in its full intellectual (and sometimes blue) glory was on LP (long playing) record.

The convention continues to defy explanation: Invariably, you didn't buy a comedy album; somebody had to give it to you (they already had it, courtesy of someone else). You then listened to it together, and the people who had already heard it watched and waited for you to laugh. Then you bought a copy of the album for someone else and watched them listen to it and laugh. And so on.

Taping them was never done; remember that cassette recorders hadn't been invented, and very few people owned a cumbersome 7-inch reel-to-reel tape recorder.

Premium cable channels such as HBO, which permit profanity, pretty much eliminated comedy albums, and basic cable "improv" shows practically destroyed the rest of stand-up comedy by demanding rapid-fire jokes and quick payoffs. Talk about cashing in on the golden eggs by throttling the goose that laid them!

Most comedy albums (*Firesign Theatre* and *Conception Corporation* being the notable exceptions) were recorded in front of a live—and often drunk—nightclub audience. Several performances were usually edited into a single flawless act, and a noted journalist/radio monologist/hep cat (Steve Allen, Nat Hentoff, Roger Price, etc.) was chosen to write the liner notes.

The talent was astonishing, for this was the era of Chicago's Second City, New York's Greenwich Village coffee houses, and San Francisco's beat clubs. The performers were intellectual, liberal, socially committed, and frequently actors first and comedians second. The performers who came out of the Hungry i (q.v.), Mister Kelly's, the Village Vanguard, and other clubs led to those who got their start at the newer Improv, Comic Strip, Laugh Factory, and Comedy Store.

As in the days of vaudeville, most of them became identified by a catchphrase they introduced and then used at least once each act to the applause of recognition. But not always; the genius of Woody Allen, Richard Pryor, Nichols and May, and Jonathan Winters could never be represented by a single expression. Nevertheless, match the one-liner with the comedian:

1. "Same to you, fella."
2. "Riiiiight!"
3. "Well excuuuusssse me"
4. "Is there anybody here I haven't offended tonight?"
5. "Yes, hello, operator?"
6. "The devil made me do it."
7. "I don't get no respect."
8. "Yadda, yadda, faddah."
9. "Wonderful WINOooooo."
10. "Hello dere."
11. "Why not?"
12. "Booga booga!"
13. "Smok! Smok!"
14. "Would you believe . . ."
15. "Nanu, nanu."

a. Don Adams
b. Flip Wilson
c. Dayton Allen
d. Lenny Bruce
e. Steve Allen
f. George Carlin
g. Mort Sahl
h. Marty Allen
i. David Steinberg
j. Robin Williams
k. Rodney Dangerfield
l. Bill Cosby
m. Steve Martin
n. Bob Newhart
o. Shelly Berman

Quiz: Celebrity Scandals

You don't need to be a politician to have a scandal of your very own; these celebrities managed to do it without a single vote. Match the famous person with the non-talent-related reason for his/her notoriety:

1.	Robert Mitchum	a.	Allegedly flipped finger on TV
2.	Zsa Zsa Gabor	b.	Underage sex
3.	Roman Polanski	c.	On-air firing by show host
4.	Michael Jackson	d.	Alleged wife beating
5.	Marilyn Monroe	e.	Slapped a cop
6.	Richard Gere	f.	Statutory rape
7.	Larry King	g.	Nude calendar
8.	Mackenzie Phillips	h.	Alleged pederasty
9.	Richard Pryor	i.	USC football squad
10.	Julius LaRosa	j.	Walked off own TV show
11.	Jackie Mason	k.	Alleged animal abuse
12.	Jan-Michael Vincent	l.	Crack fire victim
13.	Jack Paar	m.	Financial fraud
14.	Clara Bow	n.	Coke bottle
15.	Errol Flynn	o.	Drug use
16.	Fatty Arbuckle	p.	Hollywood sign suicide
17.	Jayne Mansfield	q.	Drowned in toilet
18.	Peg Entwistle	r.	Pot bust
19.	Lupe Velez	s.	Death by decapitation

Quiz: Me, Myself, and I

Marilyn Monroe once said, "A sex symbol becomes a thing. I just hate being a thing." Yet there have been a number of celebrities who have worn their fame graciously, even with humor. Can you name them by recognizing their quotes on the subject of fame—and themselves?

1. "The only thing worse than being talked about is *not* being talked about."
2. "I enjoy the way I look, but it's a joke."
3. I'm a controversial figure. My friends either dislike me or hate me."
4. "Everyone tells me I've had such an interesting life, but sometimes I think it's been nothing but stomach disturbances and self-concern."
5. "Making movies is better than cleaning toilets."
6. "For me, life has been either a wake or a wedding."
7. "Nothing is beneath me if it pays well."
8. "Can you imagine being wonderfully overpaid for dressing up and playing games?"
9. "Actors often behave like children and so we're taken for children. I want to be grown up."
10. "Behind all art is ego, and I am an artist and I am unique."

Quiz: Loose Lips

"Gossip is the new pornography," opined a character in Woody Allen's *Manhattan*. But even the most cynical social commentator couldn't have been so prescient as to predict how effectively gossip would obscure legitimate journalism in the 1990s.

If, as the tea bag remarks, "Small minds talk about people, large minds talk about things, and great minds talk about ideas," where does that leave gossip? Gossip proves nothing but the bad taste of the gossiper, but that never stopped people from specializing in reporting it over the years. Identify these spiritual fathers and mothers of Geraldo, Jerry, Tanya, and Liz:

1. Jimmie Fidler
2. Hedda Hopper
3. Louella Parsons
4. Adela Rodgers St. Johns
5. Dorothy Kilgallen
6. Walter Winchell
7. Ed Sullivan
8. Radie Harris

Quiz: What a Way to Go

Some people are famous for the way they lived, others for the way they died, and sometimes for both. Match these well-known people with the ways they met their maker:

1.	Christopher Columbus	a.	Typhus
2.	Isadora Duncan	b.	Suicide
3.	Saint Lawrence	c.	"Lead poisoning"
4.	Jean Harlow	d.	Lung abscess
5.	Joseph R. McCarthy	e.	Uremic poisoning
6.	Margaret Mitchell	f.	Strangulation
7.	Bugsy Siegel	g.	Alcoholic liver failure
8.	Peter Ilych Tchaikovsky	h.	Heart disease
9.	Pontius Pilate	i.	Roasting
10.	Benjamin Franklin	j.	Automobile accident

Quiz: Your Fifteen Minutes Are Up

Andy Warhol, whose life and art earned him notoriety in equal measure, opined in 1968 (for a Stockholm exhibition catalogue), "In the future, everyone will be world-famous for fifteen minutes." Warhol's lasted far longer than fifteen minutes, ending in 1987, when he died at the age of fifty-one. Can you identify these people who also enjoyed their fifteen minutes:

1. Janet Cooke
2. Rosie Ruiz
3. Robert Opel
4. Sasheen Little-Feather (Maria Cruz)
5. Valerie Solanas
6. Arnold Zenker
7. Jean Karakos and Oliver Lorsac
8. Rob Pilatus and Fab Morvan
9. Van McCoy
10. Nina Van Pallandt

Answers

What's in a Name? (Answers)

1. Fred Astaire	14. Irving Berlin
2. Eve Arden	15. Jack Benny
3. Lauren Bacall	16. Rita Hayworth
4. Ann Bancroft	17. William Holden
5. Mel Brooks	18. Rock Hudson
6. Doris Day	19. Roy Rogers
7. Al Jolson	20. Shelley Winters
8. Boris Karloff	21. Danny Thomas
9. Danny Kaye	22. Dean Martin
10. Larry King	23. Ginger Rogers
11. Kirk Douglas	24. Tennesee Williams
12. George Burns	25. Monty Hall
13. Red Buttons	

Insults (Answers)

1. Walter Matthau to Barbra Streisand on the occasion of *Hello Dolly*
2. Billy Wilder about Marilyn Monroe
3. Greer Garson about Marlon Brando
4. Elsa Lanchester about Maureen O'Hara
5. Dorothy Parker on Basil Rathbone
6. Jack Nicholson on Jessica Lange
7. Billy Wilder on fellow director Otto Preminger
8. Noel Coward on James Cagney
9. Rock Hudson on James Dean
10. Orson Welles on Steven Spielberg after Spielberg paid $50,000 for a "Rosebud" sled from *Citizen Kane*

Praise (Answers)

1. Ethel Merman (no slouch herself) about Mary Martin
2. Marlene Dietrich on Orson Welles
3. Kevin Brownlow on Lillian Gish
4. Believe it or not, this is praise, and it's from George Burns about Gary Cooper.
5. Clark Gable on Spencer Tracy
6. Cybill Shepherd on Marilyn Monroe
7. Groucho Marx on Margaret Dumont
8. Director John Ford on director Sam Peckinpah (supposedly)
9. Fred MacMurray on Barbara Stanwyck
10. Unknown writer on Humphrey Bogart—but it's such a good quote, we couldn't leave it out.

Scandals (Answers)

1. John Profumo, member of Parliament and Minister of War, under British Prime Minister Harold MacMillan, had a fling with Christine Keeler, a purported call girl who, at the same time, was having an affair with Assistant Russian Naval Attaché Eugene Ivanov. Despite the appearance of impropriety, what forced Profumo to resign in 1963 was that he lied about the affair when questioned about it in the House of Commons.

2. Among the scandals that dogged President Lyndon Baines Johnson to his grave in 1973 (everything from allegations of stealing elections in Texas to ordering the assassination of JFK) was the fraud conviction, in 1964, of his friend Billy Sol Estes and whispers of complicity in fundraising swindles by Estes *compadre* Bobby Baker. Combined with sexual allegations against another associate, Walter Jenkins, the Republicans had a field day announcing the initials *LBJ* stood for "Lyndon-Baker-Jenkins." Johnson won the 1964 election anyway.

3. In the summer of 1969, a car ran off a bridge into the water off a Massachusetts island called Chappaquiddick. Inside were Senator Ted Kennedy of Massachusetts, who was driving, and one of his staffers, Mary Jo Kopechne. The senator swam to safety while Ms. Kopechne, apparently trapped inside the car, drowned. The senator's delay in reporting her death—he insisted he was in a daze and called the police as soon as his mind cleared—seriously damaged his presidential ambitions.

4. Anthony Blunt, Keeper of the Queen's Pictures, had been linked to British double agents Kim Philby and Guy Burgess, yet he was so valuable to MI-5, British Intelligence, that he was granted immunity when he confessed in 1964. The 1979 exposure of a fifteen-year government cover-up (during which time the Queen had knighted Blunt) was an embarrassment to Prime Minister Margaret Thatcher.

5. Janet Cooke is the *Washington Post* reporter who won a Pulitzer Prize in 1981 for her heart-rending newspaper series about an eight-year-old heroin addict. Coming on the heels of the *Post*'s Pulitzer for their Watergate coverage, this consolidated the paper's position as the national leader. That prestige was seriously tarnished when Ms. Cooke confessed that she had invented the young addict and fabricated her articles. She was summarily dismissed but was located in 1995 by a magazine writer who found her working in a Michigan department store.

6. Clifford Irving counted on bashful billionaire Howard Hughes keeping quiet when Irving offered Hughes's fake biography to *Life Magazine* and McGraw-Hill publishers in 1972. He was wrong, although the way Hughes refuted their alleged contract—he testified through speakerphone—hardly calmed the waters. Postal handwriting experts subsequently convinced the court of the fakery. Since Irving had used the papers to land publishing deals, everything evaporated—including Irving's credibility and freedom—when the forgeries hit the fan.

7. A former agent who became head of Columbia Pictures, David Begelman was skillful at deal-making and beloved by all Hollywood insiders—even after he admitted forging $40,000 worth of checks in 1977 in the names of actor Cliff Robertson, director Martin Ritt, and LA restaurateur Pierre Grolieu. What made the scandal even more so was that the studio held off firing him, so valuable were his talents. He was finally ousted from Columbia, atoned by making a documentary about drug abuse, and later ran MGM for a short time. In 1995, when new financial questions began to surface, he took his own life in a Los Angeles hotel room.

8. Checkers, the cocker spaniel owned by Trisha Nixon, was cited by Vice President Richard M. Nixon as a freebie he got as part of some shady contributions to his election slush fund in 1952. In denying the allegations, the future ex-president also named his wife's "good Republican cloth coat" as an attribute. The so-called "Checkers Speech" deflected public criticism at the time but was thereafter cited as the first of many scandals to befall Nixon.

9. Herb Stempel, in 1958, blew the whistle on the TV game show *Twenty-One*. He stated that he and other contestants—including the highly successful Charles Van Doren—had been provided with answers ahead of time. In the "Quiz Show Scandals" that followed, the TV networks maintained that since nobody was hurt—the money belonged to the sponsors, who encouraged the deception—no harm was done. This, of course, ignored the incalculable damage that was inflicted upon the credibility of the medium itself.

10. When Kathy Evelyn Smith confessed (but only to a tabloid newspaper) to giving John Belushi the drug injection that killed him in 1982, she touched off a criminal investigation that resulted in, among other things, a (temporarily) raised consciousness over drug use in Hollywood. She later fought extradition from Canada to the U.S. to face second-degree murder charges.

Biographies (Answers)

1. Mae West
2. Desi Arnaz
3. Charles Chaplin
4. Dorothy Lamour
5. Fay Wray
6. Marian Davies
7. Peter O'Toole
8. Sammy Davis, Jr.
9. John Wayne
10. William Friedkin (a shameless plug by the author for his own book)

John Travolta (Answers)

1. *Perfect*
2. *Basements*
3. *Blow Out*
4. *Eyes of an Angel*
5. *Urban Cowboy*
6. *Phenomenon*
7. *Broken Arrow*
8. *Two of a Kind*
9. *Primary Colors*
10. *Get Shorty*

Extra credit answer: James Ubriacco directed the later *Look Who's Talking* pictures.

Comic Catchphrases (Answers)

1. n
2. l
3. m
4. g
5. o
6. b
7. k
8. d
9. f
10. h
11. c
12. i
13. e
14. a
15. j

Celebrity Scandals (Answers)

1. r
2. e
3. b
4. h
5. g
6. k
7. m
8. o
9. l
10. c
11. a
12. d
13. j
14. i
15. f
16. n
17. s
18. p
19. q

Answers

Me, Myself, and I (Answers)

1. Oscar Wilde
2. Dolly Parton
3. Oscar Levant
4. Cary Grant
5. Klaus Kinski
6. Peter O'Toole
7. Laurence Olivier
8. David Niven
9. Jeremy Irons
10. Richard Dreyfuss

Loose Lips (Answers)

1. One of the first newspaper columnists to branch out to radio, Fidler covered the Hollywood studios.
2. Most often contrasted with Louella Parsons, Hedda Hopper—famous for her hats—held the movies in her unforgiving grasp in newspaper columns and on radio.
3. Louella "Lolly" Parsons covered show business for the Hearst papers, usually in competition for scoops with Hedda Hopper.
4. A hard-working journalist and sometimes-screen-writer, Adela Rodgers St. Johns brought legitimacy to covering Hollywood for newspapers and, later, TV.
5. Feared and respected, Dorothy Kilgallen's beat was Broadway, broadcast, and movies; she was famous for her feud with TV's Jack Paar.
6. With his rat-a-tat delivery (both on radio and in print), powerful syndicated New York columnist Walter Winchell was famous for espousing causes, even when he was wrong.
7. Before he was a TV host/producer, Ed Sullivan wrote Broadway's "Toast of the Town" column with a knowing and sympathetic sensibility.
8. Demanding and imperious, syndicated Hollywood columnist Radie Harris played the studios like a harp to get morsels of news.

What a Way to Go (Answers)

1. h
2. f
3. i
4. e
5. g
6. j
7. c
8. a
9. b
10. d

Your Fifteen Minutes Are Up (Answers)

1. Janet Cooke won the Pulitzer Prize for her 1980 *Washington Post* series on Jimmy, a young ghetto drug addict. She then had to return the award, when she revealed she faked the stories. At last report, she was a sales clerk.
2. Rosie Ruiz looked like the fastest woman on earth when she won the Boston Marathon in 1980. The only problem was that she hadn't run the whole 26 miles; she started 2 miles from the finish line. In 1984 she was arrested in Miami on cocaine charges.
3. Robert Opel was the streaker who buffed David Niven during the 1974 Academy Award show. He had a fling at acting and stand-up comedy and was found murdered in 1979.
4. Sasheen Little-Feather accepted Marlon Brando's Oscar® for *The Godfather* in 1972, castigating the Academy for racism against Native Americans. An actress, her real name was Maria Cruz.
5. The founder of SCUM (Society for Cutting Up Men), Valerie Solanas shot Andy Warhol in 1968. She went to jail and Warhol recovered.
6. When AFTRA, the broadcast union, went on strike in the 1960s, Arnold Zenker substituted for CBS newsman (and cultural icon) Walter Cronkite. He is now a corporate media consultant.
7. French record producers Jean Karakos and Oliver Lorsac introduced the lambada in 1989. Um, remember the lambada? (Does "the forbidden dance" ring a bell?)
8. Better known as Milli Vanilli, Rob Pilatus and Fab Morvan were spared no disdain when it turned out that the model-handsome singers did not, in fact, sing their own tracks on their 1989 album, *Girl You Know It's True*.
9. Van McCoy, backed by the Soul City Symphony, recorded a song called "The Hustle" in 1975. The song is credited with kicking off the disco craze. He died of a heart attack at age thirty-five.
10. Nina Van Pallandt was romantically linked with author Clifford Irving, whose "authorized biography" of billionaire Howard Hughes forced Hughes to break his silence in 1972 to deny its authenticity. When Irving was jailed for fraud, the icily beautiful Van Pallandt became an actress, debuting in Robert Altman's *The Long Goodbye* in 1973.

Chapter 12

MiNUTiAe

One of the most distressing trends as the twentieth century draws to a close is what can only be described as the isolation of the American community. One incident is revealing: It was reported casually in a Boston newspaper feature in the early 1980s that students from a suburban high school took a supervised field trip into the city and were asked to write about it when they returned later that same day. The teacher was shocked to read, in a majority of the essays, that her students had expected to be attacked, kidnaped, raped, or murdered during their five-hour stay in an urban environment and were relieved when they got home again.

The teacher may have been astonished at the teenagers' attitude, but social observers were, sadly, not surprised. They added the student's paranoia to a growing list of observations that have come to characterize a society in which mere human interaction has become a volatile commodity.

Humans gain experience by the simple act of speaking with fellow humans. When Marco Polo "opened" China, when Admiral Perry "unlocked" Japan, when Columbus "discovered," America, and, indeed, when primitive man merely moved from one cave to another, the more important result wasn't the act itself (how can you "find" a place that other people have already been living in?) but, rather, the exchange of knowledge between disparate civilizations.

What happened between the time that Sir Richard Burton reported his adventures along the Nile to a curious world and those sub-urban Boston teenagers breathing easier after returning from their "dangerous" foray into the neighboring city? Ironically, the answer is "communication." Or lack of it.

The Internet is, in theory, the greatest tool for education since the invention of movable type. Within moments, anyone can access information from around the world. And that's the problem.

The wealth of information itself on the Internet becomes a danger. Weigh this: A ninth grader is assigned to write a report on World War II. In years past, a student would walk into his/her school library and ask the librarian to suggest perhaps half a dozen books. The student would then skim from chapter to chapter before deciding on a focus for his/her paper and then would settle down to write it. The Internet is more powerful than any librarian, yet has no discretion. The student typing the search phrase "World War II" is equally likely to turn up William L. Shirer's *The Rise and Fall of the Third Reich* as she is to stumble across the Web site of the Aryan Nations.

Of course, freedom of thought is one of the cornerstones of American democracy. The theory is that people, when shown the fallacy of their ideas, will amend them. In practice, however, the effect is that enlightenment produces intransigence. Dogmatic people cherish their dogmas, and in such cases truth can be horrendously threatening.

If, as the old saying goes, "the truth shall set ye free," why is so much time and effort spent on lying? The question is not whether new ideas are valid but why people resort to violence in lieu of considering them.

Quiz: Secret Identities

Nowadays they call it multiple personality disorder, but time was—if you were a superhero—you just *had* to have another name for those days when your tights were at the cleaner's. Of course, both "real" and "secret" identities were fictitious. Match the following. (Extra credit: Identify Lamont Cranston's other secret ID.)

Civies	**Tights**
1. Bruce Banner	a. Mighty Thor
2. Mike Waring	b. The Shadow
3. Clark Kent	c. The Thcarlet Pumpernickel (*sic*)
4. Bruce Wayne	d. Iron Man
5. Peter Parker	e. Green Lantern
6. Don Blake	f. The Incredible Hulk
7. Lamont Cranston	g. Batman
8. Tony Stark	h. The Falcon
9. Britt Reid	i. The Lone Ranger
10. Alan Scott	j. Spider-Man
11. Dan Reid	k. Green Hornet
12. Daffy Duck	l. Superman

Quiz: Bar Bets

These are trick questions and are presented here without warranty of any kind:

1. How many grooves are there on one side of a standard 33 1/3 rpm record?
2. What is Smokey the Bear's middle name?
3. Which weighs more, a pound of feathers or a pound of steel?
4. According to international law, if a plane crashes on the border between the United States and Mexico, in which country must the survivors be buried?
5. Name at least six actors who played Ian Fleming's superagent James Bond.
6. Why can't you Xerox a Xerox of a Xerox?
7. Name at least three U.S. Presidents who are NOT buried inside the continental United States.
8. When does the millennium begin?
9. Which has more calories, 4 ounces of corn flakes or 4 ounces of sugar-frosted flakes?
10. Is there any such thing as a U.S. penny?

Quiz: Don't Quote Me

Sometimes quotes became famous by being misused, or misapplied, or misquoted. These quotes aren't what they used to be, but in some ways have been improved (or at least made funnier) in the translation. Who is credited with having spoken them?

1. "If all the debutantes in Connecticut were laid end on end, it wouldn't surprise me in the least."
2. "You can lead a horse to water, but a pencil must be lead."
3. "You can lead a horticulture, but you can't make her think."
4. "Anybody who sees a psychiatrist ought to have his head examined."
5. "May the bird of paradise lay an egg in your beer."
6. "The way to a man's heart is right through his chest."
7. "If you can't say something nice about someone, sit next to me."
8. "More fun than human beings are legally allowed to have."
9. "Love between two people is beautiful. Between three it's fantastic."
10. "Consider that two wrongs never make a right, but that three do."

Quiz: Advertising Catchphrases

Advertising is so pervasive that very often it registers a new expression in our language. Name the products that were originally sold using these phrases or that popularized these phrases to the extent of being forever identified with them.

1. "Cool, calm, and collected"
2. "It's what's up front that counts."
3. "You've come a long way, baby."
4. "No matter what shape you're stomach's in . . ."
5. "Mama mia, that's some spicy meatball."
6. "Mother, please, I'd rather do it myself!"
7. "They laughed when I sat down to play the piano."
8. "Don't leave home without it."
9. "——— has been shown to be an effective decay-preventive dentifrice that can be of significant value when used in a conscientiously applied program of oral hygiene and regular preventative care."
10. "Takes the worry out of being close"
11. "Aren't you glad you used———? Don't you wish everybody did?"
12. "99 and 44/100 percent pure"

The Three Stooges

There are two things in American society that men reserve for themselves: hogging the TV remote and liking the Three Stooges. The former is best explained by men's short attention spans, weak sense of loyalty, frustration with things they cannot instantly comprehend, and instinct to constantly forage for food (in this case, programming).

On the other hand, nothing can explain the Three Stooges. You either like them or you don't. Women don't. Men do.

Formed in vaudeville in 1923, the original stooges were Moe Howard (born Moses Horowitz) and his brother Shemp (born Samuel) Howard, who served as Ted Healey's "second bananas" in an act called Ted Healey and His Stooges. Two years later, Moe, Shemp, and Ted were joined by comedian Larry Fine (Finestein) and continued to tour the vaudeville circuits with enough success that they were signed to make a film, *Soup to Nuts*, in 1930 in which they were called The Racketeers. After their film debut, Shemp left the act and was replaced by another Howard brother, Curly (born Jerome).

By 1934 Moe, Larry, and Curly left Ted Healey and embarked on their own career, starring in a succession of "two-reelers" (twenty-minute comedy short subjects) for Columbia Pictures. Between 1934 and 1958 they starred in some two hundred titles including experimental entries in 3-D and with rhyming dialogue. Curly continued to appear until 1946 when he suffered a stroke; he was replaced by Shemp, who died in 1955 and was replaced by Joe Besser.

The advent of double features in the economically strapped Hollywood of the mid-'50s drove two-reelers out of business, and the Three Stooges suddenly found themselves unemployed. It was then that television revived them, when TV's backlog of comedies was sold to local stations by Screen Gems, the TV distribution arm of Columbia Pictures. The twenty-minute running time, awkward in theatres, proved perfect to fill a half-hour TV slot, with commercials. Programmed for a youth audience (over the strenuous objection of parents who found the shorts horribly violent), the Three Stooges were back.

Their revival, however, produced bitterness: Since they had always been employees of the studio, Fine and the Messrs. Howard received no residuals from Columbia's windfall income. It was only when Columbia decided to capitalize on the Stooges' renewed popularity by starring them in hurriedly made feature films that the Stooges saw some money. By the time they were back making TV guest appearances, cutting children's records, and shooting *Have Rocket Will Travel* in 1959, Joe Besser was replaced by Joe de Rita (born Joseph Wardell; a.k.a. Curly Joe) and the old two-reelers were being booked theatrically in "all-Stooge" festivals. Their last film was *The Outlaws Is* (sic) *Coming!* in 1965.

What made the Stooges funny? To many, that's begging the question. Their humor is the lowest of the low: gouging eyes (except where [usually] prevented by the well-timed barrier of a hand held sideways), running saws across each other's heads (either crosscut with the teeth or slapping full blade on the face), hitting one fist so that it bounces and makes contact, waving a hand in front of someone's face to distract and then to hit him, putting each other's heads in vices, hooking a pinky under someone's nostril and pulling, pinching someone's nose, slapping the palm against someone's forehead, dragging someone by the ear, ripping out a clump of Larry's curly hair, finger-snap-to-hand-on-fist, and other injurious behavior. These are usually accompanied by such phrases as "soitenly," "woop, woop, woop," "pick two," "woof-woof," "ma-ha?/a-ha!," "Moe! Larry! the cheese!," and the crowd-pleasing "nyuck, nyuck, nyuck."

When the Stooges did it, they never got hurt. When kids did it to each other on the playground, they wiped each other out. No wonder parents disapproved. Which, of course, explains why kids loved the Three Stooges: They stood for everything Mom and Dad feared.

They were eternal children (especially not-as-invulnerable-as-we-thought Curly). There was no art to their antics, only the consummate skill of years spent honing the craft of timing and delivery. Kids growing up in the 1950s were first exposed to them on television, where there were no laugh tracks—so something inherent in the Stooges must have been instantly recognizable as being "funny." The best bet is that Moe, Larry, and the various Curlys were grown-ups who acted like children, had a ball, didn't bleed, and, in the end, escaped to nyuck another day (it seemed that most of their films closed with the trio running off into the distance).

Notably, although the Stooges were always the recipients of violence from one another, they seldom unleashed it against others—and then it was either by accident or by pastry.

They were guiltless of the mayhem that swirled around them. Best of all, they never had to clean up their room (assuming that it wasn't thoroughly destroyed anyway). They were gloriously incorrigible.

On the other hand, they were also soulless. They relied on speed and intensity rather than empathy. Compared with, say, the work of Stan Laurel and Oliver Hardy (who are regarded by some as the most sublime of movie comedy teams), the Three Stooges films are virtually indistinguishable from each other; once you've seen one Stooge picture, you've seen them all.

They also carry a great deal of baggage. Exhibitors in college towns are often reluctant to program Stooge festivals, particularly for midnight shows, because, as one manager said, "I got tired of guys getting drunk and throwing up in my theatre."

But the best discourse appeared on the TV series *Alien Nation,* in which an earth policeman, paired with a police woman from another planet, proved unable to define why the Three Stooges were funny. Finally, he had to admit, "I can't explain it; it's a *guy* thing."

"I see," the alien police woman said, not convinced. Then she added, "But if you knew what *nyuck, nyuck, nyuck* meant in *my* language, you wouldn't think they were funny, either."

Get a Life: Trekker

Question: What is the difference between a *Trekker* and a *Trekkie*?

Answer: Although neither term is appreciated by the millions of fans who follow *Star Trek*® and its various generations, a *Trekker* is often described as someone who merely likes to watch the show, and a *Trekkie* is someone who owns a set of Spock ears.

Quiz: Teams

Sometimes A plus B equals fame and fortune, and sometimes it equals zero. When producer Hal Roach paired Stan Laurel with Oliver Hardy in 1926, did he think he was creating movie history? No. When CBS paired Dan Rather and Connie Chung, did they think they were making TV history? Yes. Go figure. Match the pairs:

1.	Mutt	a.	99
2.	Siskel	b.	Hutch
3.	Lucy	c.	Ethel
4.	Bert	d.	Lacey
5.	Bert	e.	Crosby
6.	Jeeves	f.	Maria
7.	Hope	g.	Reddy
8.	Thelma	h.	Willbuurrrr
9.	Bonnie	i.	Banky
10.	J. Edgar	j.	Gracie
11.	Fred	k.	Ernie
12.	Dee	l.	Lou
13.	Bud	m.	Desi
14.	Starsky	n.	Ebert
15.	Max	o.	Jeff
16.	Chad	p.	Wooster
17.	Cagney	q.	DeNiro
18.	Spock	r.	I
19.	Nick	s.	Louise
20.	Colman	t.	Clyde
21.	Ruff	u.	Kirk
22.	Yogi	v.	Clyde
23.	Scorsese	w.	Dum
24.	George	x.	Booboo
25.	Ed	y.	Jeremy
26.	Tony	z.	Nora

Quiz: They, Robots

Robots can be helpful, heroic, and menacing. Match the following robots with their owners. (Extra credit: Name the actors who played the owners and the film or TV show title.)

1. Rosey	a. Klaatu
2. Robot	b. John Connor
3. Robby	c. Luke Skywalker
4. Maria	d. James A. Corry
5. Gort	e. Rotwang
6. T-1000	f. Space Family Robinson
7. Terminator	g. Stephanie Speck
8. R2-D2 and C-3PO	h. George and Jane Jetson
9. Number 5	i. Skynet
10. Alicia	j. Dr. Morbius

Quiz: Slanguage

Technically, slang is unofficial speech; the moment it enters the formal lexicon, it can no longer be considered slang. Thus, such words as *hip, cool, jerk, stoned, pad,* and *camp*, for example, acquire new meaning when used in a new context.

It may be a statement of the times that current slang includes not just words, such as *crib* (home), *later* (see you soon), and *the 411* (facts), but also sounds, such as *yo* (hey there), *dis* (disrespect), and *bro* (brother). All of these slang words reflect their era; they even *look* dated, don't they? If they seem archaic now, that's the happy result of having a living, growing language. Define the following. (Note: no obscenities are included.)

1. Cherry picker	11. Get it together
2. A-okay	12. Hassle
3. Hairy	13. 24/7
4. Drag	14. Freak out
5. Rap	15. Shine on
6. Bogart	16. Booty
7. Passion pit	17. Mosh pit
8. Bread	18. Scarf
9. Hog	19. No problemo
10. Hit on	

Quiz: Acronyms

An acronym is a word formed from the initials of a phrase that is useful in speaking or writing about the phrase. In addition to being an abbreviation, it can be spoken as a word. An example is "AWOL," which means "Absent Without Leave." We see these all the time, but what do they really mean?

1. NASCAR
2. CORE
3. MASH
4. UNESCO
5. NATO
6. GATT
7. NAFTA
8. NASDAQ (pronounced Naz-dak)
9. WYSIWYG (pronounced Wizzy-wig)
10. SNAFU

Get a Life: Tally

Question: What is "Tally"

Answer: "Tally" is a tradition—said to have been invented by Roland A. Linger, the legendary scoutmaster of Boy Scout Troop 87 in Hillandale, Maryland, in the 1960s—to reduce litter. Its implementation was instantaneous, and its enforcement was a badge of honor. A boy seeing another boy carelessly discard a piece of trash—candy bar wrapper, pop bottle, etc.—would rush to scoop it up and yell "Tally!" The litterbug was then compelled to pay the finder the cash value of the trash.

Who's Minding the Store?

Before market research led to investors calling their businesses "J. J. Beanpot's," "Burgermeisters," or other contrived monikers, the people who opened restaurants and department stores proudly placed their own names on their establishments. As a result, their names survived them—and so, for the most part, did their stores.

The orange-roofed guardian of the interstate highways, Howard Johnson, started in 1936 in Massachusetts, when Johnson, who sold ice cream and fried clams (not together), convinced a man named Reginald Sprague to open a restaurant in Orleans, a town on Cape Cod. The idea was that Johnson would supply Sprague with merchandise, and the idea caught on, building to a well-known twenty-eight flavors (of ice cream, that is) and the phenomenon of "clam strips."

F. W. Woolworth was also good at selling himself as well as his ideas. Incidentally, the "F. W." stood for Frank Winfield Woolworth, and he was a Watertown, Massachusetts, store clerk. In 1879 he convinced his boss to open a separate department where every item would cost 5¢. It worked for his boss, but when Woolworth tried starting his own store in Utica, New York, it failed. Undaunted, he got more investors and, next time, added 10¢ items. The "five and dime" angle took off by catering to low-income customers.

Mail-order titan Montgomery Ward started in 1872 in Chicago, when Aaron Montgomery Ward, an expert in direct mail sales, figured he could do business without owning property—he had been wiped out by the previous year's Chicago fire. As long as the post office did its job, so did Ward's.

Bloomingdale's—now known for its individuality—began as a store-within-a-store in New York's Great East Side Store in 1872. The three men behind the firm were the Bloomingdale brothers: Lyman, Joseph, and Gustave.

A less conventional origin belongs to Sears-Roebuck and Company. The story—actually, the scheme—started in 1886, when a Minneapolis and St. Louis Railroad agent named Richard Warren Sears bought a shipment of gold watches that had been refused by a Minneapolis jeweler. Sears was already making side money by shipping goods for local farmers and selling the watches at a profit to other railroad agents. The next year, Sears moved to Chicago and hired Alvah C. Roebuck to make more watches.

But the most enterprising entrepreneur was Levi Strauss, who, at age twenty, moved to San Francisco to make tents to sell to prospectors in the California gold rush. By inspiration, he got a tailor to make not tents but sturdy overalls out of the canvas material he brought with him. Strauss started his own "blue rush" by hiring every available tailor and seamstress in the Bay Area to produce Levi's Blue Jeans—held together by rivets—and sold them at market prices to countless miners. By the way, the reason that Levis started off dark blue is that it was easier to dye them that color than to try and match shades of light blue, brown, or grey canvas, and, later, denim.

Last Millennium

"Today is the first day of the rest of your millennium"—which begins, by the way, on January 1, 2001, not 2000. For a little perspective on how far we've come in the last century, here's a rundown of some of the big items in the news in 1901:

Queen Victoria dies at age eight-one after sixty-four years on the job.

President Theodore Roosevelt makes his "speak softly and carry a big stick" speech at the Minnesota State Fair, inspiring American interests abroad.

President William McKinley is shot by Leon Czolgosz.

U.S. Steel—the first billion dollar corporation—is formed by J. P. Morgan, who immediately buys off Andrew Carnegie in order to eliminate the competition.

William Normann invents the process to saturate fat in order to prevent it from becoming rancid. In other words, he invents cholesterol.

Nobel Prizes are awarded for the first time.

General Leonard Wood and Major William C. Gorgas of the U.S. Public Health Service apply mosquito controls to rid Havana of yellow fever.

Automobile factories are begun by R. E. Olds, Henry Ford, and John North Willys, among others. From them will (eventually) come the Oldsmobile, the Ford, and the Jeep.

The U.S. College Entrance Examination Board holds its first examinations.

Guglielmo Marconi receives the first transatlantic wireless message. It is the letter *S,* from Poldhu, Cornwall.

Andrew Carnegie (see J. P. Morgan) gives New York $5.2 million to start a public library.

King C. Gillette starts a safety razor company in Boston.

A building boom in upper Manhattan starts the construction of the community of Harlem.

Rhetorical Trivia Questions?

- Of all the things to make Scotch Magic Tape smell like, why did they choose celery?
- Was there ever a kid who didn't smell the purple ditto hand-out from the teacher?
- What on earth would possess anyone to make leisure suits, a type of clothing that turned sweat into stench?
- Nothing quite smells like Play-Doh, does it?
- Is there a rule book that makes school cafeterias serve "mystery meat" with "surprise sauce"? And what is with the lime Jell-O?
- Fight it out: Binaca versus Tic-tac. (Binaca, with a touch of alcohol, has a slight edge?)
- Quick, who was funnier: Shields or Yarnell?
- When was the last time somebody gave you a nougie? A hickey? A wedgie? Virginia heartburn?
- How long could you do "skins" when you played jump rope?
- Does anybody still have the tiger tail that Esso (Standard Oil, now Exxon) gave out to loop around your gas cap for their "put a tiger in your tank" promotion?
- Admit it: You looked twice at the stiff leash and muzzle that people used to walk their "invisible dogs."

- Whatever happened to those silly, thin pencils that *Time* magazine used to send out with their subscription junk mail?
- Did you ever scare the heck out of the neighbors by putting a roll of caps on the curb and hitting the whole thing with a hammer?
- What was the reason you tore the corner off of a $2 bill before passing it along (and heaven forbid you held onto it!).
- Who was hotter: Luke Duke or Bo Duke (John Schneider or Tom Wopat)? If you voted for General Lee, get a life!
- Isn't the best thing about the invention of the Sony Walkman the fact that you don't have to listen to some jerk's boom box?
- Admit it: The most frequent questions asked Ouija Boards had to do with boyfriends and girlfriends.
- Why did only male ducks in Duckburg talk that way?
- After all these years, isn't it comforting to know that the last candy in the roll of LifeSavers® is always orange?
- Why is there still Pez?
- Whose idea was it to make people sick by running scented perfume ads in magazines?
- If you bought Juicyfruits when you went to the movies, didn't you sit on the aisle seat with the light on it so you could see and, thus, avoid eating the licorice ones? (Juicyfruits and Gummi Bears: Separated at birth? You decide.)

PTM: David Feldman

According to David Feldman, who has been writing the popular Imponderables™ *books since 1986, Imponderables are "questions that cannot be answered by numbers or measurements or standard reference books . . . that haunt you for hours . . . until you forget about them before you ever find their solutions." Well, Feldman remembers, and ten bestsellers attest to his research skills. They also say something about the state of the public's curiosity, a condition that may be changing, as Feldman notes.*

Nat Segaloff: Imponderables are not Trivia, but there is still a fascination with obscure information. Is there a distinction?

David Feldman: I don't really mind when somebody calls Imponderables Trivia, but it's hard to distinguish between something that is truly valuable information and something that isn't. The implication is that the end product is all that matters. I guess I tend to think of Trivia as questions that you can nail down in a "What and When" kind of way—if you can find the right reference book.

Segaloff: What connection is there between people's affection for Trivia and their need for instant gratification?

Feldman: I think there is a correlation. One thing that's always interested me is watching people play "Solitaire." In classic "Solitaire," there's a point at which you know you've won, which is when all the cards are up. Some people continue playing, putting the six of clubs over the five of clubs, and the seven of clubs over the six of clubs, and so on. There's a kind of a childlike gratification in knowing that you've won. I think that is some of the pleasure of Trivia, and I have to admit to feeling that way myself. But, unlike answering the question "How do we solve world peace?" there *is* a finite answer.

I had a schizophrenic academic existence, where I was studying popular culture and also studying literature and philosophy, and I have to admit that it did appeal to me to get out of a field where I knew there wouldn't be ultimate answers—not that there are ultimate answers in popular culture, either.

Segaloff: Are there some subject areas where you find more concrete answers than others?

Feldman: Definitely, but sometimes this has more to do with the cooperation of experts in the field than the subject matter. The hard sciences are among the best areas to do research, in particular, physics, and I have found that people in that field have a genuine curiosity and are willing to talk about things that don't have a practical application. But I've found, when talking to people in applied fields, the personality that is necessary to do the occupation in real life makes them far from interested in talking about my kind of questions. The one that strikes me the most is medical doctors. Generally speaking, if I ask them a question that doesn't have a practical application, they're not interested, whereas if I talk to a physicist about a theoretical question, he or she is still quite willing to talk. It's not that one question is easier to answer than another; it's just the kind of training that people get. Doctors are doers, they lay on hands; physicists are more interested in the theoretical.

Segaloff: Have people become more interested in facts than in the pursuit of knowledge *per se*?

Feldman: This is a subject that really bothers me. I think I was lucky to go to schools where I was trained not just to learn a particular type of fact, but how to do research and find out new questions that would pop up that couldn't be anticipated by the teacher. When you learn how to research one little thing, and then another little thing, little things lead to big things. It makes me happy that a lot of teachers are using my books in their classes, and that they're teaching kids how to think.

David Feldman's tenth Imponderables *book is* How Do Astronauts Scratch an Itch? *from Putnam. The board game based on his series is called "Malarky"™ (sic) (Patch), and he is currently working on both his eleventh* Imponderables *book and another game. Feldman holds a degree in popular culture from Bowling Green State University and lives in New York City, where there is plenty of popular culture to go around. His website is www.imponderables.com.*

PTM: Mickey Myers

Since receiving critical praise for her first exhibition in Boston in the fall of 1966 (at age twenty-two), artist Mickey Myers has combined wit and energy in ways not usually found in contemporary art. Her graphics—which embodied bold uses of color and shape reflecting the influence of her teacher, Corita Kent—brought her to national attention during the 1970s. Her silk screen interpretations of hearts, fireworks,

Get a Life: Spice Girls

Question: Name the Spice Girls.

Answer: Posh (Victoria Adams), Scary (Melanie Brown), Baby (Emma Bunton), and Sporty (Melanie Chisholm). (Note: For a short period of time during 1997 the Spice Girls were a popular glitter music group who achieved popularity in Europe and then came to America, where they enjoyed a short burst of fame before their American fans realized that they were already over in Europe. In 1998 there were reports that many of them had married Menudo).

LifeSavers®, and, especially, Crayola crayons help form the iconography of the era.

Nat Segaloff: What connections should be made between the politics of the '60s and the pop art of the era, such as posters by Peter Max and Roy Lichtenstein and Andy Warhol?

Mickey Myers: I think that the whole thrust of the '60s had to do with throwing everything—no matter what it was—off whatever pedestal it had rested on. This was clearly happening in art, and what was being put up on the pedestal were the soup cans and the comics—mediums that reached larger groups of people. So there was a connection, inasmuch as the power was moving to the people, not only in politics but in art as well.

I was in college when pop art was "popping" onto the scene, and we used to talk about the fact that, in essence, what we were doing was no different than what the Impressionists did when they painted still lifes in their kitchens. They got the slabs of meat from the butcher, or the bowls of fruit, or Van Gogh with leather shoes—whatever was around the house. What the pop artists did was to simply say, "We're no longer limited to fruit bowls in the kitchen. Let's look at what it is that we're surrounded by. We are truly an industrial age, and we're going to focus on the things of that industry."

Segaloff: Your work has a deftness and ease. Does it come freely?

Myers: No. Ideas have to brew inside me for a long time, and then I have to work on them for a long time. Even though the work seems spontaneous, those pieces have usually developed over a long period of time. I can tell you, for example, that the idea of the crayons developed in my head for at least a year before I ever even ventured into putting it on a piece of paper.

In 1987 Myers began experimenting with water colors, then pastels, to create a series of stunning and inspirational cloudscapes. A sampling of this work can be found on her website at www.mickeymyers.com. She also produced the PBS documentary on Corita Kent titled Primary Colors.

Get a Life: Russ Meyer

Question: What Pulitzer Prize–winning film critic wrote Russ Meyer's 1970 seminudie, *Beyond the Valley of the Dolls?*

Answer: Roger Ebert wrote the screenplay for Meyer's kinetic sequel to Jacqueline Susann's *The Valley of the Dolls.* Less well known is that he has also had been involved in other Meyer films, albeit without screen credit.

Answers

Secret Identities (Answers)

1. f
2. h
3. l
4. g
5. j
6. a
7. b
8. d
9. k
10. e
11. i
12. c

Extra credit answer: This is a double-secret. Lamont Cranston's real name is Kent Allard. It was the real Cranston who gave Allard permission to use his name as well as taught him the trick of clouding men's minds, etc., to become The Shadow.

Bar Bets (Answers)

1. One (Think about it.)
2. "the"
3. They both weigh the same (1 pound).
4. You don't bury survivors.
5. George Lazenby, Barry Nelson (TV), Roger Moore, Timothy Dalton, Pierce Brosnan, David Niven (in *Casino Royale*), and Woody Allen (as "Jimmy Bond" in *Casino Royale*). Oh, yes, and Sean Connery.
6. *Xerox®* is the registered trademark of the Xerox Corporation, which goes to great lengths (including sending "reminder" letters to journalists) to protect its trademark from becoming a verb or a generic name for photocopies.
7. Jimmy Carter, Gerald Ford, Ronald Reagan, George Bush, and Bill Clinton (they're alive as of this writing).
8. January 1, 2001 (*not* 2000)
9. Since calories are determined by weight, both contain equal amounts calories.
10. Strictly speaking, the copper coin worth $.01 is "one cent," not a "penny" (look at one).

Don't Quote Me (Answers)

1. Dorothy Parker
2. Stan Laurel
3. George S. Kaufman
4. Samuel Goldwyn
5. Johnny Carson
6. Roseanne
7. Alice Roosevelt Longworth
8. David Letterman

9. Woody Allen
10. Tony Hendra

Advertising Catchphrases (Answers)

1. Secret® deodorant
2. L&M® cigarettes
3. Virginia Slims® cigarettes
4. Pepto Bismol®
5. Alka-Seltzer®
6. Bayer® aspirin
7. U.S. School of Music
8. American Express® card
9. Crest® toothpaste
10. Ban® deodorant
11. Dial® soap
12. Ivory® soap

Teams (Answers)

1. o—Jeff (cartoon characters)
2. n—Ebert (the movie critics)
3. m—Desi (Arnaz)
4. k—Ernie (*Sesame Street/It's a Wonderful Life*)
5. r—I (down east comedy records)
6. p—Wooster (P. G. Wodehouse)
7. e—Crosby (Bob and Bing, the *Road* pictures)
8. s—Louise (Sarandon and Davis)
9. t/v—Clyde (gangsters)
10. v/t—Clyde (Mr. and Ms. FBI)
11. c—Ethel (Mertz)
12. w—Dum (Lewis Carroll's Wonderlanders)
13. l—Lou (Abbott and Costello)
14. b—Hutch (TV cops)
15. a—99 (*Get Smart*)
16. y—Jeremy ('60s songsters)
17. d—Lacey (TV cops)
18. u—Kirk (Vulcan and Iowan)
19. z—Nora (Charles, *The Thin Man*)
20. i—Banky (Ronald and Vilma, silent movies)
21. g—Reddy (early Hanna-Barbera TV series)
22. x—Booboo (prime Hanna-Barbera TV series)
23. q—DeNiro (brilliant director/actor team)
24. j—Gracie (Burns and Allen)
25. h—Willbuurrrr (Mr. Ed, of course, of course)
26. f—Maria (*West Side Story*)

They, Robots (Answers)

1. h—George and Jane Jetson (in the cartoon series of the same name)
2. f—Space Family Robinson (but mostly by Billy "Danger, Will Robinson" Mumy)

3. j— Dr. Morbius (Walter Pidgeon in *Forbidden Planet.* Later seen in *The Invisible Boy*)
4. e—Rotwang (Rudolf Klein-Rogge in *Metropolis;* the Robotrix Maria was played by Bridget Helm)
5. a—Klaatu (Michael Rennie in *The Day the Earth Stood Still*)
6. i—Skynet (the machine-run world of *Terminator 2: Judgement Day*)
7. b—John Connor (played by Edward Furlong in *The Terminator,* but he wouldn't own him until the future)
8. c—Luke Skywalker (although, technically, Obi-Wan Kenobe owned them, in *Star Wars*)
9. g—Stephanie Speck (played by Ally Sheedy in *Short Circuit,* and it wasn't ownership, it was, er, love)
10. d—James A. Corry (this is the ringer; Alicia was played by Jean Marsh and Corry by Jack Warden in "The Lonely," on the original 1959 *Twilight Zone* TV episode)

4. United Nations Educational, Scientific, and Cultural Organization
5. North Atlantic Treaty Organization
6. General Agreement on Tariffs and Trade
7. North American Free Trade Agreement
8. National Association of Securities Dealers Automated Quotations
9. "What You See Is What You Get" (computer argot)
10. Situation Normal: All Fouled Up (army expression)

Slanguage (Answers)

1. NASA construction crane used as an astronaut's pre-launch escape device
2. "Everything is all right." (space program)
3. Risky; tense
4. Bummer; unpleasant; also to cross-dress
5. Intimate, meaningful conversation; also urban-influenced singing without music
6. Hang onto a marijuana joint without passing it along
7. Drive-in movie theatre, where young patrons neck in their cars
8. Money
9. Harley-Davidson motorcycle; also selfishness
10. Make unwanted sexual advances
11. Gather one's emotions in anticipation of action
12. To bother or irritate
13. Twenty-four hours a day, seven days a week; workaholic
14. Lose one's composure; flip out
15. To purposely give the wrong information to someone
16. One's rear end
17. Gathering of standees near the stage at a rock music concert
18. Eat quickly; steal
19. "It is not something we need worry about."

Acronyms (Answers)

1. National Association for Stock Car Auto Racing
2. Congress of Racial Equality
3. Mobile Army Surgical Hospital

Answers

Resources

Acker, Ally. *Reel Women*. New York: Continuum Publishing Co., 1991.

Alderman, Ellen and Caroline Kennedy. *The Right to Privacy*. New York: Alfred A. Knopf, 1995.

Anger, Kenneth. *Hollywood Babylon*. San Francisco, CA: Straight Arrow Books, 1975.

Bathroom Reader's Institute. *Uncle John's Second Bathroom Reader*. New York: St. Martin's Press, 1989.

Beck, Ken and Jim Clark. *The Andy Griffith Show Book*. New York: St. Martin's Press, 1985.

Bell, Ruth. *Changing Bodies, Changing Lives* (Revised). New York: Vintage Books, 1987.

Ben Is Dead Magazine, ed. "Retrohell." Boston, MA: Little Brown and Co., 1997.

Berliner, Barbara with Melinda Corey and George Ochoa. *The Book of Answers: The New York Public Library's Most Unusual and Entertaining Questions*. New York: Prentice-Hall Press, 1990.

Bogdanovich, Peter. *John Ford*. Berkeley, CA: University of California Press, 1968.

Boller, Paul F., Jr. and John George. *They Never Said It*. New York: Barnes & Noble, 1993.

Brooks, Tim and Earle Marsh. *The Complete Directory to Prime Time Network TV Shows*. New York: Ballantine Books, 1992.

Burnam, Tom. *More Misinformation*. New York: Ballantine, 1980.

———. *The Dictionary of Misinformation*. New York: Harper & Row, 1975.

Buxton, Frank and Bill Owen. *The Big Broadcast 1920–1950* (revised). New York: Viking Press, 1972.

Chomsky, Noam. *The Chomsky Reader*, ed. James Peck. New York: Random House, 1987.

Crescent, Peter and Bob Columbe. *The Official Honeymooners Treasury*. New York: Perigee Books, 1990.

Dalton, David. *James Dean: The Mutant King*. New York: St. Martin's Press, 1974.

Dunn, Jerry. *Tricks of the Trade*. Boston, MA: Houghton Mifflin Co., 1991.

Edelstein, Andrew J. and Frank Lovece. *The Brady Bunch Book*. New York: Warner Books, 1990.

Feldman, David. *Imponderables*. NY: William Morrow, 1986, 1987.

———. *Why Do Clocks Run Clockwise?*. NY: Harper & Row, 1987.

———. *When Did Wild Poodles Roam the Earth?*. NY: HarperCollins, 1992.

———. *What are Hyenas Laughing at, Anyway?*. NY: Putnam, 1995.

———. *How Do Astronauts Scratch an Itch?*. NY: Putnam, 1996.

Fletcher, Connie. *What Cops Know*. New York: Pocket Books, 1990.

Forbes, Malcolm with Jeff Bloch. *They Went That-A-Way*. New York: Ballantine Books, 1988.

Frank, Alan. *The Science Fiction and Fantasy Film Handbook*. New Jersey: Barnes & Noble Books, 1982.

Garrison, Webb. *The Ignorance Book*. New York: William Morrow, 1971.

Goodgold, Edwin and Dan Carlinsky. *Trivia*. New York: Dell Publishers, 1965.

Griscom, Andy, Ben Rand and Scott Johnston. *The Complete Book of Beer Drinking Games*. Memphis, TN: Mustang Publishing Co., 1984, 1989.

Guterman, Jimmy. *The Best Rock 'n' Roll Records of All Time*. New York: Citadel Press, 1992.

Harmetz, Aljean. *The Making of The Wizard of Oz*. England: Pavilion Books, Ltd., 1977.

——. *Round Up the Usual Suspects: The Making of* Casablanca—*Bogart, Begman and World War II*. New York: Hyperion Books, 1992.

Hilliard, Robert L. and Michael C. Keith. *Broadcast Century: A Biography of American Broadcasting*. Stoneham, MA: Butterworth-Heinemann, 1992.

Hirsch, E.D., Jr., Joseph F. Kett and James Trefil, eds. *The Dictionary of Cultural Literacy*. Boston, MA: Houghton Mifflin Company, 1988.

Information Please, Almanac. New York: Houghton Mifflin Company, various years.

Irons, Peter and Stephanie Guitton, eds. *May It Please the Court* . . . . New York: The New Press, 1991.

Katz, Ephriam. *The Film Encyclopedia* (rev). New York: HarperCollins, 1994.

Kisch, John and Edward Mapp. *A Separate Cinema*. New York: Farrar, Straus and Giroux, 1992.

Kohn, Alfie. *You Know What They Say* . . . . New York: HarperCollins, 1990.

Lamparski, Richard. *Whatever Became Of* . . . . New York: Bantam Books, 1976.

Landy, Eugene E., Ph.D. *The Underground Dictionary*. New York: Simon & Schuster, 1971.

Malmuth, Neil M. and Edward Donnerstein, eds. *Pornography and Sexual Aggression*. Orlando, FL: Academic Press, 1984.

Marsh, Fave and Kevin Stein. *The Book of Rock Lists*. New York: Dell/Rolling Stone Press, 1981.

McCarthy, John and Brian Kelleher. *Alfred Hitchcock Presents*. New York: St. Martin's Press, 1985.

McGee, Harold. *On Food and Cooking*. New York: Charles Scribner's Sons, 1984.

——. *The Curious Cook*. New York: Macmillan Publishing Company, 1990.

McGilligan, Patrick, ed. *Backstory 3*. Berkeley, California: University of California Press, 1997.

Morris, William and Mary. *Harper Dictionary of Contemporary Usage*, Second Edition. New York: Harper & Row, 1985.

Murphy, Bessie Randall. *A Hundred Recipes from the Old South*. Columbus, Ohio: National Association of Margarine Manufacturers, 1938.

New York Public Library. *The New York Public Library Desk Reference*, Second Edition. New York: Prentice Hall General Reference, 1989, 1993.

Panati, Charles. *Panati's Parade of Fads, Follies, and Manias*. New York: HarperCollins, 1991.

Patterson Lindsay, ed. *Black Films and Film-makers*. New York: Dodd, Mead & Company, 1975.

Pinkham, Mary Ellen. *Mary Ellen's Giant Book of Helpful Hints*. Avenel, New Jersey: Wings Books, (1976, 1979, 1980, 1981) 1994.

Poundstone, William. *Big Secrets*. New York: Quill Publishers, 1983.

Reader's Digest. *Reader's Digest Book of Facts*. Pleasantville, New York: The Reader's Digest Association, Inc., 1987.

Robertson, Patrick. *The Guinness Book of Movie Facts & Feats*. Fifth Edition, New York: Abbeville Press, 1993.

Rosenman, Joel, John Roberts and Robert Pilpel. *Young Men With Unlimited Capital*. New York: Bantam Books, 1974, (revised) 1989.

Rovin, Jeff. *In Search of Trivia*. New York: New American Library, 1984.

———. *TV Babylon*. New York: New American Library, 1984.

Sagan, Carl. *The Demon-Haunted World: Science as a Candle in the Dark*. New York: Random House, 1995.

Sandler, Adam. *Daily Variety*. Los Angeles, CA: Cahners Publishing, August 2, 1994.

Schickel, Richard. *The Disney Version*. New York: Simon & Schuster, 1968.

Schumacher, Michael. *There But For Fortune: The Life of Phil Ochs*. New York: Hyperion Books, 1996.

Segaloff, Ruth S. *Collected Recipes*. unpublished.

Sifakis, Carl. *The Encyclopedia of American Crime*. New York: Facts on File, Inc., 1982.

Smith, Dave. *Disney A-Z*. New York: Hyperion, 1996.

Spiegel, Celina and Peter Kupfer, eds. *Great First Lines*. New York: Fawcett Columbine, 1992.

Spignesi, Stephen J. *The Odd Index*. New York: Plume (Penguin), 1994.

Staten, Vince. *Can You Trust a Tomato in January?*. New York: Simon & Schuster, 1993.

Stern, Jane and Michael. *Square Meals*. New York: Alfred A. Knopf, Inc., 1984.

Strunk, William, Jr. and E.B. White. *The Elements of Style*, Third Edition, New York: Macmillan Publishing Co., 1979.

Sutton, Caroline. *How Did They Do That?*. New York: Quill Publishers, 1984.

Thomey, Tedd. *The Glorious Decade*. New York: Ace Books, 1971.

Trager, James. *The People's Chronology*. New York: Holt, Rinehart & Winston, 1979.

Varasdi, J. Allen. *Myth Information*. New York: Ballantine Books, 1989.

Viorst, Milton. *Fire in the Streets*. New York: Simon & Schuster, 1979.

Walker, Samuel. *In Defense of American Liberties*. New York: Oxford University Press, 1990.

Wallace, Irving. David Wallechinsky, Amy Wallace, Sylvia Wallace. *The Book of Lists #2*. New York: William Morrow & Co., 1979.

———. *The Book of Lists #3*. New York: William Morrow & Co., 1983.

———. *The Book of Lists*. New York: William Morrow & Co., 1977.

———. *The People's Almanac #3*. New York: William Morrow & Co., 1981.

White, Patrick J. *The Complete Mission: Impossible Dossier*. New York: Avon Books, 1991.

Winokur, Jon, ed. *The Portable Curmudgeon*. New York: New American Library, 1987.

———. *Return of The Portable Curmudgeon*. New York: Plume (Penguin), 1995.

Winter, Ruth. *A Consumer's Dictionary of Food Additives* (Third Edition). New York: Crown, 1989.

Woodward, Bob. *Wired: The Short Life & Fast Times of John Belushi*. New York: Simon & Schuster, 1984.

Worth, Fred L.. *The Trivia Encyclopedia*. Los Angeles: Brook House, 1974.

Young, Mark C. ed. *Guinness Book of Records*. New York: Bantam Books, 1997.

Zicree, Marc Scott. *The Twilight Zone Companion*. New York: Bantam Books, 1982.

Zinn, Howard. *The Twentieth Century: A People's History*. New York: Harper & Row, 1980, 1984.

Index

EVERYTHING

The Everything Crossword and Puzzle Book
by Harold Cordry

Trade paperback, 352 pages
1-55850-764-7, $12.95

Whether it's crossword puzzles, acrostics, or a new fangled word game you crave, *The Everything Crossword and Puzzle Book* has the challenges you're looking for! Spend hours searching for hidden words, solving word scrambles, connecting words, creating words out of words, and enjoying hundreds of fun, mind-boggling word games. With over 300 puzzles, The Everything Crossword and Puzzle Book has a game for you!

The Everything Games Book
by Tracy Fitzsimmons and Pamela Liflander

Trade paperback, 304 pages
1-55850-643-8, $12.95

If you're looking for games to play yourself or with a group of friends, *The Everything Games Book* really does have it all! Packed with information, fully illustrated, and complete with strategy for winning play, it can help you create the special family memories you and your loved ones will treasure forever. And if not, at least you'll know how to beat them at their own game!

Available Wherever Books Are Sold

If you cannot find these titles at your favorite retail outlet, you may order them directly from the publisher. BY PHONE: Call 1-800-872-5627. We accept Visa, Mastercard, and American Express. $4.95 will be added to your total order for shipping and handling. BY MAIL: Write out the full titles of the books you'd like to order and send payment, including $4.95 for shipping and handling, to: Adams Media Corporation, 260 Center Street, Holbrook, MA 02343. 30-day money-back guarantee.

We Have

EVERYTHING

OVER ONE MILLION EVERYTHING BOOKS SOLD

More bestselling Everything titles
available from your local bookseller:

Everything **After College Book**
Everything **Astrology Book**
Everything **Baby Names Book**
Everything® **Bartender's Book**
Everything **Bedtime Story Book**
Everything **Beer Book**
Everything **Bicycle Book**
Everything **Bird Book**
Everything **Casino Gambling Book**
Everything **Cat Book**
Everything® **Christmas Book**
Everything **College Survival Book**
Everything **Crossword and Puzzle Book**
Everything **Dessert Book**
Everything **Dog Book**
Everything **Dreams Book**
Everything **Etiquette Book**
Everything **Family Tree Book**
Everything **Fly-Fishing Book**
Everything **Games Book**

Everything **Get Ready For Baby Book**
Everything **Golf Book**
Everything **Guide to Walt Disney World®,**
   Universal Studios®, and Greater Orlando
Everything **Home Buying Book**
Everything **Home Improvement Book**
Everything **Internet Book**
Everything **Jewish Wedding Book**
Everything **Low-Fat High-Flavor Cookbook**
Everything **Money Book**
Everything **Pasta Book**
Everything **Pregnancy Book**
Everything **Study Book**
Everything **Trivia Book**
Everything® **Wedding Book**
Everything® **Wedding Checklist**
Everything® **Wedding Etiquette Book**
Everything® **Wedding Organizer**
Everything® **Wedding Vows Book**
Everything **Wine Book**